Far Off Metal River

Far Off Metal River

Inuit Lands, Settler Stories, and the Making of the Contemporary Arctic

EMILIE CAMERON

UBC Press • Vancouver • Toronto

23 22 21 20 19 18 5 4 3

Printed in Canada on FSC-certified ancient-forest-free paper (100% post-consumer recycled) that is processed chlorine- and acid-free.

Library and Archives Canada Cataloguing in Publication

Cameron, Emilie, author
Far off metal river : Inuit lands, settler stories, and the making of the contemporary Arctic / Emilie Cameron.

Includes bibliographical references and index.
Issued in print and electronic formats.
ISBN 978-0-7748-2884-0 (bound). – ISBN 978-0-7748-2885-7 (pbk.). –
ISBN 978-0-7748-2886-4 (pdf). – ISBN 978-0-7748-2887-1 (epub)

1. Bloody Falls Massacre, 1771. 2. Inuit – Crimes against – Nunavut.
3. Inuit – Colonization – Nunavut. 4. Inuit – Nunavut – Social conditions.
5. Culture conflict – Nunavut. I. Title.

E99.E7C248 2015 971.9'550049712 C2015-901449-2
C2015-901450-6

Canada

UBC Press gratefully acknowledges the financial support for our publishing program of the Government of Canada (through the Canada Book Fund), the Canada Council for the Arts, and the British Columbia Arts Council.

This book has been published with the help of a grant from the Canadian Federation for the Humanities and Social Sciences, through the Awards to Scholarly Publications Program, using funds provided by the Social Sciences and Humanities Research Council of Canada.

UBC Press
The University of British Columbia
2029 West Mall
Vancouver, BC V6T 1Z2
www.ubcpress.ca

The Indians who are now appointed your guides, are to conduct you ... to a river represented by the Indians to abound with copper ore, animals of the furr kind, &c ... The river, which is called by the Northern Indians Neetha-san-san-dazey, or the Far Off Metal River, you are, if possible, to trace to the mouth ... and observe what mines are near the river, what water there is at the river's mouth, how far the woods are from the sea-side, the course of the river, the nature of the soil, and the productions of it ... If the said river is likely to be of any utility, take possession of it on behalf of the Hudson's Bay Company.

— The Hudson's Bay Company's instructions
to Samuel Hearne, 1769

Contents

Illustrations

Hivuniqhuut, Preface

Qujagitakhunga ilihaqpakkama Inuinnaqtun. Angulalikkaarmit ikajuqtauvlunga una numiktitquivlugu hamna hivuniqhuut.

Una piksaliuqtauhimajuq hivuaniittuq makpiraarmi piksaliuqhimajaa ilannarma, Mathieu Dumond-up, havaaqaqhuni huraajjanut qaujihaqtiujuq piksaliuqtiuvlunilu Qurluqtumi, Nunavunmi. Piksaliuqhimajaa aujami, Qurluqtum Kugaani, hilataani igluqpaqarvianit Mat-iup, nuliangalu Amanda, irnialu Thomas-lu, ukiuraalungmi najuqpagaat igluqpaqarviat. Mat qunniaqpakhuniuk avinngarjuaq ubluummaanmi pauqtuqhuni iluani kuugarmi, qunnialitakhugu iijikkiqhugulu, taqammuqtaaqhuni imarmi marluinnarmi ivilingnit kuukkam hinaani.

Iluani makpiraarmi aulahimajuq taimaa ihumannaqhuni uvani Qurluqtualungmi inuit inuaqhimajut qangaraalungmi, uvani kuukkami Mat-lu Amanda-uplu igluqpaqarviat, ihumannaqhuni, ihumagijara uvamnit, kuinginnaittumik nunanit nalunaiqhigialik aujami kuukkam hinaani. Hamna Qurluqturmiut tutqiqhinnaqtumik, una Qurluqtualup Inuaqhihimagaluaqtut qangaraaluk qitqaniinngittut inmikkut ilitquhirnigut inuuhirningilluuniit. Ihumagijaunngittunittauq unipkaangit ilagijauvagaat ukuninngat qurluq, Inuinnaqtun kangiqhijjuhia qurlut ilihimajaujut ilanganit, qurluqtualuk. Una Bloody Falls Qablunaanit ihumaaluutigijauvagaat.

Ilittuinnaqhimajara havakhimalihaaqhugu una Qurluqturmiut huginngitaat uuminngat Bloody Falls mik Qablunaatut taijaivaktuq, kihimi, amihut mamiahuutigivagaat qanikkut ilagihimajangit nunalingnut.

Tukihinnarnahuaqhugu uvani makpiraami ilainnaani I-mi, ahikkut haffuminngat hilataani ilitturijumajangit qurluqtualungmit ukuninngallu Qurluqturmiut ihumajait unipkaangit qanuq inikhaqaqhuni hungmangaat ihumagijara ihumagijaujukhat haffuminngat iliharnikkut. Hilataanirmiunut, una ukiuqtaqtum ilihimajauvuq aallaungmat uuminngalu hulijjuhiat nunaa maniraalu, akhuurnaqpiaqhunittauq anuria, uuminngalu unipkaaqhimajauvaktut uuminngat qurluqtualungmit. Angiglivallialiqhuni, una ukiuqtaqtuq ilitturijauvlunilu nunaa amihurjuaqaqhunilu avataa, maniraa nunattiarijauvaktuq, unalu hakuiqpakhunilu hilamut aallannguqpauhianit, inuuhirliuqhunittauq. Qanurlu hikuinnauvakhuni nunaa inuinnaillu qungattuinnaqhutiktauq, qanurmi hukkuuriakhaita ukiuqtaqtumi najugautauvluni haffuminngat avatingnit qanurilingajaunikkut unagunaittuniglu maniraat, uvaguttauq hilataani najurviqaqtugut Qulaannit taijauvaktugut ilaliutijumagaangapta aviktuqhimajumi tamainnut quvianaqtunik pinniqpiaqtunik ihumagihimajavuttauq.

Una makpiraaq titiraqhimajuq ihumagivlugit hilataarnirmiut, uvangaluttauq. Hamna ilihautigivlugu qanuq ilaliutigivaktavut Kangangnamit Inuinnainillu, uuminngattauq kiujjutait ilagijaujut. Titiraqhimagaluaqhutik Qablunaanut, Inuinnaunngittut, Itqiliunngittullu inuit ihuaqhijauvlutik nunanganit uuktuqtauvlutik hilataani Qutingnikpaamit, una makpiraaq qangaraaluk qaujihaqhimavlutik iluani hilataanilu Nunavunmi, qaphiiqhutik ublukhautainit tatqiqhiutiraalungmilu Qurluqturmiittut. Hiiguuq, kangiqhihimajarattauq Qablunaangugama, qanuq Qablunaat ihumagivagaat Inuinnainut Qutingnikpaamilu, ilagivagaattauq Inuinnait ilagiiktunut, ilihaijingillu, ihumagijauvaktunullu, nunaptingnittauq. Naahurihimajatka Inuinnait taiguaqpaktut ikpiginiaqhimajait takutquivlutik hamna ilihautiniq tahapkuattauq ilagijaillu ihumagittiaqhugillu hamna qaujihaqhimajatka Qablunaat ilagijaillu Qutingnikpaami ukuninngalu Inuinnainut tuhaumavigilaaqtangit kangiqhujjuhianit inuuhianillu. Hamna makpiraaq titiraqhimajuq ihumagivlugit Qablunaanut tuhaumajait nipaanillu, ilihimajara, naahurihimatkalu taiguaqqangit tautuktuumijaaqqangit tumingit takunnaqhutik inikhangillu tukiliutainillu.

Uvani makpiraanmi takunnaqtut, tukimuarutihimajatka qanuq Qablunaat ihumaaluutigiinnaqtait Qurluktup Kugaani inuaqhijauhimajut unipkaarutait. Hamna ihumagijara unipkaarut qanurilingajauhimagaluaqtut, ikpingnaqhivlunilu pittailinahuaqhutik hakuirutaangillu. Ihivriuqhihimajarali inikhaat qanurilinganingillu Qablunaat ihumagijait inuglugihimavlutik Nunaqaqqaaqhimajut ajuqhautihimajaraluangit tautukhimajauvlutik inuaqhihimajut, qangaraaluk ukpirijauhimajaujuq unipkaarijauhimajut hilarjuarmit nanminirijaraluangit ukpiruhuutait qutingnikpaamit, ukiuqtaqtumilu qaujihalihaaqhutik, ihumagijauvakhutiktauq qutingnikpaami ujaraqtarviuvakhunilu. Hamna ihumagiliqpakhugu unipkaaqtauvaktuq unipkaarijaujuq kihimi ihumagijungnaiqhugu. Niplirihuutigivakhugu qanuq Inuit kiuliqpakhugit Qablunaat ihumaaluutigivagaat Qurluqtup Kugaa mikhaagut, qanurilingajauvakhutik unipkaaqtauhimavakhugit ukpiruhuutingillu puiguqtauvaktuni, ihumagijauhuiqhugillu ahinunngauliqpakhutik ilagijauvaktait unipkaarutait hulivakhugillu. Ihumagiliqhugit Inuit akhuurnahuaqpakhutik nunagijaillu ingutaaqhutik ikaarutigivakhugillu Qurluqtup Kugaa, qanurlu inikhaliuqhimavaktait Qurluqturmiut ihumagijauvagaat unipkaaqtauvagaat, qanurilingajauhimavlutik akhuuqtauvakhutik Inuinnait Itqiliillu atauttimut katittaraangamik unipkaaliqpakhutik aviktuqhimajumi nunaanit qangaraalungmi. Atauttimut pivlutik, unipkaaqhimajara hapkuat nunanganit Qurluqtum Kugaa inuaqhihimajaujut unipkaarutaat ikajuutauliqpakhuni qanuq ihumagijauvaktut Qablunaat ilagijait ublumimut ukiuqtaqtumi.

Mat-ip piksaliuqhimajaa ikajuutauvlunilu ukuninngat havaktauhimajunit inikhaliuqhugu ihuaqhaijaqhugulu. Hamna ihumagijauvakhuni Qurluqtum Kugaa angitqijauvlunilu kuugainnit ilagijauvlunilu inungnut huraanillu kuugarmiutauvaktuni. Taimaa ihumagijauvakhunilu ukiuqtaqtumi nunagijauvluni inungnut huraadjanullu ingilrautivagaat inuuvlutik qaujihaiviuvakhunilu nunagijamingnit tautungnaqhunilu, inuuvigijaraluangit qangaraalungmi inuuttiarniq. Kuinnginnaittumi, qajangnaqtumilu, ukiunnguraangat, unipkaaqtauvakhuni hamna nunagijaat qangaraalungmi ikajuutauliqpagaat ilagijaujunut uuktuqattaqhutik taimaa akturnaittunilu iluani ihumannaqtumi ukuninngat Qablunaat ilitturihimavlutik ilagiingniq nunami. Uuktuqhimaittumik ilauqatauhimaittumik takunnaittunilu ihumagijaunngittut, uuminngaluniit Qablunaat ilitturilimaittut ahiqanngittuni.

Hamani ilainnaatigut qujagivlugit amihuujut inuit ikajuqhimagamik uvamnut makpiraaliurnigut. Ikpingnaqhunilu amihuugamik. Kihimi, Qurluqturmiut qujagitakhugit ikajuqhimagamik uvamnut haphuma havaatigut quanaqpiaqquhi Qurluqturmiuttat ikajuqhimagaminga havaatigut mikhaagut, qaujihaijullu qujagitatka qaiqattaramit nunanut ihumagijauvlutik. Quanaquhi.

The photograph on the cover of this book was taken by a friend, Mathieu Dumond, who works as a wildlife biologist and freelance photographer in Kugluktuk, Nunavut. It was taken in the summer, on the Coppermine River, just outside the cabin where Mat; his wife, Amanda; and their son, Thomas, live year round. Mat had been watching a muskrat all afternoon as it paddled in the river, drawn, as his eye was, to the partially submerged thicket of mud and grass and sticks along the shore.

In a book that directs a great deal of attention to the Bloody Falls massacre, alleged to have occurred more than two centuries ago just a short way upstream of Mat and Amanda's cabin, it's important, I think, to begin with the more quiet geographies of a summer afternoon along the river. As Kugluktukmiut have repeatedly made clear, the Bloody Falls massacre is not the centre of their own histories or experiences. It is not even the most important story associated with Kugluk, the Inuinnaqtun name for the rapids, known to some as Bloody Falls. Bloody Falls is primarily a preoccupation of non-Inuit outsiders.

I knew when I started this project that Kugluktukmiut are not particularly interested in Bloody Falls, and, in fact, many are annoyed by its close association with their community. As I explain in Chapter 1, the contrast between outside interest in Bloody Falls and the ways in which Kugluktukmiut relate to the story and the place itself is one of the reasons I thought it was an important starting point for this study. To outsiders, the Arctic is known for its difference and its drama – for stark landscapes, harsh climate, and for harrowing stories like that of the Bloody Falls massacre. Increasingly, the Arctic is also known for its resource riches, its geopolitical significance, its vulnerability to climate change, and its social suffering. Whether drawing on long-standing tropes of icy lands and smiling Inuit, or more recent turns to the Arctic as a site of environmental precarity and immense energy reserves, those of us who live outside the North are continually called upon to engage with all that is extreme, exotic, and sensational about the region.

This book was written for these outsiders, among whom I count myself. It is a study of how we relate to the North and to Inuit, and the consequences of these relations. Although it has been written primarily for and about Qablunaat (those non-Inuit, non-Indigenous peoples who are anchored in places and practices outside the North), the book is based on many years of research within and outside Nunavut, including many weeks and months in Kugluktuk. Indeed, most of what I understand about being Qablunaaq, and about how Qablunaat relate to Inuit and the North, comes from relationships with Inuit friends, mentors, intellectuals, and lands. I hope that Inuit readers will feel I have represented this learning and these relationships with integrity, and that my analysis of Qablunaaq relations with the North and with Inuit will resonate with their understandings and experiences. Most of this book is written in a distinctly Qablunaaq voice and tone, I know, but I hope readers will see traces of other ways and forms.

In the chapters that follow, I describe how and why Qablunaat are so preoccupied with the Bloody Falls massacre story. I consider both what this story makes possible and what it suppresses, avoids, and undermines. I examine its role in the formation of Qablunaaq ideas of race and indigeneity, efforts to order imperial violence and witnessing, and the production of historical truth, and I trace the ways in which the story has shaped nationalist claims to the North, early Arctic exploration, and ongoing interest in northern mineral resources. But I also pay attention to the occasions and contexts within which the story *does not matter.* I discuss the range of ways Inuit have responded to Qablunaaq obsessions with Bloody Falls, including not only purposeful rejection of the story but also practices of forgetting, ignoring, and moving away from all that is associated with this story and event. I consider how Inuit self-determination and land claim movements have intersected with Bloody Falls, how Kugluktukmiut direct attention away from the story, and how recent efforts on the part of Inuit and Dene to come together around shared concerns interweave with regional histories. Taken together, I argue, these geographies of the Bloody Falls massacre story help to both *place* and *displace* Qablunaaq relations with the contemporary North.

Mat's photograph helps with this project of placing and displacing. It places Bloody Falls in a larger river system and in relation to the people and animals that rely on that river. It reminds us that the Arctic is a place where people and animals go about the daily motions of living, and that the land is not merely a backdrop for the drama of exploration or a source of hydrocarbons or a vista for the tourist gaze but also a lived and living place. For Kugluktukmiut, the Coppermine is not a "Far Off Metal River" but rather the place where they live, the water they drink, a cherished part of the *nuna* (land). Quiet, careful, seasonal, storied engagement with that land, over and over and over again, nurtures relationships and practices and possibilities that simply do not register within the dominant frames through which Qablunaat are taught to engage with this place. But this does not mean such practices and relationships do not exist or do not matter, or that Qablunaat cannot learn to relate differently.

In the acknowledgments, I thank some of the many, many people who helped me with this book. It is humbling to see just how many there are. But, here, I want to specifically thank the people of Kugluktuk, who have not only gently helped me along with this project but also withstood the continual flow of researchers in and out of their community with grace and generosity. Quanaquhi.

A Note on Language and Spelling

Inuktut (an umbrella term for Inuit languages spoken throughout Canada) has a number of dialects and orthographies. This variation is partly related to histories of migration and settlement across the circumpolar region, and the associated development of regionally distinct vocabulary and pronunciation. It is also partly due to histories of contact with missionaries, who developed and imposed different orthographies in different regions. Inuinnaqtun is spoken in Kugluktuk and the broader Kitikmeot region and is written using a roman orthography. Elsewhere in Nunavut, different dialects of Inuktitut are spoken and are written in either roman lettering or syllabics. In 1976, the Inuit Cultural Institute (ICI) developed a dual writing system of syllabics and roman orthography, which was intended to standardize spellings across dialects and to allow for easy conversion across orthographies. In the Kitikmeot region, ICI orthography is increasingly in use, but many people continue to spell words in the ways they are most comfortable and that reflect past practice. Thus, there are often multiple spellings in circulation; "Kugluktuk," for example, is also spelled "Qurluqtuq."

In this book, I primarily use ICI roman orthography, but where other spellings or orthographies are preferred or are in primary use, I use them. Furthermore, because I have studied Inuktut in both Kugluktuk (where I learned Inuinnaqtun vocabulary and orthographies) and Ottawa (where I learned Inuktitut vocabulary and orthographies used in the Kivalliq region of Nunavut), I use the spelling with which I am most familiar in a given context. For example, I first learned the word "Qablunaaq" in Kugluktuk, where it is often spelled "Kablunak" and sometimes "Qaplunaaq." In Eastern Nunavut, it is more often written as "Qallunaaq," and in all contexts, it is sometimes capitalized and sometimes not. I capitalize "Qablunaaq" to gesture toward my understanding of the word as referring not only to non-Inuit individuals or characteristics but also to a distinct subject position and collectivity defined in relation to Inuit (see Chapter 1 for further discussion). "Qablunaaq" is an accepted ICI mode of spelling the word as it is pronounced in Kugluktuk ("Qaplunaaq" is also used in ICI).

In cases where I quote from texts, I use the orthography of the original, except for quotes from Maurice Métayer's *Unipkat.* Métayer developed his own rather idiosyncratic orthography, and it is not in current use. Given this, passages from *Unipkat* have been transliterated into ICI orthography so that those who read Inuinnaqtun can more easily engage with them. I gratefully acknowledge Janet Tamalik McGrath's extensive translation, transliteration, and language consultation; Mona Tiktalek's language interpretation work in Kugluktuk; and Emily Angulalik's translation of the preface.

I have also made an effort to use the terms and orthographies preferred by the Dene nations referred to in this book. When I quote from a historical text, I use the terms as they appear in the original, but elsewhere I use the contemporary Sahtú, Tłı̨chǫ, Dënesųłiné, and T'satsąot'ınę terms, characters, and spellings. In his travel narrative, for example, Samuel Hearne refers to both the "Northern Indians" and the "Copper Indians," peoples who subsequently came to be known by settlers as the "Chipewyan" and "Yellowknives" Dene and have always been known to themselves as Dënesųłiné and T'satsąot'ınę, respectively. All of these terms appear in this book. Similarly, the people whom early anthropologists referred to as "Copper Inuit" are also known as Inuinnait, but "Inuinnait" is itself a collective term for a range of "-miut" who historically lived and travelled in various parts of the Central Arctic (see map, page xxii). Although extended family networks continue to connect Inuinnait living in Ulukhaktok (Holman), Northwest Territories, with Kugluktuk, Iqaluktuuttiaq (Cambridge Bay), and other settlements in Nunavut, Ulukhaktok is part of the Northwest Territories and the Inuvialuit Land Claim Agreement, whereas those living in Kugluktuk and other Kitikmeot communities are beneficiaries of the Nunavut Land Claim Agreement.

Acknowledgments

I want to begin with huge, warm thanks to Allen and Grace Niptanatiak, Amanda and Mathieu Dumond, Catherine Niptanatiak, and Ace, Jon, and Jeff Niptanatiak for their friendship, care, and generosity. You have housed me, schooled me, transported me, fed me, and laughed at me for many years, and I love you all dearly. I would not have met the Nips or even visited Kugluktuk had it not been for Rebecca Craigie and Catherine Minshull, whose journeys to Kugluktuk initiated my connection to the community. Thank you. Thank you to Millie Kuliktana, who continually challenged and inspired me and played an important role in ensuring this book got written. Thanks, too, to all the people in Kugluktuk who guided me, met with me, hosted me, and otherwise shaped this project: Colin and Mavis Adjun; Aime Ahegona; Richard Akana; Jerry Atatahak; Miranda Atatahak; Alice Ayalik; Ida Ayalik-McWilliam; Marion Bolt; Sandy Buchan; Geoff Clark; Joe Allen Evyagotailak; Natalie Griller; Nellie Hikok; Margo Kadlun-Jones; Peter Kamingoak; Ann Rose Kerkovius; Twyla and Konrad Kryger; Pauline MacKinnon; Rosemarie Meyok; Joseph Niptanatiak; Red Pedersen; Derrick Powers; Donna, Mitch, and Jenny Rand; Lucy Taipana; Peter Taptuna; Mona Tiktalek; Becky and Luigi Torretti; Rob and Deb Walton; and Larry Whittaker.

At various stages, this book has been shaped by conversation, critique, or engagement with the writing of a number of scholars, many of whom I also count as friends. I owe a huge debt to Julie Cruikshank, Dan Clayton, Bruce Braun, Janet Tamalik McGrath, and Janice Cavell, all of whom read the manuscript in full and offered the most thorough, challenging, and insightful feedback I could hope to receive. Janet Tamalik McGrath shaped this book in more ways than I can describe, not only as a friend and Inuktitut teacher but also by holding me to a high standard of care in writing. Nagligivagit. I am also grateful to Jackie Price and Becky Mearns, whose thinking, writing, and friendship run through the text. Warm thanks, too, to Laura Cameron and Audrey Kobayashi, who have supported my work for many years. Critical feedback was also provided along the way by Andrew Baldwin, Trevor Barnes, Noel Castree, Rosemary-Claire Collard, Deborah Conners, Joyce Davidson, Sarah de Leeuw, Jessica Dempsey, Matt Farish, Anne Godlewska, Josh Gladstone, Tom Gleeson, Jack Hicks, Tina Loo, Beverley Mullings, Dana Olwan, Ted Rutland, Ann Secord, Mick Smith, Frank Tester, and Theresa Wong. Thank you.

Joanna Reid provided amazing editorial feedback on the entire text, and I would not have finished without her. Special thanks to Darcy Cullen at UBC Press for her continual support in moving the book to completion and to Lesley Erickson and Deborah Kerr for such close editorial attention. I also gratefully acknowledge research assistance provided by Stephanie Kittmer, Jay Malette, and Tara Cater. A slew of archivists and librarians at Library and Archives Canada, the Prince of Wales Northern Heritage Centre (PWNHC), the NWT Territorial Government Archives, the Hudson's Bay Company Archives, the University of Saskatchewan Archives, the Canadian Museum of Civilization, Kew Gardens Library and Archives, the Warwickshire County Records Office, the British Library, the Royal Society, the Linnaean Society, the Antiquarian Society, the City of London Archives, and Queen's University Special Collections were essential. Special thanks to Robin Weber at the PWNHC and to Mary Margaret Johnston Miller at Library and Archives Canada for their assistance. While doing archival research, I was generously hosted by a number of people, including Suzanne and Darcy Henderson, Bertie Mandelblatt, Jessica Mace, Spencer Tracey, and Carie Woods. Funding from a number of sources is also gratefully acknowledged: the Social Sciences and Humanities Research Council, ArcticNet, the Canadian Polar Commission, the Ontario Graduate Scholarship program, the Northern Scientific Training Program, the Network in Canadian History and Environment (NiCHE), *Antipode*'s Graduate Student Scholarship, as well as support from both Queen's University and Carleton University.

I have presented pieces of this book on several occasions but would like to particularly thank audiences at the University of Toronto, Memorial University, and the University of Wisconsin-Madison for their helpful feedback. I would also like to thank the UBC home seminar crew. Parts of Chapter 3 appeared in *Emotion, Place, and Culture,* edited by Liz Bondi et al., and parts of Chapter 4 were published in *Rethinking the Great White North,* edited by Andrew Baldwin, Laura Cameron, and Audrey Kobayashi.

In Ottawa, I have landed in the most wonderful community, and life without Kathryn Trevenen, Leslie Robertson, Frédérique Chabot, Karen Cocq, David Moffette, and Paul Saurette is unimaginable to me. Thank you not only for your friendship but also for pushing this book in so many ways. Huge thanks, too, to Jen Ridgley, Pablo Mendez, Fiona Jeffries, Rebecca Schein, Justin Paulson, Stacy Douglas, David Hugill, Danielle DiNovelli-Lang, Sonya Gray, Ummni Khan, Jill Wigle, and Theresa Wong for making life at Carleton so vibrant and for sustaining me during the final push. Warm thanks, too, to my family, who have watched this project unfold over almost ten years, with special thanks to my mom, Hélène Cameron, who read the entire text and offered such thoughtful feedback.

Finally, I would like to acknowledge that this book was largely written on unceded Anishnaabe lands. The complex relationship between settler colonial occupation of southern Canada, the writings of non-Inuit Indigenous scholars and intellectuals, and my own understanding of Qablunaaq relations with the Arctic deserves more attention than I give it here. But I gratefully acknowledge that my ability to live and work on these lands begins with the hospitality of the Anishnaabeg.

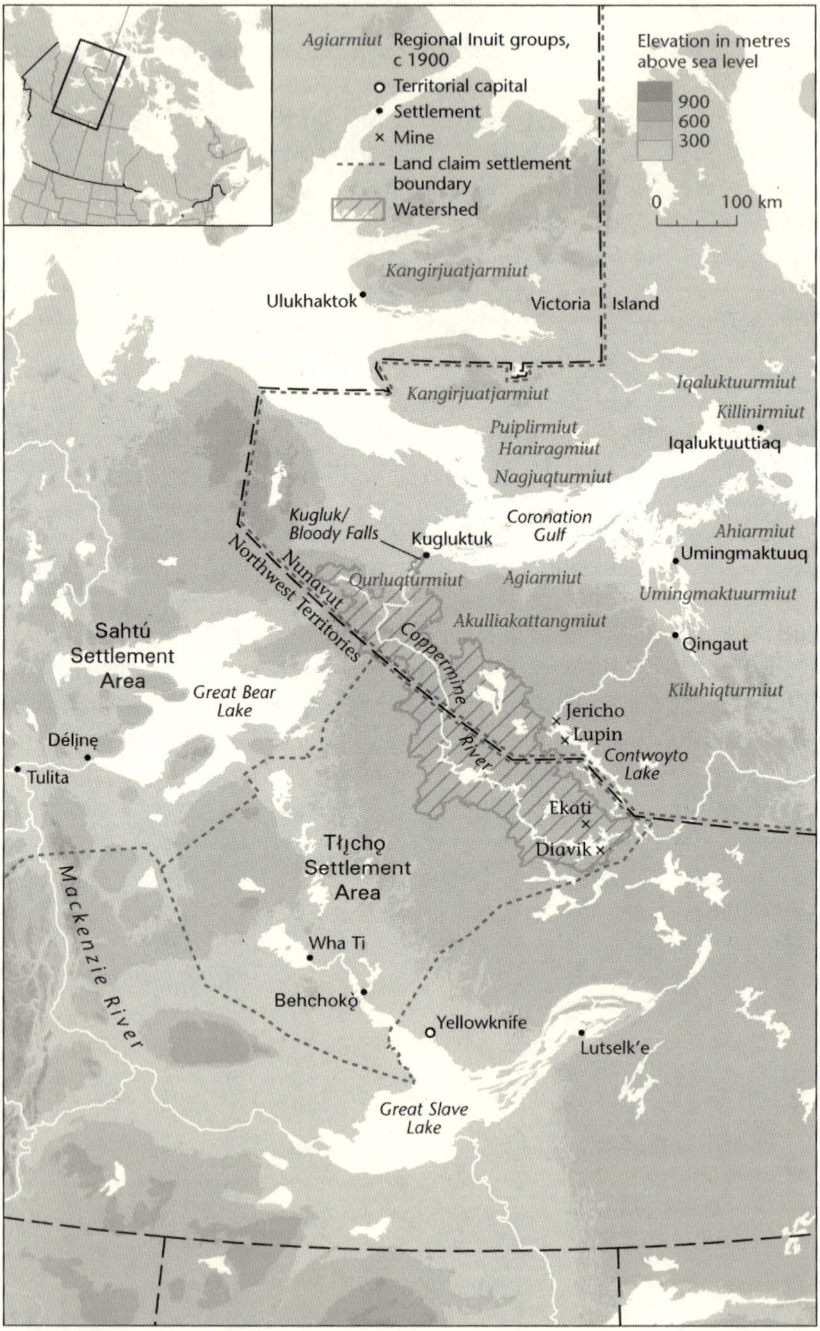

The Central Arctic

Far Off Metal River

I
Summer Stories

If settlers took their story seriously ... they would be required to confront the inherent injustice in their claim of any rights or authority over indigenous peoples and to their unconquered and unceded territory.
– Johnny Mack, "Hoquotist"

Imagine interpreting for us your own people's thinking toward us, instead of interpreting for us, our thinking, our lives, our stories.
– Jeannette Armstrong, in Paulette Regan, *Unsettling the Settler Within*

No living generation of Arctic narrator will ever get enough satisfaction out of spinning yarns about the Arctic and its cast of thousands, from the bygone days to this very moment. I am standing here in front of you to announce, unfortunately, that none of us will ever live long enough to finally complete the elusive final book on the Arctic and its people ... The Great White Arctic will remain an unfinished story to the very end of human habitation on planet Earth. How sad.
– Alootook Ipellie, "Thirsty for Life"

At the height of summer, when the Northern Store in Kugluktuk, Nunavut, is stocking outboard motors and the airport buzzes with mineral survey teams, Kugluk, a stretch of rapids on the Coppermine River, is teeming with fish. Waves of char, whitefish, and grayling make their way up and down the river, so numerous at times that even a teenager practising with a *kakivak* can spear a fish pretty much every time. Inuit have been fishing at this spot for centuries. The narrowing of the river here forces the fish together, and there are perfect little notches in the rocks along its edge for spearing. A gravel clearing upstream on the eastern bank of the river, Onoagahiovik (Unnuagaqhiurvik), used to be ideal for camping, setting up drying racks, and turning all that fish into *biffi* (dried fish).[1] From time to time, an elder from Kugluktuk will come to the falls to stock up and dry fish, but as the riverbed has become increasingly shallow, it's more and more difficult to reach the falls by boat.

Many years ago, or so the story goes, a group of Inuit camped at Kugluk were killed in their sleep by a group of Dene who had travelled well beyond their own territory at the behest of the Hudson's Bay Company (HBC). In the 1760s and '70s, Dene living in the lands west and northwest of Hudson Bay were already enrolled in the fur trade, journeying regularly to the forts on the west coast of the bay and struggling to maintain their lives and livelihoods as territories shifted, beaver populations fluctuated, diseases wreaked havoc, and missionaries began their steady creep north. It was from Dene trappers that Moses Norton, chief factor at Prince of Wales Fort (present-day Churchill, Manitoba) from 1762 to 1773, first heard of a "Far Off Metal River" teeming with copper riches, on lands that had yet to be traversed by Europeans and that remained largely blank on their slowly expanding maps.[2] At this time, it was not yet clear to Europeans whether there was a passage from Europe to Asia by way of the Arctic; it was not even clear where, exactly, the northern reaches of the continent fell away, if at all. And so it was that, in 1769, Norton arranged for Dene guides to lead Samuel Hearne, a young but ambitious HBC employee, to the copper deposits rumoured to exist in the Far Northwest. Hearne's task was to locate and determine the richness of the copper deposits, to make peace with local Indigenous groups, and to report any findings that might contribute to the discovery of a northwest passage.

Hearne's journey was essentially a failure on all three counts. After two unsuccessful attempts, he finally reached the river (prematurely named the Coppermine) and, once there, he and more than thirty men spent hours searching for copper, only to discover a single sizeable lump. Hearne and his guides promptly turned around and walked home. In his travel narrative, Hearne compensated for this highly anti-climactic turn of events by recounting in great detail a "massacre" that he claimed to have witnessed at Kugluk, a place he named Bloody Fall, the day before his futile search for copper.[3] According to Hearne, in the middle of the Arctic summer

"Kumuktahk Splitting Trout (Char)," Bloody Falls, Northwest Territories, June 1931. The photographer, Richard Finnie, did not provide biographical details about the man in the shot, but elders in Kugluktuk recognize him as Kumuktaaq. *Photo by Richard S. Finnie, Library and Archives Canada, Accession 1987–154, MIKAN 3607370.*

Bloody Falls, looking north, August 2008. *Photo by Emilie Cameron.*

night, 17 July 1771, a group of Indians led by Hearne's widely respected Dënesųłiné guide, Matonabbee, killed "upward of twenty" Inuit camped along the Coppermine River while Hearne himself stood "neuter in the rear." His account of the massacre – published twenty-four years later, although in limited circulation long before this – went on to become an iconic Arctic story. It has been anthologized in northern literature collections; reproduced in documentaries, plays, and poems; memorialized in stamps, murals, and street names; and even commemorated in song.[4] Hearne himself has been hailed as the "Marco Polo of the sub-Arctic" and as a sensitive and unusually perceptive explorer whose depiction of northern Indigenous life represents "one of the best ... in the early contact phase."[5]

The massacre itself occurs near the end of Hearne's narrative, seven months after his departure from Prince of Wales Fort. According to Hearne, as he and his crew followed the Coppermine River north toward the Arctic Ocean, spies were sent ahead to determine "if any Esquimaux were inhabiting the river-side between us and the sea." Five tents of Inuit were discovered, and "when the Indians received this intelligence, no farther attendance or attention was paid to my survey, but their whole thoughts were immediately engaged in planning ... how they might steal on the poor Esquimaux the ensuing night, and kill them all while asleep." After describing the Indians' preparations for battle, Hearne provides an account of the notorious massacre scene:

> In a few ſeconds the horrible ſcene commenced; it was ſhocking beyond deſcription; the poor unhappy victims were ſurpriſed in the midſt of their ſleep, and had neither time nor power to make any reſiſtance; men, women, and children, in all upward of twenty, ran out of their tents ſtark naked, and endeavoured to make their eſcape; but the Indians having poſſeſſion of all the land-ſide, to no place could they fly for ſhelter. One alternative only remained, that of jumping into the river; but, as none of them attempted it, they all fell a ſacrifice to Indian barbarity!

Excerpt from *A Journey*, 1795.

The account continues:

> The shrieks and groans of the poor expiring wretches were truly dreadful; and my horror was much increased at seeing a young girl, seemingly

> about eighteen years of age, killed so near me, that when the first spear was stuck into her side she fell down at my feet, and twisted round my legs, so that it was with difficulty that I could disengage myself from her dying grasps. As two Indian men pursued this unfortunate victim, I solicited very hard for her life; but the murderers made no reply till they had stuck both their spears through her body and transfixed her to the ground. They then looked me sternly in the face, and began to ridicule me, by asking if I wanted an Esquimaux wife; and paid not the smallest regard to the shrieks and agony of the poor wretch, who was twining round their spears like an eel! Indeed, after receiving much abusive language from them on the occasion, I was at length obliged to desire that they would be more expeditious in dispatching their victim out of her misery, otherwise I should be obliged, out of pity, to assist in the friendly office of putting an end to the existence of a fellow-creature who was so cruelly wounded. On this request being made, one of the Indians hastily drew his spear from the place where it was first lodged, and pierced it through her breast near the heart. The love of live, however, even in this most miserable state, was so predominant, that though this might justly be called the most merciful act that could be done for the poor creature, it seemed to be unwelcome, for though much exhausted by pain and loss of blood, she made several efforts to ward off the friendly blow. My situation and the terror of my mind at beholding this butchery, cannot easily be conceived, much less described; though I summed up all the fortitude I was master of on the occasion, it was with difficulty that I could refrain from tears; and I am confident that my features must have feelingly expressed how sincerely I was affected at the barbarous scene I then witnessed; even at this hour I cannot reflect on the transactions of that horrid day without shedding tears.

Hearne's published account goes on for several more pages. The scene becomes ever more horrifying as he describes the mob stabbing of an old man (his body reduced to little more than a "cullender") and the "butchering" of an old woman who had remained oblivious to the massacre because of her failing eyesight and poor hearing. Afterward, the Indians having "completed this piece of wantonness," Hearne and his companions "sat down, and made a good meal of fresh salmon," and Hearne "instantly" resumed his land survey and search for copper.[6] Disappointed in the copper resources of the region but heartened to spot the Northern Ocean, he and his guides headed back to Prince of Wales Fort.

Although the reliability of Hearne's account of the massacre has been questioned for at least two centuries, the story continues to circulate as though it is an accurate portrayal of a historical event. There are good reasons to side with the skeptics. According to historian and literature scholar Ian MacLaren, the version of the massacre story that appeared in Hearne's published travel narrative is in fact a fourth iteration. The first, Hearne's field notes, is now lost, but transcriptions of what are believed to be his original notes have survived, and as I discuss in subsequent chapters, these differ in important respects from the published version. Not only is there no "original" account to consult, then, but scholars have long believed that the published narrative was heavily edited to suit the interests of eighteenth-century readers and that the most graphic and evocative elements of the massacre scene were fabricated. Others have challenged Hearne's account by drawing on Dene and Inuit testimony. The members of the first Franklin expedition (1819–22) were told by their Dënesųłiné guides that Hearne was not present at the massacre, and they believed their guides. Despite their doubts about Hearne's account, they assembled a series of materials that were pivotal in confirming the "truth" of the Bloody Falls massacre, albeit without explicit confirmation of Hearne's presence at the scene. This truth was achieved, in part, through production of the first image of Bloody Falls, attributed to George Back, complete with skulls and bones (see the engraving on page 72). Scholars have since insisted that it, too, is a fabrication. Drawing on interviews with Kugluktukmiut and a study of Inuit oral traditions, literature scholar Robin McGrath suggests that Inuit were unlikely to have camped where the bones are placed and that any remains would have been washed away by yearly flooding. As I argue in Chapter 3, the Franklin expedition members would likely have agreed that the bones are in the wrong spot, if indeed they existed, but the image continues to circulate as though it is an accurate depiction of the site in 1821.[7]

Hearne's story, then, whatever its correspondence with historical events, is a *story.* But even those who concede that the story was probably embellished maintain the truth of the event itself, and the insistent materiality of the alleged massacre site plays a role in this process. Bloody Falls not only anchors Hearne's story; it has continued to gather stories of encounter, violence, and witness over the past two centuries. John Franklin and subsequent explorers did not just claim to find bones at Bloody Falls: they named a flower in honour of the massacre and reproduced Hearne's mounting sense of anxiety as they, too, drew their Dene guides closer to Inuit lands. Ethnologist Vilhjalmur Stefansson described Bloody Falls as "the center of the story of the North" and, recalling his own visit, declared the "basaltic gorge through which the Coppermine was now rushing ... one of the deadliest rapids in the world."[8] The wilderness canoeists who paddle the Coppermine River every summer retrace Hearne's steps and describe Bloody Falls as a transition point between barren wilderness and Inuit encounter. The murder of two Catholic missionaries in 1913 by Sinisiak and Uluksuk has been localized at Bloody Falls, though it almost certainly did not occur there, and the falls became a site for Richard S. Finnie's 1931 film, *Among the Igloo Dwellers,* as Finnie joined a long line of visitors before and since who have endeavoured to piece together the historical details of the massacre.[9] Marked on regional maps, Bloody Falls is central to Qablunaaq imaginative geographies of the North. Even a wolf attack on the Canadian Arctic Expedition (1913–18) was oriented in terms of its distance from the falls.

In a sense, for Qablunaat (sing. "Qablunaaq," a term I define in more detail later in this chapter but can be taken to mean "non-Inuit, non-Indigenous peoples or settlers"), *history itself* begins at Bloody Falls. The massacre is continually invoked as the region's first "historical" event, the moment in which Inuit "prehistory" gave way and a triumphant, deeply colonial claim to the land and its stories was first articulated ("history," in such formulations, begins with European arrival and witnessing). Indeed, as I describe in this book, the story of the Bloody Falls massacre has played an important role in defining the ways in which Qablunaat relate to northern lands and peoples. It has made legible a distinctly Qablunaaq sense of being innocent witnesses to the suffering of northern Indigenous peoples, it has shaped northern resource extraction and land claims, it interweaves with the production of racialized classificatory schemes, and it helps anchor Qablunaaq claims to the history of the North. Bloody Falls is also a target of conscious efforts among Inuit and Dene to forget and reorder imperial histories and geographies, and to assert jurisdiction over their lands, lives, histories, and futures. The story, in other words, *matters,* although not necessarily in the ways one might expect.

Although it is rarely remarked upon, Hearne's account of the Bloody Falls massacre is a summer story. It unfolds under a midnight sun, amid blueberry bushes and willows, alongside a river teeming with fish. While much is made of Arctic winters, this story is shaped by the summer trails of the Bluenose, Bathurst, and Dolphin and Union caribou herds and the incessant buzzing of mosquitoes, not by igloos or ice or northern lights. Its circulation, moreover, has been propelled by the summer journeys of subsequent explorers and prospectors, the summer swarms of southern researchers, and the summer travels of canoeists who paddle the length of the Coppermine River as much as by those who know the land in all its seasons. But one need not *know* the North in a "corporeal, bodily sense," as Stephen Leacock mused in 1936, need not know the intimate details of the Coppermine River bottom or the habits of Arctic char, to assert a claim to its stories:

> When I write about the North I speak with a certain authority. For I know the North, as few people know it. In the corporeal, bodily sense, I have never been there. But in my arm chair, in front of the fire in my house on Côte des Neiges Road in Montreal, I have traversed it all, from the portages back of Lake Superior to where the Mackenzie delta washes into the tidal seas. I have been with Franklin on the Coppermine and Coronation Gulf, with Hudson till I lost him owing to his own folly, with Mackenzie over the divide, in Red River ox-carts with Butler, and in the foothills with Milton and Cheadle. In the snow-storms and Arctic blizzards I feel perfectly at home; if it gets really bad I just lie down in the snow, along with Stefansson, and let it bury me completely and lie there for a day or two and read a book till it moderates. But I must say I don't think I ever felt such intense cold as on crossing the Coppermine running hard with ice through barren treeless country of slate and stone. Imagine trusting oneself on a river like that on a sort of raft or boat made of willow sticks, wet to the skin, in piercing cold. I had to get up and mix a hot whiskey and stir the fire and leave Franklin and Richardson to freeze awhile till I rejoined them.[10]

Leacock's tongue is planted firmly in cheek here, but he nevertheless evokes a persistent and profoundly arrogant claim to "know" the North from afar, one that continues to underwrite the authority of a range of northern relations and practices. As a number of scholars have noted, the "idea of North" is both central to nationalist imaginations in Canada and based on radically limited experience; North is, indeed, an *idea* for most Qablunaat, an idea constituted by the stories we tell.[11] Claims to properly know the North from afar have been occasionally rebuffed, occasionally mocked, and mostly ignored by Inuit. Inuit are keenly aware that Bloody Falls is a profoundly invented place, that it has been constituted overwhelmingly by people who have never actually *been* – "in the corporeal, bodily sense" – to the spot where the Coppermine River narrows. But this inventedness, as Inuit are also keenly aware, should not be mistaken for falsity or immateriality. Stories matter, and as I demonstrate in the chapters that follow, Bloody Falls has a remarkable capacity to gather and order Qablunaaq experiences and relations with the North and with Inuit. But neither should the immense imaginative resonance of the story be assumed to encapsulate the place itself. If, as I argue in this book, stories are material, relational practices through which we order our relations with each other and with the land, then it becomes possible to consider that there is more than one place anchored by the gabbro walls that force the Coppermine through its narrow channel here, and more than one story through which this place is made meaningful. And if we begin by acknowledging that the Bloody Falls massacre story is a summer story – that, like the myriad other summer stories that constitute this prototypically wintry place, it is situated, partial, specific, and placed – we can begin to think differently about the North.

GEOGRAPHIES OF QABLUNAAQ RELATIONS WITH THE CANADIAN ARCTIC

This book was written during a time of immense interest in the Canadian North. Spurred in large part by evidence of climatic change and expectations that global warming will transform the environmental, economic, and geopolitical significance of the Arctic region, international attention is trained on northern people, places, and things to an unprecedented degree. As the prospect of an increasingly ice-free Arctic raises possibilities of expanded shipping, mining, and drilling, both polar and non-polar nations are scrambling to map and claim the region's riches. Buoyed by reports of retreating sea ice, resource developers and ship builders and pension fund investors have turned their gaze northward, along with the federal government, whose intention to transform northern "potential into prosperity" is only lightly veiled with promises to attend to the social, cultural, environmental, and economic well-being of those who call the North home.[12]

Amid these geopolitical rumblings, Inuit struggle to place their concerns at the forefront of northern "development" and repeatedly reassert their authority over northern lands and seas.[13] They insist that the federal government live up to the promises of the northern land claim agreements, devolve jurisdictional controls to northerners, and account for the well-being of its northern citizens. Struggling to address not only rapid environmental change but also the social, economic, political, and cultural legacies of colonization, northerners are simultaneously under immense scrutiny and frequently sidelined in the "new North" heralded by politicians and investors. Poverty, intergenerational trauma, and overcrowded housing combine with pressures to promote massive resource development, even while the very lands and animals that have sustained life in the North for millennia shift under rapidly changing environmental conditions. Far from being the timeless, mythic place of nationalist imaginations, the Arctic is in fact a site of great political, cultural, economic, environmental, and social change.

While much may be shifting in and beyond the North today, these shifts are not wholly novel, and we should be mindful of all that is swept aside when the North is produced as "new." Contemporary Arctic geographies are shaped by histories of imperialism and colonialism, by the specific racializations elaborated in settler societies, by historical and contemporary flows of capital and resources, by state and missionary activities in the region, by traditional cultural, economic, and ecological practices, by Inuit and other Indigenous political movements, and by changes in the *nuna* (land) itself. Although some continue to imagine the Canadian North as an isolated, timeless, and far-flung region whose very isolation and starkness anchors the nation's symbolic economy, the Arctic is in fact deeply relational and always has been; it is constituted both imaginatively and materially by networks of people, ideas, and things. These networks, moreover, are made sensible, legible, and political through stories. That is, the stories we tell about our relations with one another and with the land matter, or so I contend throughout this book. I am particularly interested in how Qablunaaq relations with northern peoples and places are made possible through the stories we practise. Qablunaaq stories differ from those that emerge from the ancient and intimate relations that northern Indigenous peoples have nurtured with the land, but they do teach us how to relate to the North, and they inform us of our claims to the land and its resources. In so doing, they foster some forms of life and not others.

I am interested in understanding how, why, and where Qablunaaq stories come to matter, and for whom. I understand stories as relational and material ordering practices, as practices that are not merely representative but also constitutive of our relations with one another and with the land. Stories, I argue, are not separate from, nor merely representative of, the world around us; they are themselves material, and they have material effects on the lives we live. From such a perspective, the stories that anchor understandings of the Arctic are significant not only because of their imaginative force but also because of their influence over the very material conditions of life both within and beyond the North. Stories matter, in other words, and not just in imaginative terms. To the extent that the shifting geographies of capital, resources, governance structures, and climate in the contemporary Arctic are made sensible, legible, and political through stories, we must pay close attention to the stories that anchor and authorize Qablunaaq claims.

I examine Qablunaaq relations with the Canadian Arctic through close study of a particular story, the story of the Bloody Falls massacre. Although conventionally told as an account of Inuit-Dene conflict, this story, I argue, is a Qablunaaq story: it is told by, for, and about Qablunaat (however much it claims otherwise), and it advances Qablunaaq claims and interests. Although I focus on specific practices of the story, and although I advance a series of arguments about Bloody Falls, I employ the story primarily as a methodological tool, a kind of organizing focus that draws attention to some of the complex relations through which past, present, and future Norths have been made possible, sensible, and legible. In many ways, tracing the geographies of the Bloody Falls massacre story was itself a methodology for exploring a larger set of questions and concerns. That is, it was only by immersing myself in the specificities of the story and by working with the proposition that story is a relational and material ordering practice that I was able to examine the larger processes and practices that interested me. In asking when, where, and for whom the massacre story matters, I was in fact attempting to understand what it means to relate to the North as Qablunaat, what our inheritances are, and what our knowledges do. In a context where such questions are either not posed at all or are posed in such a way as to reinscribe Qablunaat as the centre of colonial and decolonizing processes, I was not only interested in asking this question, but also in problematizing the terms upon which I might seek to answer it.

Why this particular story, then? In part, I was interested in the contrast between efforts to memorialize, materialize, and celebrate the story, and efforts to ignore, refuse, and forget it. Hearne's account of the massacre has been told and retold for centuries and is still invoked today as a kind of instructive parable for making sense of Inuit, Dene, and Qablunaat relations. The story's persistence and reach have a great deal to teach us about the shape of Qablunaaq relations with the North. But I have known from the beginning that the Bloody Falls massacre story is not a "good story" among Inuit and that Kugluktukmiut are not particularly interested in engaging with it. It is not told when Kugluktukmiut head to the falls to fish. It is not told when a teenager shoots his first *tuktu* (caribou), when elders get together over tea, or even when Inuit and Dene gather in each other's communities to work toward better futures for themselves, their young people, and the land. Occasionally, when a researcher or tourist passes through Kugluktuk, an elder will accept the standard honorarium and half-heartedly tell the story, passing the cash on to grandchildren who, in turn, use it to buy gas, smokes, food. There are better stories to tell, for better purposes. Tracing these limits and refusals and moves away from Bloody Falls was thus as important to me as tracing its iconic impact and reach. It seems to me that Qablunaat need to learn not only the shape of our influence and claims and inheritances but also the limits of those claims and all the ways in which we do not matter and do not know. The geographies of the Bloody Falls massacre story help us to do that.

The story also naturalizes a subject position that I think is enormously important and that continues to shape Qablunaaq relations with the North and with Inuit. In Qablunaaq tellings, Hearne is a neutral witness to the violence and suffering of Indigenous peoples, and neither his witnessing nor his constitutive role in that violence and suffering are acknowledged as themselves consequential. This neutrality is false; not only was Hearne responsible for the journey that brought Dene to Inuit lands in the first place, his witnessing was also deeply invested and impactful. Stories like Hearne's enable Qablunaat to pretend that our witnessing is benevolent, objective, and appropriate, and I aim, here, to unpack the significance of this form of relation to northern lands and peoples. Hearne's subject position, moreover, resonates with that of contemporary Qablunaaq researchers, many of whom continue to conceptualize their gaze as neutral, helpful, objective, and necessary. The story of the Bloody Falls massacre enables us to understand not only how witnessing, neutrality, and benevolence have shaped Qablunaaq relations with Inuit during the last several centuries but also how these play out in contemporary research relations.

Furthermore, although numerous researchers have attempted to unearth an Inuit "counter-story" that could complicate or challenge Hearne's account, such efforts have largely been in vain.[14] As I discuss in Chapter 6, Kugluktukmiut extensively story their relations with Dene, including past violent encounters, but no single, definitive, "local" version of the Bloody Falls massacre has been shared with and documented by Qablunaat. Such stories may well exist, of course, but the fact that Kugluktukmiut continually fail to satisfy this desire among Qablunaat is both instructive and suggestive. As I detail later in this chapter, part of my interest in writing this book stemmed from my desire to challenge the conceit that "counter-stories" represent the scope of Indigenous responses to colonial discourses and, more broadly, that efforts to address or change the colonial nature of contemporary Inuit-Qablunaat relations require Inuit to resist, talk back, or renarrate in direct response to Qablunaaq stories. This is not only an exceedingly narrow framework within which to conceptualize Inuit subjectivity, it also reproduces colonial relations in that Inuit are called upon to respond to Qablunaat in modes, formats, and terms that are dictated by, and legible to, Qablunaat. The absence of a clear counter-story to Hearne's account of the Bloody Falls massacre provides an opening to consider the limits of this framing and to work toward other modes of relation.

Qablunaaq Geographies: Not Quite Not Inuit

Studying Qablunaaq stories is not necessarily the same thing as studying settler or white stories. Although the term "Qablunaaq" is often understood to mean "white" or "white person," this is not exactly what it means in Inuktut and not precisely how I invoke it here. "Qablunaaq" is a relational term.[15] It is a term in Inuktut for a non-Inuk, and though the non-Inuit who have ventured onto Inuit lands are often white, "Qablunaaq," as Minnie Freeman notes, "does not mean white man – there is no meaning in it at all pertaining to colour or white or man. I know for sure, too, that it was the *qallunaat* who named themselves white men, to distinguish themselves from other colours, for it is they who have always been aware of different racial colours."[16] Morphologically, there is a connection between the word "Qablunaaq" and facial hair: in Inuktitut (a dialect of the Inuit language), *qablu* means "eyebrow," leading some to suggest that "Qablunaaq" refers to those who have more facial hair than the typical Inuk; Freeman was told that it referred to those who are particularly inclined to groom their facial hair. Historically, politically, economically, culturally, socially, spiritually, and emotionally, "Qablunaaq" means much more than this, of course, but it is important to begin by noting that the term is not centrally concerned with skin colour.

The other non-Inuit who periodically ventured onto Inuit lands, as the story of the Bloody Falls massacre details, are, of course, "Indians" (Itqiliq [singular]; Itqiliit [plural] in Inuinnaqtun), including Gwich'in, Dene, Cree, Innu, and other Indigenous peoples whose traditional territories abut and overlap Inuit Nunangat (Inuit homelands). "Qablunaat" thus refers to the non-Itqiliq, non-Inuit peoples whom Inuit have encountered over the years, from the earliest explorers, whalers, traders, and missionaries to the government, academic, and corporate figures of the present.

Although the word "Qablunaaq" does not directly refer to skin colour or imply a racialized hierarchy (as Western attributions of skin colour have done since at least the eighteenth century), Inuit are acutely aware of the hierarchical, racialized conceptualizations that Qablunaat carry with them when they head north and the structures of power that authorize their claims and actions. But it is not solely their obsessions with race that distinguish Qablunaat. Freeman, for example, doubts that *qallunaat* refers to "people who pamper their eyebrows" and points instead to its etymological links with the word *qallunaaraaluit,* which means "very respectable, avaricious, materialistic, who could do anything with material, or those who fear for their ability to manufacture material." This meaning, Freeman suggests, is more reflective of what it means to be qallunaaq among Inuit. Zebedee Nungak's imagined "Institute of Qallunology" has documented a range of Qablunaaq characteristics, from an obsession with small talk to a competitive and classed organization of social relations. Alootook Ipellie has commented on the Qablunaaq appetite for the rich resources of his homeland, and Tommy Akulukjuk on the experience of "looking up through the microscope" that Qablunaaq researchers so unself-consciously direct at Inuit lives, bodies, and communities.[17] Martha Flaherty, too, has observed that Qablunaat "interpret the concept of 'freedom of expression' as 'freedom of exploitation' – the freedom to exploit Inuit knowledge for one's own gain."[18] These are just some of the embodied, specific, relational understandings of what it means to be Qablunaaq. Its meaning emerges from Inuit languages, values, and ways of being in the world and the ways in which traders, trappers, missionaries, explorers, governments, academics, corporations, writers, journalists, teachers, and tourists have jarred against what it is to be *inummarik,* a real Inuk.

My interest here is not precisely in how Inuit understand Qablunaat – Inuit have expressed this eloquently, in a range of contexts, for generations – but rather what it means to relate to the North as a named, relationally constituted, historically and geographically specific people. Many Qablunaat relate to the North as Canadians, some as white people, but more often, I think, as the unnamed, unmarked beings their whiteness authorizes.[19] This book examines the textures and patterns of Qablunaaq relations with the North, with Inuit, and with the land, but it is important to clarify that it is not precisely *about* Inuit. Although it is deeply informed by the insights and perspectives that Inuit have shared with me, or that I have been touched by in the writings and teachings of Inuit and non-Inuit alike, it is an inquiry into the contours of a relationship, one that has shifted over time and will continue to shift, and one that has been politically and materially consequential.

Indeed, whether we recognize it or not, Qablunaat are constituted relationally; we are not received as neutral or benevolent beings, unencumbered by the histories that we have inherited and the structures that authorize our speech, our actions, and our wealth. Part of what the Bloody Falls massacre story teaches us, in fact, is that the habit among Qablunaat of imagining that we are somehow not involved, not responsible, and not named by our relations with the North has a long and ongoing history. The stories we tell trace these relations for us. It is the relations – the structures, the forces, the material reordering of worlds – that are at stake in this book. To trace Qablunaaq geographies is not, then, to engage in "white studies" or to feed the settler appetite for guilty, fascinated horror at colonial wrongs. It is not meant to encourage what Daniel David Moses so compellingly describes as a settler compulsion to "dance around the wound" of colonialism. That is not my intention here. It is, instead, to attend to the relations that have made us and to begin to work toward relations that are more just, more kind, more humble, and more life giving.

Colonial Geographies

In discussions of the contemporary North, the dynamics of colonization and decolonization are rarely named, but they are my primary interest here, including the ways in which the stories Qablunaat tell allow us to turn away from this defining feature of our relations with Inuit and with northern lands and resources. I understand colonialism to involve the dispossession and occupation of Indigenous lands, the establishment and maintenance of economic and political domination, and the production and promulgation of knowledge and ideas that naturalize uneven, hierarchical, exploitative relations. In Canada, the colonial project is defined by the specific dynamics of settler colonialism, in that the colonizing group not only occupies and extracts wealth from Indigenous lands but also has settled on them. As Patrick Wolfe observes, this requires ongoing political, economic, and cultural work; in settler colonial contexts, "invasion is a structure not an event."[20] Naturalizing invasion and producing a sense of settler "indigeneity" thus characterizes settler colonial contexts. Settlers aim to feel, finally, *settled,* to be "post" colonial, and this involves a persistent denial of the ongoing displacement and dispossession of Indigenous lands, claims, knowledges, and lives. In Canada, the "idea of North" has been central to this dynamic; Qablunaaq claims to be fundamentally "northern," to locate our dreams of national unity in Arctic lands, and to perennially "go north" to discover ourselves reflect the ongoing and impossible desire in settler colonial contexts to legitimize the unresolved, unjust relations that underpin dispossession and settlement.

Colonial and settler colonial relations in northern Canada have unfolded differently than those in the South, not least because Qablunaat have never *settled* the Arctic in precisely the same ways as they have other parts of the country. Although Inuit lands, resources, practices, bodies, and knowledges have been the target of whalers, traders, missionaries, explorers, scholars, doctors, and police for centuries, Inuit experienced rapid and intensive state intervention primarily by way of a modernist welfare state following the Second World War. They continued to live primarily on the land until the mid-twentieth century, never signed historical treaties, were never forced onto reserves, and always far outnumbered Qablunaat on their lands. Furthermore, Inuit have always been held apart as a different Indigenous group in Canada, mostly governed as Canadian citizens (although in deeply racialized and paternalistic terms) and only briefly administered as wards of the state under the Indian Act.[21] This is not to say that Inuit have not experienced many of the same colonial incursions as other Indigenous peoples in Canada; they have, including residential schooling, forced relocation, the shooting of sled dogs, Christianization, unauthorized exploitation of their lands, the undermining and outlawing of cultural and economic practices, and other forms of dispossession. But the historical geographies and contemporary articulations of colonization in the North differ in important ways from those in the South.

Further complicating understandings of colonialism in the Arctic is the widespread misapprehension that, with the signing of comprehensive land claim agreements (such as the Nunavut Land Claim Agreement), colonial relations were somehow resolved, in that Indigenous peoples were "given" parcels of land by the state. This is not so. Comprehensive land claim agreements in northern Canada are premised on the state's recognition that Indigenous peoples hold a primary and unceded claim to their lands, as acknowledged in the Royal Proclamation of 1763.[22] The property relations, institutions, and interactions that are formalized through land claim agreements are not gifts from a benevolent state; the agreements require Indigenous signatories to formally cede their claims to the land in exchange for specific types of compensation, title, and the establishment of forms of governance that might more substantially account for their interests than existing structures. As many Nunavummiut have observed, the institutions established through land claim agreements often reinforce and perpetuate colonial relations. They also, as is clear in Nunavut today, facilitate and accelerate the accumulation of capital by formalizing title to Indigenous lands and implementing property and governance regimes that enable resource extraction.

Although there is no "after" or "beyond" colonialism in the contemporary North, this is not to say that colonial relations wholly define the lives of northerners. This, too, is a colonial conceit. Not only are there active, ongoing efforts to decolonize northern institutions, practices, and relations; Inuit ways of being-knowing-doing-accounting also persist and thrive in spite of colonial relations.[23] As Audra Simpson observes, "the condition of Indigeneity in North America is to have survived" colonization and thus "to have called up the failure of the project itself."[24] But if Indigenous survival attests to the fact that colonization is never complete, this does not mean that colonialism is not persistent, insidious, and resolutely present. Rather, it is to hold together what settler colonialism continually denies – its own existence and the deeply violent geographies that sustain it – and to refuse a totalizing account of colonization in which "the Settler's power is the fundamental reference and assumption, inherently limiting Indigenous freedom and imposing a view of the world that is but an outcome or perspective on that power."[25]

I understand this "holding together" of both rigorous acknowledgment of colonial relations and a refusal of totalizing, encompassing accounts of colonization as an essential orientation to the colonial present. It requires both honest remembering and conscious forgetting, detailed tracing and imaginative leaps. It involves an impossible but necessary turn both toward and away from colonial relations, however contradictory and paradoxical this may seem. This is as closely as I can approximate what it means for me to orient toward "decolonization," a word I use with caution and that I understand as a critical mode of relating to pasts, presents, and futures that cannot be wholly defined in relation to the colonial, and as a dismantling of colonial institutions, laws, claims, and occupation. As a number of Indigenous scholars and leaders have insisted, decolonization not only demands reckoning with colonial practices, structures, knowledges, and relations but also requires nourishing practices, subjectivities, and aspirations grounded elsewhere. In sociologist Boaventura de Sousa Santos's terms, it means attending to that which does not exist, that which has been produced as absent through colonial modes of ordering.[26]

"Decolonization" necessarily means something different for Indigenous peoples than it does for the state, for the descendants of settlers, and for those who continue to profit from the dispossession of Indigenous lands and resources. Indeed, many Indigenous writers and scholars insist that their capacity to live their lives otherwise, to nourish the worlds they desire, is limited not only by colonial legal and institutional structures and radically limited access to their lands, but also by the enormous cultural, economic, and political investment of settlers in colonial knowledges, subjectivities, and material relations. For settlers, *unsettling* – imaginatively, materially, politically – is an essential and ongoing task.[27] We must learn to know less, claim less, to listen, and to stop. This is one of the reasons I approach the concept of decolonization with caution and do not claim to be undertaking decolonizing work in this book. For me, such a claim nudges too closely toward settler desires to be "good" in the face of colonial relations and moves too quickly toward a reconciliation or resolution that is not mine to claim.[28] As Audra Simpson notes regarding the possibilities of engaging in a shared process of critical interrogation, "we don't have to reconcile, we don't have to be great friends, we don't even have to be friends ... [but] it would be nice if we each had a substantive and triangulated sense of things – together – and were unsettled by that – together – and uncomfortable – together. We don't have to actually like it, or like each other." But to "join in the process of critical interrogation ... to ask questions together ... is part of a kind of citizenship that could be quite productive."[29]

For me, joining in a process of shared, unsettling interrogation, in the context of this book, involves both radically *placing* and *displacing* Qablunaaq practices and claims, as I understand them. It demands both scaling back on the reach of established modes of apprehending colonial relations and taking up different modes of apprehension. Although I begin with the premise that colonialism significantly shapes Qablunaaq relations with Inuit and the North, I aim to engage with colonial relations and the storying of the North differently here.

STORY AS A RELATIONAL AND MATERIAL ORDERING PRACTICE

My first encounter with the Bloody Falls massacre story was accidental. I was visiting a friend in Kugluktuk and came across a reference to *Senecio lugens,* a species of ragweed named in honour of the massacre, while lazily flipping through a field guide to northern wildflowers (*lugens* means "to mourn" in Latin; see Chapter 3). I had never heard of Bloody Falls or Samuel Hearne. I had no intention of undertaking research in

Kugluktuk, and though I was intrigued and appalled by this little flower, I did not anticipate that it would become the basis for a larger study. This accidental encounter with Bloody Falls, in the form of a photo of a little yellow flower, in a field guide, in an overheated house in New Town, is instructive. It suggests that stories are not isolated texts or wholly imaginative devices. Stories are not simply *about* people or places. They are themselves composed of networks of relations between people, places, and things, and specific practices of stories matter.

Although it is conventional to refer to the North as a particularly storied place – and a number of scholars have done remarkable work examining Qablunaaq literature, the "idea" of North in the southern imagination, and Inuit storytelling and literary traditions – scholars have tended to invoke very different theoretical frameworks for understanding the narrative geographies of the region depending on *whose* stories are under discussion. Indeed, part of what I aim to do in this book is challenge the vastly differing ways scholars have approached story when dealing with Indigenous peoples as a "traditional culture," as opposed to a colonized group. When Indigenous peoples are addressed in relation to the traditional, "story" is understood as a repository of traditional knowledge, as a form of wisdom that is intimately tied to place, and as an ancient oral practice. The role played by stories and storytelling in forming Indigenous social, cultural, and environmental relationships, in teaching appropriate conduct, and in nurturing spiritual ties is emphasized. Colonialism rarely makes an appearance, except as a historical process that undermined the capacity of Indigenous peoples to sustain their oral traditions.

In studies that conceptualize Indigenous peoples as colonized, on the other hand, the stories told by Indigenous peoples tend to fall away. Studies of the narrative dimensions of colonization typically focus, instead, on the *colonizers'* stories and their capacity to naturalize colonial domination and to discursively mark the limits of an imperial project.[30] Stories are primarily approached as texts, not as embodied material practices shaped by the social, cultural, environmental, and political contexts within which they are told. It is the imaginative, representational importance of colonial discourses that is of most acute interest. In studies of colonial discourse, in other words, the stories told by Indigenous peoples do not matter (except insofar as they might "counter" dominant discourses), whereas in studies of Indigenous storytelling, "story" tends to name practices and knowledges rooted in the traditional, oral, and local, practices and knowledges whose relations with the complex geographies of the present are often left unexplored. This contrast in theoretical and conceptual approaches to "storying" the North is no accident. It reflects both the temporal fantasies that underpin imaginative geographies of indigeneity (in which contemporary Indigenous people and cultures are assessed in terms of the persistence of the traditional and "premodern") as well as the extent to which story has been stripped of its contextual and material specificity in discursive analyses.

Although a great deal of northern research proceeds within this racialized and colonial division of labour, there are notable exceptions, including the work of Julie Cruikshank, who has long studied not only the narrative dimensions of non-Indigenous knowledge production but also the rich social relations shaping storytelling in Indigenous oral traditions. Working with Tlingit and Tutchone women in the Yukon through the 1980s and '90s, Cruikshank explored "how narrative provides a framework for experiencing the material world and how local stories intersect with larger social, historical, and political processes." She also critically interrogated the uses to which Indigenous narratives were being put, including the rise of the traditional ecological knowledge (TEK) industry and the use of Indigenous stories as historical evidence. Her more recent work, along with that of anthropologists Paul Nadasdy, Nancy Wachowich, Lisa Stevenson, and Ann Fienup-Riordan, offers nuanced investigations of the complex ways in which Indigenous and non-Indigenous knowledges, practices, and claims intersect in the contemporary North. Similarly, Keavy Martin's recent work discusses Inuit storytelling as a diverse, complex, and evolving cultural, philosophical, and literary tradition, one that is best examined within Inuit interpretative frameworks rather than Qablunaaq theories. Furthermore, although the knowledges, philosophies, analyses, and methodologies articulated by Inuit intellectuals remain largely absent from most academic work, a number of scholars from Inuit Nunangat have mobilized Inuit intellectual traditions within the Qablunaaq academy, including Janet Tamalik McGrath, Jackie Price, Rebecca Mearns, and Looee Okalik.[31]

Despite these important interventions, technocratic, essentialist, and profoundly colonial engagements with "story" in the North remain remarkably tenacious. "Traditional knowledge" continues to be understood as a source of data, Indigenous knowledge systems continue to be approached by bureaucrats and researchers without due regard to epistemological and ontological difference, and the "story of the North" as site of nationalist becoming continues to underwrite geopolitical claims to northern lands and resources. Much of this work unfolds, moreover, without any acknowledgment of or attention to colonial pasts and presents, including the ways in which colonial relations shape the production, reproduction, distribution, dissemination, and erasure of various forms of knowledge. It thus remains important to continually articulate methodological and theoretical spaces within which both the reach and limits of Qablunaaq practices might be apprehended, and within which Inuit are not simply positioned as "local" informants, purveyors of traditional knowledge, or stylized figures in a well-worn account of colonial domination and resistance. It remains important, in other words, to attend to the "storying of the North" in ways that respect and account for Inuit not only as complex, diverse individuals but also as self-determining people who have themselves been undertaking analyses of Qablunaat for centuries and who, crucially, do not live wholly on the terms or within the horizons of Qablunaaq imaginations, policies, claims, and practices.

To do so, I think, requires a different understanding of what stories are and what they do, not just in the context of specific social relations, but also as they figure within dominant theoretical paradigms. That is, part of my aim in this book is to approach story as a site and mode of colonial encounter, one in which conceptual, historical, political, and material geographies collide and interweave. As a geographer whose training was heavily influenced by poststructuralist approaches to colonial and postcolonial studies, for example, I am both indebted to and deeply dissatisfied with the ways in which the concept of discourse has been rallied to make sense of colonial relations. Readers will note both an engagement with this tradition and a kind of chafing against its principal lines of argument, particularly the practice of extrapolating broad cultural, political, and social patterns by way of colonial texts.[32] The analysis of colonial texts and discourses has been central to postcolonial studies. As Edward Said made clear, cultural production is intimately related to imperial domination. One must imaginatively conquer distant peoples and lands, Said argued, in order to validate and carry out that domination in more material terms.[33] This foundational premise of postcolonial studies enabled a generation of scholars to draw productive links between culture, literature, ideas, and processes of imperial domination, and work in this tradition has helped us to appreciate and articulate how important stories can be. It has helped us understand that stories matter, that they are not innocent, not "just" stories. Colonial texts and the imaginative geographies they help constitute may be partial, constructed, and misleading, but they are nevertheless materially consequential.

But postcolonial approaches to the narrative dimensions of colonization have their limitations. In taking seriously the role of stories in colonial and imperial formations, colonial and postcolonial scholars have tended to assume that the ideas and relations they can diagnose in stories are themselves the scope and terms of colonization, as well as the appropriate terrain of anti-colonial struggle. They have tended to rely too heavily on a theoretical rendering of colonial relations in which colonizer and colonized occupy agonistic, placeless, timeless positions, and in which colonial texts are invariably understood to be hegemonic. They have overemphasized the representational and have underestimated the messy, material, placed contexts in which colonial relations are continually made and remade.[34] Within such a framework, for example, I could argue (as others have effectively done) that the Bloody Falls massacre story elaborates and naturalizes the whiteness of the North, reproduces colonial tropes of savagery and civility, perpetuates a harsh landscape aesthetic, dehumanizes Indigenous peoples, and advances settler claims to northern space.[35] Such analyses are not wrong; they are compelling and important. But they are also partial. They can be articulated without ever setting foot in Nunavut, without ever talking to an Indigenous northerner, and without paying attention to the specific places and contexts within which the story of the Bloody Falls massacre is actually practised. As much as critical research into Hearne's narrative (and the narrative constitution of colonial relations more broadly) aims to trouble and unsettle geographies of colonialism, whiteness, and racism in Canada, in many ways it reinscribes the very relations of power that it hopes to disrupt. The actions and imaginaries of the colonizing culture are foregrounded, and no accounts of Inuit and Dene relations with the story are provided. The textual, representational dimensions of the story are presumed to be contiguous with its social and political importance, and the actual *practices* of storying the North fall from view. It is the text, understood as words and ideas, that is highlighted in such analyses, while familiar lines between Indigenous and settler, colonized and colonizer, are assumed and reinforced. My point is not that examining colonial texts and discourses is unimportant but rather that it is insufficient; it relies too little on geographic context, too readily conjures homogenized, stylized constituencies, and too easily accepts a timeless, static rendering of colonial relations.

In response to these limitations, I was interested in studying stories in all their material specificity and in paying attention to how people practise stories in specific settings. I did not want to assume, in advance, that the discursive relations that can be diagnosed in Hearne's text necessarily correspond with the ways in which relations are made and unmade in place. I initially pursued this interest by engaging with actor-network and posthumanist approaches to story.[36] These approaches have provided helpful tools for destabilizing prevailing assumptions and explanations in the social sciences and humanities about power, agency, representation, and the human. Scholars working in these traditions have reimagined "story" as a material practice through which relations are ordered and reordered, not as a wholly representational phenomenon. Stories are understood not so much as discrete objects of analysis or texts (as they are in postcolonial studies) but rather as modes of relation and intervention. As sociologist John Law argues, stories do not merely represent some outside reality; they are "ordering strategies" that are intimately bound up with "the materials in which they are carried."[37] Stories are complex assemblages of people, places, and things; some may be narratively performed by humans, but they must be understood as relational networks of humans and non-humans, not as representations that somehow sit apart from the materials they represent.

Methodologically, approaching story in this way demands not only careful attention to the specific "things" involved in a given practice of a story but also a willingness to suspend the notion that particular forces or structures are at stake. Rather than assuming to know in advance who and what matters in a given context, one proceeds by patiently tracing relations. With these provocations in mind, instead of asking what broader discursive formations the Bloody Falls massacre story exemplifies, I turned my attention to the relations that are made possible by particular tellings of the story, even while I understand these specific relations and practices as embedded in broader political, social, and economic contexts. By emphasizing the material and relational, and by focusing on specific *practices* of storying Bloody Falls, I was able to suspend the assumption that Qablunaaq stories matter always and everywhere, that they are necessarily politically consequential, and that Qablunaat are the primary and most powerful actors in the past or present North. I was able to take seriously the importance of "things" such as flowers, plumbing, and plaques in various orderings of Bloody Falls, as well as the role of silence, refusal, and forgetting. It was by paying attention to the materiality of story, for example, that I came to understand Hearne's account as one in a series of copper stories that have been instrumental in opening the North to industrial resource extraction (see Chapter 4).

Bruno Latour describes this approach as requiring a certain agnosticism, a refusal to subscribe to established lines of social and political explanation and a rigorous commitment to empiricism.[38] It is an agnosticism and empiricism that, for me, works best in friction with other lines of thought. I am not agnostic on the matter of Qablunaaq relations with the North, and I am not willing to abandon analysis of how prevailing structures and practices shape these relations. I suspend conventional assumptions about colonial relations and structures in the North not because they are not compelling, but rather to sharpen my analysis of exactly how power operates, how relations are made and undermined, and with what consequences. As political theorist Timothy Mitchell (who has himself engaged these bodies of thought) reminds us, the point is not simply to trace heterogeneous relations but rather to ask who wins and who loses by arranging the "mixed way things happen" into coherent and sensible explanation. This is what story helps make possible, and this is why the persistence, reach, and durability of "iconic" stories like those about Bloody Falls are of much more than literary significance. Stories like Hearne's do not simply order and naturalize forms of violence, domination, extraction, and dispossession in representational terms; they also intervene in the material ordering of lives and livelihoods, and they make such orderings make sense. While analyzing Inuit-Qablunaat relations solely in terms of colonial discourse risks both overstating and oversimplifying those relations, there are also serious risks in characterizing Inuit-Qablunaat relations as heterogeneous assemblages of humans and non-humans. Conceptualizing stories as networks of relations helped me to work in tension with postcolonial approaches to story and discourse, but ultimately I was interested in taking sides on the question of who and what matters in the ordering of the contemporary North.

It is important to note, moreover, that the capacity for stories to order the material world and to sustain human and non-human relations is well established in Inuit and other Indigenous traditions, however much Qablunaat tend to attribute these insights to European thinkers.[39] Indeed, it is radical in Qablunaaq epistemologies to suggest, as feminist science studies scholar Donna Haraway does, that we can intervene in the relations that make us in both imaginative and material terms by way of the stories we trace, or to note, as philosopher Walter Benjamin did, the capacity for stories to unleash radically different pasts.[40] But this is simply common sense for Joseph Niptanatiak, an elder in Kugluktuk, who notes that stories have kept him warm while on the land.[41] He is not speaking metaphorically. I do not assert any kind of equivalence between Inuit storytelling epistemologies and recent attempts among Qablunaaq scholars to take seriously the constitutive importance of "things" in social and political life, to trouble the line between the human and non-human, and to link the imaginative world with more material geographies. Not only is my understanding of Inuit epistemologies radically limited and itself shaped by Qablunaaq structures of thought and practice, but I also have no interest in reconciling these vastly different traditions. My intention, here, is to acknowledge what Inuit and other Indigenous intellectuals have told and shown Qablunaat for centuries, and to note that the ontological and epistemological snags that have mired a generation of Qablunaaq scholars – those of us with interests in the relations between knowledge, power, practice, representation, and materiality – simply do not arise in other intellectual traditions. It is to point to a space between knowledges and the limits of what can be known while at the same time acknowledging the rich contributions of Inuit intellectuals to understandings of story.[42]

There are other limits to the ways in which Indigenous peoples and knowledges are apprehended within studies of colonial discourse that motivated me to seek out a different approach to story. As I discuss above, most studies of colonial discourse do not engage with the stories told by "the colonized," but if they do, these stories tend to be conceptualized either as "counter-stories" or "stories from the margins" that might be extracted from Indigenous informants. Anti-colonial and Indigenous scholars have long emphasized the importance of reclaiming their imaginative, psychic space as much as their lands, bodies, and resources, and they have specifically pointed to the importance of telling their own stories as part of this process.[43] But it seems to me that there is an important distinction between counter-storying – responding directly to dominant stories – and nourishing the ideas and practices that promote physical, emotional, and spiritual wellness and autonomy. The former addresses colonial representations and relations directly and purposefully; the latter engages a much wider set of practices and relations that are not necessarily legible to (or aimed at) colonial figures. But this is not to say they do not exist or do not matter. When postcolonial scholars conceptualize talking back, writing back, and counter-storying as central to decolonization, they risk reinforcing an exceedingly narrow and narcissistic rendering of Indigenous subjectivities, practices, and politics.

Here, again, approaching story as a relational and material practice loosened this expectant, scripted framing of how Inuit and Inuit storytelling might be apprehended by a Qablunaaq scholar. It allowed me to pay attention not just to enunciations of the Bloody Falls massacre story, or to explicit efforts to "counter" Hearne's version, but also to a series of other stories and practices through which Bloody Falls is ignored, refused, and forgotten. In other words, paying attention to how the story is *practised* in Kugluktuk and beyond, rather than simply examining the contexts in which Hearne's account is narrated, allowed me to place counter-stories and direct responses to colonial orderings of Bloody Falls in a much larger frame. But more than this, understanding story as a *relational* practice drew my attention to the relationships that nourish stories and that shaped the ones I tell in this book. My tracing of these stories was influenced not only by postcolonial, actor-network, and posthumanist theories but also by relationships with Inuit intellectuals, friends, mentors, language, lands, and research participants, and by the writings of Indigenous, anti-racist, anti-colonial, and feminist scholars. These relationships and writings directed my attention to the production of knowledge itself, to my own relational and material ordering practices, and to the terms upon which a Qablunaaq scholar might engage in relationships with Inuit communities, knowledges, and knowledge systems.

That engagement partly took the form of interviews, focus groups, and informal conversations with residents and visitors in Kugluktuk over a period of five years, and partly involved the development of relationships with Inuit friends and mentors who were not formal research participants but who significantly guided the ethical, methodological, political, and intellectual unfolding of this project.[44] I learned different things in formal interviews than I did on the land, in people's living rooms, at community hearings for various mineral development proposals, at family and community celebrations, by studying Inuktut, or by reading and listening to Inuit intellectuals. I want to emphasize, too, that my knowledge and understanding is situated and limited; the academy has its share of well-meaning Qablunaat whose claim to know the North and to know Inuit is based on their invariably limited visits, friendships, and studies. As Martha Flaherty notes, this partial and relational knowledge is too often mobilized as universal, declarative, and expert. But if my understanding is partial, situated, and political, this does not mean that it has no place in this study. Instead, it underscores how important it is for that engagement to be named as partial and political, for it to be overseen and checked for accuracy, for boundaries and protocols around knowledge to be respected, for it to be sincere, serious, and long-term, and for it to be grounded in relationships.[45]

My intention was never to represent Inuit or study Inuit, but rather to *learn to learn* from and with Inuit intellectuals, friends, research participants, and language about what it means to be Qablunaat and how we might relate differently.[46] There is an important distinction here between learning and knowing. By learning to learn, I do not mean that Inuit possess knowledge that might simply be conveyed to me and that I might then apply to this study. I mean, instead, that what I have learned is itself relational. This learning has been shaped by my relationships with others, and it has required not just an openness to knowledge but also the development of a capacity to learn and know within a different epistemology, however partial. I did not believe that it was possible, as a Qablunaaq scholar embedded in a deeply colonial structure of knowledge production, to undertake a study that was not itself shaped by colonial relations, but I also did not believe that it was possible or ethical to attempt to learn about Qablunaat and our relations with Inuit wholly from within Qablunaaq theories, knowledge systems, methodologies, and structures. It was from this uneasy space that I began to study Inuktut intensively and began to learn to learn how Qablunaat might approach knowledge differently.

NALUNARUIRUMAAQTUQ: NOT KNOWING

Late one winter evening, during a long conversation about knowledge, research, Qablunaat, Inuit, and the academy, Inuktitut scholar Janet Tamalik McGrath told me about a Nattilingmiut expression, "*naluna-ruirumaaqtuq.*"[47] Taken in its entirety, "nalunaruirumaaqtuq" roughly translates as "confusion usually resolves itself," or "things come clear eventually," but it does so by way of a rich and complex articulation of knowing and not knowing, certainty and confusion, present and future. I had been studying Inuktitut with Tamalik for several months by then, long enough to understand basic grammar and phrasing but only beginning to get a sense of the meaning of this rich phrase. That understanding is still unfolding. It should be emphasized, moreover, that although my discussion of nalunaruirumaaqtuq is informed by studies of Inuktitut grammar and language, and by conversations with Inuktitut speakers and teachers, my understanding is grounded in my own encounter with this word and should not be read as a definition. Relating to (and representing my relationship to) nalunaruirumaaqtuq carries with it the same dangers as any ethnographic encounter – my relationship says as much about me as it does about Inuktitut. Nor is nalunaruirumaaqtuq an authentic Inuit solution to the struggles over knowing and being in settler colonies, one that might be "applied" in a range of settings. But given that it is precisely Qablunaaq relationships with knowing and not knowing Inuit that I trace in this book, and work toward tracing differently, I hope that my encounter with nalunaruirumaaqtuq can be instructive. As I outline below, Inuktitut concepts of knowing and not knowing make strange some of the ways in which Qablunaat relate to knowledge and knowledge production, and my encounter with nalunaruirumaaqtuq has helped me to name some of the key methodological, epistemological, and ethical challenges that have driven this project. I hope that encounter might provide readers with a firmer sense of what I mean when I invite Qablunaat to relate differently to the North and to Inuit.

It is now well established that knowing and knowledge are an important terrain of colonization. Much postcolonial and anti-colonial scholarship turns on the premise that the production of knowledge about Indigenous peoples and other targets of colonization is fundamental to imperial and colonial practice; students of colonialism take it as given that knowledge enables, buttresses, validates, extends, and naturalizes colonial relations. Although such insights have been mobilized to make sense of the colonial dimensions of a range of knowledge practices, both past and present, and although the knowledge claims of critical scholars have themselves been subject to important critiques, to be a scholar is to produce knowledge. This is the paradox that structures our practice, the impasse that we cannot overcome. What would it mean to "not know" in the face of such a condition? This question is rarely posed, I think, because of the ways in which "not knowing" structures academic knowledge production and because of the ways in which knowledge is conceptualized in Qablunaaq epistemologies. Although we accept that knowledge is itself the terrain of colonization, we do so – unsurprisingly – within the terms of our own epistemologies and with an understanding of knowledge as something that can be accessed, accumulated, interpreted, and conveyed without attention to its relational context. This understanding of knowledge reinforces the notion that we might identify particular topics, methodologies, theoretical frameworks, or modes of writing that will somehow avoid reproducing and retrenching colonial relations. But in conceptualizing knowledge and knowledge production on these terms, it seems to me that we reinforce an understanding of knowledge that is itself problematic. In seeking to *replace* troubling forms of knowledge production with new, better, correct alternatives, we continue to relate to knowledge as information, rather than understanding it as "a relational and inter-relational series of networks that generate, validate and critique information."[48] And we continue to misapprehend *not knowing* as absence, lack, or failure, rather than as an epistemology and mode of relation in its own right.

This relationship with knowing and not knowing is a very specific one – so specific, in fact, that there is a distinction drawn in Inuktitut between Qablunaaq ways of learning and knowing and Inuit relationships with knowledge.[49] In Inuktitut, to *ilisaq-* is to learn in the context of Qablunaaq schooling (*ilinniaq-* in other dialects). It builds on the root *ili-*, which is to put or place; thus, to ilisaq- is to put things in place. It is to adopt a style of learning in which things have their proper place and perform a set of "right" answers to known problems. But there are other ways to learn and know in Inuktitut. To *pilimmaksaq-* is to engage toward becoming competent. It is to develop skills through observation, mentoring, practice, and effort, so as to ensure the participation and involvement of all community members. Relatedly, to *ajurungniiqsaq-* is to engage to become more independent. Literally, to ajurungniiqsaq- is to remove an inability, which, it is important to note, is approached with compassion and humour in Inuktitut, not judgment. To ajurungniiqsaq- is to become more capable and self-reliant, so that one might help others to be capable.

Learning in Inuktitut, from what I understand, involves cultivating one's *isuma* – one's wisdom and judgment. It involves being placed in situations that force you to exercise your own mind as you seek knowledge and understanding. Learners are neither directly told what they should learn nor encouraged to ask questions about how to correctly perform a task or behaviour. They are expected to learn through keen observation and the cultivation of their own capacities to discern, judge, and act. There is no final, correct state at which one arrives, although practised, careful skills are greatly valued and respected. Learning is highly specific to the learner and deeply relational. Indeed, within such a framework of values, relations, and practices, it is not surprising that the Inuktitut verb stem for knowing, *qaujima-*, has as its roots the verb *qau-* (to rise and be light, bright, as in the sun), *-ji-* (which refers to being an agent), and *–ma* (a reference to a continual and stable state).[50] In a morphological sense, qaujima- evokes a relationship with learning and knowledge wherein people take ownership of their capacity to rise and be bright, like the sun. Knowing, in Inuktitut, involves taking up one's responsibility within a set of relations and working to refine one's skills and understanding for both personal and collective benefit.[51]

Just as there is no single path to knowledge, there is more than one way to *not know* in Inuktitut. The literal opposite of qaujima- is *qaujimanngit-*, where the *–nngit* indicates a negative, a not knowing. It signals a lack of capacity or absence of knowledge. From what I understand, qaujimanngit- accords more closely with what we think of in English as "not knowing," as an absence or limitation in knowledge. But there is another verb for not knowing, *nalunaq-*, that refers less to having wrong or limited knowledge and more to a relationship with an uncertain state. Consider Rachel Qitsualik's description of *"nalunaktuq,"* articulated as part of a broader discussion of how Qablunaat might approach the changes unfolding in the Arctic today:

> The root word of *nalunaktuq* is *nalu,* or "not knowing." In Inuktitut ... *nalunaktuq* loosely means "difficult to comprehend" or "unpredictable." But why should the Inuit perspective on such a thing matter? Well, besides the fact that their burgeoning population makes up 86 per cent of Nunavut, Inuit have learned the harshest lessons from the Land. The best such lesson has been that of *nalunaktuq:* the fact that general trends serve as poor indicators of what the Arctic will actually *do.* Many people believe that Inuit survivability and Land-knowledge are one, but few suspect that both hinge upon an acceptance of the Land's protean nature.[52]

To not know in the sense of nalunaktuq is not to have failed, to have no value, or to be wrong, and neither is it to embark on an active quest to master a given set of circumstances. Such associations with not knowing are specific to Qablunaaq relations with that which we do not understand. But neither is it to throw up one's hands, to give up, or to suggest that one has no responsibilities or agency. As I discuss below, Inuit relations with not knowing in the nalunaktuq sense demand a very different set of responses.

In Inuktut, a single word can express an entire sentence or thought; words are formed by combining morphemes that signify what we think of in English as subjects, objects, verbs, adjectives, and other parts of speech. So, "I am going to the store" can be expressed in Inuktitut as *niuvirvingmunngauniaqtunga.* Each component of the word provides a different dimension of the sentence. In literal terms, "nalunaruirumaaqtuq" breaks down into the following morphemes:

Morpheme	Language component	Meaning
nalu-	Verb	To not know, to be confused
-naq-	Verb	To have the feeling of, or to cause
-ruiq-	Verb	To no longer have the ability or capacity
-rumaaq-	Adverb	Expression of time; distant future; uncertain truth
-tuq	Agreement or person suffix	Third-person singular present indicative (he/she/it); also refers to a general condition

If you unpack the meaning of "nalunaruirumaaqtuq" literally, by piecing together the individual morphemes, the term expresses a feeling or experience of not knowing, of being confused, and then eventually no longer having that experience. Structurally, the word includes a double negative, both the not knowing of nalu- and the not having the capacity or ability of -ruiq-, and although we are taught to steer away from double negatives in English, in nalunaruirumaaqtuq something very important is conveyed. Nalu- is not, in fact, the negative form of knowing in Inuktitut; it is not precisely about not knowing or knowing incorrectly. The verb nalu-, as Qitsualik explains, expresses more of a sense of being confused, of not knowing quite what to do or how to respond to a situation. It expresses a moment of uncertainty, an awareness that one does not quite know how to relate to a set of circumstances. Similarly, -ruiq- suggests a cessation of action or lost capacity, a state of "not any more" that implies a prior state of having or knowing. Both "negatives" suggest, in that sense, an awareness of how ability, knowledge, and capacity relate to time and to circumstances, and by their very nature suggest that things have been and could be otherwise.

To –naq- is to be in a state of feeling and experiencing a verb; it draws attention to the emotional, spiritual, and physical experience of a verb. To nalunaq-, then, is to experience a state of not knowing something, of being confused. Together with –ruiq- and –rumaaq-, though, nalunaruirumaaqtuq conveys a shift in this state, an indication that eventually, one will no longer be in a state of unknowing and confusion. The infix –rumaaq- is particularly suggestive in this regard. It not only refers to the distant future, but also to an uncertain certainty (another seemingly contradictory concept that is poorly conveyed in English but makes sense in Inuktitut). It conveys a sense that in the long run, something is certain to happen, even if it is also uncertain and open to change. In a way, it conveys confidence in both change and the contours of well-known patterns; some things are certain to happen, even if they don't necessarily happen in ways we can control or predict. As many Inuit intellectuals have made clear, accepting and finding ways of responding to a fundamentally changing set of circumstances is central to Inuit modes and practices of knowledge.[53]

Altogether, from what I understand, "nalunaruirumaaqtuq" expresses a kind of confidence that somehow, one will know what one needs to know, in time. It expresses a kind of openness to a present that is uncertain, confusing, and in which the best way forward is not clear, but neither does it need to be clear; there is a reassurance in the expression that confusion will be resolved. This openness is not passive; to acknowledge a state of "not knowing" in Inuktitut is not to claim a lack of capacity or agency, but neither is it to rush to action. The most appropriate response to a state of nalunaq- is, first, to acknowledge the way things are. It is foolhardy to pretend to know or understand when one does not. Similarly, to act quickly without an understanding of a situation is to risk great danger; acting without keen knowledge and understanding is worse than doing nothing at all. To acknowledge nalunaq- is not to throw up one's hands, though; this, too, is foolish. Instead, it is to remain open, attentive, and prepared to respond to the moment. Importantly, there is no value attached to being in a state of not knowing. It simply is, and one simply responds to the situation as it is.

Nalunaruirumaaqtuq not only expresses a state of not knowing, then, it also implies a response and a relationship with that state, one that is instructive for Qablunaat who are interested in reshaping their relations with Inuit and the North. When one is confused, when one does not know how to proceed, one acknowledges that state and cultivates a kind of relaxed but alert openness to the knowledge that will come. This is the "doing" appropriate to a state of nalunaq-. It is a purposeful and respectful way of relating to a set of circumstances. In Inuktitut, the kinds of things that one can come to know through Qablunaaq styles of problematization, analysis, and argumentation are valuable only insofar as they help us to rise and respond to a given set of circumstances. Wise, careful action in specific situations is contingent on how carefully one has observed, practised, and responded in past circumstances, how closely one has listened to and learned from others, and how accurately one has assessed the conjuncture of the present. There is no "right" way in an abstract, universal sense, even if there are more practised and wise responses. There is only more and less confidence in one's wisdom and judgment, more and less respect for silence, observation, feeling, relationship, patience, accuracy, and humility. This relationship with knowing and not knowing makes strange the academic conceit that the scope of the literature is the scope of knowledge on a given topic, that there is a "right" way through any learning endeavour, and unsettles the voice and the style that Qablunaat are encouraged to take up as scholars.

Indeed, for me, engaging with the concept of nalunaruirumaaqtuq makes apparent the specificity of Qablunaaq relationships with knowledge and the consequences of this way of relating to knowing (and not knowing). I have found it particularly helpful for conceptualizing how I want to produce knowledge in this colonial present and how to locate my "substantive, triangulated sense of things." Nalunaruirumaaqtuq reminds me of the importance of acknowledging all that I do not know and of relating to that not knowing respectfully. Qablunaat (especially Qablunaaq scholars) are particularly bad at this; we are continually trained to do otherwise. As Tamalik McGrath observes, "Qablunaat have enjoyed, and continue to enjoy, economic and systemic privilege in Inuit lands. This has led to an ingrained epistemic privileging that, in my observation, is hard for qablunaat to see or acknowledge."[54] But it also reminds me of the importance of what Qablunaat *do know* and *must know*, of our responsibility to continually learn and observe so that we might better respond to the dangers and possibilities we face. Nalunaruirumaaqtuq reminds me that knowing and not knowing have consequences, that knowledge is embedded in relationships, and that our task is not to seek a perfect or final knowledge about our shared relations, but instead to be wise, humble, accountable, respectful, hopeful, and alive in the face of the specific, placed moments in which we all act. It is to acknowledge that there is no conclusive, linear, or eternal form of relation with each other or with the land, but neither can we expect our relations to change without conscious, quiet effort to learn, practise, and respond to the demands of this colonial present. And it is to be alert, to anticipate that we will act, that we must act. If Qablunaat are to take up their "substantive and triangulated sense of things" in this colonial and decolonizing present, it seems to me that we must learn to both acknowledge the limits of what we know and can know *and* take greater responsibility for what we do know and must know. To be actively humble, to know without speaking, to be silent, to engage our not knowing respectfully – these are the skills we have not yet learned to learn.

My engagement with nalunaruirumaaqtuq has also helped me to name something that is almost impossible to express in Qablunaaq epistemologies but that I have tried to enact in this book. Our task as Qablunaat, it seems to me, is not to find newer and better ways of producing knowledge, or to replace all that is troubling in the story of the Bloody Falls massacre. We can try, and the trying is important. But my intention here is not to *replace* Qablunaaq imaginative geographies with more accurate or comprehensive alternatives. My intention is to enact an altogether different relationship with knowing and not knowing that involves both radically *placing* what we do know and relating more respectfully, responsibly, attentively, and quietly to all that we do not know. By "placing," I refer not just to subject position or perspective, but to placing in a more fundamental relational, contextual, material sense, which invariably means acknowledging that we know far less than we think we do. Such a placing is the beginning of a process of *displacing* Qablunaaq knowledges and claims, and of relating differently to knowledge. Nalunaruirumaaqtuq helps me to conceptualize, validate, and name these intentions. It provides a framework for relating differently to confusion, uncertainty, and limits. It provides a framework within which one can listen to and learn from and with Inuit rather than extracting knowledge for use in other places.

I aim, in the chapters that follow, to trace the contours of what Qablunaat know and do not know, what we understand and misunderstand, without filling that space with new claims to knowledge. To refuse to know and to signal the limits of what I know is not to suggest that everything Qablunaat misapprehend and misunderstand does not exist, but rather to acknowledge that it *does* and that it is neither mine to understand nor to claim. In refusing to know, in marking out the limits of what I know and do not know, I hope to highlight some of the ways in which Qablunaat and Inuit might story and enact our relations differently. But I also invite readers to consider what we do know and must know and not to be content with what Sami political scientist Rauna Kuokkanen terms the "position of the politically correct dominant, who argues that they can no longer speak" lest they be construed as speaking for the Other.[55] Learning to learn from and with each other requires Qablunaat to confront the sanctioned epistemic ignorance that continues to structure the academy and to find ways of respectfully and responsibly engaging Inuit epistemologies, ontologies, methodologies, and axiologies. The chapters that follow attempt to enact this movement between knowing and not knowing, placing and displacing the story of the Bloody Falls massacre. My hope is that readers will not only be compelled by the stories I trace but also begin to consider the broader possibilities of relating differently.

OVERVIEW OF CHAPTERS

One of the primary ways in which the Bloody Falls massacre story structures Qablunaaq relations with the North and with Inuit is through its creation of a subject position from which Qablunaat can witness the suffering of northern Indigenous peoples without feeling involved or implicated in that suffering. This positionality remains compelling, I argue, and underpins settler colonial desires to both witness and deny colonial violence today. I trace the emergence and implications of this subject position in Chapter 2. Through close study of the geographies of publication, circulation, and reception of Hearne's narrative in the late eighteenth and early nineteenth centuries, I demonstrate how the massacre story was used to order Qablunaaq bodies as neutral witnesses to the "savagery" of Indigenous peoples. I focus on the ways in which Hearne's contemporaries took up his story as they struggled to make sense of the violence of the French Revolution and imperial expansion. The popularity of his narrative at the time, I argue, can be partially attributed to its engagement with concerns about mass violence, race, and the precarity of empire. Hearne's story offered readers a place from which they could both intimately experience the violence of empire and deny their constitutive role in its formation. It is a subject position that remains compelling and continues to structure Qablunaaq relations with northern Indigenous peoples.

Is the Bloody Falls massacre story "true"? The reliability of Hearne's account has been questioned for centuries, but Hearne's defenders insist that he was both present and accurately recorded the event. Dene members of the first Franklin expedition claimed that Hearne was twenty miles back when the massacre unfolded, armed with a pair of scissors tied to a pole, and that he had neither participated in nor witnessed the event. The Franklin expedition members believed their Dene guides, and in their private notes and letters confessed as much. And yet, as I argue in Chapter 3, the expedition members played a pivotal role in confirming the truth of the massacre. They invented a series of "things" that worked to establish the massacre as a historical event, even while its primary witness quietly retreated from view. These things – particularly a species of ragweed identified at Bloody Falls and the skulls and bones that appear in the first visual depiction of the site – acted as material proof of what was hitherto merely a story; they worked to order Hearne's account as history. Chapter 3 thus examines the ways in which historical truth is produced and maintained through the ordering of people, places, and things and reminds us that stories need not be "true" to have profound effects. What is at stake here is not so much the actual truth of the massacre but rather the capacity for truth to be produced through situated, specific efforts to make sense.

In a way, then, it does not matter whether Hearne's account is true. The story continues to structure Qablunaaq relations with the North and with Inuit, regardless of its historical veracity. Among these relations is the naturalization and racialization of northern mineral development. Both Hearne's journey and his account of the massacre played a formative role in opening the Central Arctic to mineral exploration and mine development, and if the story of the Bloody Falls massacre is approached as a copper story, its implication in past and present efforts to extract copper from northern lands becomes apparent. In Chapter 4, I consider the ways in which the production of knowledge about "Copper Inuit" (Inuinnait) and "Copper Indians" (T'satsąot'ınę or Yellowknives Dene) – those who, along with the Northern Indians (Dënesųłiné or Chipewyan Dene) are alleged to have led the attack at Bloody Falls – relates to the naturalization of imperial dispossession.[56] The chapter presents a range of copper stories about pre-contact use of native copper, early imperial mineral exploration, relations between Inuit and Dene, the use of copper knives and tools, and more recent mineral exploration and extraction in the region. I argue that the production of anthropological knowledge about Inuit, stories of Qablunaaq adventure and exploration, and the massacre itself must be considered in relation to the geographies of mining, past and present, and that attending to copper stories is useful in this regard. Chapter 4 is an effort, in that sense, to trace the ways in which Qablunaaq stories work to naturalize a progression from "traditional" relations with the land to those underpinning industrial extractive economies. It also points to the ways in which forging relations with copper has made certain kinds of life possible in the North, and considers how contemporary struggles around mine development in Nunavut relate to a broader effort to make and sustain life in the territory.

If stories can both sustain and undermine life, how, then, might we respond to the ordering capacities of stories like Hearne's and their implication in colonial formations? In Chapter 5, I challenge the notion that counter-stories are the most appropriate means of rejecting or re-working hegemonic narratives. Counter-stories can advance certain objectives, I argue, but to reduce Indigenous relations with colonial stories to these terms is to overlook the range of Indigenous responses to colonial relations and to reinforce colonial subjectivities. The chapter focuses on the proposed erection of federal and territorial heritage plaques to commemorate Samuel Hearne and the Bloody Falls massacre in the early 1970s, a scheme that Kugluktukmiut firmly rejected. In resisting the commemoration, Kugluktukmiut were not so much rejecting abstract claims to the story of the North, I argue, but rather rejecting the capacity for such claims to enable much more material interventions into their lives and lands. Their resistance was shaped by shifts in federal and territorial governance, northern Indigenous political movements, and the rise of industrial resource extraction in the North, as well as by relations with the land and with each other that exceed the reach and understanding of both past and present Qablunaaq observers. Just as Richardson's mournful flower says a great deal more about the culture within which he operated than it does about Inuit responses to the Bloody Falls massacre, it seems to me that the celebration of counter-stories and resistance stories among Qablunaat says a great deal more about us than it does about Inuit relations with our shared stories and histories.

Chapter 6 considers the ways in which Kugluktukmiut engage with both the site and the massacre story as part of an active ordering of the worlds in which they wish to live. The chapter works through a series of moments and practices of not knowing, including the ways in which Kugluktukmiut actively forget and refuse to know the story of the Bloody Falls massacre. Through analysis of interviews with Kugluktukmiut, I consider the range of ways in which people move away from Bloody Falls, physically, narratively, temporally, and symbolically, including efforts to draw my attention to practices of survival, practices of knowledge production and transmission, and practices of forgetting. I also consider broader efforts to forget, ignore, and reinvent the story as part of a process of renewing relations with Sahtú and Tłı̨chǫ Dene communities south of Kugluktuk and of articulating a shared commitment to protecting northern lands. These relationships with Bloody Falls, I argue, are anchored in geographies of responsibility and care and involve creative, active efforts to story a desired future. They have little to do with Qablunaat; even the effects of colonial intervention (a form of involvement critical Qablunaaq scholars are inclined to emphasize) do not wholly account for what is at stake here. If we are to understand and reshape our relations with northern peoples and lands, I argue, we must relinquish the belief that our responsibilities are the only ones that matter in this shared colonial present, and we must come to terms with the fact that there are profound ancestral responsibilities animating the ordering of northern relations.

I draw attention to practices of ignoring and forgetting Bloody Falls, not just to situate the ways in which Kugluktukmiut story the massacre in broader terms, but also to remind Qablunaat that the burden of decolonizing Qablunaaq stories and relations with the North does not fall wholly to Inuit or Dene. There is no authentic counter-story from the colonial margins that will dismantle the practices and relations made possible by the Bloody Falls massacre story. I make this claim for both empirical and political reasons. There are stories about Bloody Falls that both Inuit and Dene refuse to tell Qablunaat, and I firmly believe in the importance of naming this limit to Qablunaaq knowledge production. But many Kugluktukmiut also insist on the peripheral nature of the story and its Qablunaaq origins and purposes. Many first heard the story at residential school and learned of their apparent hostility toward Dene not from their elders but from their textbooks. This is not to say that the hostility did not exist or is not storied; it did and it is, alongside stories of cooperation, mutual aid, intermarriage, trade, and sharing. But many Kugluktukmiut suspect that, because so few Inuit likely survived the massacre (if, indeed, it occurred), specific accounts of the event did not occupy a prominent place in oral histories. Other violent encounters did. Bloody Falls has been prototypical for Qablunaat since Hearne's account first circulated, but its place in Inuit and Dene understandings of their respective and shared histories is more complex, and such understandings interweave with colonial institutions and texts. I only gesture toward this complexity here. It is not my place to delve into how Inuit and Dene story their own histories, and the relationships I have developed have not authorized or encouraged such a study. I name such limits, instead, to complicate the notion of an authentic Indigenous response to hegemonic colonial narratives (and to place desires for such responses squarely among Qablunaat) and also as part of a politics of acknowledging the limits of what Qablunaat think they know or have a right to know.

Chapter 7 turns away from the notion that gathering authentic Indigenous counter-stories from the colonial margins will somehow resolve or reorder colonial relations and turns toward an examination of the driving Qablunaaq interest in the North – land. Our stories, I argue, continually aim at advancing and legitimizing settler colonial dispossession. I revisit the three objectives that guided Hearne's mission – to locate and assess the region's mineral riches, to make peace with Indigenous peoples, and to advance knowledge of the Northwest Passage – and trace the ways in which these objectives have structured Qablunaaq relations with the North and with Inuit over time. Although Qablunaat tend to conceptualize the North as a site of Inuit struggle and suffering (and we have a practised capacity to position ourselves as benevolent, neutral, and helpful witnesses to that struggle and suffering), it is our own struggle to control and profit from northern lands and resources, I argue, that demands attention. The chapter examines contemporary struggles over Arctic resource extraction and reflects on the possibilities of reordering Qablunaaq relations with northern peoples and northern lands. Ultimately, I argue, our task is not simply to tell better stories about the North but rather to intervene in the structures of dispossession and domination that are made sensible, legible, and possible by the stories we tell.

2
Ordering Violence

How is one to lend one's ear to the recital of abominable scenes without sinning oneself, that is, taking pleasure oneself?
– Alain Grosrichard, in conversation with Michel Foucault, *Power/Knowledge*

Let us leave this Europe which never stops talking of man yet massacres him at every one of its street corners, at every corner of the world.
– Frantz Fanon, *The Wretched of the Earth*

"And the Esquimaux?" It was Matonabbee himself who asked the question. "You do not want to know why I walked so far to kill them?"
His words resounded in the silence like the booming of distant ice.
"I have my people to care for ... No leader would do less."
"Or no savage." Norton's laugh was solitary.
– Pauline Holdstock, *Into the Heart of the Country*[1]

In the closing pages of their 2008 attack on the "Aboriginal industry," Frances Widdowson and Albert Howard invoke the Bloody Falls massacre as evidence of the "genocidal intentions" that follow from Indigenous "kinship-based systems" and "tribalism." The massacre, they argue, "occurred because the Chipewyan and Inuit were not connected by kinship," and it is proof that violence inevitably flows from Indigenous political, cultural, and economic systems. "The perception that primitive peoples were peaceful is merely due to romantic wishful thinking on the part of many academics studying tribal societies," argue Widdowson and Howard. "If we really want to achieve the aspirations of the Enlightenment, the answer does not lie with tribalism ... There would be no such thing as the public sphere, where everyone is supposedly equal under the law, since kin would be favoured over others in the distribution of goods and services." The book ends with an appeal to become "a global tribe," where the "world can live as one" and no single group's "special interests" would prevail.[2]

This chapter examines the implication of Hearne's travel narrative in the development of late-eighteenth-century discourses of violence, order, and savagery, beginning with its publication in 1795. If Widdowson and Howard can mobilize Hearne's account of the Bloody Falls massacre today as evidence of the inherent violence of Indigenous peoples, that mobilization takes its cue from much earlier engagements with Hearne's tale. Like Widdowson and Howard, moreover, Hearne's contemporaries were interested not only in equating indigeneity with violence but also in emphasizing the extremity and distinctiveness of that violence. Widdowson and Howard's framing of the massacre as a "genocidal" act is not incidental; it is consistent with a long-standing practice of *ordering* violence according to the interests of empire.

The question of what can and cannot be deemed violence remains a preoccupation of critical scholars, particularly as it relates to empire.[3] Many scholars have observed that the foundations of imperial and colonial "order" are themselves grounded in tremendous violence, a point that Frantz Fanon made with respect to the imperial project more widely. He argued that empire has always been about denying the violence that underpins it, not just through the identification of non-European peoples and practices as inherently and extraordinarily violent, but also through the constitution and celebration of civilized man as somehow not implicated in the violence of imperial dispossession and rule. I want to highlight two implications that flow from Fanon's insight. First, if ordering violence in the interests of empire requires a reframing of particular violent acts and ideas as *not* violent, then ordering violence is as much about constituting a non-violent, civilized observer as it is about naming violence as such. In other words, it is not only knowledge of Indigenous peoples that is produced in descriptions of Indigenous violence but also conceptualizations of the civilized observer. Second, given that ordering violence involves differentiating between particular acts and particular peoples, it requires ongoing work that should be identifiable and analyzable. I pay attention in this chapter to ordering as practice and not to the more static and transcendent notion of order. My concern, in other words, is the ways in which relations between Indigenous and non-Indigenous peoples have been staked out through the ordering of violence.

HEARNE'S *JOURNEY TO THE NORTHERN OCEAN* (1795)

Hearne's travel narrative, *A Journey to the Northern Ocean,* was published almost three years after his death and twenty-four years after the massacre. Versions of his journal had already circulated, however, among several "learned and curious gentlemen" in London and beyond, as manuscripts, excerpts, pamphlets, and no doubt, orally.[4] Hearne first reported on his journey to his employers at the Hudson's Bay Company (HBC) headquarters in London in a letter sent 28 August 1772, two months after his return to Prince of Wales Fort and as part of the fort's annual mailing to London.[5] Captain James Cook was given access to Hearne's reports and his maps when he set out on his third voyage in 1776, along with other explorers and scientists, as the HBC allowed Royal Society members to consult its records through the 1770s and '80s.[6] French explorer La Pérouse is famously alleged to have read Hearne's journal while the two sailed back to London from the fort in 1782. He had sacked the fort after Hearne (who was its acting governor at the time) surrendered to the French offensive. According to the Preface of the French edition of Hearne's narrative, La Pérouse had seized the manuscript as bounty upon conquering the fort but had generously returned it to Hearne "à la condition expresse de le faire imprimer et publier" (on the express condition that it be printed and published).[7]

Indeed, there were several calls for the publication of his journals, calls that Hearne claimed not to have anticipated when he initially put his travel notes together:

> When I was on that Journey, and for several years after, I little thought that any remarks made in [my journal] would ever have attracted the notice of the Public: if I had, greater pains might and would have been taken to render it more worthy of their attention than it now is. At that time my ideas and ambition extended no farther than to give my employers such an account of my proceedings as might be satisfactory to them, and answer the purpose which they had in view ... But as the case has turned out otherwise, I have at my leisure hours recopied all my Journals into one book, and in some instances added to the remarks I had before made;

> not so much for the information of those who are critics in geography, as for the amusement of candid and indulgent readers, who may perhaps feel themselves in some measure gratified, by having the face of a country brought to their view, which has hitherto been entirely unknown to every European except myself.[8]

Hearne may not have anticipated much interest in his travels in 1772, but by 1792, when his completed manuscript was handed over to publishers Strahan and Cadell, things had indeed "turned out otherwise." Cook had begun to publish his travel narratives through the 1770s, and by 1800 more than one hundred editions of various reports from Cook's voyages had been released.[9] Cook's journeys were not only landmarks in establishing a particular tradition of scientific travel, but were also central to the emerging market for scientific travel narratives that would rapidly expand in the late eighteenth century. Hearne was paid the remarkable sum of £200 for his manuscript, indicating that Strahan and Cadell foresaw healthy sales.[10] By 1799, *A Journey* had been translated into German, Dutch, and French, and English-language editions had been published in Ireland and the United States. The book was enthusiastically and extensively reviewed, and many notable figures of the day purchased copies for their libraries.

Hearne's Preface to *A Journey* reveals some of his motives for publication. He begins with a long response to his critics, particularly geographer Alexander Dalrymple, who had questioned the accuracy of Hearne's cartographic readings and, by extension, his general credibility.[11] Hearne presents lengthy refutations of Dalrymple in an effort to "convince the Public that his objections are in a great measure without foundation" and to re-establish himself as a reliable writer.[12] As historian Simon Schaffer observes, eighteenth-century "travelers' tales ... were notoriously hard to credit. So it became important independently to establish the credibility of the storyteller apart from the content of the story."[13] Having addressed and dismissed Dalrymple, Hearne resolves to "quit the disagreeable subject with declaring, that if any part of the following sheets should afford amusement to Mr. Dalrymple, or any other of my readers, it will be the highest gratification I can receive, and the only recompense I desire to obtain for the hardships and fatigue which I underwent in procuring the information contained in them." Despite his best efforts in the Preface and throughout the book, Hearne was not entirely successful in recuperating his credibility, and the question of whether to read *A Journey* as an authoritative source of knowledge or a literary "curiosity" remains unresolved to this day.[14]

Hearne was defensive not only of himself but also of the HBC, whose failure to extensively explore the land under its control had been critiqued by those who challenged its economic monopoly. Hearne's journey had been undertaken in part to defuse such criticisms, and the publication of his narrative was aimed at vindicating his former employer. Publication was itself enabled by the HBC's growing willingness to share its extensive holdings with explorers, scientists, and other "learned gentlemen" and, indeed, with Hearne himself. At the time of his journey, Hearne would not have been encouraged or even permitted to publish his narrative, but, beginning in the 1770s, Samuel Wegg (HBC deputy governor and governor between 1774 and 1799, and treasurer of the Royal Society from 1768 to 1802) began to grant Royal Society members unprecedented access to HBC journals, reports, letters, charts, and maps.[15] It was Wegg who gave Hearne access to his own and other records at the HBC headquarters, Wegg who introduced him to Andrew Pennant in 1782–83 (Pennant wrote *Arctic Zoology* in 1784, drawing on Hearne's findings), and Wegg who would have allowed his close friend Dalrymple to scrutinize Hearne's unpublished notes.[16]

Reviews of *A Journey*, although mostly enthusiastic, were informed by reviewers' stances with respect to the HBC, Hearne's credibility, and the scientific merits of his trip. Whereas the popular monthly *Gentleman's Magazine* took pains to note that *A Journey* was accompanied by an "*accurate* map of Mr. Hearne's track," the more conservative and high-brow *British Critic* opened its review by stating that "little accession has resulted either to commerce or to the stores of knowledge" from Hearne's travels, and it questioned "the importance of the publication itself, or the discoveries and information it professes to communicate."[17] Historical geographer Felix Driver suggests that the boundaries between "scientific exploration and adventurous travel, the sober and the sensational, or the analytical and the aesthetic," were in the process of negotiation during these years, and one can certainly observe this in reviews of *A Journey*.[18] While the *English Review* (a more popular magazine) praised Hearne's work as a stand-out example in the sea of "books of travels and voyages" on the market, describing him as "a judicious observer, and ... a candid and faithful reporter of facts; facts new, striking, and highly important," others, such as the *Critical Review*, which was known for its Tory and High Church sensibilities, dismissed it as appealing to "persons of leisure" and to those "who are desirous of becoming acquainted with savage manners," not scientific or commercial fact.[19] Certainly, Hearne's working-class, unlettered background would have limited his authority as a scientific gentleman, and the more highbrow, conservative journals tended to question his reliability, whereas their more populist counterparts lauded the book's importance. But these stances were about more than policing the boundaries between learned gentlemen and men of curiosity. As the *British Critic* stated, Hearne's "opinion against a north-west passage" was "decided," and it was this conviction that upset the interests of those who advocated for extensive and ongoing Arctic exploration.[20] Dalrymple was himself agitating for another expedition to find the Northwest Passage (that he would command), and the HBC recognized the importance of positioning itself as a promoter of such expeditions, following allegations that it was concealing the existence of the passage.[21] To undercut Hearne was to enhance the case for additional exploration at a time when state funding was explicitly sought, and it would seem that many made public statements about Hearne's reliability for precisely this reason.

Assessments of Hearne's contribution to cartography, science, and commerce were divergent, but almost all critics agreed that he was a reliable and credible source regarding the "savage state."[22] Commentators seized on Hearne's account of the massacre as a particularly evocative portrayal of savagery, and it was reproduced at length in a number of reviews and for many years following.[23] For instance, the first published reference to Hearne's manuscript (as yet itself unpublished), a 1784 review of Cook's *Voyage to the Pacific Ocean,* focused almost entirely on the massacre, even though the review's discussion of Hearne's journey was ostensibly intended only to contextualize the state of knowledge regarding the Northwest Passage at the time of the Cook voyages.[24] From this first mention of Hearne's findings through to reviews of *A Journey,* the didactic importance of the massacre for delineating civilized and savage ways is emphasized. The *Critical Review,* for example, positioned Hearne's narrative as an antidote to the "praises of savage life" and as a corrective to those who "foolishly ... take pleasure in contrasting the defects of civilization with the little solid comfort to be found in their favourite state of independence." Few such romanticized accounts, it claimed, "are founded on an accurate examination of the facts," and if nothing else, *A Journey* was "a plain narration of incidents ... in the wildest part of North America."[25]

Scholars have extensively examined the use of "savagery" to shore up the civilized British self.[26] Its mobilization in reviews of *A Journey,* however, was arguably informed as much by concerns about the French Revolution as about indigeneity. The French Revolution and the Revolutionary Wars were of urgent concern to the British in the closing years of the eighteenth century, raising questions about violence, war, and social order that

Hearne's *Journey* addressed. His nuanced and conflicted descriptions of Matonabbee, his guide, were particularly fruitful sources of contemplation regarding the inherent nature of men and their vulnerability to violence and mob behaviour. The *Critical Review,* for instance, dwelled upon Hearne's contributions to the moral geographies of murder, claiming that among the Northern Indians murder was "in some cases, held dishonorable" and that murderers were shunned, although "the women, it is true, sometimes receive an unlucky blow from their husbands for misbehaviour, which occasions their death; but this is thought nothing of." The reviewer quoted Hearne's anxious comment that Matonabbee had killed one of his wives in this manner:

> And he is, in every other respect, a man of such universal good sense, and, as an Indian, of such great humanity, that I am at a loss how to account for his having been guilty of such a crime, unless it be by his having lived among the Southern Indians too long, as to become tainted with their blood-thirsty, revengeful, and vindictive disposition.

While Hearne struggles to account for the violence of a man who is otherwise "of such great humanity," the reviewer scoffs at his sympathies. "This Matonabbee," he writes, "is the author's favourite: and besides pummeling one of his wives to death, he stabbed the husband of another woman several times, and made no scruple to be in a party with his brethren to assassinate a company of a different tribe, sleeping quietly in their huts." The source of the reviewer's apprehensions about humanizing savage murder is revealed in the sentence that immediately follows: "The profusion of the rich, in civilized life, is often and deservedly cried out against: but it bears no proportion to that of the savages. A savage family frequently *wastes* more in one day, than the richest family in London or Paris does in a dozen years. Of this we have had frequent proofs in the narration of this journey."[27]

This rather bizarre appeal to the relative scruples of the rich in comparison to the habits of Northern Indians likely made perfect sense to readers in 1797. Penned as the Revolutionary Wars continued to wreak havoc in France, and as revolutionary sentiments spread in England, anxieties about violence, murder, and their justification were of more than passing interest.[28] The possibility that the masses might rise up against the "richest families in London" was urgently considered as Hearne's narrative circulated. As Edmund Burke warned in his widely read *Reflections on the Revolution in France,*

> Plots, massacres, assassinations, seem to some people a trivial price for obtaining a revolution. A cheap, bloodless reformation, a guiltless liberty, appear flat and vapid to their taste. There must be a great change of scene; there must be a magnificent stage effect; there must be a grand spectacle to rouze the imagination, grown torpid with lazy enjoyment of sixty years security, and the still unanimating repose of public prosperity.[29]

Stories about death, torture, violence, and mass murder gained unprecedented appeal in Britain during the 1790s. The conditions under which people might be swept into collective, violent action, and the bloody consequences of such actions, spoke to pressing social and political concerns both at home and abroad. These themes are amply evoked in Hearne's narrative. Consider his published description of the preparations for the massacre, a passage that does not appear in earlier versions and was no doubt shaped by his editors:

> It is perhaps worth remarking, that my crew, though an undisciplined rabble, and by no means accustomed to war or command, seemingly acted on this horrid occasion with the utmost uniformity of sentiment. There was not among them the least altercation or separate opinion; *all were united in the general cause,* and as ready to follow where Matonabbee led, as he appeared ready to lead ... Never was reciprocity of interest more generally regarded among a number of people, than it was on the present occasion by my crew, for not one was a moment in want of anything that another could spare; and if ever the spirit of disinterested friendship expanded the heart of a Northern Indian, it was here exhibited in the most extensive meaning of the word. *Property of every kind that could be of general use now ceased to be private,* and every one who had any thing which came under that description, seemed proud of an opportunity of giving it, or lending it to those who had none, or were most in want of it. The number of my crew was so much greater than that which five tents could contain, and the warlike manner in which they were equipped so greatly superior to what could be expected of the poor Esquimaux, that no less than a total massacre of every one of them was likely to be the case, unless Providence should work a miracle for their deliverance.[30]

This passage evokes the pull of the "violent mob, the many-headed beast" that scholars argue was a defining image of the late eighteenth century, as Britons worried about the possibility of a republican revolution at home.[31] Hearne's struggle to make sense of Matonabbee's violence resonated with debates about whether the Jacobins were justified in their own violent, mob-like overthrow of the aristocracy. For the editors of the *Critical Review,* at least, to sympathize with Matonabbee was not just to sympathize with the savages of the Americas, it was to cast the violence of the French Revolution in a positive light and to accept savage behaviour in civilized Europe. Indeed, Anti-Jacobins were specifically concerned about the influence of texts such as Hearne's on the public. As McCann writes, "they saw the public consumption of literary texts, political pamphlets, popular journals and philosophical tracts as the means by which a gullible and manipulable audience could be swayed from passivity to the violence and atavism of revolution."[32]

It was not only the eruption of violence in Europe that worried Hearne's contemporaries. The late eighteenth century was a spectacularly violent period in British imperial history, as wars, rebellions, and uprisings around the world resulted in death and torture on a massive scale, and were also described in unprecedented detail in the growing news and publishing industries. The British were making sense not only of the "massacres [that] were taking place in France" and the threat that "violent republicanism" posed to the "mythic image of Britannia," but also of their own "savagery" in the Americas throughout the Indian Wars, the American War of Independence, and the slave rebellions across the West Indies.[33] Reports of violent repression, murder, and torture by British subjects had begun to undercut public support for colonial expansion, as had accounts of scalping, rape, cannibalism, and other "savage" acts carried out by Britain's Indian allies in the American War of Independence.[34] Late-eighteenth-century interest in tales of Indian savagery was informed, in that sense, not simply by some straightforward confrontation with the colonial, Indigenous Other, but by a complex mixture of anti-colonial sentiment in Britain, the rise of the abolitionist movement, successive violent uprisings in England and Ireland, and growing public awareness of the atrocities committed by British subjects in the name of empire. Stories of Indian savagery, in other words, were not always and only about Indians but rather were ways of making sense of complex political, economic, and social crises in a tumultuous time.

Indeed, some of the most celebrated Romantic poets drew on Hearne's writing as they grappled with the uncertainties of late-eighteenth-century Britain.[35] Literature scholar Tim Fulford proposes, for example, that Coleridge's "The Rime of the Ancient Mariner," written in 1798, was directly inspired by *A Journey.* Basing his argument in part on Coleridge's annotations in his copy of *A Journey* and his remark that it prompted him to show that superstition was "not peculiar to savage or barbarous tribes," Fulford suggests that the poem was in fact a commentary inspired by imperial and domestic crisis.[36] In the "Rime," he argues,

> Coleridge had generated a poetry which collapsed the assumed superiority of Briton to slave, European to Indian, using the ethnographical information provided by travelers to lay bare the mechanisms by which fear and desire are produced and internalized, the mechanisms by which, in response to the culture they lived in, people shaped themselves in subservience to and/or in power over others.[37]

Fulford also finds traces of Hearne in Wordsworth's "The Complaint of the Forsaken Indian Woman" (1798) and in the uncompleted Wordsworth-Coleridge project "The Three Graves" (c. 1797). Similarly, Carl Edward Thompson argues that Wordsworth's "The Excursion" (1814) was based on Hearne's travel narrative. But if the Romantics were questioning the assumed differences between slaves, Indians, and British subjects in the late eighteenth century, Wordsworth had become, by 1814, a firm proponent of the "civilizing mission" and the notion that "other cultures [were] backward and savage, in need of British guidance both practically and morally."[38] Using the figure of the "Solitary," who returns from a voyage to America, where he expected to find "a Rousseauistic idyll, and living examples of the Noble Savage," Wordsworth writes that Indians are in fact

> A creature squalid, vengeful, and impure
> Remorseless, and submissive to no law
> But superstitious fear, and abject sloth.[39]

Just as reviewers of Hearne's narrative warned against romanticizing savagery, Wordsworth's poem makes clear the importance of distinguishing between civilized and savage ways.

What, then, separated the savagery of the British from that of the Northern Indians? Staking out these differences was central to late-eighteenth-century responses to *A Journey*, as the *Critical Review*'s anxious reference to revolutionary sentiments reveals. Hearne himself offered answers in a lengthy chapter regarding "the persons and tempers of the Northern Indians." In it, he dwells on the Northern Indian "heart" and particularly Indian responses to violence, a theme that also informs his description of the massacre. For instance, although Hearne observes that the Northern Indians "are by no means a bold or warlike people" and that their attack at Bloody Falls represented their only act "of wanton cruelty on any other part of the human race," he states,

> Their hearts, however, are in general so unsusceptible of tenderness, that they can view the deepest distress in those that are not immediately related to them, without the least emotion; not even half as much as the generality of mankind feel for the sufferings of the meanest of the brute creation. I have been present when one of them, imitating the groans, distorted features, and contracted position of a man who had died in the most excruciating pain, put the whole company, except myself, into the most violent fit of laughter.[40]

Response to the suffering of others is a key theme in Hearne's writings. He uses it time and again to differentiate himself from the Northern Indians, not least at Bloody Falls, where his horror at the torture of a young woman stands in contrast to the Indians' mocking question as to whether he "wanted an Esquimaux wife."[41] Hearne's self-conscious display of pity, disgust, and tears at the sight of the massacre – tears that were allegedly triggered again and again as he recollected the event years later (in what Robert McGhee suggests "would today be diagnosed as post-traumatic stress") – was a sentimental outpouring that signified the humanity of his "heart."[42] Indeed, reviews of *A Journey* praised it as an "affecting narrative" and particularly noted Hearne's reaction to the "barbarous" massacre, which was deemed "a proper mixture of indignation at the brutalities, and of compassion for the miseries, of those wretched savages."[43] In contrast to later gendered and racialized associations of sentimentality with irrationality, to be civilized in the face of savage violence was to be overcome with emotion, and to be dispassionate was to reveal the savagery of one's heart.

Fulford makes the important observation that Hearne's tears not only separated civilized from savage, they also helped him evade responsibility for the massacre:

> To his fellow white men, he was supposedly in command of the expedition and should, therefore, have been able to prevent the attack, imposing civilized leadership on savage followers ... [but] "Neuter in the rear" he was not so much neutral as impotent – his manliness in question not only by the Dene warriors who ridiculed him for pitying the girl they had speared but also by readers who expected him to take control. Hearne's tears save

> him. They re-establish his difference from his fellow assailants, re-impose civilized values on the text. They show that the white man feels guilt and pity when Indians do not. If Hearne was complicit with murder, he purges his guilt by compassion of which tears are the bodily proof ... Sensibility and compassion ... were imposed on the narrative to redeem it from the danger of aligning the white man with the Indian.[44]

As Fulford makes clear, Hearne's carefully managed performance of sentiment in relation to specific forms of violence marks his civility and masculinity and diverts attention from his complicity in and responsibility for that violence. To pity the girl, to shed tears at the barbarous scene, was to confirm his difference and his innocence. His performance was defined by a self-conscious expression of feeling, involving a tense struggle between containing emotion and being overcome by it:

> The terror of my mind at beholding this butchery, cannot easily be conceived, much less described; though I summoned up all the fortitude I was master of on this occasion, it was with difficulty that I could refrain from tears; and I am confident that my features must have feelingly expressed how sincerely I was affected at the barbarous scene I then witnessed; even at this hour I cannot reflect on the transactions of that horrid day without shedding tears.[45]

This passage was repeatedly quoted in reviews and has been a cornerstone of efforts to absolve Hearne of responsibility for the massacre. During the 1970s, for example, a government official who wished to erect heritage plaques at Bloody Falls countered community objections to commemorating Hearne and the massacre by noting that Hearne "did not take part in the massacre and actually wished very sincerely that he could have prevented it."[46] But as Kugluktukmiut made clear, Hearne was understood to be both directly and indirectly responsible for the events of 17 July 1771, regardless of his tears.

Hearne's tears not only absolve him of responsibility for the barbarous scene; they also produce a place from which to view the event in all its gory detail and yet *not be involved.* To be civilized, in the context of Hearne's account, is not only to be affected by violence, it is to be a neutral (if reluctant) witness to the violence of others. To be savage is to revel in violence, to lose oneself and one's conscience to the pull of the savage mob, and to experience no emotional distress when "reflecting" on such violent acts. These are profoundly relational subject positions: Hearne's emotional state differentiates him as a civilized, neutral witness capable of documenting the dispassionate, savage violence unfolding before him. His ability to order violence is contingent on his constitution as an observing and sentimental witness whose "proper" emotional response signals his civilized *difference* and *distance* from the scene rather than his culpability or responsibility.

Witnessing, classifying, and remediating the violence of Indians was a responsibility that Hearne extended to the HBC more broadly, one that involved acute attention to the Indian heart. Commenting on hostilities between Northern Indians and Esquimaux along the northwestern shore of Hudson Bay, Hearne wrote that HBC efforts to smooth relations between them

> have at length so far humanized the hearts of those two tribes, that at present they can meet each other in a friendly manner; whereas a few years since, whenever they met, each party premeditated the destruction of the other; and what made their war more shocking was, they never gave quarter: so that the strongest party always killed the weakest, without sparing either man, woman, or child.[47]

Here, again, imperial violence is distinguished from the "shocking" acts of Indigenous people, enabling the HBC to be framed as a civilizing, benevolent force in the region that had, in fact, incurred "great expense ... by introducing those strangers."[48] Emblematic of the "anti-conquest" style of travel writing that Mary Louise Pratt associates with this era, such a tack not only naturalizes the civilizing mission that would dominate subsequent imperial activities in the region, it also masks the ways in which colonial expansion and the fur trade in particular had thoroughly disrupted northern land use, territory, and trade, leading to the kinds of conflicts that Hearne and others decried as inherent to savage life.[49] Consigning violence in the Americas to savages was an immensely disingenuous act, but one with significant discursive power.

Indeed, much more was at stake in Hearne's description of the massacre than the amusement of "persons of leisure" or the absolution of one man from complicity in a violent act. *A Journey* was published during a crucial moment in the formation of modern racial classificatory schemes that would become sedimented in subsequent decades.[50] Prominent racial theorists of the day consumed travel narratives like Hearne's and used them to delineate racial typologies.[51] Linnaeus himself posited five taxa of *Homo sapiens* in his 1769 *Systema Naturae* (Europeans, Americans, Asians,

Africans, and the "monstrous") and based this typology on the reports of his colleagues and other travellers. Notably, he classified Americans based on their "choleric" and "combative" tempers and characterized Europeans as "sanguine" and "clever." Hearne's study of the character of Northern Indians, in other words, was not read solely for its insights into life on the barrenlands but also because it supplied geographical evidence for the formulation of racial typologies. It buttressed emergent and shifting understandings of the essence of indigeneity and, by comparison, the essential nature of civilized humanity.

Ordering violence in the late eighteenth century was thus informed by, and contributed to, ideas about race and nature. As Terry Goldie observes, the violence of the Northern Indians was seen as "an essential characteristic" and an "expression of nature," not as a "human response by the indigenes to oppression."[52] In this context, Hearne could be presented as merely a witness, documenting the habits of the Northern Indians and measuring their divergence from civilized humanity. He could be judged on the basis on his accuracy and reliability rather than his complicity. For their part, the Indigenous figures conjured in Hearne's travel narrative could appear only as instances of a more generalized type, supporting the broader orderings of peoples and things at stake in *A Journey*. Their humanity and individuality mattered only to the extent that they illuminated the underlying essence of indigeneity. These practices of ordering race and nature were thus profoundly relational; they produced the subjectivities of the ordering witness as much as understandings of racialized Others.

CIRCULATING TYPES

The relational subjectivities delineated by Hearne's tears have been remarkably tenacious. Not only has the positionality of passive yet horrified witness to Indigenous violence continued to this day, it is deeply reliant on the production of generic Indigenous "types" that fulfill the fantasy of non-complicity in Hearne's story and that so appealed (and continue to appeal) to those who wish to deny the constitutive violence underpinning colonial acquisition and domination. One of the most famous of these "types" is the young, naked Inuk woman whom Hearne describes as twisting around his legs during the massacre. According to Ian MacLaren, her torture is "the entire book's climax and most memorable moment ... The figure of Hearne in Canadian literature can not free himself from the Inuit girl who is always there."[53] Indeed, this scene

This story is taken from the diary of Samuel Hearne, the first white man to cross the Arctic Circle in North America. It is a story of dogged determination and unbelievable privation

The Far Away Metal River

BY ROBERT E. PINKERTON

Illustrated by John Clymer

Samuel Hearne, the first white man to go north of the Arctic Circle on this continent, first to reach the polar sea by land, had a peculiar courage.

One of the great early explorers in America, though long forgotten, he carried through to completion a remarkable journey. He faced hardships with such fortitude as to arouse wonder at man's capacity to endure. He pressed on even when he could not hope, because he could not quit. For two and a half years he accepted intimate association with savages whose brutality is appalling.

Yet Hearne's greater courage is revealed in what he suffered emotionally. Hunger and privation brought no such test as when he stood at the shore of the polar sea and did not raise a finger while a girl, twisting about his legs and begging for her life, was jabbed to death by spears in the hands of his Indian companions.

Starvation could not cause the anguish of seeing men, women and children murdered, women the victims of mass rape, defenseless people plundered. Hearne even submitted to being robbed, starved, belittled and abandoned by Indians in his service. He was revolted and stung to anger by the atrocities he was forced to witness, but he made only mild protests. Therein lies the peculiar quality of his courage. Samuel Hearne held fast to what he felt was most important—submergence of self in the performance of duty.

In its physical accomplishment, Hearne's journey was extraordinary. He started from Prince of Wales Fort, now Churchill, halfway up the west coast of Hudson Bay, near latitude 59 and only a few miles farther south than Skagway, Alaska. He went as far west as the longitude of Montana's western border and north past the Arctic Circle to the western end of Coronation Gulf, on the Arctic Ocean.

An Eskimo girl about 18 years old fled up the hill to Hearne. As she twisted about his legs in terror, the horrified white man shouted a plea for her life.

A True Book-Length Feature

69

The opening pages of Robert E. Pinkerton's "The Far Away Metal River," *True: The Man's Magazine*, 1947.

has been excerpted, reimagined, and serialized innumerable times, and these various invocations of "the girl" provide important insights into the persistence of Hearne's story.

Consider the opening pages of a May 1947 article written by Robert Pinkerton for *True: The Man's Magazine.* The accompanying image shows the moment in which the young woman "twisted about [Hearne's] legs in terror" as the "horrified white man shouted a plea for her life." In the 1795 edition of *A Journey,* the Dene laughed at Hearne's plea and proceeded to stick "both their spears through her body and [transfix] her to the ground ... [paying] not the smallest regard to the shrieks and agony of the poor wretch, who was twining round their spears like an eel!"[54] Pinkerton reproduces this account and dwells extensively on the "courage" required of Hearne to witness the massacre without intervening:

> Hearne had orders from his superiors to cross the Barren Grounds. Obedience came before all else. If he had not stood idly by while Indians murdered, raped, and plundered, he would have been killed or left to starve. As an Englishman of his time and training, he chose to live that he might finish his job. He chose to obey regardless. The man wasn't hardened. He had compassion, sympathy and understanding beyond the ordinary. His revulsion at the scenes of savage cruelty was great. Years after the girl was slain at his feet he wept when he recalled the incident. Undoubtedly there were times when Hearne was prompted to run amok and achieve some measure of justice and decency, and perhaps more guts are required to sink one's desires and keep duty foremost.[55]

Aimed at men returning from the Second World War, this article clearly emphasizes the aspects of Hearne's experience that might resonate with veterans, including the emotional intricacies of obedience and duty. Pinkerton's retelling goes on to repeatedly invoke scenes of rape and even mass rape, even though Hearne's own sensational account contains no references to either.

Moreover, what matters in Pinkerton's version is not so much that rape occurred but that Hearne was forced to helplessly witness it. The magazine considers the physical hardships he endured but insists that

> Hearne's greater courage is revealed in what he suffered emotionally. Hunger and privation brought no such test as when he stood at the shore of the polar sea and did not raise a finger while a girl, twisting about his legs

> and begging for her life, was jabbed to death by spears in the hands of his Indian companions.
>
> Starvation could not cause the anguish of seeing men, women and children murdered, women the victims of mass rape, defenseless people plundered ... He was revolted and stung to anger by the atrocities he was forced to witness, but he made only mild protests. Therein lies the peculiar quality of his courage. Samuel Hearne held fast to what he felt was most important – submergence of self in the performance of duty.[56]

Violence against Indigenous women is both pervasive and naturalized in imperial contexts, and the very fact that the attack on "the girl" has been invoked and reimagined so many times, and so graphically, reinforces claims that the perpetuation and denial of sexualized, racialized violence is constitutive of this colonial present.[57] That Pinkerton could simply add rape to the scene, as a kind of appropriate and expected component of a violent Indigenous encounter, is itself notable. But the magazine's engagement with Hearne's story does more than naturalize and eroticize violence against Indigenous women. It also stakes out a familiar subject position: Hearne is the anguished, helpless, reluctant witness to Indigenous violence, the figure who recognizes suffering but is not responsible for it. The fate of "the girl" and the suggestion of rape more generally are used to amplify the savagery of the event and to secure its classification as an act of *Indigenous* violence: "Hearne knew what was coming," writes Pinkerton. "This would not be a war. It would be a massacre ... And even with superior numbers and weapons, the Chipewyans, in typical Indian fashion, took no chances. They wanted to kill but they didn't want to run the least risk of getting hurt. It never occurred to them to give the Eskimos a sporting chance."[58]

In *True*'s invocation of "the girl" – intended for war veterans who were struggling with their own implication in the violence of empire – readers are asked to identify with Hearne's suffering, not hers, and in so doing to explore the emotional geographies of white masculinity. What matters is Hearne's response to violence, not his complicity or responsibility, and certainly not the pain or humanity of the young girl, who here lacks a "sporting chance" of protecting herself. The magazine is not alone in using her for this purpose. Don Gutteridge similarly trains his attention on the relational subjectivities of white masculinity, dispossession, and rape. His book-length poetic rendering of the massacre, published in 1973 as *Coppermine: The Quest for North,* exemplifies the dynamic I describe in this chapter:

Last victim:
girl, maybe eighteen,
sacrificial virgin,
snow like a
bloodied altar
ringed with priests
(Matonabbee like Jason
eyes on the fleece)
their stiff spears
are a halo at her throat,
they thrust with all
the religious lust
with all the rage
of their twisted love:
her body a host
for the visiting sword
flies apart like a
shattered vessel,
blood a veil of
scarlet, everywhere
(flesh is victim to
everyman's darkness,
the victor's dance
on the scarlet snow
this rare immaculate
moment)

But
why don't they see
she's still alive,
flesh at my feet:
a torn coat!

blood sucked up
by snow like a
sponge, on my boots
now, like a blotter
sucked up my trousers
shirt clean collar,
pink sweat on my

arms, salt taste
on the tongue:
eyes burning with
fresh sight

O see the blade
break her heart open
like a new cunt

see her hump
like mad on
its copper tip

O look at her
fucking Death
like crazy
til they both
die!

(Blood is scarlet
its sound is the
slash of scimitar
sword hatchet
singing in the
flesh historic:
perpetual answer
to our chaos
of questioning,
we wear its wound
like Cain's badge –
blood on our guilt:
a scarlet tunic)

I look at
Matonabbee, he
laughs, blood
juggling on his lip.[59]

Ian MacLaren describes this poem as "uncreatively, unavailingly, and shamelessly obscene."[60] It is a deeply violent, misogynist, and racialized celebration of rape, one that draws on old and persistent geographies of violence, responsibility, and guilt, and MacLaren is right to condemn it. Here, as in *True*'s rendering, rape is merely a device through which we come to know Matonabbee and Hearne, savage and civilized. Gutteridge's rendering is almost frantically graphic, but it is by no means unique, and if anything it makes explicit what other accounts offer indirectly. Hearne, and by extension the "we" whom Gutteridge names as inheritors of his legacy, wears responsibility for the violence of empire like a stain or a wound, something passively and reluctantly soaked up like a sponge, merely by being present, whereas the Indian aggressors remorselessly wear the violence they have actively carried out on their laughing, bloody lips. Hearne is the allegedly reluctant Qablunaaq observer with whom subsequent readers have so easily identified as they, too, position themselves as innocent, horrified, and yet riveted witnesses to sexualized, racialized violence. As in *A Journey,* Hearne is the star of this story, not Matonabbee and most especially not the girl, who is indeed a "host" for a parable of colonial erotics and violent dispossession. Therein lies an essential violence of imperial orderings. If modern epistemologies involved, above all, new ways of translating the specific into translocal classifications and orders, these orderings had profound consequences for both masking and perpetuating the violence of empire. Ultimately, stories such as Gutteridge's say nothing about their ostensible victims; they offer metaphoric, generalized renderings of imperial violence in which the specific pain of specific people – here, the "young girl" – is relevant only to the extent that it illuminates the experience of the civilized witness or confirms racialized classificatory schemes. Indeed, "the girl" has appeared almost as often as Hearne in northern literature, yet she remains a nameless generic figure, produced for the enjoyment of the observer while underwriting a whole economy of racialized and sexualized possession in the North.

Postcolonial scholar Ian Baucom insists that this failure to register the specificity and humanity of racialized victims of violence was central to the circulation of stories from the imperial periphery throughout the late eighteenth and early nineteenth centuries. For all their sensational currency, stories of imperial violence circulated most effectively (and affectively) when stripped of their geographic, historical, and personal specificities. In a study of how accounts of the *Zong* massacre, the forced drowning of 132 slaves by an English ship captain in 1781, circulated in imperial Britain, Baucom argues that "the story of the massacre was retold ... not as the story of a particular historical event ... but as one in a series of equivalent stories." He traces the ways in which abolitionist William Wilberforce mobilized the story by grounding "the value of memory in the substitution of the generic for the singular, the series for the event." Wilberforce did not mention the *Zong* by name and did not give the precise dates or location of the incident, or the names of those who had been killed. Instead, he presented the massacre as a generalized *kind* of story, one revealing the underlying truths of slavery:

> What Wilberforce seems to have sensed was that his story was imperiled by its very specificity, that its "value" would attenuate to a zero point the more unique it became. The story, in other words, had to become generic if it was to have any use, if Wilberforce was to inspire in his audience anything but melancholy, anything but a paralyzed regret before the absolute specificity of a scene of irreversible human damage.[61]

Here, just as in Hearne's narrative, there is a relationship between emotion, specificity, and complicity. To focus on the specific details of the *Zong* massacre would lead to emotional paralysis in the face of the irreversible *human* damage for which Britons were collectively responsible. An abstracted *kind* of story, however, provided emotional distance and enabled listeners to extract generalized truths about slavery and their own benevolent relation to the victims of the slave trade. The only details of the Zong massacre that mattered were those that illuminated Wilberforce's conceptualization of slavery, not those that attended to the specific experiences of the slaves in question.

Hearne's story, too, was populated with generalized figures that would assist in its circulation. Although presented in painstaking detail, its torture scenes are almost certainly inventions, inserted by savvy publishers and editors. Hearne's earlier unpublished account of the massacre states that the Dene "ran on the tent on a sudden & killed every soul before they had power to rise in the whole 21 persons ... The massacre was soon accomplished, the inhabitants being all asleep."[62] There is no naked girl, no desperate pleas, no horrified tears. MacLaren argues that "readers of the day" and Hearne's "ghost-writer" would have found "the massacre of people merely in their sleep both too meager an event to serve as the climax of an entire work, and too good an opportunity for Gothic enhancement to be left untouched." He contends that the murder of the girl, of a deaf old woman by the rapids, and of a man stabbed so many times that he resembled a "cullender" comprise a classic Gothic triangle: "Here is stark terror, but it came from the publishing house in London, not from the wilderness of North America."[63] What is crucial to understand here is that these figures – graphically detailed but nonetheless wholly generic – were not just good for selling books; they were equivalent "types" that could be combined with other stories to confirm and secure the essential truths of imperial domination.

Upon publication, then, and for the general audience that consumed it, Hearne's description of the Bloody Falls massacre was valuable because it could be combined with other accounts of violence, torture, and war to derive general insights into savagery, order, and civilization. Its circulation and value were contingent on its dislocation from its geographical, cultural, and historical context. Although ostensibly about the *particularities* of Northern Indians and northern landscapes, it was taken up for what it revealed about savagery and violence *in general.* This ordering was by no means distinct from the immense violence that marked the late eighteenth century, but was rather a crucial discursive strategy aimed at recuperating the civility and innocence of an imperial project in crisis. "Story" was essential to these orderings, not simply in imaginative or textual terms, but as a situated, material, and relational practice. Hearne's story ordered relations between savage and civilized, violent and innocent, that have persisted to this day. However much the Bloody Falls massacre story continues to be offered as a prototypical account of the violent relations between Inuit and Dene, then, its repeated invocation tells us much more about Qablunaat and their uneasy, eroticized relations with the violence of empire.

3
To Mourn

Scientists are scrupulous representatives of the facts. Who is speaking when they speak? The facts themselves, beyond all question, but also their authorized spokespersons. Who is speaking, then, nature or human beings? ... The scientists declare that they themselves are not speaking; rather, facts speak for themselves. These mute entities are thus capable of speaking, writing, signifying ... Little groups of gentlemen take testimony from natural forces, and they testify to each other that they are not betraying but translating the silent behavior of objects.

– Bruno Latour, *We Have Never Been Modern*

Objects arise as the figures in the landscape of empire; narratives and actions put them in motion.

– W.J.T. Mitchell, *What Do Pictures Want?*

What then is truth? A mobile army of metaphors, metonyms, and anthropomorphisms – in short, a sum of human relations, which have been enhanced, transposed, and embellished poetically and rhetorically, and which after long use seem firm, canonical, and obligatory to a people: truths are illusions about which one has forgotten that is what they are; metaphors which are worn out and without sensuous power; coins which have lost their pictures and now matter only as metal, no longer as coins.

– Friedrich Nietzsche, "On Truth and Lies in an Extra-Moral Sense"

In Kugluktuk, in spring, things change fast. Days swell with more and more sunlight, and everyone's mood lifts steadily toward a kind of smiling exuberance after months of darkness, until it seems that nobody can recall the dull weight of winter. Sleds are strapped with jerry cans, furs, foam mattresses, and canvas tents as people make for the land. The air is still cold, but some days it creeps above zero, and it seems as though everything is on the increase. Talk turns to birds – someone says that the geese will be back any day now – and children play all night under golden twilight, resting their heads through math class. Humour sides with the surreal; nothing makes sense and it's funny that way. Everything is aggressively, insistently, crazy-making backwards.

By summer, though, a balance has been struck. Rhythms return, the sun grows hotter, giddiness eases as people take shape again. ATVs are hauled out of storage, and the drone of their engines advances and recedes throughout the day. The ice melts for good, at least for now, and the best sealing spots melt with it. Some still travel upriver to Kugluk and Onoagahiovik to scoop char from the rapids, the place their ancestors stayed all night fishing. Along the banks of the river, wildflowers bloom, shots of yellow and purple in a rich ruddy carpet of willow, sedge, and lichen, and soon the berries will appear. By mid-July, a small, unremarkable ragweed, *Senecio lugens,* has begun to flower in scattered patches along the Coppermine River and along the shore in front of town. Few people notice. The plant has no distinct name in Inuinnaqtun, no specific use and no story, and is thus referred to simply as *nautsiaq,* a flower, one of many that light up the land, along with stands of lupin, Arctic cotton, and lousewort.[1]

For some, though, and at other places along the river, this little yellow flower is both notable and specific. Known also as the black-tipped groundsel, *Senecio lugens* was named by John Richardson, surgeon-naturalist with the first Franklin expedition (1819–22), the first expedition to retrace Hearne's steps through the Central Arctic. Its species name is derived from the Latin word *"lugeo,"* meaning "to mourn."[2] The name *lugens* was accepted among early nineteenth-century botanists as a kind of double entendre. Officially, it referred to the colour black, but *lugens* was also understood as a reference to the mourning dress that was increasingly common in Europe from the late eighteenth century onward.[3] Indeed, although "lugens" appears to be a reference to the plant's black-tipped involucral bracts, the name's more oblique evocation of mourning was also intentional. Richardson's botanical appendix to the expedition's travel narrative did not explain how a flower might be conceived of as mourning, but it did emphasize that the expedition had collected the plant's type specimen

Senecio lugens. Photograph by Robert D. Bull. Canadian Museum of Nature.

at "Bloody Fall, where the Esquimaux were destroyed by the Northern Indians that accompanied Hearne, whence the specified name."[4]

Senecio lugens was just one of many objects that the Franklin expedition assembled as physical proof of the massacre, and it is the production of historical truth through the ordering of "things" that concerns me here. Although they privately doubted the veracity of Hearne's account, the expedition members played a pivotal role in confirming Hearne's story. They did so, moreover, without ever explicitly declaring his account to be true; instead, they assembled a series of objects that stood as proof of the massacre where words fell short. This chapter thus intervenes in the long-standing Qablunaaq debate about whether Hearne's account of the Bloody Falls massacre is true. I do so not by rallying historical or material evidence, and not by contrasting fact and fiction, but rather by exploring the geographies of truth making itself, and the ways in which stories produce truth-effects that become concretized as history.

I understand truth as a produced, relational, and socio-material effect rather than as a transcendent condition, and I am particularly interested in the ways in which material objects become enrolled in its production. Truth, I argue, is constituted relationally and contextually. Truths emerge in place, through particular assemblages of people, ideas, and things and must be continually reproduced and reinscribed through practice.[5] Indeed, the orderings described in this chapter are not reducible to a blunt interest in confirming Hearne's story. The Franklin expedition's storying of Bloody Falls emerged from, and contributed to, a range of interests and contexts, including the men's very personal travails throughout their journey but also a series of military, political, publishing, and scientific communities in Britain that interpreted and engaged their findings. This chapter thus attends to the ways in which complex, situated efforts to make sense can contribute to the production of historical truth. What is at stake here is not so much the "actual" truth of the massacre but rather the capacity for truth to be produced through specific, situated practices and, ultimately, the capacity to order and make legible different, less deadly truths.

ANIMATE NATURES

Samuel Hearne was not the only impotent witness to the Bloody Falls massacre. He writes,

> I did not see any birds peculiar to those parts, except what the Copper Indians call the "Alarm Bird," or "Bird of Warning." In size and colour it resembles a Cobadekoock, and is of the owl genus. The name is said to be well adapted to its qualities; for when it perceives any people, or beast, it directs its way towards them immediately, and after hovering over them some time, flies round them in circles, or goes a-head in the same direction in which they walk. They repeat their visits frequently; and if they see any other moving objects, fly alternately from one party to the other, hover over them for some time, and make a loud screaming noise like the crying of a child. In this manner they are said sometimes to follow passengers a whole day. The Copper Indians put great confidence in those birds, and say they are frequently apprized by them of the approach of strangers, and conducted by them to herds of deer and musk-oxen; which, without their assistance, in all probability, they never could have found. The Esquimaux seem not to have imbibed the same opinion of these birds; for if they had, they must have been apprized of our approach toward their tent, because all the time the Indians lay in ambush, (before they began the massacre), a large flock of those birds were continually flying about, and hovering alternately over them and the tents, making a noise sufficient to awaken any man out of the soundest sleep.[6]

In this passage, Hearne's preoccupation with the "superstitious" beliefs of the Copper Indians, which recurs throughout *A Journey*, is only half-hearted. Clearly, the bird's capacity to prevent the Bloody Falls massacre, described in detail only a few pages before, adds pathos to Hearne's account, and the bird's classification into Linnaean taxonomies does little to diminish its evocative power. Although Hearne's alarm bird did not stand up to scientific scrutiny (there are no alarm birds or cobadekoocks to be found in subsequent catalogues of northern fauna), the interweaving of animate nature, violence, pathos, and witnessing that it expressed most certainly lived on.

Fifty years after Hearne's cobadekoocks issued their futile warning, the Franklin expedition retraced Hearne's footsteps and set about identifying, classifying, and naming the flora and fauna of the region. The expedition was assembled after a long hiatus in polar exploration. Following the defeat of Napoleon in 1815, the British redirected their attention toward the discovery of a northwest passage. Debates over Hearne's reliability were renewed in order to justify extensive state-sponsored exploration in northern North America, including a retracing of his overland journey from Hudson Bay and along the Coppermine River. Of particular significance was John Barrow's continual and forceful insistence that Hearne's latitudinal measurements were unreliable. In an extended 1816 attack on the HBC's failure to adequately explore its Arctic lands, Barrow (second secretary of the Admiralty) condemned Hearne's deficiencies as a cartographer. Despite having been "selected for the journey *because* he could take an observation for the latitude," Barrow noted incredulously, Hearne simply "did not think it worthwhile" to await fair weather upon arriving at the Arctic Ocean to take an accurate measurement. "In the whole of the journey of thirteen hundred miles and back again," he exclaimed, "he takes but *one* single observation!" As a result, Barrow insisted, and as agreed upon by leading geographers such as Dalrymple, Hearne's measurements were off by almost three degrees.[7] Barrow's efforts to secure a renewed polar exploration program ultimately succeeded. In order to "amend the very defective geography of the Northern part of North America" that Hearne had provided, John Franklin was dispatched in 1818, along with surgeon-naturalist John Richardson, expedition artist George Back, and midshipman Robert Hood, to be joined by a sizeable party of assistants, guides, and voyageurs upon reaching North America.

Richardson's responsibility on the voyage was to collect, preserve, and transport "various subjects of Natural History, which can be allowed consistently with the primary object of the Exploration."[8] Identifying plants, in other words, was valued as much as discovering geological deposits, charting transportation routes, and producing accurate maps. Although Richardson was not particularly well versed in Arctic flora, he was an ambitious and talented naturalist. Trained at the University of Edinburgh in botany, zoology, and geology, he studied under naturalist Robert Jameson and associated with other leading scientists throughout his university and early naval career.[9] In an 1819 letter to William Hooker, Richardson, who had spent the previous years working as a naval surgeon, not a botanist, worried about his "inexperienced eye" and lack of botanical expertise but also claimed to have great energy and enthusiasm for the task ahead. "The only quality I have in common with a Botanist is zeal for the advancement of science," he wrote, and so began a long relationship with Hooker and other leading botanists of the day.[10]

The early nineteenth century was a fascinating and dynamic time to be practising botany. Imperial exploration and trade had greatly expanded the scope and volume of plants available for study, motivating the development of a more systematic means of classifying and naming flora. Scientific bodies such as the Royal Society adopted the Linnaean system of plant and animal taxonomy during this time, a decision that was not without controversy.[11] The Linnaean system was intended to replace the long and unwieldy scientific naming systems that preceded it and to universalize the diversity of local, Indigenous names. Botanists were to classify plants according to their visible sexual features, stamens and pistils, and to assign binomial Latin names (*Genus,* followed by *species*) to the proliferation of plants pouring in from around the world. Linnaeus insisted that names be issued in Latin and that species names be assigned either in tribute to naturalists or prominent public figures, or to describe the appearance or habitat of the organism. They were not to reflect Indigenous names, languages, or medicinal or other uses, and were not to be biographical except in the form of attribution.[12]

The very efficiency of the Linnaean system was a source of concern for some critics, who charged that it was overly mechanistic and that it sacrificed the evocative power of common plant names. Indeed, the adoption of Linnaean taxonomy can be understood as part of a broader move toward the rationalization and secularization of scientific practice, a process well under way before the 1859 publication of Darwin's *On the Origin of Species.*[13] Linnaean names did not so much challenge theologically based understandings of the natural world as sidestep them, and it was this lack of explicit reference to the divine qualities of plants that made some botanists uneasy. The gradual secularization of botanical practice does not necessarily indicate a corresponding secularism among botanists themselves, of course, or even an immediate challenge to theological understandings of plant morphology, distribution, and origin.[14] Early-nineteenth-century botanical theory was deeply informed by theology and metaphysics. Belief in God as nature's designer was largely unquestioned, and the nascent sciences were understood, in part, as a process of revealing his work. Indeed, natural philosophy – the precursor to the modern natural sciences – was devoted both to the study of the natural world and to philosophical ruminations on the origins and causes of natural phenomena. The study of plant life, in that sense, was understood not only as a descriptive practice but also as an engagement with meaning, cause, and origin.

One of the ways in which the divine properties and origins of plants were discerned by botanists was through their own reactions to the natural world. Scientific figures have expressed a sense of wonder at the workings of God for centuries, and botanists are no exception. But historian David Elliston Allen argues that from the late eighteenth century onward, naturalists were expected not only to document "what one saw plainly and accurately" but also "to record one's reactions – and the livelier these reactions appeared, the more beneficial, the more exalting, the more 'tasteful' the contract with nature was assumed to have been."[15] A personal involvement with plant specimens was encouraged, and emotional engagement was particularly valued. Indeed, contemporary notions of objectivity, understood as requiring suppression of the self and the emotional, emerged as a model of scientific practice only in the mid-nineteenth century; the scientific climate in which Richardson operated was not only tolerant but to some extent supportive of emotional reactions to the natural world, whether in a religious or a more generalized Romantic register.[16] Plants, it was believed, could affect people, but it was also believed that plants were themselves effects, physical manifestations of God's mysterious universal design.

Richardson himself has been memorialized as a generally emotional and sensitive man who stored up "the best poems and songs of Burns ... ready to be poured forth when his feelings were touched by either the pathetic or the humourous."[17] Such a characterization perhaps attests more to the Romantic atmosphere in which this 1868 comment was written than to Richardson's own sensibilities, but it nevertheless suggests that feeling and emotional engagement with the world did not diminish, and perhaps contributed to, his status as an upstanding man of science. He became a fellow of the Royal Society in 1825 and maintained close relations with the major figures of nineteenth-century botany throughout his career; even today, he is celebrated as an important figure in the history of science.[18]

Richardson was also a devout Christian, filling his letters to his family and colleagues with theological interpretations of everyday life.[19] He was convinced that the Arctic landscape was "inhospitable to atheists" and that only his Christian faith saved him from despair on the arduous journey. As he wrote to his wife from Bloody Falls in July 1821, "I must now my Dear Mary conclude this hurried letter recommending you to the Almighty disposer of events, his protecting care is equally necessary in a crowded city as in a dreary waste – That he may watch over you is the daily prayer of your affectionate husband."[20] This reference to the "Almighty disposer of events" appears in much of Richardson's correspondence with colleagues and family, and the expedition members with whom he traversed the Central Arctic remarked upon the strength of his faith. But his sense that God was watching over the "dreary waste" of Bloody Falls is significant, as is his conceptualization of God's essential role in death, loss, and mourning. In an 1824 letter to Franklin, Richardson commented on Franklin's sister, Isabella Cracroft, who was bearing the death of her husband

> with a resignation so truly Christian. Time, the grand physician of the mind will soften down the poignancy of her grief into a tender remembrance of the excellent qualities and benevolent disposition of her departed husband. In the mean time her pious frame of mind will enable her to contend with the anguish inseparable from so recent and severe a deprivation by directing her to the contemplation of the Almighty disposer of Events who orders every thing according to his pleasure and all for the best. It is in the power of him who hath taken away to blunt the sting of death, destroy the victory of the grave and in another and a better world bring about that reunion which is the hope to which a Christian most fondly clings when the ties of friendship are thus suddenly swept asunder.[21]

Richardson did not question God's capacity to "order every thing," and his certainty shaped his botanical practice.

According to historians Philip Rehbock and John Hedley Brooke, the botanical sciences in Britain remained thoroughly teleological until the 1830s; that is, plants were believed to be designed by God and outfitted with features that reflected a specific meaning or purpose.[22] It was God, in other words, who tipped the involucral bracts of *Senecio lugens* in black, and it was the job of naturalists like Richardson to decode his reason for doing so, in part through scrutiny of their own emotional reactions. Because Richardson himself provided so little explanation about the naming of *Senecio lugens,* one cannot say with certainty who, or what, he imagined the flower to be mourning. But certainly, in the botanical community within which Richardson operated, it would have been plausible to imagine that God's own grief at the slaying of the Inuit was manifested in the features of the black-tipped groundsel and, moreover, that this grief was accessible to the close eye of the naturalist. The naming of *Senecio lugens* would have been legible as both a tribute to God and a mournful record of a savage act, a reminder that God was watching that day, as Richardson knew he was.[23]

Such a tribute did not explicitly violate Linnaean taxonomical guidelines. In one sense, the name connotes precisely the kinds of things the Linnaean system was meant to overcome: it evokes a sensational event with which the British public was amply familiar, it refers to Indigenous history, and it indexes an emotional reaction to the natural world – all of which Linnaeus aimed to eliminate from plant-naming practice.[24] And yet the species name "lugens" was also an accepted reference to black colouration.[25] The fact that the name also evoked a mournful reaction to the Bloody Falls massacre was conveniently resonant. *Senecio lugens,* it would seem, was named for both its poetry and its morphology. It was a brilliant negotiation of early-nineteenth-century botanical naming debates.

PUBLIC NATURES

The point was not simply for *Senecio lugens* to make sense to botanists, however: Richardson was collecting and naming plants for a much wider audience. Not only had plants such as coffee, sugar cane, and cotton transformed imperial commerce, but, from about the mid-eighteenth century onward, natural history had also begun to capture the imagination of writers, artists, and the rising middle class.[26] By the turn of the nineteenth century, it was not unusual for middle-class families to spend a day at the beach, identifying local species, or for ladies to wander the woods with botanical guides in hand. A few poems were written about Linnaean taxonomy, and the discovery of new species elicited interest from a much broader constituency than the network of botanists involved in the identification, circulation, and naming of plant specimens. Widespread knowledge and enthusiasm for plants occurred, in part because a separate, specialized, scientific realm had yet to be established, and in part because knowledge of the natural world grew alongside and in relation to literary and philosophical thought. Although Richardson certainly needed specialized knowledge and skills to carry out his assignment, his findings were meaningful to a wider public audience and were made accessible to that audience through the publication of the expedition's travel narrative.

Richardson was well aware of the public's interest in the expedition and was keen to augment his own reputation through the publication of his work.[27] He arranged for the production of separate bound copies of the botanical appendix for independent circulation, one of which was presented to William Hooker at Kew, and he assisted Franklin in quickly preparing the travel narrative for publication.[28] The travel narrative was written to appeal to a relatively elite but informed and enthusiastic audience, one familiar with Hearne's account of the Bloody Falls massacre and keenly interested in the expedition's encounter with the famous site.[29] On this front, the book did not disappoint. Not only did *Senecio lugens* feature prominently (as one of the few specimens that earned a full-page illustration in the botanical appendix), but the book also supplied extensive commentary on the massacre and an illustration of the site itself.

Bloody Fall, attributed to expedition artist George Back, is one of twenty-four images in Franklin's *Narrative of a Journey to the Shores of the Polar Sea.* It was the first published image of Bloody Falls (Hearne provided

Bloody Fall, by George Back. *Library and Archives Canada, 1992–547–6.*

only a written description of the site), and, furnished with skulls and bones, it functioned as a kind of nineteenth-century equivalent of the crime scene photograph. Although attributed to Back, *Bloody Fall* is a composite of sorts; Janice Cavell notes that the drawing upon which the final engraving was based would have been prepared by Robert Batty, John Barrow's son-in-law, and passed on to well-known engraver Edward Finden for final production.[30] Although Franklin had expected that Back would himself oversee the production of the travel narrative's images, Back was dispatched to the West Indies shortly after the expedition's return to Britain, leaving the task to the team assembled by Barrow and publisher John Murray. Back did not actually sketch the massacre site in his field journals, opting instead to record a more southerly part of the rapids and the mouth of the Coppermine River. According to the published narrative, *Bloody Fall* was partly based on "a sketch taken by Mr. Hood," but midshipman Hood's journals from 15 September 1820 to his death in October 1821 have been lost, along with the sketch to which Franklin refers.[31] Thus, the exact materials informing the preparation of the engraving are unclear. As expedition artist, however, Back was expected to provide realistic depictions of the landscape, and the image would have been interpreted as such.

Batty evidently took up the expedition members' claims that the area around their camp was "strewed" with human remains. In his own notes, Richardson insisted that the men had "encamped on the very spot where the Massacre of the Esquimaux was transacted by Hearne's party" and that "the ground is still strewed with human skulls."[32] Franklin only vaguely referred to skulls and bones "near the encampment" but made a point of stating that "signs of struggle" were apparent on the bones themselves.[33] Back's field journal described the bones and their picturesque placement in some detail:

> The place where our tents were pitched – commanded a very beautiful view of the river – which was bounded on each side by lofty hills of clay and sand ... On the right side was the Rocky Island the natives had just quitted – with their dogs remaining harnessed – and their tents [made of deer skin] – and fish thrown down in scattered confusion. The fall filled the centre – whilst the bustling scene of tents – and armed men and the humiliating one of human bones – and fragments – occupied the foreground.[34]

This description is consistent with the final engraving, and it probably guided Batty's rendering of the scene, but it is also consistent with a sketch that Back prepared of a different part of the rapids, where the expedition members were also more likely to have camped.[35]

Over the years, scholars have argued that both the existence of the bones and their precise location are suspect, citing everything from periodic flooding of the area to a likelihood that ground squirrels would have made off with any remains.[36] More convincing are the claims of Kugluktukmiut that Inuit would almost certainly have been camped downstream on a flat, gravelly stretch known as Onoagahiovik, not on the high bluff where *Bloody Fall* locates the remains.[37] The expedition members' notes also contradict Batty's placement of the bones and support the claims of Kugluktukmiut that the massacre would have occurred downstream. Both Back's and Richardson's field journals describe the massacre site as located on a low stretch of land closer to the foot of the rapids, not on the bluff featured in the engraving.[38] Franklin also specified that bones were found below the rapids. It is more likely that Batty, not Back or Hood, placed the skulls and bones on the bluff, either because of a misreading of the expedition reports and sketches or for aesthetic reasons. According to Ian MacLaren, the placement of the bones is consistent with the picturesque ruins motif; Arctic landscape art of the era was defined by the picturesque aesthetic, and the bones offered a "historical emblem investing the landscape with temporal depth."[39] Just as the journals of expedition leaders were sometimes heavily edited during their preparation for publication, MacLaren argues, illustrators and engravers would have created a "carefully managed" image of Bloody Falls, with "several stages of composition interven[ing] between the first effort with pen or brush" and the final engraving. Image and text were both managed, MacLaren suggests, to maximize their capacity to circulate as a "commodity for public consumption."[40]

In the text of the published narrative, Franklin himself subtly disowned the engraving's placement of the bones, remarking that "the surrounding scenery is accurately delineated in the annexed sketch taken by Mr. Hood but finished by Mr. Back."[41] In other words, he vouched for the accuracy of the "surrounding scenery" but remained silent about the campsite and the bones. The inference is that the rest is not accurate, and certainly *Narrative of a Journey* and the journals of the other expedition members contradict the placement of both. Franklin would understandably have been reluctant to directly challenge Batty's work, which Barrow (Batty's father-in-law) described as developed "in a very beautiful manner," adding, "on the whole I have no doubt but that they will produce a very excellent set of plates."[42] Whatever their location, however, the expedition members went out of their way to confirm the presence of bones at the site, bones that explorers Peter Warren Dease and Thomas Simpson also reported finding in 1838.[43] Although it is possible that the bones were fictional or not actually human (and their position in the engraving is certainly suspect), it seems unlikely that Franklin, Richardson, and Back would have entirely invented them, though they may have exaggerated their quantity and the "signs of struggle" supposedly evident on the bones themselves.

Although the precise "truth" of each is somewhat uncertain, the engraving, the bones, and *Senecio lugens* functioned together as a kind of material evidence for the massacre, and each was invested with evocative, emotional detail. Franklin stated that he could see signs of struggle and violence on the bones themselves, and his travel narrative made a point of reaffirming Hearne's naming of the place as Bloody Fall. He emphasized the increasing anxiety of his Indian guides as they approached the falls and his own futile attempts to engineer peace between groups of Esquimaux and Indians in the region. The engraving provided a "commanding view" of the massacre site that conformed with both aesthetic convention and the expectations of readers (if not the expedition members' own records of the scene), and Richardson conjured a seasonal botanical witness to the tragedy; wildflowers mourning a wild grave, flowers black with the blood of the massacre victims. Indeed, although Richardson would have seen stands of black-tipped groundsel throughout his travels in the Central Arctic, he chose "Bloody Fall" as its type locality, forever linking it with the "historic" site and appealing to public knowledge of Hearne's journey. It would seem that the flower, bones, and engraving worked together within botanical and aesthetic conventions of the times to dramatize and *materialize* the massacre. They ordered the places and things of the region into relations that would confirm Hearne's story.

Their ordering was consequential. Even today, *Senecio lugens* is presented as a kind of evidence for the massacre, and the presence of bones remains largely unchallenged.[44] Historian Glyn Williams's 2009 discussion of the Bloody Falls massacre, for example, concedes that

> doubts have recently arisen about the authenticity of some of the details given by Hearne, and especially his gruesome description of the death of a young Inuit girl ... but of the reality of the killings there can be no doubt, for when Lieutenant John Franklin's party reached the spot fifty years later they found skulls and other bones still scattered on the ground.[45]

If Hearne's word has always been subject to some doubt, the "material evidence" presented by the Franklin expedition seems to stand as testimony to the historical truth of the event itself.

What makes this ordering particularly remarkable, however, is not so much its effectiveness, but rather its departure from the expedition members' *own* stances with regard to the truth of Hearne's account. As much as Hearne's cartographic findings may have been in doubt, he was the only European who had travelled the region, and both his official reports and his narrative were consulted extensively by the expedition members. As the first Europeans to visit the Coppermine River since Hearne, they carried a copy of his journal with them and made frequent notes in their own field journals about the accuracy of his cartographic, geographic, and anthropological observations. In a July 1821 letter to his wife written from Bloody Falls, for example, Richardson conceded that Hearne's latitudinal measurements were most certainly wrong but stated,

> I do not think his mistake willful, but the same excuse cannot be made as to his description of the Eskimaux girl clinging to his knees for his protection in his account of that bloody transaction, for the Indians assure us that he was left twenty miles or upwards in the river at a spot which they pointed out to us, and that when the war party was returning they met Hearne advancing alone having made a spear for himself by tying one leg of a pair of scissors to the end of a long pole ... The Indian account[s] of this transaction ... agree so well with each other that I believe it.[46]

This observation was never made public. In fact, the expedition members did their best to confirm Hearne's story rather than calling it into question, albeit by avoiding explicit reference to his presence at the scene. Franklin specifically noted of Bloody Falls, "As the spot exactly answers the description given by Mr. Hearne, of the place where the Chipewyans who accompanied him perpetrated the dreadful massacre on the Esquimaux, we had no doubt of this being the place, notwithstanding the difference in its position as to latitude and longitude given by him, and ascertained by our observation."[47]

And yet, the expedition members clearly *did* doubt the veracity of Hearne's story. Richardson *believed* the "Indian accounts" that Hearne's detailed description of the massacre was an invention. Back, too, noted in his field journal that "the most interesting part" of the "shocking scene" described by Hearne "I imagine to be unfounded."[48] Even Franklin's recounting of the testimony of an expedition member named Rabbit's

Head, a stepson of Matonabbee who was a young boy at the time of Hearne's trip, failed to explicitly confirm the massacre. Although he noted that Rabbit's Head had confirmed "the leading incidents recounted by Hearne," Franklin avoided direct reference to Hearne's status as a witness at the scene.[49] Such openings in Hearne's account were left unmarked by the expedition members in all but their private notes and letters. It would seem that the truth of the massacre was allowed to prevail even as its primary witness was quietly removed from the scene.

What to make of these concealments and doubts? Ann Laura Stoler argues that "imperial formations *require* specific 'procedures' of bad faith that cultivate scrutiny and disregard." She suggests, drawing on Jean-Paul Sartre, that "one never wholly believes what one believes" and that the dispositions of imperial agents hinge on a capacity to sincerely advance truths that they also, at the same time, believe to be untrue.[50] From such a perspective, the enormously detailed, scrutinizing practices that gave authority to *Senecio lugens,* to descriptions of marked bones, and to the 1823 engraving simultaneously cultivated a strategic dis-regard, a look away from the uncertainty and contradictions underpinning these orderings. If, in fact, the expedition members found little or no material trace of the massacre (which seems at least plausible), if they had lost faith in its most famous witness, and if the bones, rank grass, and mournful flowers presented in the travel narrative were in some sense overdetermined, it would seem that they nevertheless *believed* in the massacre itself. Its truth as an event and as a site was allowed to rise above any contradictory inclinations. It was a massacre that demanded "fitting tribute," and it would seem that the truth of the bones and the black-tipped groundsel emerged from the relations they traced as much as from their actual existence. They attested to what *must* be true, what demanded material witness.

But these orderings of plants and bones were about more than confirming a historical event. As much as it performs a kind of tribute to the massacre and its victims, *Senecio lugens* also seems to reference Richardson's own sense of apprehension and disorientation in what he felt was an incomplete, unsettling landscape. Not only was Bloody Falls lacking in a suitable monument to its past (the expedition members remarked on Hearne's failure to place his own permanent mark on the landscape), but Richardson also regularly commented on the isolation, sterility, and barrenness of the land, its absence of depth, boundaries, and human life. The Arctic landscape was famously bewildering to the British in this way, as was the culture of those who inhabited it.[51] *Senecio lugens,* named more than a year after Richardson had left the Coppermine River, seems to capture the great sense of loss and incoherence that he experienced on his journey, the failure of the land to make sense and remember, and the land's seeming indifference to human survival.

Indeed, it was precisely the Franklin expedition members' failure to meet with Inuit at Bloody Falls, as they had hoped to do, that contributed to the harrowing events that followed. Ancitipating that Inuit would provide food and information to support his explorations on the Arctic coast, Franklin was dismayed when a group of Inuit spotted at Bloody Falls fled as soon as they saw the approaching strangers (a decision that Back later attributed to memories of "Their Fathers scalped by Matonnabbe's hand").[52] Lacking supplies and an understanding of regional wildlife patterns, but nevertheless committed to continuing along the coast, the party began to starve in the weeks after its stay at the rapids. Winter came early, the herds of caribou upon which the expedition had relied headed south, and the crew was forced to subsist on lichen and the leather from their moccasins. Nine of the twenty crew members died of starvation that fall as they walked southward across the open tundra. The survivors are widely believed to have eaten the fallen. On 20 October 1821, Iroquois (Haudenosaunee) voyageur Michel Teroahauté, mad with hunger, shot and killed midshipman Robert Hood, an expedition member. Richardson responded by shooting Teroahauté in the back of the head.[53] Days later, finally reaching Fort Enterprise, where the men anticipated finding stores of meat left for them by Akaitcho, a Yellowknives (T'satsąot'ıṇę) chief, they found an empty, snowed-in cabin, but no supplies. Franklin described this moment as one of "infinite disappointment and grief," but he also suggested that "it would be impossible to describe our sensations after entering [the] miserable abode, and discovering how we had been neglected."[54] Franklin may have been unable to express his deeply felt sensations in the pages of his travel narrative, but Richardson managed to find words in its botanical appendix. Richardson named a plant found in the woods near Fort Enterprise *Geocaulon lividum.* In this case, there is no hiding the very personal, emotional reasons for the name. Although "lividum" usually refers to a bluish-black or lead colour, there is nothing black or blue about the plant.[55] Also known as false toadflax, *Geocaulon lividum* is bright green, its leaves are frequently streaked with yellow, and its berries range from scarlet to orange. "Lividum" also means "livid," "spiteful," or "envious," and it seems that this second meaning is what Richardson aimed to express in the naming of the plant. Richardson was livid at Akaitcho's apparent betrayal of his promise to provision the fort, livid with the man who had murdered Hood and with his own decision to take a life, and his heart was black with the state of the decaying crew.

Journal entries documenting this stretch of the expedition do not appear in *Narrative of a Journey*, and given the weakened state of the crew, the entries likely never existed. Instead, "Dr. Richardson's Narrative" was inserted, a carefully worded account of the events leading up to and following the deaths of Hood and Teroahauté, first drafted at Fort Resolution. In it, Richardson distinguishes his own violence from that of Teroahauté. Although Teroahauté had for the most part been "good and respectful" throughout the trip, Richardson claimed that "his principles, however, unsupported by a belief in the divine truths of Christianity, were unable to withstand the pressures of severe distress." If Teroahauté's violence could be traced back to his spiritual weakness, Richardson's own violence was framed as a rational, responsible, and necessary act:

> Hepburn and I were now left together for the first time since Mr. Hood's death, and he acquainted me with several material circumstances which he had observed of Michel's behaviour, and which confirmed me in the opinion that there was no safety for us except in his death, and he offered to be the instrument of it. I determined, however, as I was thoroughly convinced of the necessity of such a dreadful act, to take the whole responsibility upon myself; and immediately upon Michel's coming up, I put an end to his life by shooting him through the head with a pistol. Had my own life alone been threatened, I would not have purchased it by such a measure; but I considered myself as intrusted also with the protection of Hepburn's, a man, who, by his humane attentions and devotedness, had so endeared himself to me, that I felt more anxiety for his safety than for my own.[56]

Here, Richardson's framing of his act as necessary, carefully reasoned, and responsible distinguishes it from the reckless, unfeeling, wanton violence of Teroahauté, and indeed, from that of the "Indians" at Bloody Falls. In an April 1822 letter to his wife, describing the expedition's ordeal since his letter from Bloody Falls in July 1821, Richardson was even more explicit about God's role in ordering the violent events of October 1821:

> Bless the Almighty Protector of the Universe that he was pleased to comfort me under every trial by the consolations of religion – the consciousness of being constantly under his all seeing eye and forever an object of his paternal care, conjoined with his glorious declaration that all things work together for good to those who love him supported me under every

> trial and produced a calmness of mind and resignation to his will under the prospect of approaching death that I could not have previously hoped to attain ... If it were possible that any man could remain an infidel in such a situation how dreadful would his sufferings be.[57]

As in Hearne's narrative, moreover, those "infidels" who expressed sympathy for the suffering of others seemed to Richardson to be inadequately named by the word "savage." Writing to his wife, he described the care provided by a group of Dene to the starving expedition members: "These savages, *as they have been termed,* wept upon beholding the deplorable condition to which we were reduced. They nursed us and fed us with the same tenderness they would have bestowed on their own infants."[58] Whereas Teroahauté's spiritual weakness both accounted for and ordered the savagery of his actions, Dene who exhibited "tenderness" seemed to undermine their categorization as savages.[59]

Richardson apparently suffered greatly in subsequent years, as the burden of having taken a life weighed heavily on him. Harriet Martineau, who knew him well in his later years, wrote that "the sufferings of that fearful time, and especially the necessary homicide, left their traces for life on [his] countenance ... The frequent remark of strangers, to the end of his life, was that his face had the expression of a man who had suffered to excess."[60] Whatever his personal struggles with the events of October 1821, editors and reviewers, Barrow included, seized on his description as they worked to recuperate the honour and upstanding character of the expedition members, now subject to rumours of having succumbed not only to murder but also to cannibalism. Ultimately, reviewers were effusive in their celebration of *Narrative of a Journey,* declaring it an appropriately sober, pious, modest, and accurate description of the voyage, and a new standard against which subsequent travel narratives would be measured.[61]

Richardson clearly had a very personal interest in the ordering of feeling, witness, race, and violence throughout the journey, and he had at his disposal an idiom within which to make sense of the harrowing events of 1821. The notion that God, "the Almighty disposer of Events who orders every thing according to his pleasure," was present both at the Bloody Falls massacre and throughout his own descent into "savagery" was unquestioned by Richardson. It was a conviction that made the naming of *Senecio lugens* a fitting tribute both to God's watchful presence in the "dreary waste" of the Central Arctic and to the ordering role of witnesses like Hearne, Richardson, and subsequent Qablunaaq observers of northern lands and peoples. If stories are practices of making sense through the tracing of relations between people and things, then the Franklin expedition's conscious and careful engagement with (and confirmation of) the Bloody Falls massacre story must be understood as itself a relational and material ordering practice. That is, the expedition members did not simply "cite" Hearne's text as they retraced his footsteps; they actively enrolled a series of things as part of a situated effort to make sense of his account and their own confrontations with the people, places, and things of the Central Arctic. Those things, in turn, were enrolled in broader sets of relations with publishers, engravers, reviewers, and the reading public, propelling the "truth" of the massacre along even while it continued to be marked by doubts.

TRUE NATURES

The truths produced by the Franklin expedition are relational and contextual effects; they do not hold everywhere, for everyone, and they require repeated reinscription to be effective. Indeed, periodic efforts to defend Hearne's account of the massacre – regardless of whether they have been convincing – have been crucial in maintaining its importance and relevance.[62] Discourses are partially sustained through commentary, and commentary on whether to read Hearne's narrative as an authoritative source of historical facts or as a more literary, general source of curiosities has been central to its circulation and sedimentation.

The various editions of Hearne's *Journey* that have appeared since 1795 have invariably been edited and prefaced by defenders of Hearne's truthfulness. Geologist and explorer J.B. Tyrrell's Preface to the 1911 edition states that Hearne's narrative is invaluable "not so much because of its geographical information, but because it is an accurate, sympathetic, and patently truthful record of life among the Chipewyan Indians at that time."[63] Tyrrell acknowledges that, "when endeavouring to overcome the criticisms or objections of others, [Hearne] was liable to be carried beyond points of strict accuracy and, in order to strengthen his argument, to fill in blanks in his record from his imagination." But Tyrrell insists that "in the ordinary quietude of his tent or office, when thinking of nothing but the subject which he was describing, he undoubtedly recorded his observations with accuracy."[64] Non-fiction writer Ken McGoogan, Hearne's most recent champion, similarly notes in the 2007 edition of *A Journey* that Hearne is known to have invented an account of the demise of James Knight's 1719 expedition in Hudson Bay – "Hearne conjured both eyewitnesses and survivors out of his imagination. He created a fiction." As for the Bloody Falls massacre, McGoogan concedes that Hearne "may have exaggerated 'the truth' beyond what would today be regarded as acceptable limits." But, like Tyrrell, McGoogan insists that Hearne's narrative remains an important historical document and that his account of the massacre is the only written record "of one of the most controversial moments in Canadian history."[65] It may be exaggerated and possibly even invented, but McGoogan nevertheless maintains that Hearne's account of the massacre records a moment of historical truth.

While Tyrrell and McGoogan concede that Hearne was prone to exaggeration, Richard Glover, editor of the 1958 edition of *A Journey,* devoted a portion of his academic career to the defence of Hearne's "good name."[66] In addition to writing a celebratory preface to the 1958 edition of *A Journey,* Glover published a series of articles aimed at undermining the credibility of historical figures who had questioned Hearne's claims.[67] According to historian Janice Cavell, "Glover's approach to exploration history was partisan in the extreme," and his attacks on David Thompson and John Richardson, in particular, were not only vicious but based on a highly selective use of historical evidence.[68] They were also quite influential, however, owing in large part to Glover's prominence as a Canadian historian. Until very recently, scholars have accepted and reiterated Glover's claims regarding Franklin, Richardson, and Thompson without significant challenge.

While Glover has recently been found wanting in his assessment of primary historical records, he himself levelled exactly this charge against Thompson and Richardson.[69] Thompson, for example, who claimed that Hearne had been dismissed from the HBC for "cowardice" following his surrender to La Pérouse at Prince of Wales Fort, was accused by Glover of self-serving and selective engagement with historical facts: "Where facts are neutral, or tend to Hearne's discredit, Thompson has them at his fingertips – no lapse in the old man's memory there; but when there are facts to justify Hearne's conduct, then Thompson's amnesia is complete. Here, for whatever reason, is *suppressio veri, suggestio falsi* on a handsome scale."[70] Later, Glover called Thompson quite simply "a malicious liar."[71] Richardson, who publicly argued that Hearne had deliberately misled readers about the accuracy of his cartographical observations, was described by Glover as "a deceiver" with "an unhappy talent for jumping to hasty conclusions."[72] Contemporary historians have carefully and convincingly countered a number of Glover's claims through a close reading of the historical record, thus advancing another round of debate regarding the truth of Hearne's story.

No lasting consensus on the veracity of Hearne's massacre account has been achieved, of course. Despite repeated suggestions that it is partially and perhaps wholly invented, the "truth" of Bloody Falls as an event and a place has not been undone. The geographies of the Franklin expedition reveal, moreover, how the truth of Bloody Falls has interwoven with, and been propelled alongside of, doubt. Although support for mounting the expedition hinged on claims that Hearne's cartographic findings were unreliable, and the expedition was expected to find that his latitudinal measurements were inaccurate, the reading public would have been gravely disappointed if Bloody Falls, too, had been called into question. As I argue in Chapter 2, this was a story whose truth extended far beyond the barrenlands; it confirmed and validated much broader understandings of civilization, savagery, empire, and violence. Whether the expedition members were themselves compelled by this larger truth, or concealed their doubts out of respect for Hearne, or were genuinely uncertain as to the truth of the event and its most famous witness, is not clear. Their doubts register, however, alongside the various material witnesses they conjured through their travel narrative. This interweaving of truth and doubt suggests that storying the Bloody Falls massacre as partial or as something other than *true* would require much more than a close reading of the historical record. It would demand the production of truth-effects that trace different relations between all that is anchored at the rapids. In Donna Haraway's terms, it would require "materialized refiguration" and "participation in the processes" that authorize Hearne's account.[73] The task, in that sense, is not to reveal a stable and universally true account of the massacre so much as to tell different stories, better stories. That is my task in the chapters that follow.

4
Copper Stories

Place making ... relies on the hard work of nature making. This is not just because nature, in its biophysicality, is never in stasis, although it does have something to do with the way this forces a constant reinvestment and reinvention of labor, debate, and knowledge. Nature, also, becomes a vibrant actor in the contemporary politics of place making and the ongoing struggle to mark and claim ... As individuals travel with their stories, narrating this placed nature and its associated histories, so these proliferations spread, becoming mobilized simultaneously in different contexts and with disparate meanings.
– Hugh Raffles, "'Local Theory'"

The living person and the land are actually tied up together, because without one the other doesn't survive and vice versa.
– Aupilaarjuk, in John R. Bennett and Susan Rowley, *Uqalurait*

We have a lot of activity around Kugluktuk. Seems like our community doesn't profit from the mines. We need old folks home and community infrastructure. We need to start seeing some benefits.
– Colin Adjun, NTI Lands Policy Advisory Committee meeting, Kugluktuk, May 2007

Mining is big business in Nunavut today. Every summer, airplanes and helicopters filled with mineral survey teams zoom in and out of the hamlet of Kugluktuk. Most families have someone who works in the mines south of town, and a significant proportion of Nunavut is either under claim, exploration, or active extraction. By 2017, as many as eight mines are expected to open in the Kitikmeot region, several of which will extract copper. As Millie Kuliktana, former director of the Tahiuqtiit Society and Kitikmeot School Operations, made clear to me, moreover, the current scale of mineral development in Nunavut may be unprecedented, but outside interest in the region's mineral resources is by no means a recent phenomenon. When asked about the significance of the Bloody Falls massacre in local history, Kuliktana replied that Hearne was the first of a long line of outsiders who have exploited and colonized her people and the people's land. "It's the monster of economy that made this happen," she said. "It was the first act of colonization."[1]

This is not generally how Bloody Falls is storied outside of Kugluktuk. In the South, it is primarily known as the location of a savage act of violence committed by a barbarous tribe of "Indians." It is an event narrated by a supposedly neutral, civilized, and horrified European witness, Samuel Hearne, who looks on as the poor, innocent "Esquimaux" are ruthlessly murdered by their "Indian" attackers. Hearne goes to great lengths to establish not only his neutrality but also his efforts to prevent the killings, and in so doing he sidesteps the possibility that he might have been in some way responsible for the event. Kuliktana, on the other hand, along with a number of other Kugluktukmiut, considers Hearne both personally responsible for the massacre (because he led the Dene into Inuit territory and failed to control their behaviour) and representative of a broader history of economic exploitation and colonialism in the North.

Kuliktana's critique of Hearne is based on the fact that he was in her people's territory only because he was looking for copper. Although Hearne's journey is memorialized outside of Kugluktuk as an act of immense physical endurance (not so much as an economic venture), and his book is known primarily for its eyewitness account of the massacre, Kuliktana rightly pinpoints European interest in copper as the principal motive for his journey. Throughout the 1760s, the HBC had heard reports from Dene trappers and traders of a "Far Off Metal River" where lumps of native copper were so abundant as to ballast a ship. Facing mounting pressure to make better use of its economic monopoly and bolstered by a 1767 map produced by Dënesųłiné leaders Matonabbee and Idotliaze, the HBC dispatched Hearne to locate and determine the richness of this potential "Copper-mine."

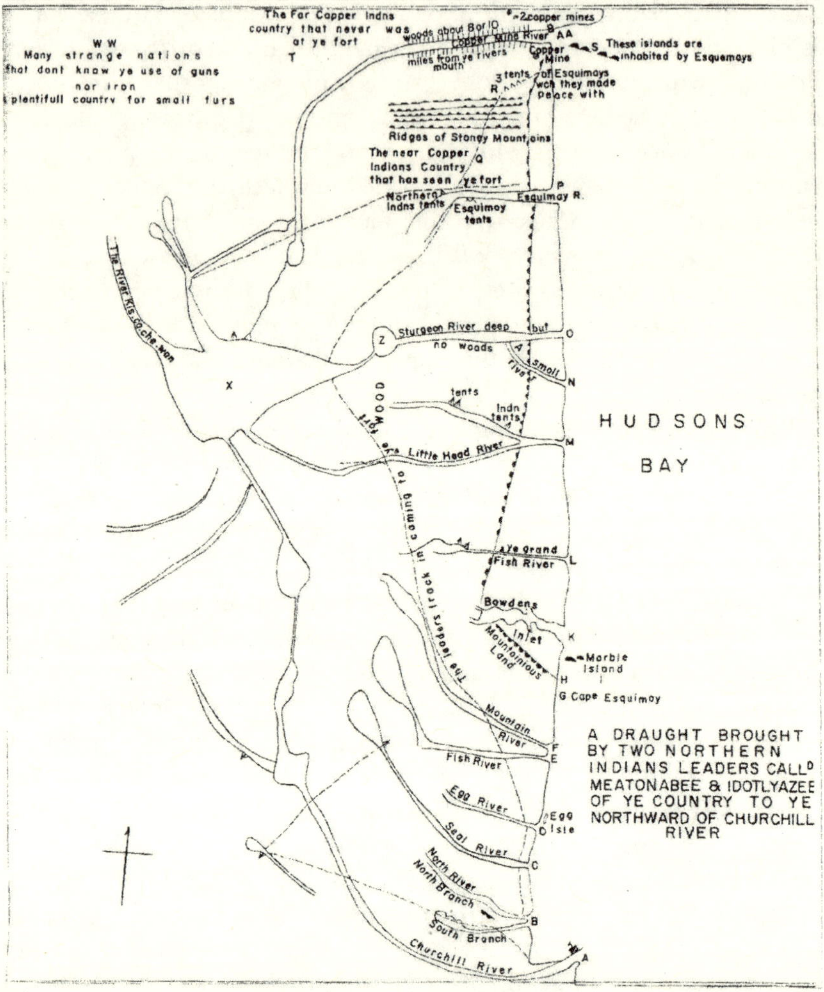

A Redrawing of a Copy by Moses Norton of the Deer-Skin Map Brought to Churchill by the Northern Indian "Captains," Mattonabee and Idotliaze, in 1767. The "A" at the base of the map indicates Prince of Wales Fort, and "B," just above it, the present-day location of Kugluktuk, where the Coppermine River meets the Arctic Ocean. Bloody Falls (not yet named as such) is just upstream. Note the location of "copper mines" on both sides of the river, as well as "3 tents of Esquimays wch they made peace with," in itself calling into question claims that Dene and Inuit were perennially hostile toward each other. The lake in the centre of the map, "X," is Great Slave, and the Sturgeon River was later named the Back River. Although the map does not follow European cartographic conventions, it is a tremendously accurate representation of a vast stretch of land. *Reproduced with permission from the Manitoba Heritage Society and the Hudson's Bay Company Archives.*

Hearne's mission, as we know, was largely a failure. It was his alleged witness of a massacre at Bloody Falls the day before his fruitless search for copper that recuperated what would otherwise have been a profoundly anti-climactic travel narrative. But his failure to locate an economically viable copper deposit was nevertheless productive: his would be the first of innumerable subsequent attempts to enrol Kitikmeot copper into international networks of extraction and trade, and his narrative ordered relations with copper in significant ways. Indeed, although it is not generally memorialized as such, Hearne's account of the Bloody Falls massacre, I suggest here, is a *copper* story; it emerged from and ordered particular relations with copper.

This chapter traces the making of copper as a particular kind of nature – one most appropriately extracted from the land and converted into capital – and the ways in which the Bloody Falls massacre story has participated in this ordering of relations. Although the production of copper as an industrial resource represents, at first glance, its ultimate abstraction and removal from the sets of relations animating its traditional importance to "Copper Inuit," such an assessment belies both the dense and profoundly material relations underpinning Inuit relations with contemporary resource extraction in the region, as well as the complex historical geographies of producing Inuit as inherently and exclusively "traditional" users of this metal. In fact, the production and naturalization of Inuit as a traditional copper culture coincided with the acceleration of industrial mining in the region, and these developments, I argue, are intimately related. What follows, then, is a series of "copper stories" that not only offer a different reading of the massacre itself but also highlight the ongoing importance of copper in constituting and undermining life in the region.

Key to the drama of Hearne's massacre story is the supposed senselessness of the Dene attack and their lack of a rational motive. The Dene are described as caught up in a kind of collective, bloodthirsty trance, intent on murder and torture; no arguments can dissuade them, and they delight in the suffering of their victims. If one reads the narrative closely, however, and particularly in comparison with transcriptions of Hearne's unpublished travel notes, it becomes clear that Hearne was not the only member of the exploration party with an intense interest in copper. Immediately after the massacre, the Dene raided the Inuit tents "of all the Copper Work and any other trifling things they thought worthwhile to take." Hearne made extensive notes on the importance of copper in local trading economies, remarking on the annual journey undertaken by the Northern Indians to the region in search of copper to "shoe their arrows and make other necessary tools such as hatchets, Ice Chizzels, etc."[2] He recorded a list of trading ratios for copper tools and noted that the Indians of the region valued copper almost as much as iron, employing it for both personal use and trade. More than once, Hearne recorded the plundering of neighbouring groups, depicting such events as economically motivated theft intended to amass goods sufficient to trade for copper and iron tools, not as the acts of an inherently uncivilized people. In fact, his field journal is littered with references to his "surprise" at the civility of his companions and his admiration for their character traits. Clearly, the very metal Hearne had hoped to locate and claim for the British Crown was already circulating in a regional economy, embroiled in acts of war and trade throughout the Central Arctic and Subarctic. It would seem that the Bloody Falls massacre was motivated as much by copper as the "violent tendencies" attributed to Dënesųłiné and T'satsąot'ınę men.[3]

Until very recently, however, explorers, missionaries, and scholars have persisted in the racialized belief that copper use was not centrally important to the Indigenous peoples of the Arctic and Subarctic, believing instead that their interest in metals emerged with the European introduction of iron. Recent research challenges this long-standing belief and suggests that throughout Arctic Canada metal was in use long before even indirect contact with Europeans.[4] The Thule, who preceded Inuit in the region, are known to have relied on metals traded over hundreds and even thousands of kilometres, and members of the Franklin expedition made extensive notes about Dene copper-prospecting practices, including the detailed topographical and geological information used by the Dene to locate sources of the metal.[5] Notably, according to John Richardson, who was responsible for the expedition's "geognostical [geological]" findings, Dene had ceased, by 1821, to make their annual journey northward in search of copper. "The establishment of trading posts near their hunting grounds," he suggested, had enabled them "to obtain a supply of ice-chisels and other instruments of iron," and thus they no longer needed to make "weapons and utensils" with copper.[6]

Stories of the discovery of metals, particularly copper, have been recorded by Arctic explorers and missionaries for the last two centuries. John Franklin recorded a story told by Rabbit's Head, a Dene member of the Franklin expedition, regarding the origin of copper in their lands. "In the earliest ages of the world," Rabbit's Head allegedly recounted, a party of Inuit men came over to Dene lands "and stole a woman from their tribe, whom they carried to [their] distant country and kept in a state of slavery." She eventually escaped and, after many days of wandering, was assisted by a wolf in crossing the ocean that separated Inuit and Dene lands. She survived for a winter by killing some caribou and building herself a house "after the manner she had learned from the Esquimaux." When spring came,

> she emerged from her subterraneous dwelling ... [and] was astonished by observing a luminous glittering appearance on a distant hill, which she knew was not produced by the reflection of the sun, and being at a loss to assign any other cause for it, she resolved on going up to the shining object, and then found the hill was entirely composed of metal.

The woman broke off several pieces, and "perceiving that it yielded so readily to her beating, it occurred to her this copper (for that was the metal), would be very serviceable to her countrymen, if she could find them again." She eventually found them, "and the young men, elated with the account she had given of the hill, made her instantly return with them; which she was enabled to do, having taken the precaution of putting up marks to indicate the path." Here, the story took a turn that Franklin determined to be a "melancholy catastrophe":

> These youths, overcome by excess of joy, gave loose to their unrestrained passions, and offered the grossest insults to their kind benefactress. She powerfully resisted them for some time, and when her strength was failing, she fled to the point of the mountain, as the only place of security. Immediately she had gained the summit, the earth opened, and ingulphed both herself and the mountain, to the utter dismay of the men, who were not more astonished at its sudden disappearance, than sorrowful for this just punishment of their wickedness. Ever since this event, the copper has only been found in small detached pieces on the surface of the earth.[7]

Missionary Émile Petitot recorded a similar story from Dënesųłiné storytellers in the 1880s.[8]

Although surely reworked in the idiom of nineteenth-century explorers and missionaries, these stories allude to both a pre-contact copper economy in the region and indicate that copper was "good to think with" in Dene oral traditions; copper and other stories helped convey a broader legal and moral framework within which the Dene operated.[9] Copper remains good to think with. Rachel Qitsualik's recent story "Skraeling" imagines a meeting of Inuit, Tuniit, and Vikings long before the British or French were even aware of the Arctic, from the perspective of Kannujaq (Inuktitut for copper or metal), an Inuk who stumbles on a Tuniq community in crisis. The community has been experiencing attacks from Siarailli (Skraelings), as well as manipulation by one of its own members, who uses a stash of treasures gleaned from the invaders to secure his power. His collection includes remarkable knives, one that shines "like a fish belly, handle decorated with yellow-hued *kannujaq*" and others that, though rusty, make Kannujaq's heart "beat faster ... This was not *kannujaq* but something far better." Qitsualik refuses to tease out the meaning of the story for those who are not familiar with Inuit histories, practices, values, and lands; to do so, she states, would be to offer the "cognitive equivalent of living on marshmallows." But the story's nuanced exploration of the relations made possible by copper – the dangers of hoarding, the survival made possible by carefully crafted tools, the "trepidation, uncertainty, and outright horror that early peoples knew" – exposes the folly and insult of imagining that northern Indigenous peoples came to value metals only through contact with Europeans.[10]

Copper was an important part of the regional economies and imaginative geographies of the Central Arctic and Subarctic long before Qablunaaq involvement in the area, but it was also implicated in longer and larger networks of technology, labour, and trade. Copper was mined across the Americas and in Britain from pre-industrial times to the early industrial era.[11] The British copper-mining industry expanded rapidly in the mid-eighteenth century due to an influx of capital and technological expertise from Europe, and by the time Hearne left on his mission, Britain had become one of the world's leading producers.[12] In Britain – not unlike in the Arctic – copper was used primarily for household utensils such as pots, pans, and pewter mugs, as well as in roofing, guttering, piping, and cisterns. But unlike the relatively circumscribed networks of copper extraction, manufacture, and trade in the Arctic at the time of Hearne's journey, copper in Britain, influenced by international capital and imperial acquisitions, moved through more widely dispersed and longer networks of mines, smelters, manufacturers, distributors, and consumers. What had once been a very local industry in Britain was extending into other places and involving more and more things. Hearne's journey must be understood in relation to this expansion. His mission was to connect Arctic copper with industrial and imperial networks extending outside the region; doing so would ultimately require not only the discovery of sufficient deposits but also the displacement of Indigenous uses and claims to the resource. Consider the following observation, recounted shortly after his futile search for copper:

> The Indians imagine that every bit of copper they find resembles some object in nature; but by what I saw of the large piece, and some smaller ones which were found by my companions, it requires a great share of invention to make this out. I found that different people had different ideas on the subject, for the large piece of copper above mentioned had not been found long before it had twenty different names. One saying that it resembled this animal, and another that it represented a particular part of another; at last it was generally allowed to resemble an Alpine hare couchant: for my part I must confess that I could not see it had the least resemblance to any thing to which they compared it. It would be endless to enumerate the different parts of a deer, and other animals, which the Indians say the best pieces of copper resemble: it may therefore be sufficient to say, that the largest pieces, with the fewest branches and the least dross, are the best for their use; as by the help of fire, and two stones, they can beat it out to any shape they wish.[13]

Hearne intended this passage as a curiosity for the reader and used it to underscore his own reliability and precision as an observer. But it can be read in quite another way: it also exemplifies the different narrative geographies within which eighteenth-century copper circulated. By storying the copper as deer, the Dene made connections between the piece of metal in their hands and a diverse network of relations that enabled them to hunt, eat, and imagine their world. Their co-existence with copper enrolled a particular network of things. Hearne, on the other hand, was more interested in connecting copper to international networks of trade and manufacture, to his own reputation as an explorer, and to the esteem and wealth that would surely follow. Indeed, Kugluktukmiut consistently criticize him for "wanting to make a name for himself," and in a sense their indictment gestures toward the very different narrative geography within which Hearne operated, even as these geographies overlapped in 1771.[14]

Exploration for copper deposits in the Coppermine River region continued after Hearne's time. Although the Hudson's Bay Company abandoned the venture, subsequent British, American, and Canadian expeditions were inspired by Hearne's effort and continued the project of identifying and mapping copper resources in the Far North. The Franklin expedition report included an appendix on "geognostical" findings, penned with "economic importance" in mind and emphasizing copper formations.[15] Geologists were dispatched by various government and private organizations throughout the nineteenth century, including a venture by well-known geologist J.B. Tyrrell, sponsored in 1893 by the Geological Survey of Canada, a trip that was widely publicized and that amplified expectations of "great mineral wealth" in the barrenlands, particularly in the form of copper. Tyrrell (who went on to edit the 1911 version of Hearne's *Journey*) was quoted in an imperial report on world copper reserves that anticipated the Canadian Arctic and Subarctic would yield "as much copper as is now mined in Northern Michigan," thus reviving imperial dreams of copper riches in the region.[16]

In the summer of 1900, geologists Charles Camsell and James Mackintosh Bell explored the Great Bear Lake region in search of mineral resources and replayed Hearne's fearsome descent into Inuit territory. "As we proceeded farther into the barren lands we saw more and more signs of Eskimo," Camsell recorded. "These signs were rather disturbing to Johnny Sanderson, who like all the local Indians had at that time a wholesome fear of Eskimo, just as the Eskimo had a fear of the Indians." As more and more Indians abandoned their party "for fear of meeting some Eskimo," Camsell and Bell found themselves alone and hungry, and came upon a group of thirty or forty Inuit. "Johnny Sanderson had always told us that the Eskimo we might meet in this country would certainly be dangerous and might want to kill us," Camsell recalled, but he and Bell decided to approach them. The Eskimo fled, abandoning a stash of caribou meat and various supplies, including "arrows tipped with native copper." Camsell and Bell ate the meat but left two steel needles and a tin plate as a gesture of friendship. Throughout their journey back to Great Bear Lake, the men "felt certain that they would be watching us from a safe distance away and might even be looking for an opportunity to kill us. These same people actually did kill the next two visitors to this locality, Fathers LeRoux and Rouviere, by sticking a knife into them." In the end, Camsell and Bell survived and saw no further signs of Inuit. Three decades later, however, Camsell would learn from fur-trapper D'Arcy Arden that the Inuit party had indeed followed them all the way back to Great Bear Lake:

> The experience of August, 1900 was gradually becoming little more than an interesting memory until actively revived in August, 1936, by a conversation with D'Arcy Arden during a brief visit that I made to Great Bear Lake. Some years after my visit to that country Arden had gone on a fur-trading expedition to the same region, and in the course of his operations established friendly relations with the Eskimo of the Coppermine River ... When in time he was able to converse with them, they told him the story

> of the visit of two white men to their camp some years previous – possibly the first many of them had ever seen. They told Arden that on catching sight of us they first took us to be Indians, but when they found that we did not run away at the sight of them, they came to the conclusion that we must belong to the same race of people who had visited the country many years ago of which their fathers had told them ... They were naturally suspicious of all strangers, for the locality was not far from Bloody Falls on the Coppermine River where Samuel Hearne's party of Chipeywan Indians had, in 1772 [sic], slaughtered a band of Eskimo men, women, and children in their sleep, and no doubt the story of this massacre had been handed down to these people from one generation to another. They told Arden of having watched us from behind some rocks as we ate our meal in their camp. They were determined to kill us if it could be done without risking their own lives; but as their only weapons were arrows and broad, foot-long knives beaten out of native copper found in the neighboring hills, this could not be done without coming to close quarters. When we left their camp in the evening some of the men followed us ... looking for an opportunity to stick a knife into us. The chance did not come ... In the mean time our needles had been found in the camp, and from that time on our lives were safe ... Human life has never been held in very high regard by these Eskimo, and killings were perpetuated sometimes for very trivial reasons. A few years after the visit of Bell and myself to this locality, two Roman Catholic missionaries were killed in almost the same locality, and possibly the murderers of these two priests may have been the same men who watched for an opportunity to murder us also. Death by the thrust of a blunt, copper knife is not one of the pleasantest things to contemplate, and it makes one shiver even after a lapse of fifty years to think what might have been the result if we had not left those two needles behind us in the Eskimo camp.[17]

This passage not only emphasizes the importance of story in constituting both Inuit and Qablunaat knowledges; it also traces the significance of copper in constituting and undermining life in the region. Camsell and Bell lived to tell their own copper stories in part because "sticking a knife" into them would have required a dangerous proximity, and according to their account, copper knives were the only weapons the Inuit party had. The fact that, a few decades later, Inuit possessed rifles and thus "were no longer a Stone Age people" amplifies the drama of Camsell's recollection, transformed from "little more than an interesting memory" to a moment of historical significance.[18]

Inuit, Dene, and Qablunaaq copper stories would increasingly converge throughout the first decades of the twentieth century. The use of copper tools among Inuinnait had virtually disappeared by the early twentieth century as iron and other metals became more readily available. Ironically, it was at this time that anthropologists first visited the area and assigned the name "Copper Inuit" to the people living in the vicinity of Coronation Gulf, in reference to their historic use of copper tools. While Diamond Jenness, anthropologist with the Canadian Arctic Expedition, catalogued Copper Inuit language and culture in 1915 and 1916, expedition geologist J.J. O'Neill searched for copper deposits in the Coppermine River and Bathurst Inlet region. In addition to producing a detailed map of the deposits, both O'Neill and Jenness relayed stories of copper trade, theft, and usage, including accounts of copper-related trade and conflict with Dene.[19]

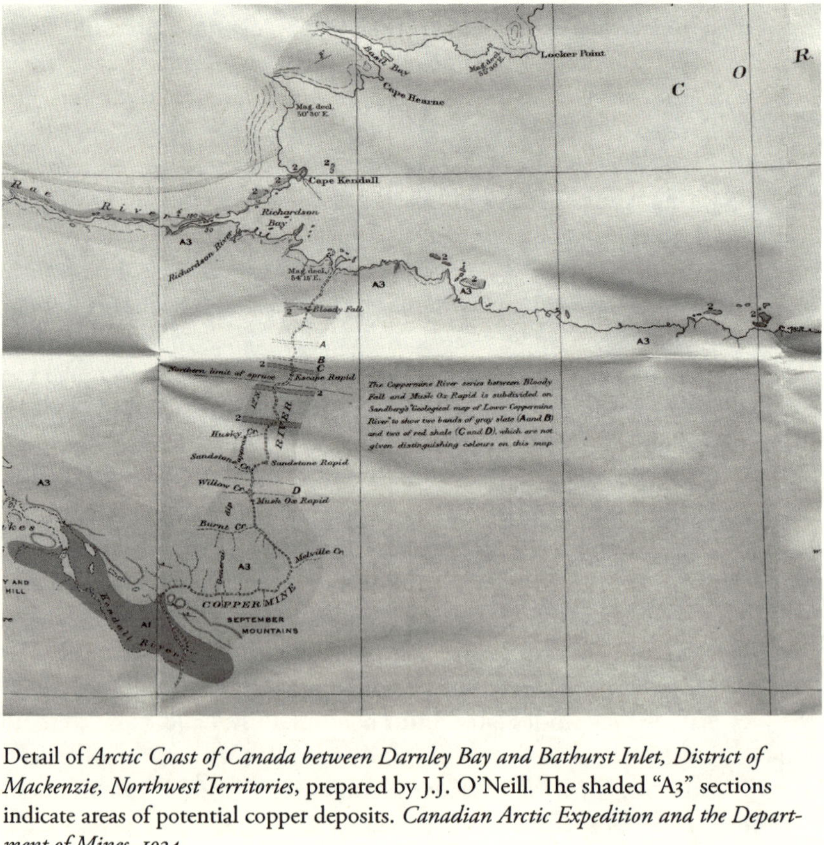

Detail of *Arctic Coast of Canada between Darnley Bay and Bathurst Inlet, District of Mackenzie, Northwest Territories*, prepared by J.J. O'Neill. The shaded "A3" sections indicate areas of potential copper deposits. *Canadian Arctic Expedition and the Department of Mines, 1924.*

But these "historical" stories, which dealt with post-contact events, were merely anecdotes to the expedition members. Jenness was primarily interested in "traditional" Copper Inuit stories, and it was through his work that they came to be cordoned off from other forms of knowledge, along with the economies that underpinned their telling.[20] Jenness's field diary reveals some of the exchanges involved in extracting stories from his informants. In January 1916, when Uloqsaq proved reluctant to tell him stories, Jenness

> told him that he could not expect me to treat him very liberally if he did not tell me any stories. He said there was someone always hanging about the tent and he was afraid to tell. However, he came over late in the evening and told us a few shamanistic stories. I asked him whether he would care to have Ikpuk present, and he said no, Ikpuk would be angry with him.[21]

Uloqsaq, who went on to become one of Jenness's primary informants, was soon coming to Jenness's tent "each evening to tell me stories," under the arrangement that he would "have his .44 rifle changed to a .30–30 if I am satisfied with him." Satisfaction came to be contingent on whether Uloqsaq would tell decisively contemporary stories, however. On 17 January 1916, after a rifle was stolen from the camp, Jenness made clear to Uloqsaq that any information he might have regarding its whereabouts would be rewarded. Two days later, "the rifle was discovered – by Uloksak." Later, Royal North-West Mounted Police inspectors used intelligence gleaned by Jenness to locate Uluksuk and Sinisiak, who had allegedly murdered two Catholic priests in 1913, though Jenness made clear his wish "to have my name kept out of the case altogether." His request was granted, and "the Corporal in stating his case for the prosecution made no mention of my part in acquiring evidence and the property of the murdered men." Jenness went on to write a "document containing information concerning the Copper Eskimos for the benefit of the Police Department in their future dealings with the natives." Clearly, his ability to "worm out a little information" from the people with whom he lived for so many years facilitated more than merely anthropological goals.[22] The intimate, long-term, power-laden relations Jenness had developed with Inuit to extract traditional stories from them also enabled him to produce authoritative information that could be used in the extension and imposition of Qablunaaq legal and judicial structures. It is no surprise that missionaries and anthropologists were so heavily consulted in efforts to impose the "rule of law" in the Arctic.

"Copper Nugget Weighing about 40 Pounds, Found in Hills on West Side of Coppermine River between Bloody Fall and Dismal Lake, Taken to Coast by Mupfa ..." *Photo by Rudolph Martin Anderson for the Canadian Arctic Expedition, 12 May 1916, Canadian Museum of History, 38798.*

Indeed, the production of knowledge about Copper Inuit in the first decades of the twentieth century was informed by a particularly colonial interweaving of anthropological, economic, legal, and scientific interests.[23] As Vilhjalmur Stefansson and Diamond Jenness published the first detailed anthropological studies of Copper Inuit culture, traders, prospectors, and missionaries arrived in the region.[24] Archaeologist Donald Cadzow travelled throughout the Northwest Territories between 1917 and 1919 and produced a leaflet describing the various copper artifacts that he collected. The leaflet presents Inuit copper tool use as a kind of primitive iteration of more "civilized" natural resource economies, which were inaugurated by the "discovery" of copper for Europeans by Samuel Hearne. Indeed, Cadzow's short history of the region begins with the Bloody Falls massacre, an event, he claims, that unfolded while Hearne was busy surveying and identifying copper reserves. After page upon page of photos and descriptions of copper artifacts, the report closes with the following comment:

> The Copper Eskimo are at present rapidly becoming semi-civilized. The Hudson's Bay Company has opened a trading-post near the mouth of the

> Coppermine river, and the Northern Trading Company operates a trading schooner along the shores of Coronation gulf. Within a few years the utilization of native copper by these Eskimo for making weapons and utensils will have ceased, the white man's handy and practical materials having taken its place.[25]

Copper tools are made to make sense, in this publication, by situating them in a historical progression from savagery to "semi" civility, a progression that involves a shift from making copper snow knives and *uluit* (knives with broad, rounded blades used for skinning and cutting) toward mapping and mining copper as a capitalist resource.

Indeed, by the 1930s, as stories of a traditional copper culture proliferated in the South, airplanes had arrived in the North, revolutionizing mineral survey practices and enabling aerial identification of copper reserves.[26] In the early 1960s, Echo Bay Mines began to mine silver and copper near the headwaters of the Coppermine River, and with a few lulls, mineral exploration has only intensified since then. In the late 1950s, as miners and prospectors scoured the region for promising deposits, missionary-anthropologist Maurice Métayer recorded a series of stories in Coppermine (Kugluktuk) that included "Texte 80," told by James Qoerhuk, regarding a group of seal hunters that suddenly became stranded on an ice floe. The full story was recorded in Inuinnaqtun and summarized by Métayer for English readers, leading to a distinctive interpretation of its meaning and particularly its revelations about Inuit relations with copper. The English summary is worth quoting in its entirety:

> It probably happened before I was born. A group of seal hunters were out on the ice when it broke loose from the shore and a thick vapor filled the sky. Ulukhaq realized the danger they were in and cried: "The ice is broken." They started running towards the shore but it was too late: they were already drifting westward along with the ice. They built a snow house the following day, by the time the ice had stopped drifting, Nualiak urged them to try again to reach the land. However, they did not succeed and had to come back to their igloo where they remained for a good part of the winter. They were lucky enough to have among them real shamans who saved them from disaster by preventing the ice they were on to be crushed by an iceberg and by performing the rites that would bring them a good wind. One by one they let their knives sink in the water and offered them to the spirit of the sea. The last knife to be offered was a weapon made of solid raw copper; it floated a while before

> sinking. Qorvik also took a small block of ice and threw it towards the land. At the same time he asked the spirits to return them home, safe and sound. A short while afterwards the wind changed direction and brought them back home. The men leapt from an ice block to another finally making their way back to the shore. They reached it by the time darkness was falling. They yelled with joy, ate snow, cried, laughed, and walked home where they found their wives. Some of them, thinking that they were dead, had taken other husbands. Qinglorqana felt for a long time as though the roll of the ocean was still in his body, waking him up during the night.[27]

The elements of the story that Métayer chose to emphasize in this abridged translation are revealing. The copper "weapon" (which was more than likely a snow knife used to build igloos, the loss of which was particularly difficult for Qinglorqana because the knife *audlartijjutiplu,* or "enabled him to travel") is understood by Métayer to be more valuable than the other knives, and its sacrifice is a central element of the summary. Although Qinglorqana laments its loss in the longer Inuinnaqtun version, and it is, indeed, considered the most valuable tool in their possession, he agrees to offer it because "ajornarhingman utilimaermik ... pingneramegoq audlartijun ... kivijaugame utqutilertainnarqaingoq kinranun kingunranun" (because there is no more hope, and they are not returning ... because it is beautiful and it was used for travelling ... [and then] because they let it sink, it brought them behind, to the land left behind).[28] The knife, in the Inuinnaqtun version, has agency; it is the knife that brings them home, not a sea god, as in Métayer's understanding of "sacrifice" to the "spirit of the sea." Furthermore, the fact that the knife leads them home is noted but not dwelled upon in Qoerhuk's account. The bulk of the story is devoted to extended descriptions of snow and ice conditions, to the subtleties of decisions about how to travel and under what conditions, and to the painful separation and complications of reunion with their wives.

"Texte 80" is thus as revealing of Qablunaaq interests as it is of Copper Inuit oral traditions. As a story told in Inuinnaqtun to a Qablunaaq missionary in the late 1950s, recorded on tape, transcribed, translated into French and subsequently into a short English summary, this text has undergone multiple twists and translations. It is a story that draws lines between the spiritual and the real, and places copper in an abstracted material hierarchy in which a copper knife is always more valuable than an iron or other tool, rather than conceptualizing copper's value relationally and contextually. In Qoerhuk's version, the knife's value is relational; he suggests that Qinglorqana drops it into the sea because its value as a survival tool has shifted. The men no longer need it as an igloo-building survival tool – they need to get off the ice floe – and the copper knife can lead them home from under the sea. By contrast, Métayer implies that the absolute value of copper knives makes Qinglorqana's "offering" the ultimate sacrifice and appeasement of the spirits of the sea.

Métayer's abridged version thus produces a particular relationship between Inuit and copper in which copper is an inert natural resource whose value derives from its relative scarcity and its material properties, thereby rendering the metal object a particularly compelling sacrifice to external spirits that exert control over the fate of Inuit. The story conveys an essentially Qablunaaq resource model of copper with a slightly Christianized pan-Indigenous spiritual realm layered upon it, a reading that should come as no surprise given the active mineral surveying taking place in Coppermine at the time, and a reading that works to naturalize industrial resource extraction in the region as a more sophisticated iteration of a traditional copper culture. To story Inuit relations with copper as more primitive iterations of industrial or modern relations, and to imply that Inuit, too, relate to copper in terms of its absolute, hierarchical, exchange value, was both inaccurate and ideological. This narrative strategy remains persistent and productive, however, not least in corporate histories of mining in the Arctic. As a recent brochure produced by multinational mining conglomerate Rio Tinto begins, "For centuries, people of the North have used the resources wisely ... Diavik is continuing this tradition."[29]

Prior to the 1990s, mining in the Coppermine River watershed was limited to the Lupin mine, on the northwest arm of Contwoyto Lake. In sporadic production since the early 1980s, it exploited a deposit, primarily of gold, that had been located in 1960. But the discovery of diamonds in the 1990s prompted the opening of three diamond mines in the watershed (Diavik, Ekati, and Jericho), and a network of diamond, copper, gold, nickel, and other base metal mines is proposed to open during the next several years.

Although some might wish to imagine that the "Copper Inuit" resist this shift in their ancestral relationship to copper, this wish speaks more to Southern imaginative geographies of the Arctic than to the views of Kugluktukmiut. As wary as some community members are about the impact of mining on the land, very few entirely oppose mineral development in the region. Mining offers the possibility of a viable economy in the North, if only for a short period of time and for a segment of the population, and people in Kugluktuk are gravely concerned about the future of their young

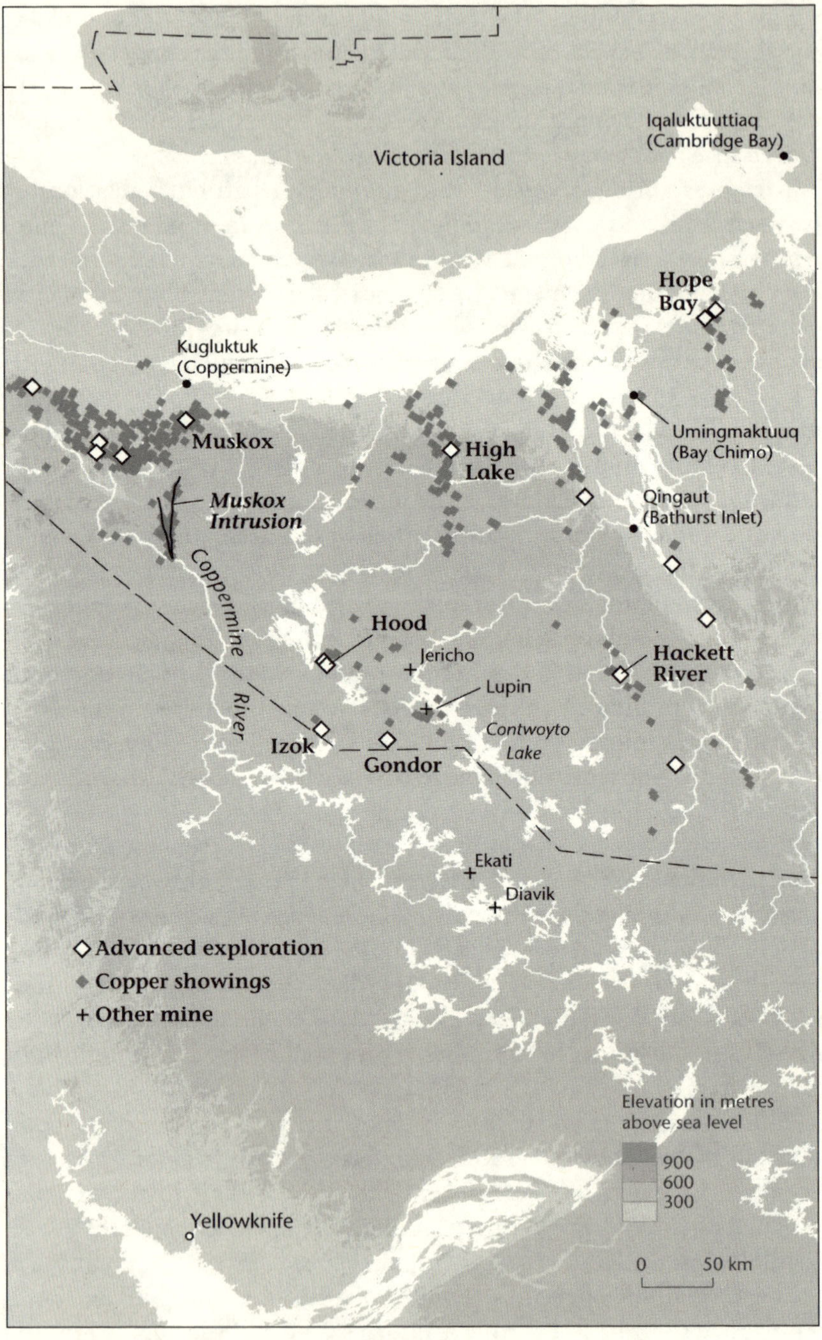

Copper showings and proposed mines in the Kugluktuk region, 2013

people. Kugluktukmiut will be hired to build the ice roads and port facility necessary to service the proposed mine at High Lake, 175 kilometres southeast of town, and they will drive the trucks carrying copper-rich ore to the sea. Ships destined for Europe will indeed be ballasted with Arctic copper within the next decade, in a sense over two centuries late.

Kugluktukmiut have been active participants in the northern mining industry for decades in fact. Some, like "the famous Inuk prospector" Noel Avadluk, made a living as grubstakers in the 1960s and were celebrated as stand-out examples of Inuit modernization.[30] As bureaucrat E.A. Schiller wrote in 1965, Avadluk's success was attributable to his "education" (which "enabled him to speak and write English well") and to his blend of traditional land skills and self-taught geological expertise:

> Noel has acquired many of the exploration talents of the modern prospector. He uses aerial photographs and geological and topographical maps. Once a mineral showing is found he investigates it with a plugger to drill a shallow hole and blast the rock with dynamite. If the showing looks attractive he will stake claims to get ownership of the minerals found. Using geology texts, Noel has acquainted himself with geological principles and his knowledge of mineralogy is adequate enough to identify the important sulphide minerals.[31]

Noel Avadluk playing cards with unidentified man, c. 1950s. *NWT Archives/Holman Photohistorical and Oral History Research Committee/N-1990–004:0040.*

So celebrated (by Qablunaaq administrators) was Avadluk that, during the Nunavut land claim negotiations, he was presented with a plaque in honour of the "significant discoveries near Bathurst Inlet, including the Pistol Lake gold occurrence" he had made in the 1960s, along with "his now-disabled wife, who had also been his prospecting partner."[32] In conversation with mining consultant Robert McPherson, Joe Allen Evyagotailak put this celebratory gesture into perspective. McPherson recalls:

> When I first mentioned Avadluk's reputation to Joe Allen Evaigotailak [sic] ... he said "Well, he hasn't anything to show for it!" since Avadluk was now a humble senior citizen but Avadluk had worked for wages in his day, and none of his discoveries had ever reached production ... Another Coppermine resident, a woman speaking through her son, told me that her husband was denied any benefit after telling prospectors about a mineral showing in the late 1960s. She was referring to a copper sulphide showing (now the Hood claims of Kidd Creek Mines Ltd.) at the south end of Takijuq Lake, reputed to contain nearly a million tons of ore. The showing was at the site of an Inuit outpost camp frequented by her husband. As the Hood claims were acquired by the Inuit at these negotiations [the Nunavut land claim negotiations], I decided to check in to the story late, using the mining recorder's archives at Yellowknife. Sure enough, the ground was staked by two prospectors during the Coppermine rush of the 1960s. However, no assessment work was done, and the claims lapsed after two years. Later, Kidd Creek Mines rediscovered the mineralization when they flew an airborne electro-magnetic survey in the region. It was explored and drilled between 1974 and 1982.[33]

Here, Qablunaaq interests in "modernizing" Inuit relations with mineral resources are laid bare. Although Inuit were prevailed upon to aid in the identification of mineral deposits from the earliest days of exploration, they were never expected to be more than assistants or labourers, and certainly not owners.

It was experiences like these that led Kugluktukmiut to agitate, as early as the 1950s, for fair access to and control of the mineral wealth in their territory. In February 1953, alarmed at the increasing presence of prospectors in the region, the people of Kugluktuk sent a petition to the federal government, outlining their concerns and demands regarding mineral exploration and staking in their territory (see figure on page 104).[34] Peter Kulchyski and Frank Tester suggest that this may have been "the first time Inuit as a group in the Canadian Arctic formally petitioned the government," and the petition states emphatically that Inuit have rights to the copper in the region.[35] The petition reads,

> Dear Sir,
>
> Father Adam asked you what was our position regarding the copper deposits some of our boys have found around Coppermine.
>
> You said that we had to follow the same laws as the whites regarding the staking and holding of the claims. We feel such a law is not right, because,
>
> (1) The land is ours and we never gave it or sold it away and never will.
>
> (2) We are one of the poorest people in the world; we have no money to buy a licence or to register a claim.
>
> (3) We are too ignorant to steak a claim according to the regulations.
>
> (4) We Eskimo feel we should be given a chance.
>
> Therefore we send you a petition requesting that any Eskimo finding ore deposit will have the right to steak it, and hold it free of taxes, and hold it free of taxes, and that he may well sell it to any Company free of taxes whenever he wants to do so.
>
> Although we have no leader amongst us our signatures will tell you that we agree on those points.
>
> Hoping that we find the Government most co-operative we sign:
>
> The Eskimos of Coppermine

This would be the beginning of a larger movement among Inuit to assert their rights to the land and resources of Nunavut, a process that gathered speed in the early 1970s, following a meeting of Inuit leaders in Coppermine that led to the creation of Inuit Tapirisat of Canada (ITC) the following year.[36] ITC (later Inuit Tapiriit Kanatami, or ITK) was instrumental in advancing Inuit demands for land claims and resource rights, demands that became particularly urgent through the 1970s as "a new breed of explorer [came] to search for oil, natural gas, and minerals" in the North.[37] The Nunavut Land Claim Agreement (NLCA) was finalized in 1993, and the territory of Nunavut was created in 1999. The NLCA outlines Inuit mineral rights (notably, Inuit retain subsurface rights over only 2 percent of the territory's 1.9 million square kilometres, although mechanisms are in place to negotiate limited benefits from mining on non-Inuit land). It also establishes protocols for environmental assessment, land use planning, and rights of entry and access to non-Inuit lands. Regardless of whether they hope to mine on Inuit or Crown land, mining companies must go through a process of community consultation and environmental impact assessment, a process that is poorly defined and in some ways moot.[38] In practice, the territorial

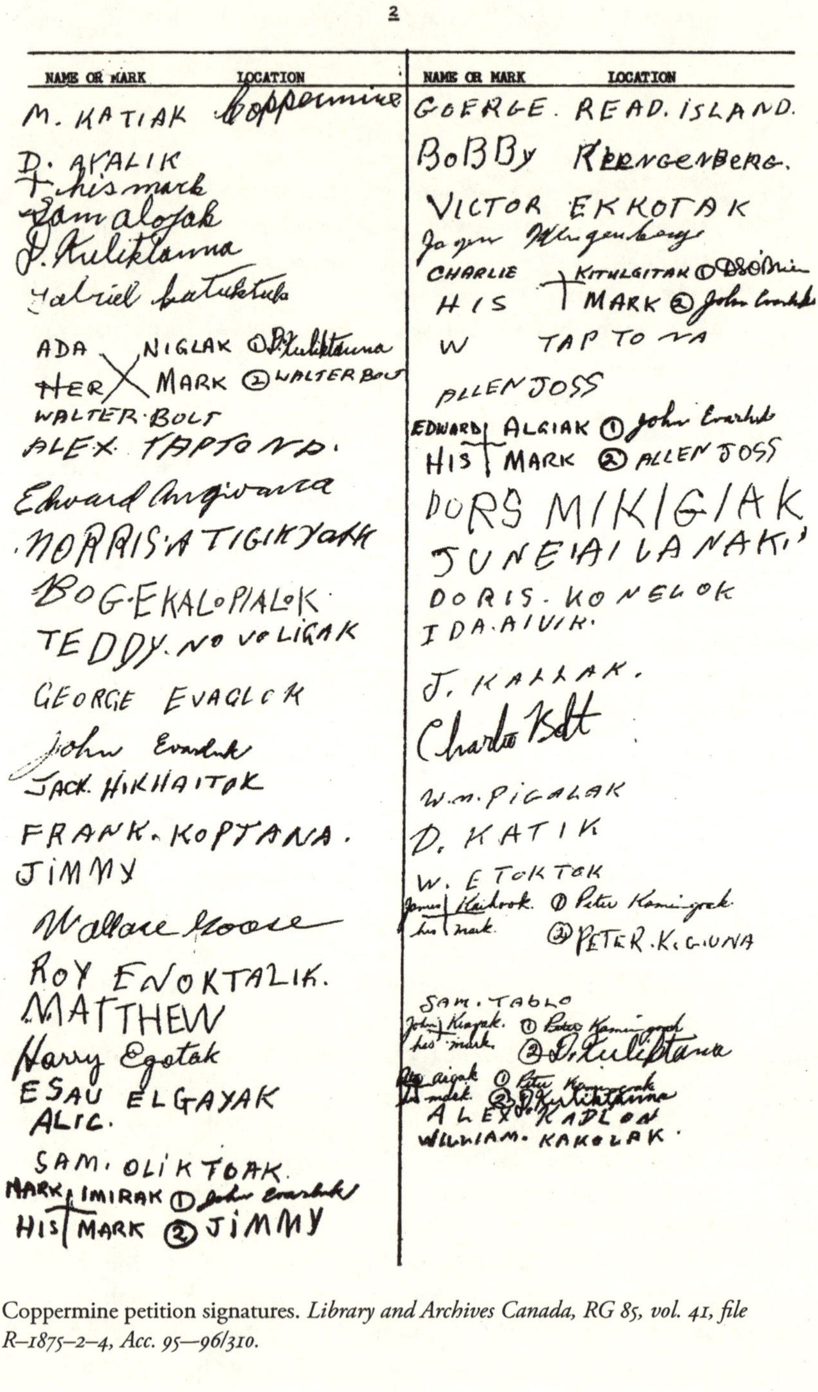

2

NAME OR MARK	LOCATION
M. KATIAK	Coppermine
D. AKALIK + his mark	
Sam alojak	
D. Kuliktanna	
Gabriel Katuktuk	
ADA NIGLAK HER X MARK	① D. Kuliktanna ② WALTER BOLT
WALTER BOLT	
ALEX TAPTONA.	
Edward Angivana	
NORRIS ATIGIKYAKK	
BOG EKALOPIALOK	
TEDDY NOVOLIGAK	
GEORGE EVAGLOK	
John Evarluk	
JACK HIKHAITOK	
FRANK KOPTANA.	
JIMMY	
Wallace Goose	
ROY ENOKTALIK.	
MATTHEW	
Harry Egotak	
ESAU ELGAYAK	
ALIC.	
SAM. OLIKTOAK.	
MARK IMIRAK HIS MARK	① John Evarluk ② JIMMY

NAME OR MARK	LOCATION
GEORGE	READ. ISLAND.
BoBBy KLENGENBERG.	
VICTOR EKKOTAK	
Jorgen Klengenberg	
CHARLIE KITHLGITAK HIS MARK	① D. O'Brien ② John Evarluk
W TAPTONA	
ALLEN JOSS	
EDWARD ALGIAK HIS MARK	① John Evarluk ② ALLEN JOSS
DORS MIKIGIAK	
JUNE AILANAKI	
DORIS KONELOK	
IDA AIVIK.	
J. KALLAK.	
Charlie Bolt	
W. M. PIGALAK	
D. KATIK	
W. ETOKTOK	
James Kailrok his mark	① Peter Kamingoak ② PETER K. GIUNA
SAM. TABLO	
John Kiayak his mark	① Peter Kamingoak ② D. Kuliktanna
[illegible] aigak his mark	① Peter Kamingoak ② D. Kuliktanna
ALEX KADLON	
WILLIAM KAKOLAK.	

Coppermine petition signatures. *Library and Archives Canada, RG 85, vol. 41, file R–1875–2–4, Acc. 95—96/310.*

and federal governments and Nunavut Tunngavik Incorporated (NTI) are all tremendously supportive of mineral exploration and extraction, seeing mining as a potentially lucrative source of employment, business and investment opportunities, education and training, and infrastructure improvements in communities.[39] Many community members express concern that regional land use plans have yet to be implemented in the Kitikmeot region (of which Kugluktuk is a part), limiting the ability of Inuit to assess mineral development activities on a regional, comprehensive basis. These concerns have become particularly urgent as plans shift from the development of an isolated mine or two toward the building of extensive road, port, and mine infrastructure in the Bathurst Inlet area, an area of great importance to Inuinnait. As it stands, environmental and socio-economic impact studies are done on a methodologically constrained and case-by-case basis, and no studies of the cumulative effect of multiple mines have been undertaken. In spite of these concerns, however, mineral exploration and mine development remain priorities in the territory.

In effect, Kugluktukmiut are as tied to copper today as they were two or three hundred years ago, although now Kitikmeot copper is connected to networks of commodity pricing, multinational investment, federal and territorial bureaucracies, and the expansion of shipping into an increasingly "warm" Arctic. Whereas in 1771, the Dene saw caribou shapes in the native copper chunks they would fashion into hunting tools, mine development today threatens the calving and feeding grounds of these same herds of caribou, even while the revenues from mines allow some Kugluktukmiut to access the capital and equipment necessary for hunting. Teenagers who occasionally steal skidoos for a night of joyriding are intimately familiar with the copper wiring systems that allow them to cut an ignition wire and jump-start the machine. The copper mined in the region will soon find its way into the GPS units they use to navigate unfamiliar lands and into the televisions that light up their living rooms. And ironically, the same copper that contributed to generations of conflict between Inuit and Dene has recently brought them together in a reconciliation process. The rapid increase of mining in their territories has motivated them to come together and resolve their conflicts in regular visits so that they might better coordinate their involvement in proposed mineral development plans (see Chapter 6). In fact, the visits began with an apology from the Sahtú Dene for past wrongdoings, including any involvement of their ancestors in the massacre at Bloody Falls.[40] Stories of cooperation, trade, and collaboration between Inuit and Dene were shared by elders in a recent visit, calling into being not only a different understanding of the past but also new terms for future relations.

MAKING LIFE

ᑕᒪᓂᒃ: ᐊ … ᐃᖅᑭᓛᑦ ᑐᓴᐅᒪᒐᒃᑭᑦ ᒪᓂᒐᖃᕐᒪᑕ ᐅᔭᕋᕐᒥᒡᔫᓐᓃᑦ ᓇᓂᓯᒃᐸᑕ ᓄᓇᒥ ᐱᐅᕆᔪᒍ ᑕᐃᒪᓐᓇ ᐃᒃᐱᐊᕐᔪᖕᒥᐅᑕᕆᑐᐃᓐᓇᓐᖏᔪᒍᒎᖅ ᑐᓂᓯᕙᕖᕐᔪᓂ ᑎᐹᑭᒥᒡᔫᓐᓃᑦ ᑕᒡᕙ ᑎᒍᔪᖕᓇᖅᓱᓂᐅᒃ …

ᐊᐅᐱᓛᕐᔮᒃ: ᐄ …

ᑕᒪᓂᒃ: ᐄ … ᑕᐃᒪᓐᓇ ᐃᓄᐃᑦ ᒪᓂᒐᖃᕐᓚᓚᐅᖅᐸᑦ ᑕᒪᐃᓐᓄᑦ ᐅᕝᕙᓗ ᐃᓚᐃᓐᓇᓐᖏᓐᓄᑦ ᓄᓇᐅᑉ ᐱᕐᑯᑎᖏᓐᓄᑦ…?

ᐊᐅᐱᓛᕐᔮᒃ: ᑕᐃᒪᓐᓇ ᖃᐅᔨᒪᔪᐊᓐᖏᑦᑕᒃᑲ ᑖᒃᑯᐊ ᑭᓯᐊᓂ ᐅᖃᖅᑐᑦ ᐊᑖᑕᒐᔪ ᐅᖃᖅᐸᓚᐅᖅᑐᑦ ᑲᓐᓄᔭᖀᖅ ᓇᓂᒍᑉᑯ ᕿ’ᒥᒻᖑᖅ ᑲᔪᖅᑑᑉ ᒥᑦᖁᐊᓄᑦ ᐊᑭᓕᓇᐊᖃᖅᑕᕋ.

ᑕᒪᓂᒃ: Hᐄ …

ᐊᐅᐱᓛᕐᔮᒃ: ᑎᒍᓂᐊᕈᑉᑯ ᓄᓇᒥᑦ ᑕᑲᓐᓇ ᐊᐅᐸᓗᒃᑐᖅ. ᓇᓂᒍᑉᑯ ᐱᑖᓇᓂᐊᕈᑉᑯ ᕿ’ᒥᕐᒥᒃ ᑲᔪᖅᑑᑎᖃᕈᒪ ᕿ’ᒥᑉ ᑲᔪᖅᑐᑉ ᒥᑦᖁᐊ ᐊᑭᓕᐅᑎᓐᓂᐊᖅᐸᕋᒎᖅ. ᑕᒡᕘᓇᓗᐊᖅ ᑐᓴᐅᒪᔭᕋ ᑖᓐᓇ. ᑕᒪᔾᔫᓐᖏᑦᑐᐊᔫᒐᓗᐊᑦ. ᐱᑕᖃᐅᖅᑐᖅ ᓇᓗᓇᓐᖏᑦᑑᒐᓗᐊᖅ. ᑕᒪᔾᔭ ᑕᐃᒪᓐᓇ ᑐᓴᖅᓱᒋᑦ ᐃᑦᕿᓛᑦᑐ ᔭᓗᓇᐃᒥ ᐃᑦᕿᓕᕐᒥᒃ ᐅᓂᒃᑳᖅᑕᐅᖅᑦᑕᓚᐅᕋᒪ ᐃᓯᒪᑕᓇ’ᑐᑎᒍᓪᓗ. ᐃᓚᖕᒥᑦ ᐃᓄᒃᑎᑑᑦᑎᐊᖃᑦᑕᖅᑐᑦ ᑕᐃᑉᓯᒪᓂ ᑐᓴᐅᒪᔭᒃᑲ. ᐃᓚᖕᒥᑦ ᐋᒃᑲᐅᒐᓗᐊᑦ.

ᑕᒪᓂᒃ: ᓲᖃ ᓄᓇᒥᒃ ᑲᒪᑦᑎᐊᕋᓱᒃᓱᑎᒃ … ᐃᓕᖅᑯᓯᖃᕐᒪᑕ …

ᐊᐅᐱᓛᕐᔮᒃ: ᐄ …

ᑕᒪᓂᒃ: ᖃᑉᓗᓈᑑᓐᖏᓪᒪᑕ. ᖃᑉᓗᓈᑦ ᐊᑐᑐᐃᓐᓇᕋᓱᒃᐸᒃᓱᑎᒃ.

ᐊᐅᐱᓛᕐᔮᒃ: ᖃᑉᓗᓈᑐᑐᐃᓐᓇᑦᑎᐊᓪᓚᓇ’ᒪᑕ ᑮᓇᐅᔾᔪᒃ ᐱᔪᒪᓂᑯᐊᓗᒃ. ᐅᕙᒍᓪᓕ ᓄᓇᖅᑲᖅᑳᖑᔪᑎᒍᑦ ᑮᓇᐅᔭᖅ ᐱᑦᑕᐃᓕᓐᖏᑕᕋᓗᐊᕙᑦ ᐃᒃᐱᕆᓚᐅᓐᖏᓇᑉᑎᒍᓪᓕ. ᑭᓯᐊᓂ ᐃᓅᓯᖅᑦᑎᐊᕐᓂᖅ ᓄᓇᓗ ᒥᐊᓂᕆᑦᑎᐊᕐᓂᖓ ᑖᒻᓇᓗ ᐊᒃᓯᕉᑎᓗᐊᓇᒐᑉᑎᒍᑦ.

Janet Tamalik McGrath: Mmm *[pause]* I have heard about the First Nations practice that if they find a rock on the land and they like it, they are not supposed to just pick it up and put it in their pockets ever, only if they give a gift in advance like a bit of tobacco, then they are free to take it *[pause]*

Aupilaarjuk: Yes *[pause]*

Tamalik: Yes ... did Inuit ever have similar rules, like in general or towards specific things of the land *[pause]*?

Aupilaarjuk: I don't know about these things but I remember that it was said, and by my father too, that if we find copper we should pay for it with a tuft of fur from a brown dog.

Tamalik: Really *[pause]*

Aupilaarjuk: If I am to take the red substance there from the land that it comes from, if I have happened across some and I want to keep it for myself and if I have a brown dog then I would be required to pay for it with the dog's tuft of fur. This is the only instance that I heard of this from. I am sure that this is not the only such instance. It is clear that there are many such rules. And just hearing about the First Nations reminds me of when I worked in Yellowknife with one First Nations man and he was our leader in that project. There were many things that I heard from them that were identical to what Inuit would do. But of course there were other things that differed too.

Tamalik: Because they lived in a way so as to care for the land *[pause]* their culture was formed by that *[pause]*

Aupilaarjuk: Yes *[pause]*

Tamalik: They are not like Qablunaat. It seems the western way is to consume.

Aupilaarjuk: Because they are operating from a western patterning that is based on acquisition of money. For us first peoples of the land, we don't reject the use of money, it's just that we never had an attachment to it. Our whole focus was on having a good life and looking after the land well.[41]

Following the settlement of the Nunavut Land Claim Agreement, Inuit became "the largest freehold owners of mineral rights in Canada." Celebrated not only as a political triumph but also as the beginning of a "new era of cooperation between the Inuit of Nunavut and mineral explorers and developers," the settlement of subsurface title in the territory was hailed as a catalyst for both Inuit economic development and an expanded multinational mineral economy.[42] The settlement would seem an occasion far removed from the Bloody Falls massacre, but, in fact, the "new era" of relations between Inuit, minerals, and "explorers and developers" initiated by the NLCA has a much longer history. Not only was Hearne's journey geared explicitly toward facilitating mineral extraction in the Central Arctic, but the massacre story itself was shaped by long-standing geographies of copper extraction, trade, and conflict. Hearne's narrative staked out relations between Inuit, Dene, Qablunaat, and copper that have shaped subsequent "copper stories" and had material consequences through to the present. If stories are material ordering practices that shape not only the imaginative but also the very tangible and concrete aspects of mineral extraction, then it would seem that these copper stories might provide insights into the ways in which "storying the North" has been implicated in opening the region to imperial capital.

Celebration of the subsurface mineral rights "awarded" through the NLCA is common but disingenuous. In fact, the settlement required Inuit to formally extinguish their rights to the entirety of Nunavut, in exchange for a cash settlement and rights to 2 percent of the territory's subsurface and 18 percent of its surface, as well as the establishment of the territory itself and its associated governance structures. It is an agreement about which many Inuit are rightly proud, but the NLCA was a conscious and strategic compromise, one that has facilitated the accumulation of capital in the North as much as it has supported Inuit interests and values. And though many Nunavummiut actively support the development of industrial mineral economies, it would be a mistake to read that support as a wholehearted endorsement of the racialized notion that Inuit must break with tradition and adopt a modern form of relation with the resources of the land. In the dialogue above, Aupilaarjuk contextualizes this for us. Inuit do not give offerings to the land in precisely the same ways as some First Nations do, he notes, but northern Indigenous peoples share a broader relational framework within which their responsibilities to the land are clear. In conversation with Tamalik, Aupilaarjuk recalls his father's teaching that if one happens upon a piece of copper and wishes to take it, then it is important to pay for it with a dog's fur. This is not payment in a capitalist sense, of course; the verb stem *aki-* signifies fair offering and exchange. The offering acknowledges the relations that sustain life on the land, and it points to the importance of copper in making life possible for Inuit. "Our whole focus," Aupilaarjuk observes, "was on having a good life and looking after the land well."

It seems to me that, for most Nunavummiut, engaging with contemporary mineral economies is not grounded in an ideological or abstract interest in opening the North to capital so much as a deeply ambivalent, hopeful effort to support life in the territory. It is about tracing very different copper stories, stories that deepen relations with money, whether in the form of royalties, wages, taxes, or commodity markets, in the hope that money and waged work might resolve some of the suffering that marks people's lives, support access to the land, and build a sense of purpose and pride for young people. This represents a qualitative shift from the relations with money that Aupilaarjuk describes. Inuit don't reject relations with money, he suggests, but such relations have always been subordinate to relations with one another and with the land, in service of a "good life."[43] Jackie Price traces similar continuities and ruptures in contemporary campaigns to promote industrial resource development: "Inuit have always understood the land to be resourceful, this new campaign understands Nunavut's resourcefulness in a different way," one that "does not respect the Inuit principle of subsistence living."[44] Indeed, industrial mineral economies transform the resourcefulness of the land into commodities for sale elsewhere, and it is precisely by maximizing the resourcefulness of an industrial mining corridor that subsistence relations with the land are threatened. There will be no tufts of dog fur placed for every piece of copper mined at the High Lake mine, should it open, as proposed, in the next several years. But to make such observations is not to hearken to a romantic or distant past. It is not to "go back." It is, instead, to call attention to what lives on in struggles to make sense of and engage with mining today, what mining promises and what it will mean for the people, the wildlife, and the land: a struggle and a yearning to sustain life.

Indeed, the fact that the Bloody Falls massacre is associated with copper in Kugluktuk but is not told as a copper story elsewhere reveals both the persistence of Qablunaaq denial about what drives our interests in the North, and the keen awareness among Inuit about how outsiders understand the value of their lives and lands. Though much academic, government, and corporate effort has gone into sustaining a narrative of progression from tradition to modernity, in which the opening of Nunavut to industrial resource extraction represents a natural and a necessary "development," the copper stories assembled here both trouble such a narrative and point toward the interests and relations it sustains. Inuit relations with industrial mineral economies are much more complex and long-standing than such a narrative implies, and their relations with copper belie any racialized containment to the "traditional past." The copper stories told by Qitsualik, Qoerhuk, Aupilaarjuk, and by those Inuit who gather to comment on proposed developments on their lands are fundamentally about *life;* they are about how life is made and sustained through the relations and practices we foster, and those we undermine. These relations are continually invoked at the community meetings and hearings of the Nunavut Impact Review Board, even if they fail to register as such in the bureaucratic accounting of "impacts" and "benefits." Relations with the land have sustained life for untold generations, even as these relations have been targeted by governments, missionaries, academics, and corporations through multiple interventions into the lives of Nunavummiut.

It seems to me, then, that the question being asked of mineral development in Nunavut today is not so much whether it should be wholeheartedly celebrated because Inuit are running the corporations and institutions that endorse it, or rejected because it represents the intensification of capitalist relations in the North, but rather whether the relations that Inuit might forge with copper or other metals through the development of mines will, indeed, support and sustain life, and if so, what kind of life, for whom, and on whose terms? I think this is the question that hangs in the air when an elder speaks at length about all that worries her about the mines (the threats to caribou and fish, the pollution of waterways, the increase in alcohol consumption and suicide, the strain of rotational work and the degrading jobs available to Inuit, the decline in hunting and land skills, and the pain of diminished sharing and social cohesion) before ultimately, reluctantly, hopefully observing that jobs might provide young people with some of what they need to continue living. It is a hope and a yearning that mining corporations actively target in their campaigns and that is continually exploited in the promise of jobs. Copper has always been central to living and dying in the North; as Qoerhuk recounted to Métayer, the relations between copper, snow, ice, and Inuit were at one time integral to survival. The point is not to revive the use of copper snow knives; Inuit survive differently today. It is, instead, to ask whether the copper stories promised in contemporary mineral development will be good stories, stories that will foster life and, if so, *whose* life, and where? It is to insist, in other words, on tracing the broader relations through which life is made in and through the North today. Regardless of whether mining enables Nunavummiut to sustain "good lives" and to continue caring for their lands, connecting Arctic copper to global markets will surely sustain the lives of Qablunaat. It will buoy our stock exchanges, grow our pensions, power our homes, transmit our e-mail. We do not emphasize these relations, but they are there to be found in our most iconic northern stories.

5
Resistance Stories

The ventriloquism of the speaking subaltern is the left intellectual's stock-in-trade.
– Gayatri Chakravorty Spivak, *A Critique of Postcolonial Reason*

Questions about the significance of resistant agency, its geo-historical reach, limits, conditions, organization and impact are all often unanswered at the very same time as the rhetoric of resistance obscures the objects against which resistant agents are said to resist.
– Matthew Sparke, "Political Geography"

Imbalance occurs when the *inummarik* way is supplanted by the *qablunaaq* way ... [Aupilaarjuk argued that] we need to consciously privilege the *inummarik* way because it helps with a critical analysis of the modern capitalist world ... The *inummarik* way has the gift of discernment, it can guide and keep everything in balance.
– Janet Tamalik McGrath, "Remembering Mariano Aupilarjuk"

On 4 August 1972, Simon Taipana sent a telex to Stuart M. Hodgson, commissioner of the Northwest Territories:

Mr Ted Boxer, Historical Committee, has advised us that there are two cairns planned to honour Samuel Hearne.

You have advised us that there is no money available to install pressure systems in new northern rental houses in Coppermine.

The Settlement Council of Coppermine has expressed strong disapproval of spending money on these historical monuments while at the same time there are greater useful needs such as bath-tubs and running water in the new northern rental housing.

Please also remember that Samuel Hearne is not regarded as a local hero, and should you insist on historic plaques, we would recommend that the plaque be in memoriam of those persons massacred at Bloody Falls.

We request preferably, that these plaques not be erected, and that the money instead be more usefully spent.

Simon Taipana
For Settlement Secretary
For Coppermine Settlement Council[1]

In what seems to have been a bureaucratic oversight, Hodgson did not see the telex in time, and territorial and federal officials arrived in Coppermine ten days later, expecting to finalize the details of a plaque ceremony. Upon landing and being made aware of the telex, Ted Boxer, secretary of the Northwest Territories Historical Advisory Board, requested a community meeting to "talk about Hearne's visit, in case it was not understood." The notion that Inuit in Coppermine must not understand the importance of Hearne's "visit" recurs throughout correspondence related to the dispute that followed. A well-attended community meeting was held a couple of hours later and was characterized by Boxer as "completely unproductive":

> The Community Council stated that Samuel Hearne meant nothing to them except in the context of the massacre. Also, that no one in Yellowknife would erect a plaque to someone from the south who came up and murdered their relatives. It was emphasized that Hearne did not take part in the massacre and actually wished very sincerely that he could have prevented it. All that was to be commemorated was Samuel Hearne's journey, and the historic fact that it had taken place. All arguments were rejected by the Council. They stated that the fact of his visit was recorded in the history books. The economic advantage of cairns to the community was also rejected on the grounds that they were arguing a principle which was related to the Land Rights issue. This outweighed any monetary gains from tourism. Nothing could be said to change their views on this point.[2]

A protracted dispute between the settlement council and the Government of the Northwest Territories (GNWT) followed. A month after Boxer's visit, the people of Coppermine voted almost unanimously against the erection of plaques commemorating Samuel Hearne and advised the

GNWT of their decision. Frustrated, Commissioner Hodgson asked Reverend John Sperry, Anglican archdeacon of the Arctic diocese and a man with long-standing ties to the community, to fly to Coppermine and speak to the people. Sperry had been a missionary in Coppermine for twenty years (from 1950 to 1970) and is still highly regarded by many in Kugluktuk today. Following his visit, members of the community reversed their decision and indicated that they would allow the commemoration to proceed, although in the end no plaques were erected.

In this chapter, I assess the intricacies of the plaque dispute to draw broader conclusions about the shifting geographies of colonial governance, federal-territorial jurisdiction, and Inuit self-determination in the 1970s and the terms upon which Kugluktukmiut have self-consciously and publicly rejected Qablunaaq obsessions with Bloody Falls. For the first time, the massacre story enrolled land claims, bathtubs, and the possibilities of exercising a measure of control over the materialities of everyday life in Coppermine, and community members responded accordingly. Their responses, I argue, are as revealing of the shape of governmental power in the early 1970s as they are of Inuit strategies to resist Qablunaaq control over settlement life. I thus examine acts of resistance as a diagnostic of power, as a means of tracing historical shifts in the intentions and methods whereby governmental, corporate, and religious figures have intervened in the lives of Kugluktukmiut. If, as I argue throughout this book, story can productively be thought of as material, then this chapter helps tease out the conditions under which stories demand direct political response, as well as the terms upon which those responses become legible to Qablunaat.

THE COPPERMINE CONFERENCE AND INUIT SELF-DETERMINATION

Charlie Gruben's account of "what can happen to your country" was one of many sobering stories of oil, gas, and mineral exploration shared at the "Coppermine Conference of Arctic Native People" in July 1970:

> Let me tell you a little about Tuktoyaktuk and what oil exploration has done for us. It's the most messed-up place. They put roads in about a mile apart and these have exposed the permafrost so that they become ditches and each spring they get deeper and deeper when they thaw out. The exploration crews dam up creeks and stop the water, block the fish. They set off explosions in shallow lakes and we see lots of dead fish. They don't provide any permanent jobs. And that's what can happen to your country.[3]

The meeting, one of the first gatherings of Inuit from across the Canadian North, was a galvanizing political moment in the history of northern land claims. The following year, Inuit Tapirisat of Canada (ITC) was founded, and the movement toward the settlement of Inuit title and the establishment of the territory of Nunavut was under way. Spurred by the rapid acceleration of resource exploration and extraction in their territories and their continued exclusion from consultation processes, resource revenues, and the employment benefits accruing from these developments, the delegates shared a sense of urgency about the cultural, economic, and environmental impacts of the booming northern resource industry and a growing interest in establishing their Aboriginal title in a context where that title was either ignored or under active threat of extinguishment.

Informed in part by a report prepared by Peter Cumming, legal adviser to the meeting, the delegates were well aware of the federal government's hostility toward Aboriginal title and Aboriginal rights, made clear in the 1969 White Paper.[4] They were particularly concerned, however, about the implications of transferring legal and jurisdictional powers from the federal to the territorial government during the preceding decades. As Kirk Cameron and Graham White observe in their history of northern political development, "in the 1950s [the Northwest Territories] was a colonial dependency, administered from Ottawa, delivering only very basic public services," and as the territory moved toward greater independence from Ottawa in the 1950s and '60s, "issues of constitutional development and governance ... were framed and resolved with almost total lack of recognition of the status, needs and values of the Aboriginal peoples."[5] Cumming highlighted this disregard for Aboriginal rights in his report to the Coppermine delegates. He pointed to specific territorial acts and amendments passed in the 1950s and 1960s that eroded Inuit control over their lands by transferring federal controls over Crown lands to the territorial commissioner and by granting the GNWT the power to "deal with the Eskimo Aboriginal title in respect to such lands."[6] In essence, the transfer of federal control over the lands and peoples of the North to the territorial government was paving the way for the extinguishment of Inuit Aboriginal title (which had never been ceded by treaty or war), much as had occurred in British Columbia. Indeed, Cumming drew the attention of the delegates to the case of the Nisga'a First Nation, who had taken the BC government to court in 1969, contesting the government's unlawful extinguishment of their Aboriginal title.[7]

The urgency of the situation was obvious to the conference participants. The pace of development was so swift and so unchecked that the delegates feared they would have no meaningful land or resources to claim if they did not act immediately. Discussion focused on Banks Island in the Beaufort Sea and the oil and gas exploration occurring there that summer. Aware that the Department of Indian Affairs and Northern Development (DIAND) had issued 308 oil and gas exploration permits for Banks Island, and having heard stories of the destruction wrought by oil and gas exploration at nearby Tuktoyaktuk, delegates such as Peter Sidney of Sachs Harbour (an Inuit settlement on the island) worried about "how much damage they will do to Banks Island ... They say they will work there four or five years. They will scare away the caribou, spoil the fox and geese."[8] Agnes Semmler of Inuvik warned that "things happen so fast, look at Tuktoyaktuk. Everything happened before the people knew what was going on ... Banks Island's a pretty small place; in five years you'll have nothing."[9] Led by delegates from Sachs Harbour, the conference members prepared a resolution on the matter, sending it by telegram to Prime Minister Pierre Trudeau and Minister of Indian Affairs and Northern Development Jean Chrétien on 16 July 1970:

> The Eskimo People of Sachs Harbour Banks Island unanimously and strongly object to any oil or gas exploration on Banks Island. Your government has issued leases for such exploration without any prior consultation whatsoever with the Eskimo people. These actions are an example of your government's continuing complete disregard for the rights of the Eskimo people and are contrary to the standards of common human decency ... Banks Island has a very delicate ecological balance which will be destroyed if exploration is allowed and the land surface disturbed, as your government will readily understand if it will only choose to consult with the Eskimo people and have biologists conduct the necessary research ... The people of Sachs Harbour urgently request that you direct that no further exploration take place until consultation can be made with the Eskimo people in these matters. Your government's failure to do so can only be interpreted as conscious consent to the destruction of the people of Sachs Harbour.[10]

Signed by all conference participants, the resolution went on to outline demands that the government must "always have prior consultation with the Eskimo people in respect to any service, exploration, or any other activities to be undertaken" and that "your government recognize our rights as Aboriginals in the lands of the North and give us fair compensation where there is expropriation of our rights in the lands." Lest the government fail to appreciate the "seriousness of the situation," the signatories warned that they were "quite prepared to take whatever action is necessary to protect their community and environment."[11] Peter Kamingoak, a respected elder from Kugluktuk and a key player in the organization of the Coppermine Conference, was a signatory of the resolution. According to Robert McPherson, the resolution caused "a furor" in southern Canada when the story reached the *Toronto Globe and Mail.*[12] Indeed, the delegates purposely aimed for media coverage, having learned that "if it doesn't get in the press, you never seem to get any action. When we wanted this school you see here in Coppermine, we didn't get any action until we drew up a petition and got it in the press – then things happened."[13]

Transcripts of the Coppermine conference sessions reveal a conscious and forceful rejection of the deferential, peaceable, "smiling Eskimo" figure and an articulation of a shared resolve to establish their rights as Indigenous peoples. As David Tukutuk of Great Whale River (Kuujjuarapik, Nunavik, Quebec) asserted,

> For a long time the whiteman has come to the Eskimo and told him to "do this, do that" and the Eskimo said "yes, yes" and did whatever he was told, no matter how menial the job. But today we are beginning to think of what's best for us and for our people and we are starting to say "no, that's not what I want to do" [Applause!]. As native people, we must stand up today and fight for our rights.[14]

The frequency with which delegates referred to the importance of speaking out, of refusing to stay silent, and of acting as a collective to resist the forces affecting Indigenous communities across the North reveals the meeting's importance in building a sense of political consciousness and shared resolve. Kamingoak himself made clear his intentions to stand up to the "whiteman," particularly in terms of land claims and treaties:

> All the provinces were Indian lands, you know and the whiteman came in and took them over. What they did in the south, now they are trying to do to our land in the north ... We don't want any treaty – this is our land. If we sign a treaty, they'll treat us like Indians – push us around. We don't want no whiteman telling us "you move over to here because I want this land."[15]

This, then, was the political context in which Inuit leaders were operating in the early 1970s, a context that the territorial and federal governments were slow to appreciate. Indeed, when the Coppermine Settlement Council was informed of the governments' intent to erect territorial and federal monuments to Samuel Hearne and the Bloody Falls massacre in 1972, its stern rejection of the monuments not only shocked government officials, it also struck them as profoundly irrational, misinformed, and out of character. Ted Boxer attributed the council's actions to the undue influence of the white settlement manager, a Mr. W. Bean. In a memo debriefing his superiors on the debacle, Boxer stated that "it was apparent ... that the Settlement Manager had had something to do with the reaction of the Settlement Council to the proposed commemorations" and insisted that Inuit resistance to the plaques was grounded in a failure to "understand" the importance of Hearne.[16] This statement was not only paternalistic and steeped in a colonial understanding of Indigenous agency; it was also naive. Inuit were actively organizing against government failures to consult, against the management of their territories as Crown lands over which they held no jurisdiction, and against the control of the North by people who had no intention "to actually *live* in the Arctic" throughout the early 1970s.[17] They were making use of the modest powers of the newly implemented settlement councils to register their concerns and were increasingly forceful in their articulation of their rights and demands.[18] The federal and territorial governments' gradual awakening to the implications of these movements is registered in the archival and oral materials documenting the dispute over the plaques.

GOVERNMENTALITY, POWER, AND RESISTANCE TO THE PROPOSED PLAQUES

Inuit were faced with a different state in the years following the Second World War. The early 1950s marked a turning point in federal relations with the NWT, as Ottawa took an unprecedented interest in its northern territory. Until that time, the territories had been governed almost exclusively from Ottawa and, as Louis St-Laurent famously observed in 1953, "in an almost continuing state of absence of mind."[19] Under St-Laurent, the federal government embarked on a massive expansion of government services in the North, motivated by concerns over Arctic sovereignty, by interests in expanding the northern resource economy, and by a postwar shift in policy making toward a more interventionist, liberal, reformist understanding of government, particularly where Indigenous peoples were concerned. Endeavouring to bring the North into its purview and to shape a particular kind of Indigenous subject, programs were launched in health, social services, education, and economic and political development.

In Foucauldian terms, we can view this shift as the beginning not so much of colonialism in the North, as political scientist Mark Dickerson argues, but of an intensified form of governmentality.[20] Foucault proposed the term "governmentality" to refer to the set of ideas, calculations, techniques, and practices concerned with the art of government at multiple scales, from concern with governing one's own conduct through to the government of populations. He was particularly interested in the ways in which the government of territory and population are imbricated with the government of self, with how modern forms of governmentality at once target the conduct of the individual and aim to manage the population as a whole. Against a long line of scholarship that had understood government as the exercise of control over a given piece of territory, and by extension over that territory's inhabitants, Foucault argued that

> What government has to do with is not territory but rather a sort of complex composed of men and things. The things with which in this sense government is to be concerned are in fact men, but men in their relations, their links, their imbrication with those other things which are wealth, resources, means of subsistence, the territory with its specific qualities, climate, irrigation, fertility, etc; men in their relation to that other kind of things, customs, habits, ways of acting and thinking, etc; lastly, men in their relation to that other kind of things, accidents and misfortunes such as famine, epidemic, death, etc.[21]

This understanding of government as an attempt to shape the conduct of populations and to exert control over the complex relations between "men and things" resonates in important ways with the shifting forms of government deployed in the North during the postwar era. For the first time, the federal government targeted Inuit as a *population,* and the minutiae of their lives and livelihoods came under government scrutiny. From the directives transmitted through the 1947 *Book of Wisdom for Eskimo* (a federal publication explaining to Inuit such things as "where sickness comes from," "before baby comes," and "planning for periods of scarcity") to government interest in transforming Inuit housing, health, education, welfare, employment, hunting, language, culture, and political organization, this was the beginning of an intensified interest in the production of Inuit as a healthy, compliant, "modern," wage-earning population.[22]

Foucault understood governmentality as distinct from what he termed "sovereign power," a form of power expressed through overt displays of force. Governmentality involves a more subtle will to govern the relations people forge with one another and with the land; it involves forms of management, consultation, participation, and documentation rather than more overt forms of violence or control. Foucault's writings on governmentality emerged from interests and studies that are relatively removed from postwar Arctic Canada, but they are nonetheless helpful in making sense of the shifting relations between the federal government, Inuit, and Inuit lands during the decades leading up to the plaque dispute, particularly when considered alongside writings by Inuit intellectuals about the postwar era. As Greenlandic poet and leader Aqqaluk Lynge wrote in the early 1970s, in a poem titled "Nunatta Akiuussutaa" (Arctic riches),

> Because cannons and war
> are ways
> not used by our people
> you use a method
> that does not, in itself,
> annihilate life
> but diminishes our strength
> With slyness and flattery
> you pretend
> it is us you are serving
> not yourselves.[23]

Lynge's words resonate with the work of David Scott, who argues that colonial forms of governmentality involve not simply a shift in modes of government, but rather the deployment of a political rationality that systematically displaces the knowledges, practices, and imaginations of the colonized group. This is not achieved through "cannons and war," as Lynge notes, but by enfolding those knowledges and practices into new modes of conduct "such that the old would now only be imaginable along paths that belong to new, always already transformed sets of coordinates, concepts, and assumptions."[24] Colonial governmentality is not just about reshaping the relations between "men and things," then, but about reshaping the very terms upon which a target population conceptualizes itself, its history, and its future. Inuit leaders who came of age during the 1970s describe a similar process: Peter Ittinuar reflects on the necessity of "becom[ing] white" to advance Inuit interests, and James Arvaluk describes the adoption of "white" politics and practices as a "trade-off" necessitated by the fact that "the traditional Inuit leaders ... were not respected historically by the government, the RCMP, the mission etc. They were not respected."[25] Ittinuar and Arvaluk characterize this transformation as a self-conscious and strategic engagement with colonial institutions, but Lynge points also to the more subtle ways in which Qablunaaq practices and modes of thinking could insinuate themselves into Inuit social, cultural, and political processes, a shift that Aupilaarjuk discusses extensively in his conversations with Tamalik McGrath.[26]

A number of scholars have taken up Foucault's ideas about governmentality in colonial contexts and suggested, as anthropologist Tania Murray Li does, that colonial forms of governmentality are characterized by a "will to improve" in which the objective is not so much to dominate others but to enhance a target population's "capacity for action, and to direct it." Its practitioners desire to make the world better, and they do so not through violence or force, but through various interventions that are made to seem like "the natural expression of the everyday interactions of individuals and groups."[27] Governing Indigenous peoples in this mode, she argues, is no less significant than more coercive, assimilative, or disciplinary forms of domination, even if those who practice it evince a genuine desire to improve the lives of those they target. Indeed, as both Li and Lynge make clear, colonial desires to improve and help are tethered to interests in Indigenous lands and resources; efforts to transform Inuit into governable subjects are inseparable from interest in northern resource extraction. Teaching Inuit to feel "disdain for ourselves," as Lynge writes, furthers the project of extracting Arctic riches.[28]

With Foucault, Lynge, Aupilaarjuk, Scott, and Li in mind, we can begin to come to terms with how improvement, benevolence, and intensified government interest in the relations between "men and things" interwove with interest in northern resource extraction and shaped the terrain of Inuit engagement with Qablunaaq practices and structures during the 1970s. Indeed, the federal government was actively concerned with reshaping relations among Inuit and between Inuit and their lands, resources, and livelihoods in the years leading up to the dispute over commemorative plaques. After decades of trying to ensure that Inuit maintained "traditional" lifestyles supplemented by trapping incomes (thus avoiding dependency on the state), the federal government reoriented its northern agenda in the face of a collapsing trapping economy, challenges to Canadian sovereignty in the Far North, famines related to changing caribou migration, and the increasingly attractive resource extraction potential of the region.[29] Whereas in previous decades, Inuit were encouraged to disperse and minimize their reliance on settlement services (which were minimal), in the 1960s and '70s (although beginning as early as the late 1940s), Inuit were pressured to settle in communities, participate in wage employment, enrol their children in schools, and adopt "Western ideas about the family, work, community, and social relations." As Frank Tester and Peter Kulchyski point out,

> the central historical dynamic that came to link Inuit to non-Inuit society politically was put in place during the period of high modernism. Unlike Indian affairs, where a pre-welfare state employed largely coercive measures, in Inuit affairs it was a liberal form of welfare state, which gave the appearance of having a more benign face and which employed a greater reliance on ideology, that became the means for attempting assimilation.[30]

Indeed, Dickerson documents the St-Laurent administration's intention to "provide northern residents with government services equivalent to, or nearly equivalent to, those services enjoyed by most Canadians" in the form of welfare and relief payments, family allowances, old age pensions, health care, education and employment training, and housing.[31] The credit system employed at fur trade posts collapsed as fur prices fell throughout the 1950s and '60s, and the federal government eventually intervened with massive relief payments and other forms of welfare as Inuit across the Arctic struggled to survive. Relief and family allowances became essential to survival as the fur economy declined, and a wave of government policies and programs were subsequently developed in hopes of transforming Inuit into modern wage earners.

The settlement of Coppermine, which had slowly grown up around a trading post established by Christian Klengenberg in 1916 and then around a Hudson's Bay post founded in 1928, only became a regional centre as medical services, the RCMP, and missionaries based themselves there through the 1920s, '30s, and '40s, and particularly after the trading posts around Coronation Gulf began to close in the 1930s, forcing Inuinnait engaged in trapping to trade at Coppermine.[32] Inuinnait established more permanent residence at Coppermine (which had been a seasonal stopping and meeting place for centuries) for a variety of reasons.[33] Some found employment at nearby DEW Line sites during the 1950s; others moved there to be closer to their children, who were attending the school built in Coppermine in 1948, and others came to be closer to medical services or to access government relief payments as fur prices fell.[34] Earlier attempts to move into town had been thwarted by government. During Christmas 1952, the annual gathering of Inuit in Coppermine lingered a little too long for the tastes of the local clergy, RCMP, and nurse, and the people were run out of town.[35] Inuit had remained in Coppermine because of the presence of caribou there and the absence of game in the interior lands, making it pointless to head back to inland camps. Concerned that Inuit were lazing about and developing slothful habits, the "white agents" worked together to ensure their dispersal. The nurse announced that "a contagious disease could come and kill all or most of them and that they should, accordingly, spread into smaller camps" and the RCMP officer "asked" the people to leave town.[36] They did. After decades of periodic outbreaks of chicken pox, measles, influenza, and tuberculosis, the threat of disease must have been an effective deterrent to remaining in town. Only a few years later, Inuinnait were prevailed upon to settle in Coppermine, in part so that medical services could be delivered more effectively. Reverend John Sperry recalls that during the latter years of his residency in Coppermine (the late 1960s), "year by year, support agencies, particularly in the medical and social assistance fields, became a part of settlement life." Tellingly, Sperry complains that these services "affected the [Inuit] sense of security even to the point of transferring some of the earlier belief in and dependence on divine assistance to dependence on a benevolent government," a comment that is as revealing of an intensifying governmentality as it is of Sperry's loosening grip on his "flock."[37]

John Amagoalik describes how, with the rise of government power in the North, Inuit encountered new forms of dispossession:

> It was around the early sixties that we started to discover that we had become powerless in our own homeland. We had become non-citizens in our own country. Our human rights were ignored and violated ... The laws were already in place. We only started finding out about these laws when some people started breaking them. It was becoming obvious that through the introduction of game laws, and through the introduction of the justice system and the education system, we had basically lost control of our lives. We found out that we were powerless. The other thing around that period in the late fifties and sixties, was that there was an exploration boom in the High Arctic for oil and gas. Multi-national corporations were coming from everywhere and they were exploring almost every foot of those islands ... We discovered that these oil companies could do whatever they wanted, with the blessing of the federal government, on our lands. We had no say about it. We had no say in how the environment was going to be

protected, or what kinds of benefits we would derive from this activity. We had no say. We looked at all these things together, and it became obvious that things had to change. That's when the idea of aboriginal rights and land claims first came on the scene.[38]

Amagoalik's phrasing is instructive: Inuit who had hitherto experienced a degree of control over their lives "found out" that they were "powerless" in relation to this new government; in this account, power is deeply relational and material. Notably, the laws and services that Amagoalik critiques were implemented in part with the intention of helping, improving, and transforming Inuit into better citizens, and Kugluktukmiut had objected to this "help" on more than one occasion. The Coppermine representative to a 1960 meeting of the Committee on Eskimo Affairs (a committee composed of various branches of government, the RCMP, the Hudson's Bay Company, the churches, and other agencies interested in governing Inuit lives and lands), Kilikavioyak, stated that "he had been asked by the people in Coppermine to say that many Eskimos there, particularly the older people, regarded the old way of life as still best for them. Only a minority of the people in Coppermine wanted to change their old way of life and the rest wanted to be left alone to make a living."[39]

But change was rapid and few Inuit managed to be left alone. Most continued to spend extended periods away from the settlement at outpost camps, where government programs, the RCMP, and missionaries exerted less influence over their daily lives. Some continue to divide their time between Kugluktuk and a range of camps and cabins across the region, but almost all Inuinnait had settled more or less permanently in Coppermine, Holman, Cambridge Bay, and Bathurst Inlet by the late 1960s and early 1970s.

An additional dynamic was introduced to northern governmental interests in the late 1960s as the newly empowered territorial government took shape. The seat of the NWT government was moved from Ottawa to Yellowknife in 1967, and the GNWT gradually assumed jurisdiction over a range of portfolios, including lands, health, education, and economic development, although portions of these portfolios remained under the purview of various federal departments. The first Yellowknife-based territorial commissioner, Stuart Hodgson, was committed to government expansion and making government relevant to northerners. He opened the November 1967 Territorial Council with telling remarks:

I take great pleasure in being able to stand before you in our new capital today, on what is indeed a historic occasion, to officially open the

> Thirty-Fifth Session of the Council of the Northwest Territories. I have always believed that people with their needs and aspirations must be the most important consideration that any government has if it is to function democratically as the servant of those it purports to govern. It is for this reason that I am so very happy to address you from this seat of government in Yellowknife – because I can say to you that the Government of the Northwest Territories has moved so much closer to our people. We are among them now, as neighbours, patrons of their businesses, and social acquaintances. And we are trying, each in his own way, to become true northerners and members of a community that stretches far wider than the confines of Yellowknife but spreads across the one and a quarter million square miles of Canada's Northwest Territories. This cannot help having a tremendous effect on the attitude of northern residents towards our government and indeed the effectiveness with which we operate.[40]

John Amagoalik, who worked under Hodgson during the early 1970s, argues that although it was the mandate of the GNWT and that of Hodgson himself to "improve the lives of our people ... their vision was one North. We are all Northerners, we are going to have a common future. That was their philosophy in Yellowknife. It was certainly not to settle land claims or create a new territory ... Their position was that aboriginal rights did not exist in northern Canada or the Northwest Territories."[41] James Arvaluk, a political leader involved in the NLCA negotiations, similarly recalls that, as much as Hodgson wanted to foster community development and local political involvement, he was primarily interested in establishing the NWT government in Yellowknife and in promoting the territory's independence from Ottawa.[42] The seat of the territorial government may have moved, but from the perspective of most Indigenous northerners it was still dominated by white men from the South, who had their own ideas about the future of the region and its Indigenous peoples.

The territorial heritage plaque program, initiated in 1970 as part of a broader move to build territorial archives, museums, and other heritage resources, was in line with the goal of building a single territory for all northerners and fostering a sense of regional and territorial identity in Northwest Territories.[43] The NWT Historical Advisory Board had selected Bloody Falls as an "impressive" site for territorial commemoration in November 1970. According to Ted Boxer, it was chosen in part because of its archaeological merits (working for the Archaeological Survey of Canada in the late 1960s, Robert McGhee had uncovered archeological evidence that Bloody Falls had been used as a fishing site for millennia) and in part because of "the historical value of the location resulting from its relation to Samuel Hearne's historic journey of 1771."[44] As federal and territorial bureaucrats strained to "explain" to the Coppermine Settlement Council, "the first white contact at Coppermine had long lasting effect on the future of the nation ... There was an achievement locating the arctic overland making the outside aware of the route. This fact is recorded in history and the plaque shows the visitors that here is the destination for that historic journey."[45] The plaque, then, which would be the first territorial heritage plaque in the NWT, would locate an event of national significance in the territory and celebrate both the importance of the NWT in Canadian history and a distinctly northern accomplishment.

Federal interest in commemorating Hearne was slightly different. Although the Trudeau administration had famously expressed its insensitivity to Indigenous interests and rights in its 1969 White Paper, it was more alert than the GNWT to the political dangers of commemorating Indigenous massacres. The Historic Sites and Monuments Board, administered through Parks Canada, was interested in honouring the "discovery of the Coppermine River" and opted to locate its own plaque at the mouth of the river, in the town of Coppermine, rather than upriver at Bloody Falls, where the territorial plaque was to be erected.[46] In a June 1972 letter to Boxer, L.H. Robinson, regional director of the National and Historic Parks Branch of DIAND, made clear that "although the Historic Sites and Monuments Board of Canada objects to historical reference to the incident at Bloody Falls, and would prefer to have our plaque located elsewhere, we were wondering about the feasibility of having a joint federal-territorial commemorative ceremony to unveil the two plaques this fall."[47] The proposed federal plaque inscription did indeed avoid explicit mention of the Bloody Falls massacre, but certainly anyone with passing knowledge of Hearne's journey would catch its oblique references to the event:

> In July 1771 Samuel Hearne of the Hudson's Bay Company and a large party of Indians led by the Chipewyan, Matonabbee, reached the Coppermine River after an arduous seven-month trek from Fort Prince of Wales (Churchill) on Hudson Bay. Hearne found neither the great mine he sought nor a direct water route to the Pacific. On the return trip Hearne became the first European to see Great Slave Lake. His narrative of this journey is a masterpiece of Canadian travel literature.[48]

Federal and territorial interests would prove to be largely aligned throughout the plaque planning process, as both sought to enrol Qablunaaq heritage sites in the distant north into the national imaginary.

The federal and territorial boards were encouraged in their efforts by Lena Pedersen, Territorial Council member for the region and a resident of Coppermine. Of Greenlandic Inuit descent, Pedersen was the first woman (and Inuk woman) to be elected to the council and had apparently requested funds from the territorial government in 1971 to "celebrate the 200th anniversary of Samuel Hearne's visit of July 17, 1771."[49] The celebration involved the erection of a cairn by the local Boy Scouts. One year later, the settlement manager described the cairn as already "somewhat deteriorated" and in need of replacement, suggesting that this "community" commemorative act might not have been as well received as territorial officials had hoped.[50] Although Boxer's correspondence indicated that Pedersen and her husband, Red, were "completely behind the erection of this monument," an internal memo to Commissioner Hodgson quoted Lena as saying that "others in the community, particularly a number of young Eskimos, are against it. The young Eskimos say we should not commemorate the visit of a white explorer, and the massacre of a number of Eskimos by the Indians who traveled with him. They have influenced the council, although Lena is still entirely in favour of the monument."[51]

Red Pedersen casts suspicion on this version of events, claiming that neither he nor Lena would have supported such an initiative.[52] In fact, the Pedersens had helped establish the very forum through which the community's "young Eskimos" were articulating their objections: the Coppermine Settlement Council.[53] Settlement councils were established by the Hodgson administration as a move toward representative government at the local level, motivated in large part by the recommendations of the federal Carrothers Commission of the mid-1960s, which studied the future of government in Northwest Territories. Carrothers identified "a strong desire, among both indigenes and whites, for local self-government and for political responsibility" and recommended the creation of a territorial "department of Local Government," which would implement representative government structures at the settlement level. He insisted that the implementation of meaningful and responsive institutions at the local level was "crucial to the economic, social, and political development of the north ... Decentralization is of first importance." Hodgson seems to have taken this recommendation to heart. Notably, both he and Carrothers saw local government structures as transformative bodies that would educate Inuit in democratic principles and processes, not as the means to articulate distinct rights or claims. Indeed, Carrothers recommended the creation of an "Institute of Political Affairs" that would engage in "grass roots political education" among Indigenous peoples; tellingly, it was to be staffed by anthropologists.[54]

With their exceedingly narrow mandates and paltry budgets, the settlement councils seemed designed to function more as practice governments than as venues for meaningful representation or self-determination.[55] Hodgson evinced a genuine commitment to their implementation, however; Amagoalik recalls that "Hodgson used to travel all over the territory. He tried to visit every single community at least once a year," and he "used to say that he was working himself out of a job. He knew that he was only filling a void in the political leadership which would one day be filled by northerners themselves."[56] The deferral of meaningful Indigenous government to a future "one day" is telling (and ongoing). As Tania Murray Li has so persuasively argued, the "will to improve" colonized peoples on the part of their self-appointed "trustees" is a hallmark of governmental power, and it is accompanied by claims that colonized peoples are unable to manage themselves.[57] She suggests, moreover, that governmental power is actually strengthened by moves to enhance the representation and agency of those being governed: "To govern means to act on the actions of subjects who retain the capacity to act otherwise."[58] Governmental power abhors the autocratic and dictatorial and instead works through persuasion, consultation, and the reorganization of relationships. Settlement councils, as conceived in the late 1960s and early 1970s, seem to exemplify this dynamic.

According to Robert McPherson, Inuit at this time were keenly aware that, even as "the people were being encouraged to assume a larger responsibility for their affairs through settlement councils ... the real power and authority remained in the hands of the government."[59] Indeed, a 1980 follow-up report to the Carrothers Commission found that

> there are ... complaints that local governments in the NWT are, in effect, administrative extensions of the GNWT, and used for the sole purpose of delivering its programs. Local councils and committees are perceived by the communities as possessing no real authority over those issues that are of vital importance to the lives of residents of the communities. The territorial and federal governments consider the local councils and committees to be their agents, or merely advisory bodies, and not part of a separate and distinct level of government. Thus, the same phenomenon occurs at the community level as at the territorial level: despite the existence of fully elected representative bodies, there is a sense of powerlessness and a feeling that government is being "administered" from afar. The principles of accountable and responsive government are not being fulfilled.[60]

Inuit nevertheless made use of the settlement councils to articulate their interests. Amagoalik suggests that Inuit involvement in the councils and other political forums expanded during the 1960s and 1970s as part of a transition in leadership:

> It was in the early sixties that we started to feel anger, not for the first time, but we started to express it openly. It was around this time that the Inuit were going through a transition in leadership. There was a younger generation becoming community leaders. This new generation of leaders was educated, not in the university sense, but was able to speak English, and had some education. They were the first generation of Inuit leaders who really started to express our frustrations.[61]

Amagoalik recalls that the generation of Inuit who attended residential schools during the 1960s and '70s were politicized by the civil rights movement, the American Indian movement, and by the realization that Inuit across the North were experiencing similar things. It was at residential school in Churchill that Amagoalik and other students started to think about "how we were going to change the Arctic."[62] Other Inuit leaders also attribute the rise of the Inuit land claim and self-determination movements in part to residential schooling, although they also insist on the high social and personal costs of this schooling.[63] As Peter Ittinuar observes, "the only way to ... stop being a colonial figure administered from afar, a colonial subservient semi-oppressed type of person ... was to become white, was through politics."[64] James Arvaluk describes the adoption of "white" politics and practices – and participation in "democratically elected [settlement] councils" specifically – as a strategic "trade-off" born out of necessity; it was a means of advancing Inuit interests at a time when traditional forms of political organization repeatedly failed to affect the decisions of government, missionaries, and the RCMP.[65] Tester and Kulchyski echo Arvaluk's observation, suggesting that "a basic lack of respect for traditional leaders and political values generally informed the judgments and approaches of government staff in Arctic administration [through the postwar era]."[66] The "young Eskimos" of Kugluktuk who used their democratically elected settlement council to resist the erection of plaques commemorating Samuel Hearne and Bloody Falls did so not so much as an exercise in the formation of territorial and national citizenship, then, but rather as part of a new strategy for the articulation of Inuit interests.

The grounds for their objection to the plaques were both practical and symbolic. As Simon Taipana outlined in his initial telex, the settlement council felt that any monies spent in Coppermine should be allocated to more urgent priorities: providing running water and bathing facilities in government rental housing. Although Qablunaaq government employees had long enjoyed homes with solid construction, effective heating, electricity, and running water, most Coppermine residents had only recently moved into "match-box" government rental housing, which was hastily built, difficult to heat, and without running water. These houses were meant to replace the scrap material structures that Kugluktukmiut had built for themselves as they settled in Coppermine. A 1963 report submitted to DIAND regarding housing conditions in Coppermine describes the housing that many Kugluktukmiut still lived in during the early 1970s and underscores the urgency of Taipana's demands for improvement:

> The scrap houses are constructed of a wood frame, generally of wood from packing cases, with canvas on the outside (the outside covering varies from canvas to sheet metal, cardboard or skins). The insides of these houses are generally floored, although in several cases they are not, and the material most generally used is the lumber from surplus packing cases. Insulation is generally lacking, although in one or two cases cardboard and moss is being used. None of the wood or scrap houses have chemical toilets or electricity. The sanitation problems caused by this are only accentuated by the fantastic overcrowding that exists ... In the homemade houses the average is only 23.3 square feet per person ... Due to the limitations of the building material, used walls must be frequently patched and buttressed, and even when banked with snow during the winter cannot keep out the wind and extreme cold. In the spring the melting snow turns the canvas and cardboard outer walls into a soggy sodden mass, and the interiors become damp and inordinately cold.[67]

This description requires contextualization. It was written by E.M. Cotterill, a Qablunaaq government official with an interest in amplifying the unsuitability of Inuit housing, and was informed by a racialized understanding of the links between housing, family, and health. His description highlights the reach of government into the minutiae of daily life and identifies a problem that government officials could then proceed to solve. Notably, his report was penned at a time when significant numbers of Kugluktukmiut were being evacuated from the community to tuberculosis hospitals in the South. Anthropologist Richard Condon suggests that 11.3 percent of Coppermine residents were sent away for treatment between 1962 and 1966, their infection rates attributed to overcrowding in the housing Cotterill described and to other "failings" in sanitation, hygiene, and diet.[68] But the report nevertheless conveys something of the contrast between the government housing provided for Qablunaat and the housing resources available to Inuit residents. Taipana's demand for pressure systems and running water in the new rental homes built for Inuit reflected community concerns about their poor quality, particularly in relation to the superior homes built for Qablunaaq residents. Although territorial officials were at pains to "explain" that the budget for settlement housing was a federal matter and that their own small heritage plaque budget would barely cover the costs of upgrading a single house, this claim did not "make much impact on the Council," which was familiar with the inertia and obfuscation made possible by the parsing of bureaucratic jurisdictions.[69]

The council's insistence that Kugluktukmiut have a say in determining budgetary priorities, including the many federal and territorial budgets that so shaped settlement life, exemplifies the clashing sense of what settlement councils were meant to achieve. While the NWT Historical Advisory Board had hoped simply to inform the people of Coppermine, via the settlement council, of its intentions to mount a plaque (over which the council had no official jurisdiction), Kugluktukmiut were using the council as a forum to convey community needs and to express their demands to government in general, regardless of jurisdiction. They were asserting their jurisdiction over their own affairs and reorienting governmental power toward their own ends. This reorientation resonates with what Peter Kulchyski describes as a "specific logic of resistance that takes place in Aboriginal politics in northern Canada: a logic of subversion, whereby structures or gestures or policies of the dominant order are turned against themselves, are operated so as to achieve an effect that is precisely the opposite of the one aimed for."[70] Tania Murray Li has similarly observed that governmental "improvement programs" stimulate their own undoing and subversion, however inadvertently, in part because they invent and address a coherent group, thus stimulating a kind of group consciousness and enhancing the legibility of the group's claims. People who had hitherto identified themselves as Nagjuqturmiut, Ahiarmiut, Uadliaruhirmiut, and other "-miut" (referring to the regional and seasonal patterns of specific groups of Inuinnait), or on other terms of affiliation and identity, had been assembled at Coppermine, and every government program that addressed them as such facilitated their ability to articulate common interests and demands.[71]

These common interests and demands extended beyond Coppermine and were increasingly articulated with a pan-Inuit movement toward land claims. Kugluktukmiut were acutely concerned that the erection of plaques at Bloody Falls or in town would compromise their "Land Rights."[72] Government officials dismissed their concerns, and Sperry later went so far as to point out the "irrelevance" of land rights to the question of heritage plaques, but the council's suspicions were well founded. Informed, no doubt, by the legal insights shared at the Coppermine Conference in 1970, Kugluktukmiut were well aware that the transfer of federal Crown land to territorial control, whether through explicit ownership or through usage, paved the way for the extinguishment of Inuit title. Kugluktukmiut were adamant that Kugluk (Bloody Falls) was Inuit land, and they feared that the erection of government monuments would compromise their control over its use and ultimately undermine their intention to claim Aboriginal title over both it and the surrounding lands.

They were right to be concerned. On 24 April 1969, the GNWT had submitted a request to DIAND to reserve federal Crown land on both sides of Bloody Falls for the creation of a "future historical and archeological site."[73] Two weeks later, the GNWT revised its submission to request "a parcel of land commencing one mile above Bloody Falls on the Coppermine River and extending downstream to the southerly boundary of the community of Coppermine," in effect requesting control over the most intensively used stretch of the Coppermine River.[74]

Use of the river and Bloody Falls was, in fact, precisely what the GNWT aimed to curtail. Robert McGhee, the archaeologist who had led excavations at Bloody Falls during the previous summers, wrote to Commissioner Stuart Hodgson in October 1968, expressing his concerns that the "archeological value of the site (which is great – it looks as if it has been an excellent fishing spot for several millennia) could be partially or largely destroyed through the construction of buildings on the site, without contravening any existing antiquities legislation."[75] Hodgson had actually visited Bloody Falls during the excavations and was apparently supportive of any measures to protect "Territorial antiquities." McGhee informed Hodgson that his efforts to have Bloody Falls declared a national historic site had been unsuccessful and that he had been advised that the GNWT "would have much greater control over the site, since you would have to issue licenses for the establishment of tourist camps or outcabins in the area," most of which would have been built by Inuit. It seems, moreover, that the notion of "preserving" the site and marking "the location of Hearne's massacre ... [with] a cairn or plaque" came directly from McGhee.[76] The GNWT's interest, then, inspired by

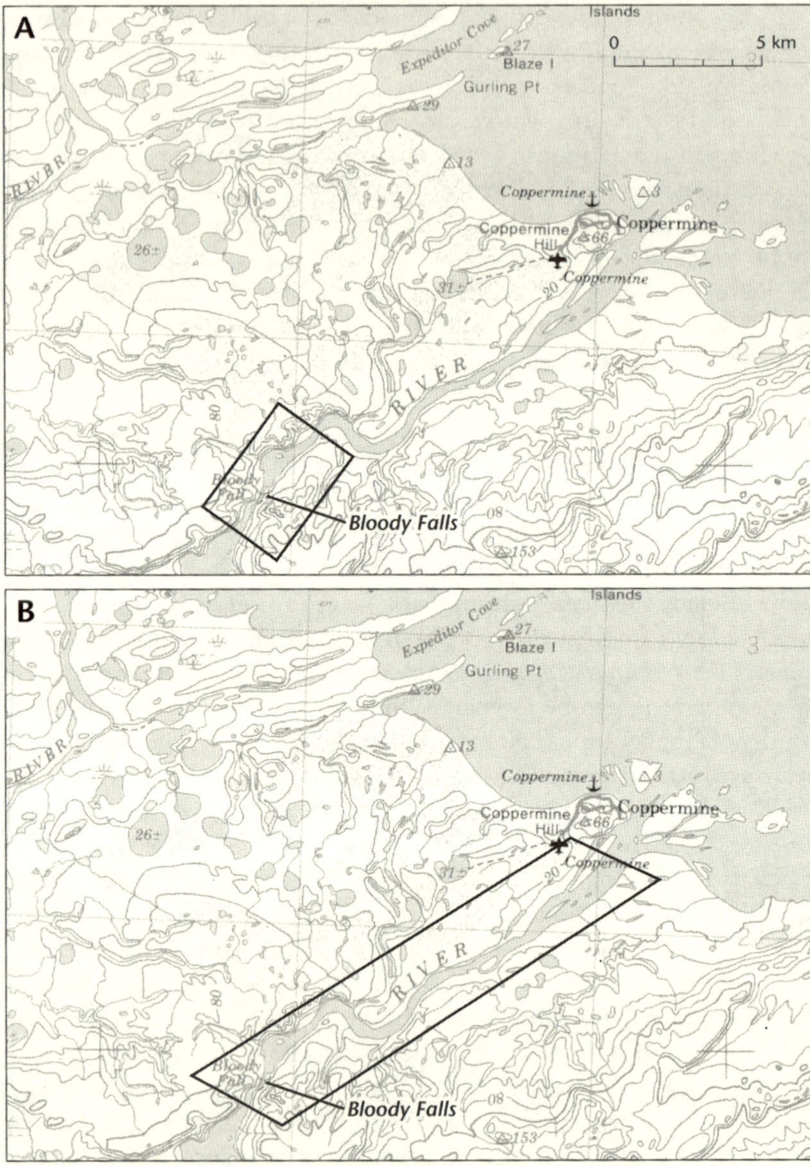

Requests to reserve federal Crown land for territorial use, as submitted by the GNWT to DIAND, 24 April 1969 ("A") and 8 May 1969 ("B").

McGhee, was not merely to mark a historical site but rather to control a roughly fifty square kilometre stretch of land and river that was crucially important to Kugluktukmiut. As Kugluktuk elder Alice Ayalik pointed out, "When white man put monument in places, they always start to do research and work, and start to say Inuit can't use that land ... It's our hunting place, our drinking water; it's our water tank and we'll have a hard time if they try to do something with Bloody Falls."[77]

Joe Allen Evyagotailak, former MLA for Kugluktuk, recalls that opposition to the plaques was driven as much by the concerns of elders as by the "young Eskimos" who had "taken over" the settlement council: "The people who knew the history, the elders, they said if Samuel Hearne didn't stop them, those Chipewyan, from killing their people then why should they have a monument for him? Samuel Hearne stood back without trying to stop it, maybe he couldn't stop them, but the elders didn't want to see that monument." According to Evyagotailak, elders were particularly concerned about being confronted with unwanted, painful memories when they visited the falls: "If they wanted to go up to the falls to fish, spend the day fishing with their family or something, they didn't want to have to see something like that monument to remind them of it ... Inuit don't like to remember what really happened,"[78] a sentiment that is still commonly expressed in Kugluktuk today. Rosemarie Meyok echoed this recollection of community resistance to the plaques: "The community at the time did not want to be reminded of the massacre because so many of our ancestors were killed there, and they refused to have that monument."[79] Whether community members objected on the grounds of not wanting to be reminded of a traumatic past, or because they took exception to outsider control over their lives, lands, and histories, Kugluktukmiut were resoundingly united in their objection to the monuments. In September 1972, they voted fifty-three to two against the plaques.[80]

The rejection of government regimes by Indigenous communities is often attributed to "the people's failure to understand what is good for them," and the plaque dispute was indeed read, initially, as a matter that might be resolved if only the people could be made to understand the importance of both Hearne and the heritage monument.[81] Alarmed at the level of resistance to the proposed plaques, Hodgson asked Anglican Reverend John Sperry, a member of the NWT Historical Advisory Board who had recently completed twenty years of missionary work in Coppermine, to visit the community and "explain" their importance to the people. Sperry travelled to Coppermine and presided over a community meeting on 25 October 1972. According to Sperry's report to Hodgson,

> The [community hall] was full and after Colin [Adjun, settlement council chair] introduced me I told the story of Samuel Hearne at fair length in Eskimo ... I pointed out the irrelevance of the land settlement issues and stressed that if the plaques could be placed with honour, then there would

> be a great tourist attraction apart from the important factor of preserving history. The chairman publicly admitted that he had never heard the full story before and it was an obvious surprise to many to hear that Hearne did not organize and lead the attack on the Eskimo village!! There were a few enquiries and a lot of enthusiasm although I cautioned that perhaps they should think the whole thing out at leisure and then write to inform you of their final decision.[82]

The suggestion that the people should "think the whole thing out at leisure" is not incidental; a hallmark of governmental power is the rejection of the use of physical violence or explicit coercion to achieve its ends. Without access to violence, governmental trustees can "operate only by educating the desires and reforming the practices of the target population" under the pretense that people can choose not to be reformed; in order for governmental power to function, it is crucial that subjects "retain the capacity to act otherwise."[83] Sperry was optimistic about his education of Kugluktukmiut. He enthused that he anticipated a "favourable reply" from them regarding the monuments and hoped that "this great hero of history" would soon be "preserved forever in formal plaquing."[84] Hodgson forwarded copies of Sperry's letter to territorial and federal departments, who were indeed "encouraged to learn from Rev. Sperry's letters that the Eskimos now show a *clearer understanding* of the purpose of erecting the plaques."[85]

Upon his return to Yellowknife, Sperry also wrote to Colin Adjun to thank him for calling the community meeting and under the pretense that "perhaps I should write down a few things so that my words can be kept on your files if any should ask more questions." The letter reads rather more like a directive. It is in this letter that Sperry's effectiveness as an agent of the territorial government is laid bare, an effectiveness made possible by his intimate knowledge of Inuit language, beliefs, and concerns. Consider his opening remarks:

> All people like to remember the past and the Eskimo people have always done this. Sometimes they remember the happy things which happened and sometimes they remember sad things. Inuenigit is that island not far from Coppermine we call Dead Man's Island. That name is like a plaque which remembers an unhappy time when people died there one summer long ago. There are lakes around named after the first man who caught a fish there and so forth. Today we still name lakes and islands after people but putting up a plaque with writing on is a better way because it tells the

story better. Both the Government of the N.W.T. and the Federal Government wish to remember Samuel Hearne with plaques.[86]

Sperry went on to summarize the main points he had made at the meeting, including the claim that "on the whole trip [Hearne] was not really the boss and it seems that most of the Indians only helped Hearne because the chief Indian Matonabbee made them." According to Sperry, Hearne "could do nothing to stop the Indian war party," and when he "called for mercy they laughed at him and mocked him. After, Hearne said that he wept to see such a killing of men, women, and children." Sperry assured Adjun that no plaques would be erected without the consent of the people and that they would not mention the "unhappy killing of the Eskimos"; instead, they would "just say that Hearne was the first whiteman to see the Arctic Ocean." As a member of the Historical Advisory Committee ("a meeting of people who think about oldtime things and happenings"), Sperry assured Adjun that "putting a plaque in the Coppermine area had nothing to do with Land Settlement or land ownership. The land business is a very different matter and you can believe the Commissioner's word on this as you can on other matters."

Sperry concluded his letter with a stern observation: "One other important matter, Colin, is that if there is one plaque or two put up to remember Samuel Hearne, then this will be known everywhere outside and we can expect more tourists to visit Coppermine taking pictures and bringing trade with them; this is very important." The grandiose materiality of this claim is striking – the notion that the mere erection of a plaque would alert everyone outside of Coppermine to its existence and prompt their visits surely raised legitimate doubts among Kugluktukmiut. But Sperry's claim was not out of line with government visions. Tourism had become an increasingly important component of the GNWT's economic development plans as fur trapping declined. A tourism plan developed in the late 1960s in fact identified Coppermine as a promising site for tourism and included plans to re-create a Copper Inuit village and provide other amenities to attract tourists.[87] Tourism has never been a lucrative industry in Coppermine, however. Kerry Horn, current owner of the Coppermine Inn, claims that during his twenty-five years of managing the business, only one visitor has come to Kugluktuk specifically to see Bloody Falls, and this was archaeologist Robert McGhee.[88]

Although Sperry reported to Hodgson that he had suggested the people of Coppermine contemplate the proposed plaques at their leisure, he was much more precise in his letter to Adjun. Sperry suggested that Adjun inform the commissioner of their final decision within two weeks. Adjun took six months, ignoring several requests from the GNWT, and his eventual response is revealing:

April 25/73

Re Samuel Hearne Plaquing

At a public meeting regarding the above the people of Coppermine voted in favor of allowing this cairn to be erected after Mr Sperry had been in town telling the people of his and the Historical Advisory Board's wishes

Colin Adjun
Chairman
Coppermine Settlement Council
Coppermine NWT[89]

Clearly missing the accusatory tone of Adjun's reply, territorial officials immediately revived the plaque program and began planning for an unveiling ceremony that very summer. Internal correspondence reveals, in fact, that plans had already been made and that the GNWT was merely waiting for word from Coppermine that the people would "condone the erection of the historic marker" so that it could proceed with the arrangements.[90] The unveiling of the two plaques would be presided over by an impressive group of officials from across the country, including DIAND minister Jean Chrétien and his wife, Stuart Hodgson and his wife, the chairs of the federal and territorial historic sites boards, Lena Pedersen, Reverend Sperry, various other federal and territorial officials, and Colin Adjun, chair of the settlement council. Peter Kamingoak was identified as a translator for the event, and the agenda included time for Inuit drumming, games, and the singing of songs by local children. Plaque inscriptions were translated into Inuinnaqtun; plaque designs were debated and commissioned; and extensive memos mulled over entertainment, food, gifts, bottles of water, appropriate footwear, supplies of life jackets for the boat ride to Bloody Falls, and other sundry details.

When Ted Boxer and R.B. Mitchell of the DIAND Parks Branch travelled to Coppermine on 9–10 July 1973 to make final arrangements, however, they were informed by Adjun that he "did not wish to take an active part in the ceremonies," raising concerns that "a situation might arise [during the plaque ceremony] which would be most embarrassing to the Commissioner and the Minister."[91] According to Boxer, Adjun said that "although the community were in favour of the plaques, the Council were still opposed, but would allow the commemoration because of the wishes of the community."[92] In effect, the council members would not block the ceremonies but refused to legitimize the plaques with their presence. Informed of this development, Sperry advised the government not to proceed with the ceremony "unless someone who knows the people at Coppermine were to attend," claiming to be unavailable himself due to holidays. The NWT Executive Committee met to discuss the situation and decided that "to pursue the plaquing ceremonies at this time would not be desirable."[93] Letters were sent to inform federal, territorial, and community representatives involved in the undertaking that the ceremonies were cancelled. Hodgson hoped to revive the matter the following year, but it would be more than thirty years before any signage was erected at Bloody Falls, and then under the auspices of the Government of Nunavut.

RESISTANCE STORIES?

Is this a resistance story? And if so, for whom? In many ways the dispute challenges the spatiality of resistance insofar as it locates resistance *within* governmental power structures rather than in a realm outside of and oppositional to "power." Throughout the dispute, Kugluktukmiut used governmental power structures such as the settlement council to promote their interests, which were to undermine governmental power over their lands and their history and to assert their jurisdiction over local decision making. Although the Coppermine settlement council had no authority over the erection of federal and territorial plaques, or over the lands upon which the monuments would stand, Kugluktukmiut made use of the structure to give the impression that local governmental approval had been denied. Adjun's refusal to attend the unveiling ceremony was not the refusal of a single resident of Coppermine; it was the refusal of the settlement council chair, and as such it presented the possibility of embarrassment at what was supposed to be a celebration of local as much as territorial and national history. Colonial and postcolonial scholars have long argued that resistance is a form of relation structured by colonial power, drawing on Foucault's primary insight that "where there is power, there is resistance."[94] But as anthropologist Lila Abu-Lughod observes, scholars have tended to hang on to a romanticized understanding of resistance as "a reactive force somehow independent of or outside of the system of power," rather than attending to the ways in which acts and expressions of resistance reveal parallel acts and expressions of power. She argues that the value of studying moments of resistance lies not so much in their "hopeful confirmation of the failure – or partial failure – of systems of oppression," but rather in "letting [resistant] practices teach us about the complex interworkings of historically changing structures of power."[95] Her insight is instructive: the opposition of Kugluktukmiut to the proposed plaques reveals as much about changing forms of power in postwar NWT as it does about Inuit strategies to resist that power.

The shape of that power, moreover, can be understood as a form of colonial governmentality, "which was concerned above all with disabling old forms of life by systematically breaking down their conditions, and with constructing in their place new conditions so as to enable – indeed, so as to *oblige* – new forms of life to come into being."[96] The decades leading up to the plaque dispute were characterized by an intensification of federal and territorial interests in shaping governable subjects, in remaking the relations between Inuit and their lands, homes, and bodies so as to create a wholly new North and a wholly new Indigenous subject. It was, in Foucault's terms, a moment of intense interest in "the conduct of conduct." Settlement councils were central to this project, and they succeeded in producing new terms for the conduct of political activity. They also generated new forms of resistance insofar as they enabled Inuit to articulate their interests in terms that would be legible and effective. But as Ittinuar and Arvaluk both observe, engaging these new forms of power was a trade-off; it required "becoming white." New forms of life and new forms of being were indeed enabled through participation in settlement councils; in a sense, the very acts of resistance described here – writing letters, voting, refusing to appear as council chair at the unveiling ceremony – were themselves expressions of the reach of new forms of governmental power into the lives of Kugluktukmiut. One can read in the plaque dispute, in that sense, both the intensification of colonial governmental power in Coppermine and new strategies for resisting such incursions.

But to hold up the dispute as a story of Inuit resistance to Qablunaaq obsessions with Bloody Falls would not entirely do justice to the events of 1972–73. Such a narrative would require storying Reverend Sperry as a coercive religious authority who extracted an uneasy acquiescence from Kugluktukmiut and whose claims about a converted, enthusiastic audience were exaggerated in service of his own interests and identity. Or, perhaps, it would require figuring Sperry as a more benign agent of governmental power who aimed to educate the desires of his subjects – rendering him no less a colonial villain – and to imagine, in turn, that the people of Coppermine were ultimately unmoved by his wishes and conspired to defeat the plaques in other ways. These would make for good postcolonial resistance stories. Such stories have their place, and they may well characterize aspects of the dispute. Speaking in Inuinnaqtun and playing upon the sensibilities of the people he knew so well, Sperry was able to convince the people of Kugluktuk to consent to the erection of territorial and federal plaques commemorating Samuel Hearne and Bloody Falls, consent that a range of bureaucrats had repeatedly failed to secure. He was particularly well suited to "educating the desires" and "reforming the practices" of Kugluktukmiut because of the intimate relationship he had with so many of them, an intimacy that carried with it different risks and stakes than those informing relations between Kugluktukmiut and anonymous government officials in Yellowknife. In the early 1970s, missionaries still wielded a great deal of authority in communities like Coppermine, underlining the personal risks involved in challenging Sperry's "wishes" and the precarity associated with overt acts of resistance in a small, isolated settlement.[97]

I am inclined to argue, however, that an analysis of the events of 1972–73 can accommodate both a critique of Sperry's power and a certain hesitancy, an unwillingness to force the complexities of the dispute into a "charmed" storyline in which the good and the evil occupy clear and separate realms.[98] A charmed account of the conflict, Ann Laura Stoler notes, would rely on stock figures engaged in a transcendent rather than a specific struggle, and would require rallying analytically slack, historically inaccurate, and ultimately politically limiting storylines to make sense of its inherent complexity and contradictions. It would require, among other things, discerning a shared oppositional consciousness among Kugluktukmiut, including a shared opposition to Sperry. In such a narrative, it becomes difficult to acknowledge that Kugluktukmiut continually invoke Sperry as a trusted and respected religious figure. Peter Kamingoak, the outspoken local delegate at the Coppermine Conference, was one of Sperry's closest friends and guides, and many attribute the high proportion of Anglicans in Kugluktuk to the strength of Sperry's character and his long-term commitment to building relationships with Kugluktukmiut. This warmth and friendship did not necessarily diminish Sperry's power. On the contrary, friendship can be seen as a component of his power; it was a tactic, a modality, and it describes the shape of his influence.[99] But the affection that many Kugluktukmiut express for Sperry complicates any account that would position him as a colonial villain. Furthermore, what if we were to take seriously Sperry's claim that the room was full of enthusiasm as he spoke to the packed community hall that evening in October? If he was received as warmly as he claimed, and if a good number of Kugluktukmiut were indeed moved by his words, does this necessarily jar with prior and subsequent opposition to the plaques? For "metropolitan enthusiast[s] of 'third world resistance,'" the possibility that Kugluktukmiut changed their minds after hearing Sperry speak can figure only as a sign of their domination, for, as Spivak observes, conventional resistance stories require "self-knowing, politically canny subalterns" united against their oppressors. The possibility that some Kugluktukmiut did, indeed, change their minds following Sperry's visit can only figure as a sign of their manipulation and victimization, not as a thoughtful decision made by members of a diverse and complicated community, in complicated times.[100]

As Amagoalik notes, Inuit "discovered" their powerlessness at particular moments and under particular circumstances; they did not conceive of themselves as a wholly oppressed people, and many still do not. The formation of a coherent, resistant Inuit community is as much an *effect* of colonial governmental power as it is a shared oppositional consciousness among Inuit. "Agreeing to say no" to the intrusions of outsiders has a historical geography, one that was emergent in the decades leading up to the plaque conflict, and one that requires ongoing effort to realize.[101] In a conventional resistance narrative, it becomes inconvenient that Lena Pedersen was an Inuk – how does one account for her allegedly vehement endorsement of the plaques in a story of "Inuit" resistance? Moreover, her advocacy for the people of Coppermine was constant and often oppositional: she stated publicly in 1974 that "the NWT Government moved North in 1967 to get closer to the people, but it has achieved only to get closer in miles to some communities. It is still as far as or further removed from the people as it ever was."[102] John Amagoalik recalls that the generation of Inuit who led the "transition" in leadership of the 1960s and '70s were thoroughly alienated from their parents and grandparents, and that when they returned to their home communities after residential school, their "rebellious attitudes" distanced them from others.[103] It would be misleading to characterize the actions of the young men who sat on the Coppermine Settlement Council as wholly representative of community concerns, but in the context of charmed postcolonial resistance stories, such a portrayal is not only compelling, it is essential.

A better approach may lie in considering both the capacity and terms upon which Kugluktukmiut were able to respond to the plaques *and* the geographies informing those responses. As their correspondence with the territorial government made clear, Kugluktukmiut felt an acute sense of responsibility for the land and for ensuring a successful land claim. Their rejection of the plaques was grounded in this sense of responsibility. Kugluktukmiut responded to a situation that angered and worried them by using whatever means lay at their disposal, including the languages and structures of Qablunaaq colonial government. Their strategy was driven by their interest in *being heard;* acts of power and resistance must be legible to be effective. And although government agents operated under the colonial assumption that Inuit had no forms of political organization prior to the arrival of Qablunaat (a misapprehension that continues to circulate even today), it is crucial to acknowledge that the strategies, claims, and concerns articulated by Inuit through their involvement in Qablunaaq institutions and structures were thoroughly informed by their own knowledges, practices, values, and forms of governance.

Jackie Price notes that Inuit governance is centrally concerned with the land. It is informed by intimate relations with the land, and it aims to maintain harmonious relations among Inuit and between Inuit and the nuna. Price suggests that the sites of authority in Inuit governance systems are not governments or other formal institutions, but rather "*maligait* [things that had to be followed], relationships, family, spirituality, experience, leadership, willingness and support given by people, [and] action." Practices of governance aim at "spiritual balance [and] harmony within individuals and amongst community members," not particular policies or political gains.[104] However much Inuit were engaging Qablunaaq styles of political organization, refutation, and decision making in the 1970s, they continued to nurture forms of practice and belief that were anchored in their own cultural and political context. It is crucial to acknowledge these practices and beliefs, however much they were opaque to colonial administrators and however much they remain largely misunderstood and illegible to Qablunaat today. If "resistance" only registers when it is confrontational, oppositional, and legible, then it should come as no surprise that this dispute over heritage plaques remains one of the few formal moments of Inuit resistance to the storying of Bloody Falls. Kugluktukmiut resisted in written form, in English, and through an elected representative; their telegrams and offhand comments are logged in territorial and federal archives and filed by appropriate department; they voted. And this was precisely the point. Other responses have not been *aimed* at governmental or colonial audiences. They are anchored in geographies that cannot be reduced to colonial power relations or to the filters of institutional legibility.

STORYING RESISTANCE

In order to story the events of 1972–73 in more expansive and complex terms, a distinction must be made between the ways in which Inuit, as colonized subjects, relate to colonial institutions, figures, and practices, and the ways in which they relate to themselves and others *as Inuit,* and by way of practices, relations, and subjectivities that both predate colonial intervention and live on in this colonial present. Government efforts to reshape the conduct of Inuit conduct intersected with, and often jarred with, the conduct of conduct in Inuit governance systems. That is, the rationalities, ethics, and intentions that shaped Inuit responses to the plaques must be understood not only in relation to the rise of governmental power in the North, but also as forms of conduct grounded in Inuit beliefs, values, aspirations, and governance systems. Although, as Jackie Price documents, Inuit governance systems have long been overlooked, dismissed, and even framed as non-existent by colonial scholars and administrators, there are clear models and guidelines for how to conduct oneself in Inuit society, including not only modes of making collective decisions, regulating social behaviour, and resolving disagreements, but also ways of living in relation to other beings and the land. Arguably, finding ways to conduct onself as an Inuk – in ways that emerge from and maintain Inuit values, knowledges, and practices in the face of ongoing governmental efforts to reshape the conduct of Inuit conduct – has been a central struggle in the postwar era.[105]

Foucault understood as "counter-conduct" any mode of conducting oneself that is outside the scope of acceptable conduct. Counter-conduct, he argued, is not necessarily self-consciously oppositional or politically intentional; it can include madness, deviance, or other forms of behaviour that do not necessarily aim to challenge dominant power structures but that nevertheless fail to conform with the terms of acceptable conduct. In the context of the plaque controversy, this term is suggestive. It allows a distinction to be made between self-consciously oppositional behaviour aimed at Qablunaaq institutions, by means of Qablunaaq forms of expression and organization, and the dimensions of this conduct that exceed colonial frames of understanding or legibility. "Resistance," then, can be understood as one of many possible tactics that might be employed by people aiming to maintain or recuperate a degree of control over their lives. Kugluktukmiut did, indeed, actively and strategically resist the erection of heritage plaques in the 1970s, and though their actions must not be seen as the pinnacle of a movement to resist imaginative geographies of Bloody Falls, they nevertheless involved calculated and courageous action. This moment of resistance was shaped by an emerging political culture among Kugluktukmiut that was articulated with broader political movements across the Arctic and beyond, and these cultures and movements were themselves shaped by the intensification of governmental power in postwar NWT and related interests in economic and political development in the North. The interdigitation of governmental power and Inuit resistance does not make the latter any less compelling or authentic. Resistance involved work, practice, risk, and the creative reorientation of programs and policies designed to do otherwise. But neither should specific acts of resistance be mistaken as the pinnacle of Inuit relations with colonization, at the expense of acknowledging the spectrum of practices, relationships, and modes of life that Inuit nurtured and maintained at this time.

The ambivalences, contradictions, and questions raised by studying – and storying – this event are highly instructive and suggest that moments of Indigenous resistance to colonial incursions must be accounted for not only in relation to the broader geographies that nourish them, but also in relation to Qablunaaq desires to conjure stories of anti-colonial resistance. Indeed, it seems to me that scholars grounded in postcolonial theories of resistance risk misapprehending the very limited scope of Inuit action that was directly aimed at colonial power as the entirety of Inuit action, even consciousness. Such studies begin with an assumption of colonial domination and seek out moments of resistance to it, in an intellectual context where such resistance is thought to be always, already, futile. I argue here that Inuit in the 1970s did not conceive of themselves as wholly colonized; whenever they attempted to engage with the systems of colonial government, they would "discover," as Amagoalik put it, that they were oppressed, disadvantaged, colonized. And they strategically intervened in such settings to advance their interests, to articulate and assert command over their lands and lives. But Inuit were only produced as colonial subjects within colonial institutions and through colonial relations, which were, at this time, intensifying their scope and reach, as schools, sanatoria, police, northern administrators, welfare systems, settlement councils, and other institutions were being implemented. Through these institutions, Inuit repeatedly encountered the disadvantage they were structurally positioned to occupy. But the terms upon which colonial governments and agents recognized Inuit were not the same terms upon which Inuit recognized themselves.

It seems to me, then, that if one were to read Inuit responses to the proposed plaques as the culmination of anti-colonial sentiment about Bloody Falls, and as a rejection of the story itself, one would not only miss some of the key concerns animating their refusal – such as land claims, adequate housing, and the importance of meaningful control over local governance – but also fail to see how little this story *matters* to Kugluktukmiut. If Inuit resist the story and reject the story, they remain in conversation with Qablunaat; they remain bound to a shared story and a shared history in which Qablunaat can see themselves. If they ignore it, however, if they refuse to care or to acknowledge it, Qablunaat are exposed as peripheral, forgotten, and illegitimate. The partiality of our stories, of our brief forays onto a land that holds much more significant, rich stories, is made apparent to us. Why should "everyone outside" come to know of Bloody Falls? What rightful place does this story occupy? What would happen if it *did not matter*? The Bloody Falls massacre story has less capacity to matter without material traces: a plaque is not simply symbolic – it is a material anchor that allows Bloody Falls to matter in consequential ways. And by extension, Qablunaat have less capacity to matter, less material claim, over a land in which they have no stories.

6
Toward an Emerging Past

We cannot afford to run our lives in the small confines of the Government mind. The reason our views may seem strange and unrealistic is that no one ever bothered to take us seriously – to look closely at us as Dene people ... We are the only people who know and realize our worth as a unique people – as a people with our own land and way of living.
– Stephen Kakfwi, in Scott, *Stories Told*

There is no single, univocal way of not existing.
– Boaventura de Sousa Santos, "A Critique of Lazy Reason"

Southerners don't want to understand Inuit ways. They're ignorant about our culture, don't consider our opinion and treat us like we know nothing. Inuit culture is oral and we keep knowledge in our minds. Even without text, our culture is full of wisdom.
– Rita Nashook, in Martin, *Stories in a New Skin*

In the 1960s, if you made a trip to the Coppermine Northern Store to buy flour or ammunition, you would have been confronted with a wall-size mural recreating the Bloody Falls massacre. Complete with spurts of sand and blood, the mural now hides behind pallets of toilet paper, potato chips, and canned milk in what has become a storage building for the new Northern Store two blocks away. It's hard to find a moment in history when Qablunaat did not work to materialize Hearne's version of the Bloody Falls massacre in town. From Richardson's ragweed (see Chapter 3) to efforts to name streets and schools after Hearne,

Qablunaat have been telling and retelling the story not only in national films or postage stamps, things that are designed to circulate widely, but also through concrete, material iterations in Kugluktuk itself.

Some Qablunaaq residents of Kugluktuk claim that Inuit "don't know the storyline" of the massacre. "They know they don't like Indians, but they're not sure why." Despite their apparent lack of knowledge of the story, however, one resident claims that for Kugluktukmiut, the Bloody Falls massacre functions as a kind of signifier for animosity between Inuit and Indians, and in that sense, "Bloody Falls is still very much alive" in town. He links animosity between Inuit and Dene, as exemplified in the massacre story, to a number of political and social effects, including, most significantly, the creation of Nunavut. Not only was the movement to establish the territory of Nunavut "racially motivated" by Inuit who did not want to be represented by "Indians in Yellowknife," the resident suggests that the long years of negotiation leading up to its creation were significantly shaped by hostilities between Inuit and the Dene nations involved in the process. During the 1970s and '80s, when the Coppermine Inn hosted delegations of northern Indigenous land claims negotiators, Qablunaat allegedly spent time passing notes between the Inuit and Dene parties because they wouldn't speak to each other. And yet, even as Qablunaat acknowledge the important role they have played in glorifying and sustaining the story of the massacre, the resident suggests that the event was not necessarily that significant: "It was a nasty thing to happen, but not really that many people died ... Those were cruel times and standards of living were different." The story, in other words, has its rightful place – in history books, in murals, but not in matters of territorial politics.

The notion that Inuit knowledge of Bloody Falls is unreliable, incomplete, and an irrational basis for Inuit-Dene animosity is not uncommon among Qablunaat, both in Kugluktuk and beyond. In this chapter, I challenge both the claim that Inuit do not "know" the story of Bloody Falls and the idea that their relations with Dene have always been marked by war, whether with spears or through contemporary political disputes. I do so by calling attention to the rich and varied history of interaction between Inuit and their neighbours to the South (the Tłı̨chǫ and Sahtú Dene Nations) and by considering the ways in which Bloody Falls figures in contemporary relations between these peoples. Inuit storytelling about Bloody Falls, I argue, is shaped by geographies of responsibility and care that weave between past, present, and future, even – and perhaps especially – when that storying involves conscious acts of forgetting, refusal, and departure from the site itself. Kugluktukmiut story Bloody Falls as part of a productive, generative turn toward the worlds they want to live in; they story toward what they want to manifest, not against a hegemonic power. If story is a relational, material ordering practice, as I argue throughout this book, then here I aim to "take seriously," in Stephen Kakfwi's words, the relational, material, world-making practices through which Bloody Falls is both remembered and forgotten by Inuit, Dene, and the land.

To do so, I engage with Inuit writings about their relations with and responsibilities to the land.[1] There is a rich and diverse Qablunaaq philosophical tradition on responsibility, including reflections on the forms of responsibility that emerge from colonial and postcolonial relations. Much of this work emphasizes the responsibilities of the inheritors of colonial privilege toward those they have colonized, and understands responsibility in terms of moral and ethical obligation to redress and account for past wrongs.[2] These writings are important, but they tend not to examine the responsibilities that Indigenous peoples have to each other, to other beings, and to the land, or the ways that specific Indigenous peoples practise and conceptualize responsibility. Here, I work with an understanding of responsibility as it has been articulated by Inuit. As Jackie Price observes of Inuit relations with dog teams,

> Responsibility was treated for what it is: an everyday activity that could be broken down into practical actions. With dog teams, Inuit knew how they could support the dogs to allow them to maximize their potential. When the dog team maximized their potential, they were a critical support for Inuit survival. In short, Inuit knew what had to be done, and fit their lives around this responsibility. The goal was always survival.[3]

This understanding of responsibility as a contextual, relational, and practical orientation to the demands of the everyday, aimed at maximizing individual and collective well-being and survival, is continually invoked by Inuit in a range of settings.[4] It is a useful guide for making sense of the ways in which Kugluktukmiut both remember and forget Bloody Falls.

REMEMBERING BLOODY FALLS

What does it mean to remember the Bloody Falls massacre? I begin with Aime Ahegona, the first person who shared his understanding of the story with me. Aime grew up in Bernard Harbour, northwest of Kugluktuk, at the edges of a trading post established there in 1916. His grandparents adopted Diamond Jenness into their family during his stay at Bernard Harbour, and their daughter Qanajuq (Jennie), Aime's mother, features prominently in Jenness's notes.[5] Aime himself moved to Kugluktuk as a young man. He traces his lineage to Alaska, and although his family had maintained connections to the Kitikmeot region for almost a century by the time we spoke in 2006, he was careful to emphasize that he did not know the stories of this place:

> I don't think there would be too many [people], here, now, like, I think all these people in town now, they're mostly from outside of town and never raised in the area, so unless you wanted to talk to Peter Kamingoak, maybe he knows more about it, Bloody Falls area and that. Or Theresa Niptanatiak ... But, like, there was not too many people who had lived here before, but all I know is that Theresa Niptanatiak and Peter, they, not too many people who had lived here before except for those two. They're all coming from outside, from mainland, some people from further north ... But some people might have a history of it.

And so our conversation began with a displacement of sorts and a careful staking out of the geographies of storytelling authority. Aime would go on to share the "little bit of this and that" he had heard from others but was careful to emphasize that he did not *remember* the massacre story:

> I was never brought up here, in this area. I've heard a little bit of this and that, like *[pause]*, Samuel Hearne was a bad boy *[laughs]*. Brought all the Indian people and killed all the Inuit people *[pause]*. I don't know why these people do those things, like, you know, why they want to make war about, you know, no reason at all; it's just land, just the land. Whoever's been there before, they should be there before *[pause]*. What happened, what I've heard is that Samuel Hearne hired a guy to bring them down. So *[pause]* everyone would have been completely out, everybody would have been gone, except for a woman with a little baby on her back, and they said somebody was running after her and she fell on the ground and disappeared. Do you know how ptarmigans, grouse, ptarmigans are really camouflaged to the ground? It's what, what that story was about. She had attached a ptarmigan feather or thing like that, like, you could have been just about stepping on a bird when you were walking around; when they're nesting, you don't see them at all! So that's what

> that woman, I heard, with the baby, she just disappeared to nowhere because she had that power put into her body from those, like, old-time people, like I told you before. So I believe that somebody survived at that time. Like, I don't know much about all that Bloody Falls area, because I lived way up north, about 120 miles, where I was brought up, at Read Island and Bernard Harbour. Bernard Harbour, that's where my cabin is. That's where I was born ... I might have heard things about it, but from my kind of way, when I'm not sure I don't want to tell about it ... That's why I never wanted to say I'm telling you the story, like, you know, because I don't remember it.[6]

Aime thus laid out some of the openings and refusals, the translations and silences, and the hints and claims that shaped our meeting that day. He carefully staked out the limits of his authority; from his "kind of way," a person must not tell a story unless it can be told accurately. To remember is to remember fully and reliably, and anything short of that is to forget. From what I understand, remembering and forgetting are expressions of competency in Inuinnaqtun, not an indication of whether traces of a story or experience can be recalled.[7] If one is not competent enough to tell a story or perform a task well, it is better not to do or say anything than to do it poorly or inaccurately. Aime gestured toward stories he had heard, but did not remember them well enough to tell them.

Nellie Hikok also forgets the Bloody Falls massacre story. In the summer of 2007, she was ninety-seven years old and still living on her own. She was known to throw herself on the back of a snowmobile in the winter, and she still prepared her own caribou meat and skins. Nellie grew up and raised children on the land, and was middle-aged by the time she settled more permanently in Kugluktuk. A laughing and generous woman, she was also an enthusiastic storyteller. Like most people, moreover, Nellie did not want to tell the Bloody Falls massacre story. Through interpreter Mona Tiktalek, Nellie shared stories about travelling to the falls to fish with her husband. When asked about the massacre, she indicated she had heard the stories, but *"puiguqtunga,"* "she don't remember them quite well."[8] She offered, instead, to tell a story about "when all the females were killed out at 14 Mile Island." This was a familiar move. Nearly every elder I spoke with declined to discuss the Bloody Falls massacre but keenly recounted stories about Ikiaridlik, "Escape Hill."

Nellie told the story in rich detail. In her telling, unlike those offered by the men who shared this story with me, women and their survival are

Nellie Hikok, spring 2008. *Photo by Emilie Cameron.*

prominent themes. The story begins as women and children wait at their camp for the men to return from sealing:

> Long time ago when people started hunting seal or looking for seal, in the winter, they always used to leave the females behind. /[9] My mom used to tell me, because they never had calendars in those days, they only know when the sun is coming up and when it's starting to get warm weather all the men start going seal hunting and all the females are left behind with the children. The Indians came from the South and they poked [stabbed] all the ladies. / The kids really thought their fathers were coming, the seal hunters, but it was the Indians and they starting poking them. And when all the men came back to the camp it was really noisy because they were screaming and crying because all the ladies were killed. / Before the guys came, there was a mother and daughter, and the daughter had just had a baby and the afterbirth hadn't been put

anywhere yet because she'd just had her baby. And from the blubber lamp, you know the lamp that they used to use long ago? They started burning the afterbirth and it got really thick inside the igloo. They were trying to protect themselves, that's why they did this / … / They used to use ice blocks for windows in the igloos, and when those Indians came one by one and tried to jump inside the igloo, they opened the window and when they smelled that strong smell and they put the window back, one by one. / And when there was hardly anymore, you could hear the footsteps outside the igloo, when there was hardly anymore footsteps they started to relax. / When there was nobody around anymore, when they couldn't hear anymore footsteps, they looked outside and there was nobody around anymore. / And when it started to get dark the hunters started coming and you really could hear them screaming and crying, really crying, it was really noisy. / All the men were screaming and crying at first, and when they finally settled down they started trying to track the Indians by their trail on the snow. / From there they started to get ready with their harpoons and stuff they could use to kill. / When they were all set to go they gathered around outside and they prayed before they left. / They were standing outside praying, praying that the Indians would get heavy, so they didn't go far or fast. They really prayed for them to be heavy. / When they were all set to go they put clean clothes on and they started praying to the dead people to help them, to look after them. / When they were all set to go and they started going, this old lady was really tired. I guess she was really tired, she got really heavy and she got left behind [by the Indians]. So she started telling those guys that she's got really good something. How you call it? She's got really good stuff [vagina] and she's got really good needle and thread. I guess she didn't want to get killed when those Inuit catch up to her. Because she got really weak and heavy, I guess she got left behind. / They took her along and she started saying again that she's got really good something [vagina] and really good thimble and needle. When those people were praying to make the Indians weak, it really helped. They made this lady weak so she got left behind. / She was telling those guys that she's got everything good on her, needle and thread, thimble also, she's got everything good on her, and they kept saying "yeah yeah" and they really started poking [stabbing] her. / She kept saying that she's got really good something but I guess they got really mad at her because she was telling those Indians where all the ladies were. / When they finally stopped poking her, killing her, they said that lady was dead long ago but she came alive. / And when they finished killing that lady they started praying again so they could

> continue travelling and tracking those Indians. / They started praying again when they got all set to go. "Where's our relatives? The people who were killed?" Asking them, "Where are you? Where's our relatives so we could pray to win for you?" / And when they got to the Indians they were gathering with them. The Inuit started pointing to each other secretly that they'll kill the other ones. / There was no top on the igloo where the Indians were, the igloo the Indians had built, so they could kill them from the top. / Two Indians were saved because they ran away, they got saved and they ran up the hill, that's when they got saved. They saved themselves because they ran up the hill. And the Inuit couldn't get to them. And that hill they always call it, once in a while when we're camping we always see it, they call it Ikiaridlik. / They killed all the Indians that were staying in the igloo but two ran away and saved themselves so they started calling that land Ikiaridlik. / There was two ladies that got saved, they saved themselves, and two Indians saved themselves too because they climbed up the hill. / The End.[10]

The story of Ikiaridlik, in Nellie's telling, provides richer materials for contemplating life in the region, both past and present, than does Hearne's account of the massacre. In her story, Inuit are the central characters, and their decisions, actions, and feelings are foregrounded. The story details some of the precarity of life and the strategies Inuit employed to survive. On the face of it, Ikiaridlik is a massacre story, but it is told primarily as a survival story. The two Inuit women and the two Indian men are its heroes; in some versions, Inuit so admire the Indians' ingenuity in escaping that they allow them to live as a gesture of admiration and respect. While Hearne's account of the Bloody Falls massacre casts Inuit as helpless and hapless victims, the story of Ikiaridlik celebrates Inuit agency and resourcefulness. In Nellie's telling, the survival and ingenuity of women were particularly emphasized, and she went on to tell a series of other stories describing women's lives.

Nellie told me this story in August 2007, the morning after a young man had committed suicide in Kugluktuk. His was the ninth in a series of suicides that had rocked the small community that year.[11] Five days later, the hamlet council unanimously imposed an immediate ban on the importation and sale of alcohol in the community and began preparations for a plebiscite to impose more permanent restrictions "at the request of the community, and to ensure the safety of children and youth."[12] The community began to rally together to address the effects of suicide on their lives and to demand action. That same week, when discussing how research into the Bloody Falls massacre might intersect with community interests,

Millie Kuliktana, director of Kitikmeot School Operations and a keen proponent of Inuit-centred curriculum and Inuinnaqtun language retention, emphasized her interest in tracing the survivors of the Bloody Falls massacre and their descendants:

> It's because our elders persevered and survived the harsh world our ancestors lived in. That's why we are here today. If that could be recorded, if the young people could realize that they come from a tradition of survival, maybe that would help them avoid all these suicides ... Who are the actual descendants of those survivors [of the Bloody Falls massacre]? They should be part of that history, saying "We're the survivors." If we could celebrate survival, surviving, maybe there wouldn't be so many suicides.[13]

Marion Bolt expressed a similar need for "good stories" to share with young people struggling to survive in the contemporary North. A cherished elder in the community, Marion had also been deeply affected by the loss

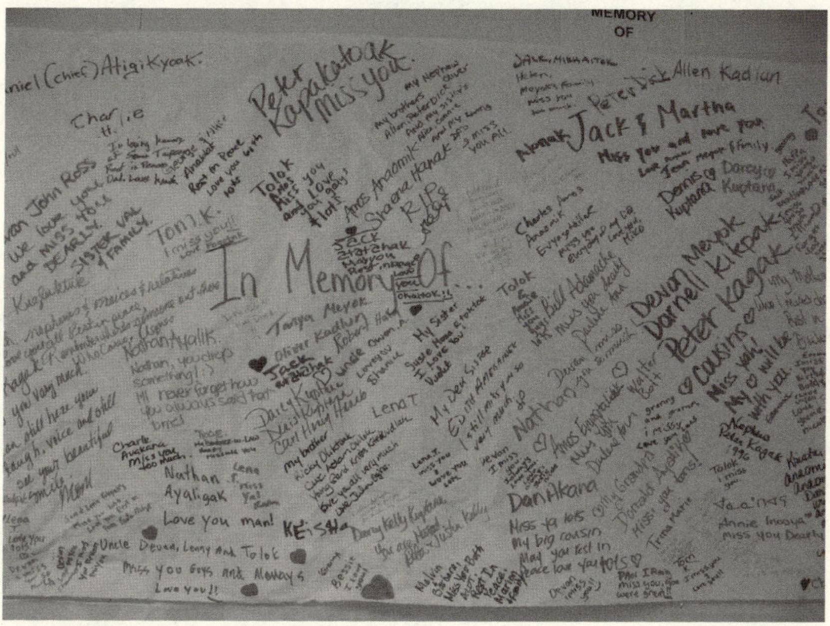

Mural installed at the Co-op store and post office, August 2007. Large sheets of paper were posted as a space to express thoughts, write notes to loved ones, and come together as a community to remember not just those who had died that summer, but all who had been lost. *Photo by Emilie Cameron.*

of so many young people. She spoke about her despair at seeing both young and old dying, and the importance of stories and the land in nourishing strong communities:

> When the old people die, the stories will be gone. It don't matter if they told their grandchildren because they may not remember or they may not have understood because of the language. They should be recorded ... It's better to share the stories. We've got to share the stories, we're losing them. Nowadays the young people don't know their language and they don't know how to hunt. I really worry about them ... They should take the young people in Kugluktuk out on the land like that, they need it ... When I was young my parents taught me how to be, just like I taught my kids how to be. I can't make them do anything, but I can talk to them. I can tell them stories and tell them the right way to be ... I'm worried about our future.

When asked what kinds of stories the young people ought to hear, Marion simply said "good stories":

> Good stories are good stories. But maybe also stories for their future, so they can know how to be. Old stories, from when we were growing up. I could tell the story of how my grandpa and granny raised me. Right from the start, from when I was born up 'til I lose them. That's a good story ... God gave us a life to live, to be happy. Our parents brought us into this world to live. We have to tell the young people that.[14]

Like Millie, Marion traced lines between stories told and lives lived, and emphasized the possibilities of staking out a more hopeful and strong future through stories that nourished histories of survival and "knowing how to be." Marion and Millie also worried deeply about the loss of the "knowledge keepers" and the permanent forgetting of "good stories." Indeed, both Marion and Nellie have passed away since I spoke with them, as have a number of other elders. While Marion insisted on the importance of recording the stories of elders, however, others were less keen. At the end of a long conversation with Joseph Niptanatiak, an elder who did not want to record his most cherished stories, I asked, "Are there stories Qablunaat shouldn't hear, only Inuit should hear?" He replied (in translation),

> *Joseph:* The traditional way, even now when the people tell stories, the government always makes a book out of it. They make money. That's what I've heard. I've heard when they make a book out of it they make lots of money. I always go anywhere, to the heritage

buildings and anywhere, when I go down south. I always see stories about my grandparents. They make lots of copies, they make money with it. Should go to [my] grandchildren ... I've got lots of stories to tell. I guess if I'm not doing anything anymore, I'll make a book out of it.

Emilie [to interpreter]: What does he think should happen to the old stories? What would he like to see?

Joseph: Long time ago these stories were told, and when I go out camping with some of my nephews or grandchildren, they always want to hear stories. And one time when we got stuck, we didn't have any camping stuff. There was Teddy, George, and Andrew. They came to where we got stuck and they had a tent, and was it ever cold at night. No blankets. And the old man started telling stories. It was really dark too. And I fell asleep! Just like I got warm from the stories and I fell asleep. And when you try to do things out there, if you start having a hard time, it's just like a story even when you're cold *[pause]*.

Emilie: [pause]. So stories are for hearing out there.

Joseph: I just love hearing stories since long ago. Even my grandparents or other people, they're really good to hear. When we go out camping, people always want to hear stories, so they always visit around and people tell stories.[15]

Joseph made it clear that stories were for telling on the land, among relatives and friends, in situations where they were meaningful, not to government or for Qablunaaq books. There is a geography of storytelling elaborated in his response that jars with the urge to record traditional knowledge before it is "lost." Joseph made it clear that he can live with the forgetting of stories; he accepts that some of his stories will die with him. He asserts the right to determine where and under what conditions his stories will be remembered, and under what terms they will be forgotten.

Peter Kamingoak took a similar stance. Like many interviewees, he declined to be recorded, preferring that I take notes during our conversation. Peter also refused to tell the Bloody Falls massacre story but offered his version of the Ikiaridlik story. In it, a single Dene boy escaped from the Inuit attack "by flying, like a bird. He must have had some magic powers too." Peter paused. "I knew a magic man like that too, when I was a boy, my friend's dad. In 1932 at Bloody Falls." And then Peter fell silent again. He went on to say that he knew a lot of stories and that his father had been a great storyteller. He used to tell him stories in the evening, when they were getting ice and melting it for tea. Sitting at the edge of the water, his father would tell lots of stories, Peter recalled. After another long pause, I asked him about the stories. He replied, simply, "They're locked up." I asked Peter whether that meant that he didn't want to tell them to me, or whether they were locked up from everyone. He said, "I'm only going to tell them to a tape recorder." "So the young people can hear them?" I asked, and he nodded. When I indicated that I had brought a recorder with me and could create recordings for that purpose if he wanted to record anything that day, Peter replied that these were the stories that the old-timers had told his dad, and they weren't meant for me.[16]

Whatever stories Peter might hold about Bloody Falls, he, too, clearly articulated the relational geographies of storytelling. As one in a long line of outsiders who had asked him about Bloody Falls, I was an irritation to withstand, not a trusted and respected friend. As he staked out the geographies of storytelling, moreover, Peter also outlined the relationalities of silence and secrecy. The pauses, the silences, and the purposeful forgetting Peter shared with me that day spoke volumes about histories of appropriation and dispossession in the North, and about the insufficiency of the temporary, superficial ties that bound us together. As Tamalik McGrath has emphasized, relationships are foundational to Inuit knowledge practices; there is a profound distinction between approaching knowledge as "information" and understanding knowledge as a "relational and interrelational series of networks that generate, validate, and critique."[17] Peter's silence was not only a gesture of refusal, but also an enactment of Inuit epistemologies, responsibilities, and intellectual authority.

Silence, here, is not absence or emptiness; the belief that Inuit silence around the Bloody Falls massacre reflects a lack of understanding and knowledge of this history is a profound misreading of what is being expressed without words. Silence can be palpable and purposeful, and not just in the context of interpersonal conversation. Indeed, the more time I spent in Kugluktuk, the more I learned to engage with silence and its resonances. Although many references to the Bloody Falls massacre were met with silence, that silence usually grew into a movement elsewhere, away from Bloody Falls, and it is this moving away that I consider next.

MOVING AWAY

The move to Ikiaridlik was a common move away from Bloody Falls. Others moved along the river, away from the rapids as massacre site and toward a longer history of relation with water, land, and animals. When asked about Bloody Falls, Joseph Niptanatiak recalled an old story about the creation of the Coppermine River:

> You may have heard this story before about the person who made the river. His name was Itiktajjak. / This Itiktajjak was getting attacked by a bear. / When he was getting attacked by the bear, he started pretending he was dead, so he saved himself. / This bear, he had a couple of cubs, they took Itiktajjak back to their den. The bears thought the person was frozen, so they started trying to thaw him out. He was pretending to be dead, but these little cubs they can't sleep, they can't fall asleep. / They put him upside down to thaw him out, his feet were up here and his head was down there. / The little cub looked at the man that they were thawing out and he said, "Dad! The person we're trying to thaw out, his other eye opened!" / Their dad said, "How can it be that the person we're thawing out, how can he open his eyes? How can a frozen person open his eyes?" / Everybody fell asleep, even the cubs, and Papa bear fell asleep also. / When the Papa bear noticed that the person had slipped out, he started tracking him. The person could hardly walk anymore. / This person was really tired, he could see the Papa bear was getting closer. And he licked his left ring finger and said, "let the river flow!" and then the river started to flow and made a big noise. / They were talking to each other [from across the river], and the Papa bear asked the man "How did you cross that river?" and the man said, "By licking it and kissing it." / That person told that bear he licked it so the water would go down so he could cross it. So the bear started licking the river and he drank so much water he burst. / When he burst, long time ago people didn't used to see clouds. / They never used to have clouds long time ago, and when that bear burst because he drank too much water, it was really foggy and became cloudy and foggy. / That's how people used to tell it, it's from way back, a long time ago. / The elders used to say if you killed a bear it would get cloudy and foggy.[18]

Joseph went on to sing an old drum dance song about Itiktajjak and his difficulties with the bear. This story, versions of which were transcribed by Jenness, Métayer, and other visitors to the region, gestures toward some of the broader and longer geographies within which Kugluk (Bloody Falls) is storied.

Indeed, Kugluk is just one of many places along a river that is crucially important to Kugluktukmiut. Like Joseph, Marion Bolt was not interested in talking about the massacre, but she insisted on the importance of the river: "It's our water tank ... They got to look after it. I want to live a long time, I want my grandchildren to live, and we need that river; we can't mess it up." "I'm worried about our future," she said. "There are too many mines, and they don't look after them. They say they look after them, but they don't always; they should be monitored. They care about 'this kind' [money]. But we need that water instead of 'this kind.' The elders say that too. We need our water. We need our fish."[19]

This move from the rapids to the wider river and beyond to the Coppermine watershed occurred in almost every conversation I had about Bloody Falls. As mining activity has accelerated in the watershed, Kugluktukmiut have grown increasingly concerned about the state of the river. Elders in particular remember the days when the water was clearer and the fish and caribou were healthier. River quality is inextricable from the health of the land and the animals and, by extension, the health of the people. Elder Alice Ayalik ended a long conversation with the following comment:

> Like I said before, a long time ago my parents used to live in Nepaktulik area, that's inland, and the caribous used to be so healthy in those days because there was no blasting, you know, the mines always use so much blasting, and nowadays sometimes the caribou are really skinny; sometimes their lungs are stuck together, stuck to their ribs. That's the most important part of what I'm saying.[20]

It seems that the river concerns Kugluktukmiut more than the rapids themselves, even though Kugluk was an important fishing site for their ancestors and remains important to many. Today, as the river silts up and its bottom becomes increasingly hazardous to propellers, few risk a trip all the way to Kugluk by boat. Most are forced to tie their boats a mile or so below the rapids and hike to Kugluk, a wet and buggy undertaking. A long and bumpy ATV trail on the west side of the river is the only practical means for most residents to access the rapids directly in the summer, rendering it a more appealing destination for teenagers looking for an escape from town than for adults, and making the journey prohibitive for elders and young children. As use of the area declines, elders strain to remember the names of the various places at the rapids. Allen Niptanatiak recalled a few while walking along the western bank of the river, including Onoagahiovik, the flat rocky area along the shore "where the people camped," and Naohiovik, which means "place to stay behind"; "it's below the falls, a nice bay for fishing near Alistair Harvey's cabin." There is Arauryak, the "place for hunting" caribou over the cliffs, beyond where the outhouse is today, and there is also an Inuinnaqtun

"Kumaiak Spearing Fish [from ledge at Bloody Falls]." Photo by Richard Finnie, 1931. *Library and Archives Canada, 1987-154 NPC, e002342735.*

name for what is referred to in English as "first hills," where a boardwalk was recently installed.[21]

Onoagahiovik is rarely used today to "stay all night and fish," although young people occasionally practise spearing fish with *kakivaat* along the edge of the rapids. Others etch messages into the picnic tables that have been placed at the site in recent years, now a well-known place to make out. These shifts have been gradual, and many Kugluktukmiut were surprised to note how long it had been since their last trip to the falls. Most fish elsewhere. At certain times of year, Kugluk is a very good fishing spot, but it is not the only one, and at many times it is inferior to other fishing sites in the area. The habits of char, grayling, and whitefish, and the gradual changes in the riverbed combine with long-standing and intimate knowledge of the region to determine where and how people fish. This move away from Bloody Falls involves not so much an act of conscious forgetting, then, but rather an active storying of other places. On a late July weekend, depending on family traditions, weather, harvesting potential, and inclination, Kugluktukmiut are more likely to travel to Locker Point or perhaps to Kugaruriak, east along the coast toward Tree River. For a day trip, people might head to one of the islands that litter Coronation Gulf, and those with more time might travel to Nagyuktuk, Read Island, or Bathurst Inlet. These movements are as invested in ancestral knowledge and family patterns as was the annual gathering of Inuinnait to fish at Kugluk, though gasoline and outboard motors render travel today faster and easier.

However much use of the area has shifted over the past several years, it would be misleading to suggest that Bloody Falls is no longer important in Kugluktuk, either as a story or a place. Nunavut Parks and the local wildlife office actively maintain the site and have been instrumental in improving the ATV trail in recent years, including installing bridges over the small creeks to protect the land. Informational placards have been installed, as have amenities such as picnic tables, a boardwalk, and an outhouse. Nunavut Parks is charged with conducting a cultural inventory for all its sites, including detailing traditional use, stories, and archaeological remains. To this end, Robert McGhee was invited to return to Kugluktuk and assist community members in identifying evidence of old tent circles, a Thule house, and other features located during his visits in the late 1960s. As the coordinator of parks planning and operations for the Kitikmeot region of Nunavut made clear, those involved in organizing archaeological work at Kugluk see it as part of a larger process grounded in community priorities, one that will involve training for youth and extensive local discussions before any archaeological identification takes place: "We see it as an end point rather than a starting point."[22]

In quite another way, Bloody Falls is an end point for the canoeists who paddle down the Coppermine River every summer. After spending weeks on the river, they reach Bloody Falls, the last campsite before they arrive in town, and many see it as a "stark transition to civilization" as much as a remote and perilous massacre site. Focus groups with canoeists revealed that only about a quarter had heard of the massacre before embarking on their trip, and they had learned of it in much the same way as many Kugluktukmiut – "through my grandfather," and "I read it in a book." Canoeists also see the falls as a significant "barrier to development" that prevents the upper reaches of the river from being transformed into "cottage country," in much the same way that McGhee worried about cabin construction in 1968 (see Chapter 5). Many were disappointed to see that the site had been signed and developed, preferring a more naturalistic experience, a claim that not only flies in the face of received wisdom about tourism to the falls but also reveals some of the imaginative geographies that inform wilderness canoe trips in the North. Comments about trash, fish remains, and other signs of human use at the site recurred as the canoeists described their disappointment upon seeing cabins lining the final stretch of river to Kugluktuk. For them, this was a prematurely peopled landscape – while the Inuk who allegedly waved as they arrived in town was a "nice touch," signs of "modern" living outside of town were inconsistent with the temporalities and geographies of nature, indigeneity, and North that inform the wilderness canoe "experience."[23]

Signage at the falls is far from obtrusive, but it does frame the site in distinctive ways. Canoeists are welcomed "to the land of the Copper Inuit" and immediately directed not to Bloody Falls as a massacre site but as a physiographic feature:

> Bloody Falls is the last set of rapids on the Coppermine River before you reach Kugluktuk on the Arctic Coast, about 13 kilometers down stream. What makes this such a unique place? Look along the steep cliffs that rise up from the rapids. This is one of the few locations along the Coppermine River where there is volcanic rock (gabbro sill) which resists the powerful forces of erosion from the ice, wind, and the never-ending flow of the river. The dark rock cliffs squeeze the wide Coppermine River into a narrow, fast flowing set of rapids. This creates a wonderful place for fishing.

Other placards draw attention to pre-Dorset and Thule use of the site and to the wildlife that live in the area today. The massacre does not earn a

A hiker approaches a signpost along the boardwalk at Bloody Falls, August 2008. *Photo by Emilie Cameron.*

placard of its own and is mentioned only as part of a longer story about "Dene Ancestors," which begins with the observation that "for thousands of years, early Indian cultures have hunted for caribou near Bloody Falls. About 1500 years ago, you would find the ancestors of the Dene setting up a caribou camp on the sandy terraced hills just downstream." Because of its riches in fish and caribou, "early Indian and Inuit cultures were attracted to this place," and occasionally, as in 1771, this "resulted in warfare." As I discuss below, situating the massacre in a longer history of relations with Dene and according ancestry to them at the very site of the conflict is part of a conscious reimagination and refiguration of regional historical geographies.

UNLEASHING PASTS, EMERGING FUTURES

In January 1998, a delegation of Sahtú Dene leaders flew to Kugluktuk from Délı̨nę, Northwest Territories. They came to begin a new era of relations with Kugluktukmiut and to put to rest, among other things, antagonisms flowing from stories about the Bloody Falls massacre. Regardless of whether their ancestors were involved, the Sahtú Dene apologized for any part they had played in the massacre. Soon afterward, Kugluktukmiut travelled to Délı̨nę to attend a healing ceremony. Millie Kuliktana suggests that the gatherings "created new friendships" and renewed longstanding relationships between the two communities.[24] In order to build on these relationships, the Sahtú were invited to travel to Kugluktuk in spring 2008 to participate in the annual Nattiq Frolics festival as well as a series of healing workshops and youth workshops responding to the community's struggles with suicide. Delegates from the Tłı̨chǫ Dene Nation were also invited to Kugluktuk for the first time. Beginning in late March, travellers from communities across the Great Bear and Great Slave Lake regions began an overland journey to Kugluktuk. They were greeted at the treeline by a group of Kugluktukmiut who guided them safely into town.

Throughout the week of feasting, dancing, workshops, and meetings that followed, the Bloody Falls massacre was never mentioned. Although histories of conflict hung in the air, and the massacre was part of the motivation behind the Tłı̨chǫ visit, this was a meeting geared explicitly towards telling different kinds of stories. Indeed, I was welcomed into the community to participate in the event but advised not to mention Bloody Falls. Millie Kuliktana noted that "nobody ever blamed them" for the massacre and that histories of conflict were not the point of the gathering.[25] I was invited to participate "as an observer of *today's* relationships, of a

A Tłı̨chǫ delegation arrives in Kugluktuk, March 2008. *Photo by Emilie Cameron.*

cultural exchange between two peoples who share a homeland." Leroy André, a leader from Délı̨nę, also emphasized the importance of remaining silent on the matter of Bloody Falls and of building relationships based on shared ties to the land rather than histories of conflict, as did Sahtú wildlife officer Ron Doctor, who travelled overland all the way from Tulit'a, southwest of Great Bear Lake, to attend the event. Doctor acknowledged that conflict had defined Inuit-Dene relations for many years, "but that's not something we want to talk about here. That's in the past."[26]

Different pasts, though, were actively nourished. Millie Kuliktana anticipated that the "stories shared will be like ones about hand games, about how many generations ago people from this region played hand games with the Dene to trade implements ... That's the kind of stories we are going to be sharing, stories of that connection." In night after night of hand games that week, people did indeed recall such stories, as women jokingly voiced their concerns about being "traded away" as their great-grandmothers may have been. Elders from the many communities gathered one afternoon to tell stories about their recollections of relations with one another, and stories centred on histories of cooperation, trade, intermarriage, and collaboration flowed between them. These were stories recollected not from a static bank of knowledge but rather as a result of meeting one another and being reminded of relations long forgotten. As George Mackenzie, grand chief of the Tłı̨chǫ Nation, observed,

> In the past our leaders have shared the caribou, have shared the land, have shared their skills to survive, to help each other. Yes, before we came, way before we came, since last year our Elders have told us many different stories, stories of how the Tłı̨chǫ, the Inuit, and the Sahtú shared the land, shared the animals, and shared their skills. We heard many stories before we came. When we announced this trip, I heard stories I had never heard before, and I'm very honoured to have heard those stories. I want to share that with you.[27]

The very act of meeting traced lines not only to the past but also to present concerns and a shared resolve to shape a future that might support northern Indigenous peoples. Speakers and storytellers moved seamlessly between past, present, and future, as in Kugluktuk MLA Joe Allen Evyagotailak's welcoming address: "Our ancestors met by walking, dog-team, and today by snowmobile. And this won't be the last time. As long as we live, we need healing and counseling to have a better life."[28] Here, Evyagotailak invokes a past that might nourish present healing, not just between nations but as peoples struggling to heal at the most intimate level. Indeed, the agenda of the visit was as much about healing from the traumas of colonial intervention in the North as from distant histories of Inuit-Dene conflict. But beyond the confines of the healing workshops, few dwelled on pain and struggle. This was a celebration meant to "empower us as people to continue with past traditions of our ancestors for the future generations as people of the land, water, and the animals."[29] Spring, Millie noted, is traditionally a time to gather in Kugluktuk and "celebrate life." In a ceremony welcoming visitors from Edmonton, she recalled histories of Inuit gathering in Kugluktuk every spring from "East as far as Tree River, from the West, from Victoria Island and from inland." The community was grieving the death of a community member that day, she noted, "but life must go on, and even now that family is expecting new family members, babies to be born. We come together to celebrate life."[30]

Millie's call to celebrate life, issued again and again throughout the week, was directed toward the youth. It was not an empty or abstract command but rather an effort to train their eyes on a more hopeful future, one made possible through grounding in their culture and land. As described in a press release read aloud during the week's closing ceremonies,

> This gathering marks the unity of leaders with the focus on youth. The youth-focused visit demonstrated the three aspects of youth incorporated in past, present, and future, ways of being as people of the North and Arctic region of Canada, where culture, language, and the land and its rich resources are changing within our communities. The original idea was to focus on youth empowerment through healing and grieving. This allowed for separate workshops to be held for both adults and youth, and was enhanced by the involvement of Dene visitors. The cultural significance of exchanges of clothing, language, and the drumming traditions of the Dene and Inuit centralized the spirit of being as a people. The prayers, songs, and the beat of the drum signifies the unity of all people who gathered to celebrate. The significance is captured in a quote shared: "Hold on to our culture as long as we can."[31]

Here, youth empowerment is thoroughly embedded in the land and in collective acts of grieving and healing. Youth are seen as a responsibility inextricable from responsibilities to the land, to the past, and to the future. These responsibilities are in turn linked to mining activity in the region:

> As industry changes and reshapes our communities ... [the gathering] demonstrates the fact that Inuit and Dene have always shared the land and its resources. This was captured as "using the land to signify the power of friendship." The mining industry impacts economically on the people, the land, and its resources, the caribou, fish, and water. For the future of our people, it is beneficial that industry continue to contribute to future events that unify the youth in all aspects of northern development. Both the Inuit and Dene are working to keep their traditions strong with the land, believing it is the land that heals the spirit of living as whole Inuit and Dene.[32]

It is notable that the gathering occurred after the Nunavut, Tłı̨chǫ, and Sahtú comprehensive land claim agreements had been finalized.[33] With the settlement of land claims came the delineation of Inuit, Tłı̨chǫ, and Sahtú jurisdiction over specific lands and the implementation of protocols for consultation regarding mineral development. The Nunavut Land Claim Agreement, which was the first to be finalized, nearly foundered over disputes about shared lands in the Great Bear region. Robert McPherson, a mineral consultant to the Inuit negotiators, recalls a particularly heated exchange that took place in Kugluktuk in 1991 over the border between the Northwest Territories and Nunavut. The so-called Parker Line, proposed by former NWT commissioner (and mining consultant) John Parker, would reserve significant lands in the Contwoyto Lake area for Dene use, on the federal government assumption that "it was little used by the Inuit" (see map of Central Arctic, page xxii).[34] Elders in Kugluktuk, according to McPherson, "were furious" and "were adamant that this was their historic hunting territory." The proposal brought the land claims process to a halt and elicited impassioned stories about Inuit use of the area:

> The exact parcel of land to provide the Indians with access to Contwoyto Lake was said to lie along a traditional trail of [the Dene]. Peter Kamingoak said it was a trail from nowhere; if there was a trail, we should be able to find it on the ground. Joe Niptanatiak said that if the government could not provide facts [of Dene use], the Inuit could not accept the decision ... Many stories by Walter Topilak, John Magsagak, and others poured forth, describing the late arrival or non-arrival of the Indians there. The speakers demanded to know the names of the Indians [who claimed traditional use of the Contwoyto Lake area]. Noel Avadluk, who had taken in many of the sessions, said in his experience there were never any Indians in the area, whereas the Inuit had lived there continually. Indians had not been there since he frequented the area in 1942; otherwise, their trails and camps would be in evidence. Other speakers also related their experiences over the years and swore they had never seen any Indians. One story recounted how, in 1988, Indians were heard on the side band radio who did not know how to get to Contwoyto Lake, so an Inuk picked them up and showed them the way. This land was evidently cherished by the Inuit elders in attendance, and their chorus of protest was bringing the discussion to an impasse.[35]

The land claim negotiations, which were on the verge of completion, were forestalled as representatives from Cambridge Bay made it clear that they would not sign the agreement if the matter were not resolved to the satisfaction of the people of Coppermine. Eventually, a compromise was reached, although some Kugluktukmiut remain disgruntled about the placement of the Nunavut-Northwest Territories border.[36]

The contrast between the stories shared in 2008 and those informing boundary negotiations in the early 1990s is stark, but it by no means undercuts the reliability and accuracy of regional oral histories. If anything, these stories expose the ways in which Qablunaaq understandings of fact, truth, history, and place jar with Inuit and Dene relations with and knowledge of the land. The notion that oral traditions comprise static, fixed stories that might be recounted, documented, parsed, and analyzed as historical evidence fails to account for the active and continual *practice* of both place and story in northern Indigenous traditions.[37] Practices of place and story are grounded in efforts to tie the past to an emerging future, and different presents unleash different pasts, different stories that might be oriented toward different futures. The Contwoyto Lake region is rich with stories of both enmity and collaboration, and both have shaped relations between Inuit and Dene over the past several decades. As the political and economic landscape has shifted in the North, and as Inuit and Dene have resumed regular journeys over shared lands, stories that might support a collaborative future are being recollected. Of the many stories that might relate Inuit, Dene, and the Contwoyto Lake area, the people who gathered in Kugluktuk in 2008 trained their attention on those that emphasize commonality. As Nellie Hikok remarked while the travellers prepared to return home, "We come from one Creator, one land ... It's true of our spirit, we have one breath, we believe in that ... The land is our home, and when you travel home may you be guided by the spirit we all breathe."[38]

As elders spoke of their shared histories and cultures, they purposefully turned toward certain pasts and to the futures those pasts might make possible. Although there was certainly a measure of political rhetoric in the repeated emphasis on shared pasts and cooperative co-management, people again and again spoke of having memories and stories evoked by the act of visiting, recognizing, and sharing:

> Even though we don't speak the same language, we are all relatives. We come from the same Creator. That's why we shake hands. Here, we are all fathers, mothers, brothers, sisters, aunts and uncles. We are all related ... From Whatì an elder came; he's seventy-five years old, he came because this is our way of life. This is our culture. This is what it means to be a Native person, a Tłįchǫ. When he saw the [Inuit] elders here, he remembered his grandparents and parents and their way of life, how they used to gather together, in respect.[39]

As the week-long gathering came to a close, plans were made to build a cabin in the Hornby Lake area to facilitate future meetings and allow past and future to mingle again, this time on the land.

Although it was not mentioned over bannock and caribou stew that spring, the Bloody Falls massacre lingers in town. As Colin Adjun puts it,

"It's a sad thing but people have to live with it."[40] But living with the past does not necessarily involve "dancing around a wound," as Daniel David Moses has observed of settler relations to colonial history.[41] It involves "becoming with" the pasts that might nourish futures worth living for. Living with the massacre story does not necessarily require direct acknowledgment or opposition; there is no active project to respond to Hearne's account with an Inuit version of the event, not because such stories do not exist, and not because this is not possible, but rather because it does not matter. But it would be a grave error to read, as some have, the absence of a direct response as lack, incapacity, ignorance, or apathy. I have suggested, here, that Kugluktukmiut actively move away from, ignore, forget, and reimagine their relations with Bloody Falls, with Dene, with Qablunaat, and with each other by storying relations that might materialize lives worth living. They respond, in other words, as a form of responsibility to past, present, and future relations. Storying relations with each other and with the land is a practical and practised task, central to survival. It is not carried out for the benefit of Qablunaat, even while relations with Qablunaaq individuals, institutions, and systems so profoundly shape the conditions under which such relations are made.

7
Ptarmigan Stories

> [Qallunaat] are experts at acquiring, amassing, collecting, and steamrolling over everybody else. That's their nature. That is the way, throughout history, that their people have acquired power and authority and control over other lands and other people.
>
> – Zebedee Nungak, "History in the Making"

> *Nunavut* is a metaphysical force that influences Inuit life. Forces like the land, weather and animals are respected by Inuit, and it is understood that these forces cannot be manipulated. Therefore, Inuit study and interact with these forces, and such experience guides the formulation of Inuit survival knowledge.
>
> – Jackie Price, *Tukisivallialiqtakka*

> I've always been aware that there are people killing us.
>
> – Tanya Tagaq, CBC Radio, 24 September 2014

Buried in Maurice Métayer's three-volume collection of stories recorded in Kugluktuk in 1958 is what might be the closest thing to an Inuit version of the Bloody Falls massacre story documented by a Qablunaaq. "Texte 66," one of many stories told to Métayer by Louis Qajuina, recounts the experiences of a group of Inuit who escape an attack at Kugluk by fleeing in their *qajait* (kayaks).[1] Métayer flags the possible connection with Hearne's narrative only in an endnote to the longer Inuinnaqtun version and does not refer to Hearne or Bloody Falls at all in the shorter English summary. As a linguist, priest, and ethnologist of his day, Métayer was less interested in Inuit accounts of historical events than in characterizing a more "timeless" and traditional culture. It would be more than three decades before the oral history collections of Métayer and others were re-examined for the historical evidence they contained, as part of a broader turn among Qablunaat to Indigenous oral histories.[2] But while Métayer (like Diamond Jenness before him) was only fleetingly interested in the story's historical significance, the story does indeed resonate with elements of Hearne's account.[3]

> Hamani uadliariurmiunguuq pikunga qurluqtumun pihugiamik ubluq nappanguqhugu pihuinnaraangatik tikinnaqtuq qurluqtuq hamanngat tariurmit tatpikugaguuq qurluqtuq qagliinnaqhugu puinrannuarmik Inuit qajaqtik amilikkaqqait havalikkaqqait havaktiguuq qainan iniqhimangmata nattit amiinnik havaktait amiliurait amiqtunnguuq iniraluaqtillugit inuinnguuq quttiqhuqtut kuungmik upinraami nuikkaqqut qablunaat uadliaruhirmiunnguuq unaaqhijut nuatqatitik tuhaavagait tuhaumagamikkik imarmuliarutigiaramikkik umijjiuramik ituaqtumiinnaqhinahuakkaqqunnguuq uliliqhutik inuuqatitik arnauhitik tamatkiqhugit inutquakharuuq audlaumajungnaikkaqquq inituriirannit inuit qajaujuraaluni audlaumajungnairmanguuq qimakpan qimakhirumalirmat taamnaguuq kingunrani tuqugiaqarniqhugu timangiqhimavalikkaqqainguuq nunalikhiariliramikkik qablunaan inuinnain uadliariurmiutat taunungaguuq paangannun qurluqtup avalatquq kitauginnaqhugu qitiqhitkut hituunnahuaramik tariulinnahuaramik taunungaguuq qaglimajaugaluaqhutik qikiqtanun ailikkaqtut umiaqtuqtut umijjiuramikkik qainatik taununga qikiqtanun tuktugiajungmata ingilraannguuq qikiqtat atajut taavunga atiqaqtut qikiqtat tamatitkut tainga kiglirhiat qurluqtualuup kitaani ittuq havviurvingnahirmik atiqaqtan nungummahian mikijurnahiq aujami tuktuliqivakkamiguuq qikiqtani qajakkut annaktut annaktuqtut qimaagamik taamnaguuq uqaqpakturuuq unataqpangniktuugaluit ilangan inutquakhamik kihimi unatarniktut quanaruuq qajalgit inuit inuuhukturuuq ingilrarnitamik uqaqpaktuq taaphuminga qimaangmataguuq qajakkut uqaqpagainnguuq qablunaanut inuinnguuq quana qajalgit annaktuqtut qimaajunnguuq qikiqtanun ajujainnguuq ilanginnguuq ilait amihuraaluit inungnik inuijainahuaqtuugaluit taamnaguuqquja&&aktuq inuuhuktuq uqaqpaktuq qablunaaq ingilraat tatpaani kingumut uqaqpakturuuq hamunngaqpaktunun tahamunngaqpaktunut tuharniramikki uqarivagainnguuq talvani nunguttpangmajjuk nungutara.

> As it was told, the people of Uadliaruhiq ["the far western side"] were around here and there is the falls up there that takes about half a day's continuous walk to reach from the sea. So the people were up there,

> putting skins on their *qajaq* frames. They had workers helping and the shell coverings were completed. The shells were made of sealskins, and they had worked on them making the skins into leather and were just finished putting them on when they looked up the river, it was springtime, and they noticed Qablunaat coming. So it was told that the Uadliaruhiq people heard some of their kin being stabbed with a harpoon *[unaaq]*, they heard their cries so they went to them and took them to the water and because their boats were ready put them in the water going downstream, covering them, along with fellow Inuit and their women. Everyone was included except for an older person who was not mobile and stationed in the old tent rings. As people left by qajaq he could not travel and so they left him there because he wanted to be left behind. After that he had to be killed, because they left him ashore, and so the Qablunaat got him on the land. The Uadliaruhiq people reached the mouth of the river, making their way by managing to stay to the middle, trying to reach the ocean downriver. They were pursued closely but they made it to the islands and got some boats ready, and were not reached as they made their way to the islands down there – the islands that were said to have had many caribou in the past, a chain of islands that goes a long way. There is a farthest one from the rapids that is called Havviuvingnahiq [place to get knife metal], and the smaller one was depleted. The people would use the islands to process caribou in the summer. So they fled to the islands to escape danger. One of them spoke of it, that they escaped being fought but a single old person was fought. He was so very grateful that their qajait were ready, he was a young person at the time and he recalled this event. He said they fled by qajait, this is what he said to the Qablunaat. He said the Inuinnain were so very grateful that their qajait were just ready and they were able to escape to the islands. They just had one member that they were helpless about. There were many Inuit that were there and they were all being pursued to be killed. The young man used to recall with just gratitude, thinking about the possible fate they escaped, he'd recount this to Qablunaat that came here, because somehow they had heard of him and so he would speak to them. This is where they finish the story so I myself do the same.[4]

If read as a source of documentary evidence, Qajuina's story is provocative. It is clearly situated at Bloody Falls, and (like Hearne's narrative) it refers to a group of Inuit who flee by boat before their attackers can catch them. In Qajuina's account there is no mass killing of Inuit in tents adjacent to those who escape by qajaq, but there is reference to a group of fellow Inuit who were killed some time before and suggestion that the survivors had come to warn those at Kugluk of the approaching danger. As in Hearne's account, an old man falls prey to the attackers, but, notably, in Qajuina's telling, he does so on his own terms. Whereas Hearne conjures a kind of hapless, pathetic figure who "fell a sacrifice to [the Indians'] fury" because he was too intent on collecting his things, Qajuina's old man thought he would drown if he fled by boat and thus remained at the falls "audlaumajungnairmanguuq," because he could not travel, because he wanted to be left behind.

The old man, moreover, is only briefly mentioned in Qajuina's account. The emphasis is on those who escape, how they do it, and their gratitude that so many Inuit survived the attack. The story emphasizes skilful decision making, knowledge of the land and river, and thankfulness for having escaped. Hearne's version only briefly mentions those who escape; the focus of the drama is on three individuals who do not manage to get away – the old man (whose body is reduced to a "cullender" by "no less than twenty" attackers), the young girl, and the deaf woman at the rapids. Notably, in Qajuina's account, Inuit are warned of the impending attack by a group of Uadliaruhirmiut who had recently been attacked themselves, and the aggressors are Qablunaat, not Itqiliit (they are all white men, not Dene). Furthermore, one of the Qablunaat is known to have spoken about the event upon returning to Qablunaaq lands, and his storytelling shaped subsequent Qablunaaq travels to the region. That is, Qajuina's account is not simply an "Inuit version" of the Bloody Falls massacre story, passed down over generations and handed over, in "pure form," to an inquiring missionary. It is shaped by knowledge of other versions of the story (as well as awareness of Qablunaaq interest in these other versions) and a sense of the material effects of Qablunaaq orderings. Indeed, it is unclear how much of Qajuina's story was shaped by the recollections of Uadliaruhirmiut who escaped the attack, how much came from learning, later, of Hearne's own storytelling, and how the occasion of its telling – a cold day in January 1958 – shaped the story itself. It is entirely possible and even likely that Qajuina and the other storytellers to whom he refers had heard Hearne's version from passing Qablunaat – from Jenness or other members of the Canadian Arctic Expedition, from traders, missionaries, or administrators, or perhaps even from Métayer himself. The story, in that sense, is entangled in Inuit-Qablunaat histories; it is shaped by these relations, and it productively unravels Métayer's (and others') interest in "pure" Inuit stories, uncontaminated by past and present relations with Qablunaat.

As a source of historical evidence about the massacre, then, Qajuina's story emphasizes Inuit agency and survival, troubles aspects of Hearne's narrative, and calls into question some of the most sensationalized, melodramatic elements that have propelled its circulation among Qablunaat for so long. But as I have argued, to reduce the Inuit "perspective" or "voice" about the Bloody Falls massacre to an alternative or counterfactual "version" is not only to restrict Inuit to a tremendously narrow narrative range but also to uphold deeply colonial and ultimately dehumanizing relations. To seek out Inuit versions of contentious histories, histories over which Qablunaat retain narrative and material control, is ultimately to ask Inuit to perform prescribed roles in maintaining uneven and violent relations. Qajuina's story is not simply a source of historical evidence, one that might be used to challenge the facts of a specific event. It takes its place within a rich tradition of storying relations with the river, with qajait, with violence, with Qablunaat, and with the land. And while, for Qablunaat, Hearne's account of the Bloody Falls massacre marks a moment of original contact, one in which an innocent white leader stands as neutral and horrified witness to Indian barbarity, Qajuina's story displaces both the details of this encounter and its claims to originality. "Texte 66" is one of many stories told by Kugluktukmiut about missed encounters, narrow escapes, and strategic evasion of Qablunaaq interference. There are as many, if not more, stories about avoiding and escaping meetings with Qablunaat through disguise and ingenuity as there are of face-to-face encounters. In other words, Inuit tell "contact stories" not simply about "their side" of the same encounters but also about encounters of which Qablunaat have no knowledge, and that were strategically avoided. Qajuina's story, then, reminds us not only that Inuit were not the helpless victims conjured by Hearne but also that Qablunaaq encounter stories are profoundly limited and partial sources for understanding our shared relations.

I have argued that the Bloody Falls massacre story is much more than a text, and that we have much to learn from the geographies of its telling. By paying attention to where, when, how, and why the massacre story is told, and the relations it makes possible, we can begin to come to terms with some of the persistent structures of knowledge and practice that shape Qablunaaq relations with the North. And by paying attention to the ways in which Inuit refuse, ignore, and forget this story, we can begin to learn all the ways in which we do not matter and do not know. Our task, I have argued, is not simply to listen to stories from the margins, to write better stories, or to more adequately weave "diverse perspectives" into Qablunaaq histories. It is, instead, to account for the ways in which our stories are embedded in much larger structures and patterns of relation, and how they relate to ongoing contestation over the fate of northern peoples, bodies, lands, and livelihoods.

I have also argued that the Bloody Falls massacre story is fundamentally a Qablunaaq story. Although we invoke the story as a source of evidence about Inuit and Dene histories or as an instructive parable for making sense of the essential natures of northern Indigenous peoples, this is a story by, for, and about Qablunaat. In this concluding chapter, I examine more directly a thread that runs through every Qablunaaq telling of the massacre story but continually goes unacknowledged: land. We want the land. For all our talk of civilization and savagery, tradition and modernity, essential natures and original encounters, the Bloody Falls massacre story is fundamentally about locating, claiming, and extracting resources in the name of empire. As Patrick Wolfe observes, "whatever settlers may say – and they generally have a lot to say – the primary motive [of settler colonialism] is ... access to territory. Territoriality is settler colonialism's specific, irreducible element."[5] Although we continually claim otherwise, our laws, institutions, and structures of knowledge are deeply tethered to this imperative. Indeed, as the geographies of the massacre story make clear, whether positioning ourselves as compassionate witnesses, reliable observers, benevolent technocrats, accurate scientists, bearers of history, or champions of Inuit tradition, Qablunaat have a practised capacity to write our own interests out of the story. Throughout centuries of retellings, Hearne's account of the Bloody Falls massacre has proven remarkably effective at obscuring, again and again, Qablunaaq investments in northern dispossession.

What, then, can the various invocations of Bloody Falls examined in this book teach us about Qablunaaq interests in both advancing and legitimizing our imperial desires? And what kind of "story of the North" would we tell if we traced the HBC's appetite for resources at some "Far Off Metal River" through to contemporary relations with Inuit lands and waters? Recall that Hearne was given three instructions: to locate and assess the region's copper deposits, to make peace with local Indigenous groups, and to report any findings that might have a bearing on the discovery of a northwest passage. Each goal was central to imperial expansion in the Far North and each remains essential.

Assessing and mapping the Arctic's resource wealth is as urgent a priority as ever. The federal government has allocated hundreds of millions of dollars over the past several years to an expanded geomapping program focused on "providing the exploration industry with valuable tools to explore Canada's North."[6] Critics charge that the program amounts to a subsidy to the extractive industry, but controversy surrounding the mapping program also points to the continued importance of "making peace" with Indigenous northerners as Inuit repeatedly challenge federal approval of seismic testing (a key tool for mapping hydrocarbon reserves) in Arctic waters. Inuit assert their ongoing jurisdiction over these waters and allege that the government has failed to meaningfully consult them and respond to their concerns about the potentially devastating impact of seismic testing on marine wildlife.[7] These conflicts make clear that although the modalities and strategies for making peace with Indigenous peoples have shifted since Hearne's time, securing the consent and participation of northerners remains a precondition for extractive projects and an ongoing site of negotiation.

Similarly, far from being a historical footnote, the Northwest Passage is still at the forefront of geopolitical struggles in the Arctic. Shipping routes through the passage have long been identified, but the technical challenges of sailing through ice-fast waters remain, as do ongoing geopolitical scuffles over who "owns" this important corridor.[8] Moreover, as climate change increases the number of days the passage is ice-free each year, the centuries-old challenge of how to get mineral resources out of the Arctic is also changing; mine proponents now routinely assess a project's feasibility based on plans to ship materials through the passage rather than face the daunting prospect of airlifting or building overland routes to the south.

All three components of Hearne's mission remain relevant in the contemporary North, then, but their form and significance have changed over time. When accounts of the Bloody Falls massacre first began to circulate, the Canadian Arctic was (to the British) a largely unmapped and unknown imperial holding. Gathering basic information about its shape, extent, and resource potential was of primary importance. Indeed, as we saw in Chapter 2, locating and extracting resource wealth was the HBC's raison d'être. The company was granted a monopoly over Rupert's Land, an area spanning over one-third of present-day Canada, with the expectation that it would coordinate the region's fur trade and use its extensive holdings to map, claim, and refine imperial knowledge. But the HBC not only hoped to find a large deposit of minerals along the Coppermine River and evidence of the fabled passage; the company also wanted to be seen to be looking. Faced with accusations that it was not adequately making use of its monopoly, the HBC (along with its supporters) held up Hearne's journey as proof of the company's imperial value. Ultimately, Hearne's reliability and accuracy were found wanting, and the Crown dispatched its own naval officers under the command of John Franklin to refine and expand knowledge of the region. Armed with more advanced instruments and embedded in more authoritative scientific networks, the Franklin expedition members not only secured the truth of the Bloody Falls massacre – they also greatly expanded knowledge of Arctic flora, fauna, geology, and geography. But both journeys were consistent with the basic imperatives of early imperial expansion in the Far North: explore, "make peace," map, claim, report back.

For both Hearne and Franklin, making peace with Indigenous peoples was a practical and situational necessity: it ensured the explorers' physical well-being and assisted in acquiring crucial regional knowledge. But neither Hearne nor Franklin was authorized to negotiate any kind of lasting agreement with Indigenous northerners; the peace they sought was much more fleeting. The British had no doubt that the region's mineral wealth was theirs to claim and therefore aimed to broker a superficial and intercultural peace, not a geopolitical one. Over time, as Canada established itself as a settler colony and engaged in practices of state making, the nature and purpose of making peace would change. Settler colonialism involves a shift from resource extraction at imperial outposts to more intensive settlement, along with the development of more complex structures of settler legitimation. The settler colonial state is just as interested in extracting resources as any imperial power, but it must justify its occupation and dispossession to itself and deny the ongoing violence upon which it is built. Settler colonial states do not simply invade and extract; they are built on a structure of ongoing dispossession, and they naturalize that dispossession as a necessary transition from the Indigenous past to the settler present. The "peace" required in settler colonies is therefore both more enduring and impossible: Indigenous peoples have never and will never consent to their own elimination and marginalization, but a great deal of political and intellectual effort in Canada has been directed toward pretending they have.

In the early years of Canadian state formation, treaties were a key tool for securing and legitimizing settler claims to land.[9] With the exception of the upper reaches of Treaty 11, however, no treaties were signed in the Arctic. With neither an influx of settlers to manage nor a viable plan to get Arctic resources out of the ground, the federal government avoided negotiating any kind of formal access to Inuit lands until it was forced to in the 1970s. But as we saw in Chapter 4, the project of legitimizing northern dispossession was underway long before then. By the early decades of the twentieth century, geology, anthropology, law, theology, medicine, and policing had emerged as distinct but intertwined spheres of knowledge and practice in the North, and they would become the means through which Qablunaat gathered knowledge about northern lands and peoples and advanced their territorial interests. The series of copper stories examined in Chapter 4 demonstrate both the utility and the interdependency of this disciplinary knowledge; "opening the North" to mining, I argue, was enabled by much more than the identification of mineral reserves. The Canadian Arctic Expedition was dispatched by the Government of Canada in 1913, for example, to gather knowledge about the region's physiography, geology, biology, and peoples. Although J.J. O'Neill's geological findings would expand federal knowledge of the region's mineral wealth, Diamond Jenness's ethnological work was at least as significant in advancing northern resource extraction. Beginning with the expedition's reports, the notion that Inuit relations with the land and resources were part of a "traditional past" that would be superseded by industrial extraction became institutionalized. It remains institutionalized.

Making peace in settler colonial contexts, then, is about much more than securing physical safety at the site of extraction. It involves complex structures of legitimation that work to position Indigenous relations with the land as insufficient, ceded, or expired, and settler relations as their natural successors. As I explore in Chapter 5, settlers long to believe that their occupation of Indigenous lands is both natural and consensual, and they continually produce knowledge to secure this belief. Both the territorial and federal governments insisted that their heritage agenda was benign and even inclusive. Inuit were expected to symbolically approve the erection of heritage plaques commemorating Samuel Hearne – an initiative over which, the government representatives hastened to note, Inuit held no formal jurisdiction – and affirm Hearne's importance in both regional and national history. When Kugluktukmiut failed to play their part, citing both urgent housing needs and authority over their own lands, government officials insisted that they must not *understand*; they framed Inuit actions as both irrational and out of character. Reverend Sperry went so far as to reassure Kugluktukmiut – wrongly – that "putting a plaque in the Coppermine area had nothing to do with Land Settlement or land ownership," even while applications were underway to secure state control over a fifty-square kilometre parcel of land at the proposed heritage site. Sperry was not so much lying as adhering to a long-standing Qablunaaq belief that the formal settlement of territorial claims in the Far North was both unnecessary and irrelevant to the everyday workings of government. Indeed, as I argue above, treaty making was largely avoided by the federal government because its interest in northern resource development was not yet urgent enough to require it. But there was also a racialized dimension to federal dismissal of Inuit land rights: unlike "Indians" (that broad, all-encompassing colonial category for the hundreds of Indigenous nations across Canada who had proven to be resistant to various forms of federal intervention), "Eskimos" were expected to happily consent to their modernization and passively accept industrial development on their lands.

Here again, Qablunaaq invocations of Bloody Falls are instructive. I argue in Chapter 2 that the massacre story has long been used to advance racialized claims about both Inuit and Dene. But the production of racialized knowledge is not simply "about" race; it is used to enable and justify a larger structure of domination and dispossession. Consider the following speech by Conservative member of Parliament George A. Drew, leader of the opposition in Canada's House of Parliament in 1953. The house was debating the creation of a federal Department of Northern Affairs and National Resources that would devote itself to unlocking the resource potential of Canada's northern territories. Drew rose to express his enthusiastic support for the initiative and affirm his "conviction that great days lie ahead in the development of the northland of this country of ours."[10] After an impassioned speech about the region's mining past and future, Drew requested one small change in the proposal: that the new ministry combine the management of Indian and Eskimo affairs. Against the suggestion made by some MPs that "it is natural to place Eskimo affairs under one department and Indian affairs under another," Drew felt that a combined department would lead to both administrative efficiencies and a cross-fertilization of ideas about managing these two fundamentally different native groups. Whereas Indians, Drew noted, displayed a stubborn attachment to both their "tribal customs" and the "ancient treaties" they had signed with the Crown (treaties, he noted, that the Indians felt offered a "measure of protection ... which they would not lightly abandon"), Eskimos were neither burdened with treaties nor prone to the kind of recalcitrance Drew attributed to Indians. Those who had "seen the Eskimos along the Arctic coast and elsewhere" would agree, Drew exclaimed,

> that they have never seen such a naturally happy people anywhere at any time. That is the most distinguishing characteristic of the Eskimo. They seem to find something to laugh or to smile about in every event of their very stern life. They are brave, they are courageous, they are energetic; they are a most attractive people. We are not hampered in the plans that may be made for their advancement by any of these ancient arrangements which

> in some measure cannot be disregarded and under which the government of course must recognize its obligations.[11]

Accessing and extracting resource wealth for the nation would be much easier on Inuit lands, Drew implied, both because of the essential nature of Inuit and because the federal government had no treaty obligations in the Arctic.

Lest there be any doubt that Eskimos and Indians were, by nature, fundamentally different peoples and thus in need of different forms of federal management, Drew went on invoke the Bloody Falls massacre:

> As you travel through the Northwest Territories you pass from the land occupied by the Indians immediately into the land occupied by the Eskimos. In years gone by they used to constantly fight each other. One of the famous spots on the Coppermine river running north into the Arctic is a place known as Bloody Falls near the town of Coppermine where a tremendous battle was fought years ago between the Eskimos and the Indian Dogrib tribe occupying that area. Historic spots of that kind simply serve to emphasize that there are differences, that there are reasons for dealing with this subject in a way that recognizes the basic differences in the problem itself. Nevertheless it does seem to me that consideration might be given to the advantages that would be gained by bringing Indian affairs and Eskimo affairs together in the same department.[12]

Drew proceeded to outline the merits of jointly administering Indian and Eskimo affairs before concluding his remarks with the requisite quoting of a Robert Service poem and a reiteration of his expectation that "the future of Canada will very largely be measured by what we do in the north."[13]

The supposed difference between Indians and Eskimos has preoccupied Qablunaat for centuries. From the reports of early Arctic explorers to Diamond Jenness's taxonomy in *The Indians of Canada* to contemporary racialized accounts of "the Inuit heart and spirit," Qablunaat have maintained an ongoing interest in describing the allegedly exceptional Inuit nature.[14] In Drew's speech, delivered in support of a new federal ministry devoted to industrial extraction in the North, the driving force behind this preoccupation is laid bare. What mattered about Inuit, to Drew, was not their "nature" in and of itself but rather the relative ease with which they might be expected to part with their lands and resource riches. Although presented as a form of ethnographic and historical evidence to justify ministerial design, Drew's ordering of Bloody Falls aimed at a much more basic and long-standing Qablunaaq goal: dispossession. Burdened neither by treaty obligations nor a proclivity for direct confrontation, Inuit were expected to agreeably comply with federal plans for their "advancement" and, in so doing, provide no meaningful obstacle to industrial resource development in the Far North. Drew's speech typifies a pattern we have seen throughout this book: the Bloody Falls massacre story is continually invoked as though it is about something else (the perils of Arctic exploration, the inherent violence of Indigenous peoples, the hard-scrabble foundations of Canadian nationhood), but in almost every instance it works to advance and legitimize the relational and material ordering of settler colonial dispossession.

Inuit, as we know, failed to meet Drew's expectations. The Department of Northern Affairs and National Resources was indeed created that year (with responsibility for Eskimo but not Indian affairs), and it went on to coordinate an apparatus of dispossession and extraction in the North. But Indigenous peoples across the North refused to step aside and permit extraction on their lands, and the Canadian government was eventually forced to enter into modern treaty negotiations to address the fact that federal claims to northern lands were fundamentally illegitimate. The modern comprehensive land claim process has been described to southern Canadians as an act of state benevolence, reconciliation, and redress, but federal interest in settling land claims is, at base, the same as it was a century ago: to secure the conditions for unimpeded and consensual resource development. The James Bay and Northern Quebec Agreement, signed in 1975, enabled large-scale hydrodevelopment in northern Quebec on Inuit and Cree lands; the Inuvialuit Agreement in 1984 secured state access to oil and gas resources in the Mackenzie Delta and Beaufort Sea; and the Nunavut Land Claims Agreement in 1999 awarded the Crown subsurface rights to 98 percent of Inuit lands. Each of these agreements was contingent on the permanent surrender of Aboriginal title to the Crown. The "bottom line" federal position throughout land claim negotiations has been to establish clear, long-lasting, stable access to Indigenous lands and resources.[15] Although the Nunavut agreement contains a number of articles that outline Inuit rights and responsibilities with respect to harvesting, language, employment, land-use planning, and wildlife management, for example, the agreement also established land title systems and institutional structures that greatly facilitate the conversion of northern resources to southern wealth.

This is not to say that land claim agreements are reducible to extraction. Nor is it to say that Indigenous northerners entered into land claim agreements with the same objectives as the state.[16] As I argue in Chapter 5, the terms upon which Qablunaaq legal and political structures recognize Inuit are not the same as the terms upon which Inuit recognize themselves, and strategic engagement with those structures is not the ultimate expression of Inuit relations with and responsibilities to their lands. As Sandra Inutiq, co-president of Nunavummiut Makitagunarningit, explains, "the driving force behind our land claim agreements was control over our lands and other cultural rights like hunting, and controlling these rights on our terms."[17] Inuit asserted authority over their lands, in other words, not simply so that they might receive a greater proportion of resource revenues (although this was a clear objective) but rather to protect and support a much broader and richer set of relations. Inuit not only sought to control decision making in their homeland, but also to make decisions in the Inuit way, to design institutions based on the "past, present and future knowledge, experience and values of Inuit society."[18]

As Jaypeetee Arnakak notes, "the dream of Nunavut came about from the realization that in order to protect and preserve Inuit rights and culture, a government that reflected Inuit culture needed to be created."[19] In the years surrounding the establishment of the territory, Inuit elders and leaders formed an Inuit Qaujimajatuqangit (IQ) Task Force that met repeatedly to flesh out their vision for how to govern in the Inuit way, and the Government of Nunavut publicly promised to incorporate this vision "into all aspects of its operations – everything from policy-making to the delivery of its programs and services."[20] Alert to the potential for Inuit ways to be simply "added on" as a kind of supplement to fundamentally Qablunaaq institutions, the IQ Task Force challenged the government of Nunavut to "incorporate itself into the Inuit Culture" rather than try to incorporate Inuit culture into itself. The latter path, they feared, would break Inuit culture into discrete elements and activities, a path that "can't work and won't work." If Inuit ways were to meaningfully inform everyday life in the territory, the task force insisted, they must be the foundation upon which its institutions were built.[21]

In the fifteen years since Nunavut's creation, the territory has struggled to manifest this vision. Deluged with interest from multinational mining companies, oil and gas developers, and commercial fishing interests, the territory's resource governance institutions in particular have not managed to deliver on the promise of Inuit-centred, community-driven decision making. As Sandra Inutiq observes:

> Now that we have a land claim, we face external pressures to exploit our lands, and internal pressures of the need to deal with poverty and the political oppression that goes along with poverty. The systems in place to ensure Inuit views are heard are failing us. In my opinion the land use plan and impact review boards need to step it up as they are who we rely on for their objective and clear analysis in ultimately protecting the exploitation of our homelands. We discuss and make decisions about the land in communities and inside buildings within the confines of institutional culture and policies which can be so disconnected to the reality of what the wisdom of the land has to teach us about sustainability. To me these decisions would be very different if they were made out on the land as any Inuk who depends on the well-being of the land for food and cultural sustainability knows. We are most conscious that the land is what defines who we are. We know instinctively that what we do to the land we do to ourselves as we ourselves are an extension of that land. In not focusing on longer term sustainability needs for Nunavut leaves vital discussions out on issues such as education, social well-being, giving, and caters only to the mining sector needs.[22]

Inutiq's statement was made at a territory-wide forum initiated in response to widespread concern among Nunavummiut that the decision-making structures that were, in theory, designed to ensure their full participation and control over resource extraction were not working.[23] Attendees at the meetings held in Iqaluit, Iqaluktuuttiaq (Cambridge Bay), and Qamani'tuaq (Baker Lake) repeatedly voiced concerns about the capacity for Nunavut's environmental assessment, land-use planning, and other regulatory bodies to incorporate their knowledge, respond to their questions, and ensure that communities shape decisions about proposed developments.[24] Many participants expressed their disappointment that these institutions were not delivering on the promises that underpinned their creation; Nunavut was supposed to do and be otherwise. In spite of having settled a major land claim, negotiated creation of their own territory, and established a series of new institutions, many Nunavummiut insisted that they did not feel they had meaningful control over development on their lands.

Struggles over land and resources in Nunavut today, then, are not precisely the same as they were in Hearne's time. Inuit are heading the corporations, organizations, and government ministries that promote resource development, and many Nunavummiut support some form of mining in the territory. But many also continue to struggle against widespread resource extraction and continue to call for transparent, consensual, collective control over their lands and lives. As the Inuit Circumpolar Council's 2011 Declaration on Resource Development Principles in Inuit Nunaat makes clear, contemporary struggles over Arctic resources are not reducible to wholesale promotion or rejection of industrial development but rather involve ongoing efforts to ensure Inuit retain control over where, when, how, and to whose benefit extraction will unfold.[25] This, it seems, is the control many Nunavummiut do not feel they have. As Laakkuluk Williamson Bathory notes, "Inuit negotiators have been successful in negotiating historic land claim agreements and self-government ... [but] there is still a deeply embedded struggle to actually implement the agreements and have a lived experience of sovereignty."[26] She points to ongoing attempts to hold the federal government accountable to both the letter and spirit of the Nunavut agreement, struggles to address poverty and the intergenerational impacts of colonization, and efforts within Nunavut to live life as Inuit, in the fullest sense. She joins a number of Inuit and other northern Indigenous activists, leaders, and scholars who have begun to critically interrogate the comprehensive land claims process and call attention to some of its limits and costs. Far from resolving struggles over land and resources, they argue, land claim agreements provide a new set of frameworks within which those struggles play out.[27]

Jackie Price contends, for example, that there is a fundamental mismatch between Inuit forms of governance and Nunavut's current system for making decisions about proposed mines. Part of the struggle Nunavummiut face, she argues, is to carve out the conceptual and metaphysical space to name the ways in which Qablunaaq ways of thinking, being, and doing continue to shape life in the territory, and to re-establish Inuit ways.[28] Nurturing relations with each other and with the land is central to this process, from the intimate scales of family and community through to territorial, national, and circumpolar mobilizations. Faced with the inadequacy of the territory's environmental review of a proposed iron ore mine on Baffin Island, for example, filmmaker Zacharias Kunuk and partners launched a parallel forum in Nunavut for making decisions about proposed mines. Emphasizing oral Inuktitut, the Digital Indigenous Democracy (DID) initiative uses Internet, community radio, local TV, and social media to provide information about proposed developments and to foster much broader conversations among Nunavummiut. The initiative aims to

> amplify Inuit traditional decision-making skills at a moment of crisis and opportunity as Inuit face Environmental Review of the $6 billion Baffinland Iron Mine (BIM) on north Baffin Island. Through centuries of experience Inuit learned that *deciding together,* called *angiqatigiingniq* ... is the smartest, safest way to go forward in a dangerous environment. Through DID, Inuit adapt *deciding together* to modern transnational development – to get needed information in language they understand, talk about their concerns publicly and reach collective decisions with the power of consensus.[29]

DID is a direct response to the perceived inadequacy of the territory's environmental assessment system, particularly its failure to effectively incorporate Inuit knowledges, communicate risks and impacts, and support Inuit decision making.

As in the rest of the country, environmental assessment in Nunavut is driven by the submissions of project proponents. It is the responsibility of the corporation that wishes to develop a mine to generate studies assessing its ecosystemic and socio-economic impact, and it is the responsibility of governments, community groups, and other interveners to respond, critique, and otherwise assess the tens of thousands of pages submitted. Critiques and concerns may be voiced by organizations and community members, again and again, and these may be duly recorded in the archives of a project assessment, but there is no mechanism within the process for a community to simply reject a project.

As Kunuk made clear in his own submission to the territory's environmental impact review board, many are increasingly frustrated with the limitations of this system:

> Baffinland's Environmental Impact Statement says their railroad, port and supertanker shipping every day of the year won't have any significant impact on our wildlife and environment. They say they won't damage endangered species like bowhead whales in their shipping lane, or arctic char in lakes next to the railroad line, or walrus calving grounds just south of their port; that caribou, foxes, wolves or any of the rare or endangered birds who nest here won't be harmed by all the noise from airplanes, helicopters, trains running every day and giant ice-breaking ships. Inuit know this is impossible. We know animals already are impacted by mining activity and global warming added to it. We know our wildlife and environment will change

> forever if they go ahead with this plan. Inuit know this but most people we interviewed so far say there's nothing they can do or can say that would change anything. No one is listening to what Inuit say.[30]

Faced with the inadequacy of the formal assessment system, DID asserts and enacts Inuit authority over decisions about Inuit lands, regardless of whether Qablunaat recognize that authority. Although the initiative responds to a "moment of crisis and opportunity" that is thoroughly shaped by Qablunaaq claims and interests, it does not aim for Qablunaaq recognition; DID supports conversations by, for, and among Inuit.

Indeed, for those without a working knowledge of Inuktitut, much of the discussion is inaccessible. As I note in Chapter 6, turning away, ignoring, and forgetting Qablunaaq structures and relations has been and remains a crucial strategy for addressing colonial intervention into Inuit lands and lives; efforts to maintain relations with each other and with the land need not be legible to Qablunaat to be effective. Although the very same metals and minerals that prompted Hearne's journey continue to attract Qablunaat to the North and contemporary institutions often work to facilitate Qablunaaq access to those resources, DID rejects the notion that Inuit must either express their modernity by endorsing large-scale extraction or remain consigned to a "traditional past."

What is the relationship of Qablunaat to struggles over land and resources in the contemporary North? What is our role in their formation, perpetuation, and identification? What must we know and learn, and what must we *stop* knowing and turn away from? As I argue in Chapter 2, Qablunaat are accustomed to naming, characterizing, and analyzing Inuit struggles, and we are practised at doing so from the privileged position of neutral, reliable, compassionate witnesses. We are less practised at placing ourselves in the frame. In the first instance, then, it is essential that Qablunaat account for our *own* struggle in the contemporary North, one that we have inherited and enact every day: to advance and legitimize settler colonial relations and claims. However much we frame our present relations with northern lands and peoples in tones of respect, shared authority, and mutual prosperity, we continue to struggle to secure control over northern lands and to legitimize our knowledge, our authority, and our claims. These are the relations we have inherited and are accountable to, however much we may protest and however much we may individually abhor this configuration. If this is so, then our task as Qablunaat is not to direct our attention to identifying and solving the problems Inuit face, nor is it to cultivate our own, personal exceptionalism, in which we prove that we are somehow different or know better than to ensnare ourselves in colonial relations. Rather, our task is to continually commit ourselves to critically interrogating and remaking our shared relations, not just interpersonally but also institutionally, legally, structurally, and materially.

As I note in Chapter 1, such an undertaking requires us to unlearn our certainty, our narcissism, and our attachment to being good and to acknowledge that our learning is specific to our experiences and relationships. There is no universal, "correct" way forward. Indeed, no single person can fully understand the complexities and contradictions that shape contemporary struggles over northern lands and resources; the story I have told here is specific to my experiences and the contours of the present as I understand them. But based on what I have learned so far, there are a series of questions and themes of inquiry around which I believe Qablunaat must continually cultivate our judgment, refine our capacities, acknowledge our confusion, and learn to listen.

Many of these questions centre on the production, circulation, and legitimation of Qablunaaq knowledge about the North and about Inuit. How does the knowledge we produce today work to legitimize and advance Qablunaaq authority over northern peoples, lands, and resources? How do we account for the myriad efforts of contemporary scholars, journalists, consultants, politicians, and other observers to document, lament, and claim neutrality with respect to Inuit social, cultural, physical, economic, and political struggles, just as Hearne did? In what ways do we continue to associate Inuit communities with violence and suffering, and how does this knowledge shape the terrain of decision making related to mine development? What is the role of scientific "truth" in the North today, and how does it continue to wield authority over Inuit claims? In what ways does a strategically delimited understanding of tradition continue to dominate knowledge production about Inuit, and how does this knowledge support processes of accumulation, dispossession, degradation, and domination in the contemporary North? Whose interests are advanced when Inuit assertions of authority are framed as naive and misguided, attributed to the undue influence of southern radicals, or celebrated as the heroic refusals of canny subalterns? Finally, in smoothing out the contradictions and complexities of contemporary struggles over land and resources, and positioning ourselves as the centre of the story of the North, what do we continually fail to see?

These are just some of the questions that the geographies of the massacre story draw our attention to. As with stories about Bloody Falls, moreover, the question to pose of Qablunaaq knowledge claims is not whether they are true; knowledge need not be true to be materially consequential. What matters is what it *does,* what it makes possible and how it participates in ordering the "mixed way things happen" into accounts and explanations that advance some interests and undermine others. In coming to terms with Qablunaaq knowledge-making practices in the Arctic, then, our task is not to discern the line between neutrality and partiality, story and history, truth and fiction, tradition and modernity but rather to understand how the line itself is a site of power, one that we continually place in our favour. And in reckoning with the limits of our knowledges and claims, our task is not to assert new truths but rather to defer, to listen, to be humble, and to stop. As Terry Audla and Duane Smith recently noted, "a multigenerational and apparently continuing challenge for Inuit is raising awareness of the obligations of non-Inuit to value and respect Inuit leadership, governance, decision making, institutions, knowledge systems, and vision for the Arctic."[31] This is something that many Qablunaat aspire to do but rarely achieve.

Indeed, as I confront these questions, I am reminded of my own struggles to listen and understand what people have attempted to teach me. It was only many years after speaking with Aime Ahegona, for example, that I came to appreciate the importance of ptarmigan in the story he told me about Bloody Falls. As I note in Chapter 6, Aime told me that he believes Inuit survived the massacre because a woman and her baby turned into ptarmigan:

> She had attached a ptarmigan feather or thing like that, like, you could have been just about stepping on a bird when you were walking around; when they're nesting, you don't see them at all! So that's what that woman, I heard, with the baby, she just disappeared to nowhere because she had that power put into her body from those, like, old-time people, like I told you before. So I believe that somebody survived at that time.[32]

At the time that Aime told me this story, I had only the vaguest idea what a ptarmigan looked like. I had never seen one on the land. Indeed, when I first met Aime, I could barely spot a muskox moving in the distance, and muskox look like big hairy chesterfields when they run. Initially, even when someone showed me exactly where to look, I had a hard time picking out what I was directed to see. Over time I learned to be more attentive.

I continue to be moved by how quickly others can spot wolves, caribou, or seal in the faraway distance, from a mere flash of fur or the patterns of birds. But I learned to look for seal when seagulls circle overhead, because seagulls eat *angmagiaat* (capelin), and so do Arctic char. Where there are char, I was taught, there are usually seal. Ptarmigan, though, continued to elude me. As Aime noted that day, ptarmigan are small and designed to hide. Their only defence is to blend in, and so in winter their feathers are pure white, like the snow, and in summer they become mottled grey and brown, just like the rocks.

It was not until I saw my first ptarmigan on the land that I was reminded of Aime's reference to the woman and child who concealed themselves by bringing the power of ptarmigan into their bodies. Nellie Hikok, too, told a story about how her grandfather, Hilgoyuk, hid like a ptarmigan to evade some Itqiliit. Hilgoyuk was fearful of some approaching strangers, and "they were just about catching up to him," she said, when he "covered himself up, just like when we pull a blanket up when we're cold, that's how he did it, so they wouldn't see him, invisible." The Itqiliit walked very close to Hilgoyuk as he hid. "They were just about stepping on him, but they couldn't even see him." Telling this story reminded Nellie of another story, one about hiding from Qablunaat, and about how Inuit "used to be really scared of Qablunaat long time ago that's why."[33]

Ptarmigan stories often touch on fear. Mark Kalluak recounts a story told to him by Sam Kunuk in Arviat in the 1970s, about a time when a husband and wife were camped inland and "saw Indians appearing around the end of a mountain." The husband snuck toward the approaching strangers, and "as he started off ... he began reciting magic words." When the Indians came close, he

> fell on his belly near a small hill. As he laid, he saw ptarmigan walking swiftly toward the north. They were all surrounding saying "Nauk, Nauk, Nauk." The man had turned the Indians into ptarmigan. He later made a song about the incident. The words go like this: "All those strangers. They make us suspicious. They make us afraid. Aya yia yi yaa. Iya iya yi yaa, iyaa aiyaa."[34]

But ptarmigan stories are not only told about fearful encounters with strangers. Kalluak also recounts a story of a woman whose baby turned into a ptarmigan because it was suddenly startled. The mother entered their tent and approached her baby because she "suddenly felt a deep love for her child." But because the baby did not see her coming, it "took flight from being frightened. It flew around inside the tent trying to escape from his mother." The mother tried to catch her child, but it "finally escaped because it became a ptarmigan. The woman lost her baby."[35] Fear, loss, love, and ptarmigans also interweave in a story told by Sandra Pikujak Katsak to Nancy Wachowich in Igloolik in the 1990s, about a grandmother whose granddaughter pesters her to tell a story. The granddaughter "kept asking her and asking her" to tell a story, and finally the grandmother relented. But the grandmother told the story so effectively that the little girl was startled, and she "turned into a little bird and just flew away." The grandmother was overcome with regret and sadness:

> She cried and cried and cried until her throat became hoarse and her eyelids became really, really red. She too became a bird, but a ptarmigan. She flew off and found her grandchild. My grandmother told me that is how ptarmigan came to be, that is how they got their cry and the red under their eyes, because a granny cried so much when her grandchild turned into a bird.[36]

These are stories of love, loss, fear, camouflage, evasion, reunion, and escape in moments of danger. Ptarmigan are at once vulnerable and protective. They are skittish birds, easily startled but also able to protect themselves by remaining still. They are marked by their grief; ptarmigan wear their losses in their red eyes and hoarse cries, but their camouflage also protects and enables survival. Indeed, ptarmigan have long enabled Inuit to survive. They are available year round, at times when larger game is scarce, and even small children can hunt them. And although I was told ptarmigan stories about fear and escape from threats posed by Qablunaat or Itqiliit, there are also ptarmigan stories about shared relations over shared lands. Ptarmigan are most at home on the tundra, but also thrive around and below the treeline, in the borderlands between Inuit and Dene territories, and are thus a shared source of food. I am told there are ptarmigan stories about these shared lands and relations, but I have not heard them.

Faced with the many questions and struggles that define Qablunaaq relations with the contemporary North, I am reminded of the ptarmigan stories I have heard, those I have not, and those that I do not even know to exist. Ptarmigan have taught me patience, and to practise so that I might learn to see some of what is before me. They remind me that the land is full of stories, even if Qablunaat often can't see them. Indeed, Qablunaaq survival hasn't hinged on being able to see ptarmigan, know ptarmigan, eat ptarmigan, or become ptarmigan, although it is precisely Inuit knowledge of the land that has kept Qablunaaq missionaries, administrators, tourists, and researchers alive. My attention was initially directed to ptarmigan as sources of protection against Qablunaaq and Itqiliq attackers. In the context of conversations with a Qablunaaq researcher about Bloody Falls, I heard ptarmigan stories about encounters with people Inuit had learned to fear, and the strategies they used to escape detection. Later, I learned ptarmigan stories about how love and fear interweave in the intimacy of close relationships, about shared sources of food, and about how ptarmigan continually transform themselves in the image of the land. Together, these stories direct attention to the richness of the land and its knowledges, practices, and relations, some of which are purposely and necessarily camouflaged, and some of which Qablunaat have occasionally been taught to see. They also direct us to the fragility, precarity, and dangers of encounter; they remind us that lives are at stake and that the losses are real.

This book focuses on summer stories, but summer is, of course, only a relatively fleeting dimension of northern life. Ptarmigan live in the Arctic year round and adapt themselves to its changing seasons. There are ptarmigan stories from the dead of winter and the height of summer, and from those in-between times, when their feathers are partly white and partly mottled. In the face of such an abundance of stories, the Bloody Falls massacre story seems radically peripheral, even absurd. And it is. But this does not mean Qablunaat should simply forget Bloody Falls and turn our attention to ptarmigan. To do so would be to risk extending and deepening the colonization of Inuit lands, lives, and knowledges under the guise of mutuality, inclusion, relationship, and respect. Qablunaat must remain in conversation with Bloody Falls precisely because it is peripheral and uncomfortable. We are responsible to this story – responsible for the ways in which it implicates us and answerable to all that it makes possible. Indeed, however much we insist otherwise, Qablunaat are named by the Bloody Falls massacre story. The notion that it names people and processes that are distant from Qablunaaq realities has a historical geography with ongoing, contemporary effects. We are named and addressed by the massacre story precisely in those moments where we claim neutrality and distance, and I have attempted in this book to both place and displace this mode of relating to northern peoples, lands, knowledges, and resources.

There is no better version of the Bloody Falls massacre story that we might take up, no "correct" imaginative geography that we might replace it with. Telling different stories will not alone make any meaningful impact on the stubborn, persistent, profitable ties that bind this colonial present. To suggest otherwise would be not only naive but dangerous. What we must attend to are the relations that stories trace and make visible to us, what they authorize us to do, and what they allow us to forget. It is the relations that matter. I thus invite readers to relate differently to what we know and do not know, what we must know, and what we must forget. Our task, it seems to me, is not to seek mastery over our relations, or to extract stable and universal truths, but rather to pilimmaksaq-, to commit ourselves to becoming more competent. It is to call upon what we have learned in moments of danger, and to relate differently. Our task is to draw on what we know *in our relations,* and for that knowledge to change how we become with others, not prescriptively, but in the sense of careful, attentive, relational emergence. And it is to relate to our not knowing respectfully, with a commitment to being attentive, so that we might come to know what we need to know, in time. This is not an invitation to be passive. In the face of uncertainty and confusion, as we confront the limits and stakes of what we know and the necessity of knowing differently, we must be actively attentive, practised and wise, and continually turn toward worlds worth living in.

Notes

Chapter 1: Summer Stories

1 Onoagahiovik (Unnuagaqhiurvik in the ICI Inuit Cultural Institute system) is usually translated as "place to stay all night and fish." Thank you to Ida Ayalik-McWilliam for confirming spellings and for her observation that the name Unnuagaqhiurvik refers to the fact that "people would stay up all night catching fish while they were plentiful (before the migration upstream slowed down)." Ida Ayalik-McWilliam, pers. comm., e-mail, Kugluktuk, NU, 4 September 2013.

2 Prince of Wales Fort was an important HBC foothold in the northern fur trade. Built in 1717, it was used until 1782, when Samuel Hearne (its acting governor at the time) surrendered it to La Pérouse.

3 Although originally named "Bloody Fall" by Hearne, and later "Massacre Rapids" by the first Franklin expedition, the name gradually evolved to Bloody Falls. See John Franklin, *Narrative of a Journey to the Shores of the Polar Sea, in the Years 1819, 20, 21, and 22 ...* (London: John Murray, 1823). Technically, Bloody Falls is a rapid, not a waterfall, as its Inuinnaqtun name (Kugluk) affirms. However, because Kugluk/Bloody Falls is referred to colloquially in English as "the falls," I have maintained that usage here and refer to it as both "the rapids" and "the falls" depending on context.

4 See, for example, Germaine Warkentin, ed., *Canadian Exploration Literature: An Anthology* (Toronto: Oxford University Press, 1993); Canadian Broadcasting Corporation, *Canada, a People's History,* Episode 6, *The Pathfinders* (Toronto: CBC, 2001); E.H. Carefoot, "Matonabbee: A Play in Twenty Scenes," 1980, 25th Street Theater fonds, University of Saskatchewan Archives, Saskatoon, SK; Don Gutteridge, *Coppermine: The Quest for the North* (Ottawa: Oberon Press, 1973); Robin McGrath, *Escaped Domestics* (St. John's: Killick Press, 1998); Gumboots, *Search for a Passage* [sound recording] (Yellowknife, NT: Gumboots, 2000).

5 George J. Luste, "History, Travel, and Canoeing in the Barrens," in *Nastawgan: The Canadian North by Canoe and Snowshoe*, ed. Bruce W. Hodgins and Margaret Hobbs (Weston, ON:

Betelgeuse Books, 1985), 41; C.S. MacKinnnon, "Hearne, Samuel," *Dictionary of Canadian Biography Online,* 2000, http://www.biographi.ca/en/bio.php?BioId=36065.

6 Samuel Hearne, *A Journey from Prince of Wales's Fort, in Hudson's Bay, to the Northern Ocean* ... (London: Strahan and Cadell, 1795), 146, 148, 157–62.

7 Ian MacLaren considers the textual inconsistencies in various versions of Hearne's story, Chipewyan oral testimony recorded by the first Franklin expedition (1819–22), and the fact that Hearne's narrative was published after his death as plausible grounds for questioning the veracity of Hearne's published account. Ian S. MacLaren, "Samuel Hearne's Accounts of the Massacre at Bloody Fall, 17 July 1771," *Ariel* 22, 1 (1991): 25–51. The first version, in Hearne's field notes, is believed to be lost. The second, a transcription of Hearne's story by fellow fur trader Andrew Graham (dated anywhere between 1773 and 1792) has survived and is available at the HBC Archives in Winnipeg. It has been published as Andrew Graham, *Andrew Graham's Observations of Hudson's Bay, 1767–1791,* ed. Glyndwr Williams (London: Hudson's Bay Record Society, 1969). The third version, a draft manuscript of Hearne's book, is also believed to be lost. However, a transcription of what is believed to be his original field notes, known as the Stowe Manuscript, has survived. The transcription, by the marquis of Buckingham, is dated 1791 at its conclusion. Its fidelity to the original is not known, though MacLaren suggests that, because the three principal verb tenses appear in it, "a feature that rarely occurs except in field notes," we can assume that "no wording was changed but that spelling was likely standardized." MacLaren, "Samuel Hearne's Accounts," 44n8, 29. See also Ian S. MacLaren, "Notes on Samuel Hearne's Journey from a Bibliographical Perspective," *Papers/Cahiers of the Bibliographical Society of Canada* 31, 2 (1993): 21–45. Heather Rollason Driscoll notes the long-standing belief among scholars that Hearne's travel narrative was written by a ghostwriter and was shaped by the editorial influence of Bishop John Douglas (who had also edited Cook's travel narrative). Following close study of the various versions of his narrative, she concluded that because Hearne had the ability, motivation, and opportunity to write the book, he was indeed its sole author. Heather Rollason Driscoll, "The Genesis of 'A Journey to the Northern Ocean ...'" (PhD diss., University of Alberta, 2002). Using stories gathered through ethnographic research in the Arctic, Robin McGrath is, to my knowledge, the first and only scholar to draw upon Inuit oral history to trouble the authority of Hearne's telling. Robin McGrath, "Samuel Hearne and the Inuit Oral Tradition," *Studies in Canadian Literature* 18, 2 (1993): 94–109. She also draws on Denis St-Onge, who questions the Franklin expedition's depiction of the massacre site in 1821 as littered with skulls and bones. St-Onge contends that the massacre occurred a kilometre downstream from that portrayed in the illustration and argues that ground squirrels would have made off with any remaining bones before the expedition arrived. Denis St-Onge, "The Coppermine River: Art and Reality," *Canadian Geographic* 102, 4 (1982): 28–31. McGrath disputes this supposition, arguing that ground squirrels could not have moved large bones, but agrees that their inclusion in the image is implausible and indulgent, and suggests that any remains would more probably have been washed away by yearly flooding. Allen Niptanatiak, a resident of Kugluktuk, concurs with St-Onge that the massacre site was more than likely downstream from the location implied by the the Franklin expedition's picturesque placement of bones on the bluffs overlooking the rapids (see page 72). Allen Niptanatiak, pers. comm., Kugluktuk, NU, 5 July 2006. As I discuss in Chapter 3, the expedition members would likely agree with McGrath and Niptanatiak, and the placement of the bones probably resulted from a misreading of the expedition materials by the illustrator and engraver who produced the image.

8 Vilhjalmur Stefansson, *My Life with the Eskimo* (New York: Macmillan, 1993), 208–9. Reflecting on Stefansson's claims, Ian MacLaren notes that, "as it was for Stefansson, it is for readers of Canadian literature today *the* story of the North." Ian S. MacLaren, "Exploring Canadian Literature: Samuel Hearne and the Inuit Girl," in *Probing Canadian Culture,* ed. P. Easingwood, K. Gross, and W. Klooss (Augsburg: AV-Verlag, 1991), 91(emphasis in original).

9 Finnie also apparently produced a short film in 1932, titled *Bloody Fall.* See Peter Geller, "Visions of a Northern Nation: Richard Finnie's Views of Natives and Development in Canada's 'Last Frontier,'" *Film History* 8, 1 (1996): 18–43.

10 Stephen Leacock, "Reflections on the North," *Beaver* Outfit 267, 3 (1936): 10.

11 Lisa Bloom, *Gender on Ice: American Ideologies of Polar Expeditions* (Minneapolis: University of Minnesota Press, 1993); Sherrill Grace, *Canada and the Idea of North* (Montreal and Kingston: McGill-Queen's University Press, 2002); Renée Hulan, *Northern Experience and the Myths of Canadian Culture* (Montreal and Kingston: McGill-Queen's University Press, 2002); Francis Spufford, *I May Be Some Time: Ice and the English Imagination* (London: Faber, 1996).

12 Government of Canada, "Prime Minister Harper Delivers on Commitment to the 'New North,'" press release, Office of the Prime Minister, 10 March 2008, http://pm.gc.ca/eng/news/2008/03/10/prime-minister-harper-delivers-commitment-new-north. See also Government of Canada, *Canada's Northern Strategy: Our North, Our Heritage, Our Future* (Ottawa: Ministry of Indian Affairs and Northern Development, 2009).

13 See, for example, Inuit Circumpolar Council, *A Circumpolar Inuit Declaration on Sovereignty in the Arctic*, Inuit Circumpolar Council, on behalf of Inuit in Greenland, Canada, Alaska, and Chukotka, 2009.

14 Numerous scholars, administrators, missionaries, and writers have attempted to unearth an Inuit version of the Bloody Falls massacre story. The most significant effort was undertaken by Robin McGrath, who examined Inuit oral history collections and conducted interviews in Kugluktuk during the 1990s. She does not present just one counter-story, but instead considers a range of stories that might relate to the massacre, thematically or geographically. In Chapters 6 and 7, I discuss the issue of counter-stories in greater depth, including a story told to missionary Maurice Métayer by Louis Qajuina in 1958 that can be read as an Inuit "version" of the massacre story. See McGrath, "Samuel Hearne"; Maurice Métayer, *Unipkat: Tradition Esquimaude de Coppermine, Territoires-du-Nord-Ouest, Canada,* 3 vols. (Quebec: Université Laval, 1973).

15 So, too, is "Inuit." Although "Inuit" is often translated simply as "people," Rachel Qitsualik argues that it more precisely means the "Living Ones Who Are Here" and suggests that it "denotes a sense of place, of having arrived, a memory that Inuit knew they had kin somewhere else." Rachel Qitsualik, "Is It 'Eskimo' or 'Inuit'?" *Indian Country Today,* 11 February 2004, http://indiancountrytodaymedianetwork.com/ictarchives/2004/02/11/qitsualik-is-it-eskimo-or-inuit-89951. See also Keavy Martin's discussion of *inuujunga* as expressing, depending on context, "I am an Inuk," "I am alive," or "I am a person," and the ways in which "Inuitness" relates to understandings of humanness and being alive. Keavy Martin, *Stories in a New Skin* (Winnipeg: University of Manitoba Press, 2012), 35, 36.

16 Minnie Aodla Freeman, *Life among the Qallunaat* (Edmonton: Hurtig, 1978), 87.

17 Ibid.; Zebedee Nungak, "Qallunaat 101," *Utne Reader* (March-April 2004); Alootook Ipellie, *Arctic Dreams and Nightmares* (Penticton: Theytus Books, 1993); Tommy Akulukjuk, "Looking Up through the Microscope," *Études/Inuit/Studies* 28, 2 (2004): 211–12. See also

Janet Tamalik McGrath's conversations with Aupilaarjuk, including his reflections on Inuit efforts to take up Qablunaaq culture and practices. Janet Tamalik McGrath, "Isumaksaqsiurutigijakka: Conversations with Aupilaarjuk towards a Theory of Inuktitut Knowledge Renewal" (PhD diss., Department of Canadian Studies and Institute of Political Economy, Carleton University, 2011).

18 Martha Flaherty, "Freedom of Expression or Freedom of Exploitation?" *Northern Review* 14 (1995): 179. "Southerners," Flaherty writes, "come north, do their field research over a number of months, usually the summer, get to know people in the community, get local help, then go south to write and publish their findings, they are acknowledged as the 'experts,' more so if they have included Inuit in the data collection and can cite them in their research. The researchers are the ones policy-makers listen to when making decisions about design, delivery or funding programs for Inuit. They are also the ones with the funding sources to do such research. There is an inherent bias in government and especially funding sources to place academic and formal education credentials ahead of practice and experience of being Inuk when deciding upon expertise and identifying research priorities and research projects to fund. The inherent bias continues to undermine our inherent right to be a self-determining people and share the power." Ibid., 185.

19 I understand whiteness to refer not simply to skin colour but rather to a structure of power relations shaped by historical and geographical context. See Sara Ahmed, "Declarations of Whiteness: The Non-Performativity of Anti-Racism," *Borderlands* 3, 2 (2004); Richard Dyer, *White* (New York: Routledge, 1997); Ruth Frankenburg, *White Women, Race Matters: The Social Construction of Whiteness* (Minneapolis: University of Minnesota Press, 1993); David Roediger, *The Wages of Whiteness: Race and the Making of the American Working Class* (London: Verso, 1991); Robyn Wiegman, "Whiteness Studies and the Paradox of Particularity," *Boundary* 26, 3 (1999): 115–50. For an earlier study of white/Qablunaaq relations with Inuit, see Hugh Brody, *The People's Land: Eskimos and Whites in the Eastern Arctic* (Markham: Penguin, 1975).

20 Patrick Wolfe, *Settler Colonialism and the Transformation of Anthropology: The Politics and Poetics of an Ethnographic Event* (London: Cassell, 1999), 2.

21 In 1939, the Supreme Court *(Re: Eskimo)* determined that constitutionally, Inuit were to be classified as Indians in Canada, thereby making Inuit subject to the Indian Act. The Indian Act was amended in 1951, however, to specifically exclude Inuit. For details, see Sarah Bonesteel, *Canada's Relationship with Inuit: A History of Policy and Program Development* (Ottawa: Indian and Northern Affairs Canada, 2006).

22 For more on the Royal Proclamation and northern land claims, see Peter Usher, "Environment, Race and Nation Reconsidered: Reflections on Aboriginal Land Claims in Canada," *Canadian Geographer* 4 (2003): 365–82, and J.R. Miller, *Compact, Contract, Covenant: Aboriginal Treaty-Making in Canada* (Toronto: University of Toronto Press, 2009).

23 See McGrath, "Isumaksaqsiurutigijakka." McGrath acknowledges the connections between her phrasing of Inuit "being-knowing-doing-accounting" and Shawn Wilson's discussion of the interweaving of Indigenous epistemologies, methodologies, ontologies, and axiologies. See Shawn Wilson, *Research Is Ceremony: Indigenous Research Methods* (Halifax: Fernwood, 2008).

24 Audra Simpson, "Settlement's Secret," *Cultural Anthropology* 26, 2 (2011): 205.

25 Taiaiake Alfred and Jeff Corntassel, "Being Indigenous: Resurgences against Contemporary Colonialism," *Government and Opposition* 40, 4 (2005): 601. See also Jodi Byrd, *The*

Transit of Empire: Indigenous Critiques of Colonialism (Minneapolis: University of Minnesota Press, 2011).

26 Boaventura de Sousa Santos, "A Critique of Lazy Reason: Against the Waste of Experience," in *The Modern World-System in the Longue Durée,* ed. Immanuel Wallerstein Organization (London: Paradigm, 2004), 157–97. See also Glen Coulthard, "Subjects of Empire: Indigenous Peoples and the 'Politics of Recognition' in Canada," *Contemporary Political Theory* 6, 4 (2007): 437–60; Glen Coulthard, *Red Skin, White Masks: Rejecting the Colonial Politics of Recognition* (Minneapolis: University of Minnesota Press, 2014); Alfred and Corntassel, "Being Indigenous"; Trinh T. Minh-ha, in conversation with Annamaria Morelli, "The Undone Interval," in *The Post-Colonial Question: Common Skies, Divided Horizons,* ed. Iain Chambers and Lydia Curti (London: Routledge, 1998), 3–16; Gayatri Chakravorty Spivak, *A Critique of Postcolonial Reason: Toward a History of the Vanishing Present* (Cambridge, MA: Harvard University Press, 1999).

27 For a fuller discussion of the importance of "unsettling," see Paulette Regan, *Unsettling the Settler Within: Indian Residential Schools, Truth Telling, and Reconciliation in Canada* (Vancouver: UBC Press, 2010).

28 As Sara Ahmed observes, "critical" white subjectivity is highly dependent on a "politics of declaration" in which, by declaring one's whiteness, privilege, racism and, crucially, one's anxieties with respect to this whiteness, one can claim to be anti-racist. Ahmed insists, on the contrary, that such declarations do not do what they claim to do. Instead, they reinforce an individualized, depoliticized, psychologized understanding of racism in which white subjects aim to transcend their implication in structural, systemic forms of racism, and in so doing to "feel better." Just as self-conscious claims to be "against" racism and to be troubled by racism can reinscribe white privilege, it seems to me that self-conscious claims on the part of Qablunaaq scholars to be undertaking good, helpful, or decolonizing research in partnership with Inuit can easily veer toward the same dangers. To the extent that Qablunaaq scholars seek to be "good" in relation to the complex, contradictory geographies of this colonial present, to "get it right," they risk reinscribing the very privileges they oppose. Ahmed, "Declarations of Whiteness." See also Emilie Cameron, "Securing Indigenous Politics: A Critique of the Vulnerability and Adaptation Approach to the Human Dimensions of Climate Change in the Canadian Arctic," *Global Environmental Change* 22, 1 (2012): 103–14; Sarah de Leeuw, Emilie S. Cameron, and Margo L. Greenwood, "Participatory and Community-Based Research, Indigenous Geographies, and the Spaces of Friendship: A Critical Engagement," *Canadian Geographer* 56, 2 (2012): 180–94.

29 Audra Simpson, "Mohawk Interruptus" (presentation at the University of Victoria, Indigenous Governance Program, Victoria, BC, 7 November 2012, https://www.youtube.com/watchv=FWzXHqGfH3U). Note that this quote comes from a live question period and in response to a question regarding the role that settlers and immigrants might play in reordering Indigenous-settler relations. In the live presentation, Simpson used the word "lovely" instead of "productive." In correspondence about the recorded presentation, she indicated that though she stood by the use of the word "lovely," she would replace it with "productive" if cited in this context. Audra Simpson, pers. comm., e-mail, Ottawa, 3 August 2013. Note, too, that I interpret "triangulated" here not so much as it is typically invoked in the social sciences (as a process whereby multiple methods are used to validate data) but rather as a gesture toward the fact that all knowledge is situated, and that a shared project of critical interrogation will enhance a collective analysis precisely

because we all speak and know from different places. See also Donna Haraway, "Situated Knowledges: The Science Question in Feminism and the Privilege of Partial Perspectives," *Feminist Studies* 14, 3 (1988): 575–99.

30 See, for example, Bill Ashcroft, Gareth Griffiths, and Helen Tiffin, *The Empire Writes Back: Theory and Practice in Post-Colonial Literature* (New York: Routledge, 1989); Homi Bhabha, *Nation and Narration* (London: Routledge, 1990); Anne McClintock, *Imperial Leather: Race, Gender and Sexuality in the Colonial Contest* (New York: Routledge, 1995); Mary Louise Pratt, *Imperial Eyes: Travel Writing and Transculturation* (London: Routledge, 1992); Edward Said, *Culture and Imperialism* (New York: Knopf, 1993).

31 Julie Cruikshank, *Do Glaciers Listen? Local Knowledge, Colonial Encounters, and Social Imagination* (Vancouver: UBC Press, 2005); Paul Nadasdy, *Hunters and Bureaucrats: Power, Knowledge and Aboriginal-State Relations in the Southwest Yukon* (Vancouver: UBC Press, 2003); Nancy Wachowich, *Saqiyuq: Stories from the Lives of Three Inuit Women* (Montreal and Kingston: McGill-Queen's University Press, 2001); Lisa Stevenson, "The Psychic Life of Biopolitics: Survival, Cooperation, and Inuit Community," *American Ethnologist* 39, 3 (2012): 592–613; Ann Fienup-Riordan, *Hunting Tradition in a Changing World: Yup'ik Lives in Alaska Today* (New Brunswick, NJ: Rutgers University Press, 2000); Martin, *Stories in a New Skin;* McGrath, "Isumaksaqsiurutigijakka"; Jackie Price, "Tukisivallialiqtakka: The Things I Have Now Begun to Understand. Inuit Governance, Nunavut, and the Kitchen Consultation Model" (master's thesis, Department of Human and Social Development, University of Victoria, 2007); Rebecca Mearns, "Nunavut, Uqausivut, Piqqusivullu Najuqtiarlavut (Caring for Our Land, Language and Culture): Exploring Land Camps as an Educational and Research Tool in Gjoa Haven, Nunavut" (paper presented at ArcticNet Conference, Ottawa, 10 December 2014); Looee Okalik, "Inuujunga: The Intricacy of Indigenous and Western Epistemologies in the Arctic," in *Indigenous Pathways into Social Research,* ed. D. Mertens, F. Cram, and B. Chilesa (Vancouver: Left Coast Press, 2013), 239–48.

32 As I discuss in a longer essay on this topic, Foucault himself made clear that discourses are not just comprised of texts, and the notion that stories are micro-iterations of broader discourses comes more from the ways in which his ideas have been taken up than from a close reading of his work. See Emilie Cameron, "New Geographies of Story and Storytelling," *Progress in Human Geography* 36, 5 (2012): 572–91.

33 Edward Said, *Orientalism* (New York: Pantheon, 1978); Said, *Culture and Imperialism.* Said himself characterized his relationship with Foucault's writing as contradictory and claimed at one point that by the time he had finished writing *Orientalism,* he had developed an analysis that "was deliberately anti-Foucault." "Edward Said," in *Criticism in Society: Interviews with Jacques Derrida ...,* ed. Imre Salusinszky (London: Methuen, 1987), 137. He was also troubled by Foucault's position on Palestine and went on to write on the importance of the critic and oppositional intellectual. See, for example, Edward Said, *The World, the Text, and the Critic* (Cambridge, MA: Harvard University Press, 1983).

34 See R. Cole Harris, "How Did Colonialism Dispossess? Comments from an Edge of Empire," *Annals of the Association of American Geographers* 94, 1 (2004): 165–82.

35 See, for example, Bruce Greenfield, "The Idea of Discovery as a Source of Narrative Structure in Samuel Hearne's *Journey to the Northern Ocean,*" *Early American Literature* 21 (1986–87): 189–208; Keith Harrison, "Samuel Hearne, Matonabbee, and the 'Esquimaux Girl': Cultural Subjects, Cultural Objects," *Canadian Review of Comparative Literature* 22, 3–4 (1995): 647–57; Kevin Hutchings, "Writing Commerce and Cultural Progress

in Samuel Hearne's *A Journey ... to the Northern Ocean*," *Review of International English Literature* 28, 2 (1997): 49–78; Richard Milligan and Tyler McCreary, "Inscription, Innocence, and Invisibility: Early Contributions to the Discursive Formation of the North in Samuel Hearne's *A Journey to the Northern Ocean*," in *Rethinking the Great White North: Race, Nature, and the Historical Geographies of Whiteness in Canada*, ed. Andrew Baldwin, Laura Cameron, and Audrey Kobayashi (Vancouver: UBC Press, 2011), 147–68; Kathleen Venema, "'Under the Protection of a Principal Man': A White Man, the Hero, and His Wives in Samuel Hearne's Journey," *Essays on Canadian Writing* 70 (2000): 162–90; Kathleen Venema, "Mapping Culture onto Geography: 'Distance from the Fort' in Samuel Hearne's Journal," *Studies in Canadian Literature* 23, 1 (1998): 9–31; Terry Goldie, *Fear and Temptation: The Image of the Indigene in Canadian, Australian, and New Zealand Literatures* (Montreal and Kingston: McGill-Queen's University Press, 1989); Rob Shields, "The True North Strong and Free," in Rob Shields, *Places on the Margin: Alternative Geographies of Modernity* (London: Routledge, 1991), 162–206.

36 In thinking through the ways in which actor-network and posthumanist scholarship might work in tension with concepts of discourse, I primarily engaged with the writings of Bruno Latour, John Law, Donna Haraway, Hugh Raffles, and Timothy Mitchell. See the bibliography for titles.

37 John Law, *Organizing Modernity* (Oxford: Blackwell, 1994), 142. See also Donna Haraway, "A Game of Cat's Cradle: Science Studies, Feminist Theory, Cultural Studies," *Configurations* 2, 1 (1994): 59–71.

38 Latour advocates a kind of methodological and interpretive "agnosticism" as a means of overcoming the pull of received theoretical or explanatory frameworks in structuring the identification of truth, cause, or phenomenon. Bruno Latour, *The Pasteurization of France*, trans. Alan Sheridan and John Law (Cambridge, MA: Harvard University Press, 1988); see also Law, *Organizing Modernity;* and John Law, *After Method: Mess in Social Science Research* (New York: Routledge, 2004).

39 See, for example, Price, "Tukisivallialiqtakka"; McGrath, "Isumaksaqsiurutigijakka"; Wilson, *Research Is Ceremony*; Thomas King, *The Truth about Stories: A Native Narrative* (Toronto: House of Anansi Press, 2003); Linda Tuhiwai Smith, *Decolonizing Methodologies* (London: Zed Press, 1999); Martin, *Stories in a New Skin;* Joanne Archibald, *Indigenous Storywork* (Vancouver: UBC Press, 2008); Leanne Simpson, *Dancing on Turtle's Back* (Winnipeg: Arbeiter Ring Press, 2011); Wachowich, *Saqiyuq;* Julie Cruikshank, *The Social Life of Stories* (Lincoln: University of Nebraska Press, 1998); Cruikshank, *Do Glaciers Listen?;* Daniel Heath Justice, *Our Fire Survives the Storm: A Cherokee Literary History* (Minneapolis: University of Minnesota Press, 2006).

40 Haraway, "A Game of Cat's Cradle"; Donna Haraway, *When Species Meet* (Minneapolis: University of Minnesota Press, 2008); Walter Benjamin, "Edward Fuchs, Collector and Historian," in *Walter Benjamin: Selected Writings*, vol. 3, *1935–1938*, ed. Michael W. Jennings (Cambridge, MA: Harvard University Press, 2002), 260–302; Walter Benjamin, "On the Concept of History," in *Walter Benjamin: Selected Writings*, vol. 4, *1938–1940*, ed. Michael W. Jennings (Cambridge, MA: Harvard University Press, 2003), 389–400.

41 Joseph Niptanatiak, pers. comm., Kugluktuk, NU, 14 August 2007.

42 See, for example, Rachel Qitsualik, "Skraeling," in *Our Story: Aboriginal Voices on Canada's Past*, Tantoo Cardinal et al. (Toronto: Doubleday, 2004); Alootook Ipellie, "Thirsty for Life: A Nomad Learns to Write and Draw," in *Echoing Silence: Essays on Arctic Narrative*, ed. John Moss, 93–102 (Ottawa: University of Ottawa Press, 1997); Aqqaluk Lynge,

The Veins of the Heart to the Pinnacle of the Mind (Montreal: International Polar Institute, 2008); and Aupilaarjuk, in McGrath, "Isumaksaqsiurutigijakka."

43 See, for example, Taiaiake Alfred, *Wasáse: Indigenous Pathways of Action and Freedom* (Peterborough: Broadview, 2005); Alfred and Corntassel, "Being Indigenous"; Coulthard, "Subjects of Empire"; Frantz Fanon, *The Wretched of the Earth,* trans. Richard Philcox (New York: Grove Press, 2004); Jackie Price, "The Arctic Is My Home: Affirming the Art of Inuit Governance," *Fuse* 35, 2 (2012): 2–3; Smith, *Decolonizing Methodologies;* Leanne Simpson, "Anticolonial Strategies for the Recovery and Maintenance of Indigenous Knowledge," *American Indian Quarterly* 28, 3–4 (2004): 373–84; David Newhouse, "Telling Our Story," in *Walking a Tightrope: Aboriginal People and Their Representations,* ed. U. Lischke and D.T. McNab (Waterloo: Wilfrid Laurier University Press, 2005), 45–52; Qikiqtani Inuit Association, *QTC Final Report: Achieving Saimaqatigiingniq* (Iqaluit: Qikiqtani Inuit Association, 2010).

44 I would like to acknowledge in particular the time I spent with the Niptanatiak family over the years and the guidance provided by Millie Kuliktana, Marion Bolt, and Anomak Pauline Niptanatiak (Pauline Plamondon). I would also like to acknowledge friendships and conversations with Janet Tamalik McGrath, Jackie Price, and Becky Mearns, as well as their written work. For reflection on the ways in which friendship might shape research between Indigenous and non-Indigenous peoples, see de Leeuw, Cameron, and Greenwood, "Participatory and Community-Based Research."

45 Research is formally overseen in Nunavut by the Nunavut Research Institute, and I was granted the appropriate licences to pursue this project. I also made a number of presentations to the Kugluktuk Hamlet Council and consulted with the Kugluktuk Hunters and Trappers Organization, Kitikmeot School Operations, the Kitikmeot Inuit Association, the Kugluktuk Heritage Society, Nunavut Parks, the Kugluktuk Wildlife Office, the Ministry of Culture, Language, Elders, and Youth, and the MLAs who held office during the course of this study (Joe Allen Evyagotailak and Peter Taptuna), as well as with individual elders. Research participants cited in this book received draft copies of the text, and I presented the main outline of the book at a community meeting in 2009, as well as through one-on-one meetings with research participants. I have also discussed my understandings of Inuit culture, language, and knowledge with Inuit scholars and advisers throughout the course of the project. I have corrected errors or misrepresentations when they were pointed out to me, but the representations in this book remain my responsibility.

46 The expression "learning to learn" from and with others comes from Rauna Kuokkanen, *Reshaping the University: Responsibility, Indigenous Epistemes, and the Logic of the Gift* (Vancouver: UBC Press, 2007). Kuokkanen contrasts "learning to learn" from and with others to the dominant academic mode of learning *about* the Indigenous Other so as to "incorporate what they are saying into what we already know." To learn to learn, she argues, requires mindful attention to the "unexamined nativism," "Eurocentric arrogance," and "Romantic notions of the colonized 'other'" that non-Indigenous scholars invariably carry with them when they attempt to engage Indigenous people and knowledges. But it also, Kuokkanen emphasizes, demands more of scholars than a simplistic refusal to speak for the Other, what she terms "the position of the politically correct dominant." Instead, Kuokkanen insists, it is incumbent upon those of us positioned within academic institutions to rigorously examine our own participation in various forms of silencing.

47 Janet Tamalik McGrath is a Qablunaaq raised among Inuit in the East Kitikmeot region of Nunavut who has worked as an Inuktitut translator, interpreter, teacher,

facilitator, and consultant for over thirty years. Tamalik reviewed this passage and provided additional feedback and clarification about the Inuktitut terms I discuss. Tamalik notes that "nalunaruirumaaqtuq" is expressed here in Nattilingmiut dialect but that it is expressed similarly across dialects. In addition to Tamalik's guidance, I would also like to acknowledge the assistance of Kumiko Murasugi, in the School of Linguistics and Language Studies at Carleton University, in clarifying some of the grammatical information presented here.

48 McGrath, "Isumaksaqsiurutigijakka," 301.

49 Although, as I discuss, my attention was drawn to Inuit concepts of knowing and not knowing by way of conversations with Tamalik McGrath and by spending time in Kugluktuk, I also note Jean L. Briggs's discussion of the distinction between *ilisaiyuq* and *isumaqsaiyuq*, in *Inuit Morality Play: The Emotional Education of a Three-Year-Old* (New Haven: Yale University Press, 1998). For discussion of the importance of truthfulness and the ways in which Inuktut distinguishes between fact, supposition, matters learned first-hand, and matters learned from others, see Rosemarie Kuptana, "Ilira: Or Why It Is Unthinkable for Inuit to Challenge Qallunaat Authority," *Inuit Art Quarterly* 8 (1993): 5–7. See also Murielle Nagy, "Comment les Inuvialuit parlent de leur passé," *Anthropologie et sociétés* 26, 2–3 (2002): 193–213.

50 Tamalik McGrath also notes the connection with *qauq,* the Inuktitut word for forehead, a gesture toward the ways in which learning and wisdom connect to the prefrontal cortex. Kumiko Murasugi suggests that in contemporary Inuktitut, qaujima- is probably a combination of *qauji-* (to know or be aware of) and *ma-* (referring to a state). She adds that one would have to consider Proto-Eskimo linguistic patterns to assess whether qauji- itself was formed by combining qau- and –ji-. Both qau- and -ji- are used as morphemes in contemporary Inuktitut, however, and their meaning is suggestive for Qablunaat who are attempting to understand Inuktitut epistemologies and ontologies, particularly the ways in which knowing and learning are expressed in Inuktitut. Thus, my reflections on the morphology of qaujima- should not be read as an empirical claim about the history of Inuktitut linguistic formation.

51 For a fuller discussion of the interrelation of peoplehood, personhood, and livelihood (*inuuqatigiingniq, inuusiqattiarniq,* and *niqiqainnarniq*), see McGrath, "Isumaksaqsiurutigijakka."

52 Rachel Qitsualik, "Nalunaktuq: The Arctic as Force, instead of Resource," Canadian Broadcasting Corporation, 31 August 2006.

53 See, for example, Aupilaarjuk, in McGrath, "Isumaksaqsiurutigijakka"; John R. Bennett and Susan Rowley, eds., *Uqalurait: An Oral History of Nunavut* (Montreal and Kingston: McGill-Queen's University Press, 2004); Price, "The Arctic Is My Home"; Price, "Tukisivallialiqtakka"; Qitsualik, "Nalunaktuq."

54 McGrath develops the "Qaggiq Model" of Inuktitut knowledge renewal, a model that nourishes Inuit ways of being-knowing-doing-accounting to renew Inuit knowledge systems and relationships. She encourages Qablunaat to view the Qaggiq model as a "conceptual space in which qablunaat can listen, experience and observe the strength of Inuktitut renewal so that they understand more clearly what they need to support." McGrath, "Isumaksaqsiurutigijakka," 253.

55 Kuokkanen, *Reshaping the University,* 116.

56 Hearne's narrative refers to "Northern Indians" (Dënesųłiné, or Chipewyan Dene) and "Southern Indians" (Cree). His mostly Northern Indian companions were joined by

"Copper Indians" (T'satsąot'ınę, or Yellowknives Dene) at various points in the journey, including at the massacre scene. The participation of Copper Indians in the massacre is elided by Hearne; he notes that they were present as preparations for the massacre were made but does not mention them by name in his description of the event, referring only to the "Northern Indians" or simply to "the Indians." Venema suggests that Hearne also avoids direct reference to Matonabbee's participation in the massacre because he hoped to "[shelter] Matonabbee from the censure of European audiences by neutralizing evidence of his violent outbursts." The fact that Hearne found the Copper Indians to be remarkably "kind" and "highly pleased" at the prospect of meeting him and assisting with his survey, and that upon meeting him they determined him to be "a perfect human being," may well have contributed to Hearne's muted treatment of their role in the massacre. Venema, "'Under the Protection of a Principal Man,'" 179–80.

Chapter 2: Ordering Violence

1 Pauline Holdstock, *Into the Heart of the Country* (Toronto: Harper Collins, 2011), 38–39. Note that in Holdstock's novel, dialogue is not indicated by quotation marks. I have added them for clarity. In the novel, Matonabbee gives his reasons for the Bloody Falls massacre, but I have removed his explanation because it is imagined by Holdstock, not based on his own words. It reads, "I have my people to care for. When my people fall sick and die for no reason at all, it is the work of our enemies to the north. In the winter before the last just gone, six of my own family died, falling to their knees from where they stood and dead within two days. My own aunt who raised me and loved me and five of her family. There is no sickness in the world that does this thing. It was the work of our enemies and they could strike again with their conjuring. That was why I walked to seek them out. No leader would do less." Note that this explanation for the massacre is consistent with Heather Rollason Driscoll's dissertation, which reviews the journals and correspondence of Captain John Fowler, who briefly governed Prince of Wales Fort in the late 1760s. In early 1769, Fowler made note of "a great mortality among the Chipewyan" and the sense among them that the deaths were a result of Inuit "conjuring." Over the following months, Fowler documented "the disagreeable News that the Northern Indians ... [are] going to Kill the Usquemays [Inuit], the reason they give for it thay have had Many of the Northern Indians died, and they think the Usquemays have Cungered [conjured] them to dith [death]." Quoted in Heather Rollason Driscoll, "The Genesis of 'A Journey to the Northern Ocean ...'" (PhD diss., University of Alberta, 2002), 106. Rollason Driscoll explores the possibility that the Bloody Falls massacre was indeed intended to avenge these deaths. Although "in none of Hearne's letters, journal notes, draft narratives, or the 1795 published account does Hearne indicate that the Chipewyan (who were joined by Copper Indians) attacked the Inuit out of revenge," she notes, and "the lack of motive is part of what fuels Hearne's horror" in the published narrative, "Hearne's ignorance does not preclude the existence of motive." Rollason Driscoll, "The Genesis," 109.

2 Frances Widdowson and Albert Howard, *Disrobing the Aboriginal Industry: The Deception behind Indigenous Cultural Preservation* (Montreal and Kingston: McGill-Queen's University Press, 2008), 263, 264.

3 See, for example, Ned Blackhawk, *Violence over the Land: Indians and Empires in the Early American West* (Cambridge, MA: Harvard University Press, 2006); Nicholas Blomley, "Law, Property, and the Geography of Violence: The Frontier, the Survey, and the Grid," *Annals of the Association of American Geographers* 93, 1 (2003): 121–41; Judith Butler,

Precarious Life: The Powers of Mourning and Violence (London: Verso, 2004); Fanon, *The Wretched of the Earth;* Derek Gregory and Allen Pred, eds., *Violent Geographies: Fear, Terror, and Political Violence* (London: Routledge, 2007); Ian Haywood, *Bloody Romanticism: Spectacular Violence and the Politics of Representation* (New York: Palgrave Macmillan, 2006).

4 Samuel Hearne, *A Journey from Prince of Wales's Fort in Hudson's Bay, to the Northern Ocean ...* (London: Strahan and Cadell, 1795), viii. Oral storytelling was an important component of fur trade and fort cultures. See Michael Payne, *Prince of Wales' Fort: A Social History, 1717–1782.* Parks Canada Manuscript Report No. 371 (Ottawa: Parks Canada, 1979); Carolyn Podruchny, "Werewolves and Windigos: Narratives of Cannibal Monsters in French-Canadian Voyageur Oral Tradition," *Ethnohistory* 51, 4 (2004): 677–700. Hearne is known to have entertained Andrew Graham, chief factor at Prince of Wales Fort between 1774–75, with stories from his journey, which Graham recorded in his voluminous "Observations on Hudson's Bay," HBCA E.2/4–13; see also Andrew Graham, *Andrew Graham's Observations of Hudson's Bay, 1767–1791,* ed. Glyndwr Williams (London: Hudson's Bay Record Society, 1969). Various manuscript versions of Hearne's original travel notes have been located over the years, including the Stowe Manuscript, which dates from at least 1791 and probably earlier. Excerpts of Hearne's journal were published as early as 1784 in *Scots Magazine* as part of a review of Cook's *Voyage to the Pacific Ocean,* but public knowledge of Hearne's journey and his narrative was primarily initiated by the 1795 publication and review of his *Journey to the Northern Ocean.* Note that in the 1784 *Scots Magazine* excerpt, there are nearly thirty attackers (instead of the nearly twenty in the published narrative), and many of the particularly graphic murder scenes are not yet fleshed out (for example, the man who "fell a sacrifice to [the Indians'] fury" is mentioned but not the twenty attackers who reduce his body to a "cullender"). *Scots Magazine,* "Books: Cook's *Voyage to the Pacific Ocean,*" *Scots Magazine* 46 (June 1784): 309–17.

5 Samuel Hearne, Samuel Hearne to HBC, 28 August 1772, folder 17405, HBCA A.11/14, London Inward Correspondence from HBC Posts - Churchill, 1723–87, HBC Archives, Winnipeg, MN.

6 See James Cook, *A Voyage to the Pacific Ocean Undertaken by Command of His Majesty for Making Discoveries in the Northern Hemisphere ...* (London: Printed for John Stockdale et al., 1784), 4:57. Regarding Royal Society member access to HBC reports, see Richard Ruggles, "Governor Samuel Wegg: Intelligent Layman of the Royal Society," *Notes and Records of the Royal Society of London* 32, 2 (1978): 181–99.

7 The Preface, titled "À La Pérouse," is written in the form of a letter to the explorer by A.J.N. Lallemand: "It is you to whom Europe is indebted for the publication of this work" (C'est à vous que l'Europe est redevable de la publication de cet ouvrage). See A.J.N. Lallemand, "À La Pérouse," in *Voyage De Samuel Hearne, Du Fort Du Prince De Galles ...* (Paris: Imprimerie de Patris, 1799), n.p.

8 Hearne, *A Journey,* v-vi.

9 Simon Schaffer, "Visions of Empire: Afterword," in *Visions of Empire: Voyages, Botany, and Representations of Nature,* ed. David Philip Miller and Peter Hanns Reill (Cambridge: Cambridge University Press, 1996), 342. See also David Livingstone, *The Geographical Tradition: Episodes in the History of a Contested Enterprise* (Oxford: Blackwell, 1992).

10 "Contract between Strahan and Hearne for MSS, 8 October 1792," Coll. 48901, ff. 53–54, Strahan Papers, British Library, London. Richard Glover compares this payment to Jane Austen's receipt of £10 for the first draft of *Northanger Abbey* in 1803. Today, £200 would

be worth approximately $25,000. Richard Glover, "Editor's Introduction," in *A Journey from Prince of Wales's Fort in Hudson's Bay to the Northern Ocean in the Years 1769, 1770, 1771, and 1772,* ed. Richard Glover (Toronto: Macmillan Press, 1958), vii-xliii.

11 See Alexander Dalrymple, *Memoir of a Map of the Lands around the North-Pole, Scale 1/10 of an Inch to 1°. of Latitude* (London, 1789). Although some have suggested that Dalrymple's questioning of Hearne's measurements constituted a "venomous attack" on his reliability, Howard Tyrrell Fry argues that "there is no justification" for this claim and that Hearne was simply "upset by this questioning and tried to defend his account." Howard Tyrrell Fry, *Alexander Dalrymple (1737–1808) and the Expansion of British Trade* (Toronto: University of Toronto Press, for the Royal Commonwealth Society, 1970), 204. Dalrymple did have a habit of aggrandizing his own credibility through critiques of others, and his close relationship with HBC governor Samuel Wegg likely led Hearne to worry that Dalrymple's critique would damage his standing with the HBC. John Hawkesworth, *An Account of the Voyages Undertaken by the Order of His Present Majesty for Making Discoveries in the Southern Hemisphere ...* (London: Strahan and Cadell, 1773); see also Alexander Dalrymple, *A Letter from Mr. Dalrymple to Dr. Hawkesworth, Occasioned by Some Groundless and Illiberal Imputations in His Account of the Late Voyages to the South* (London: Printed for J. Nourse et al., 1773).

12 Hearne, *A Journey,* viii.

13 Schaffer, "Visions of Empire," 340.

14 This tension, in fact, provides occasion for repeated commentary on the text and its "defence" as a source of scientific, anthropological, and historical knowledge. See, for example, Richard Glover, "A Note on John Richardson's 'Digression concerning Hearne's Route,'" *Canadian Historical Review* 32, 3 (1951): 252–63; Robert McGhee, *The Last Imaginary Place: A Human History of the Arctic World* (Gatineau, QC: Canadian Museum of Civilization, 2004); Ken McGoogan, *Ancient Mariner: The Amazing Adventures of Samuel Hearne, the Sailor Who Walked to the Arctic Ocean* (Toronto: HarperFlamingoCanada, 2003); J. Tuzo Wilson, "New Light on Hearne," *Beaver* Outfit 280 (June 1949): 14–18. See also Chapter 3.

15 Ruggles, "Governor Samuel Wegg." See also Glyndwr Williams, "The Hudson's Bay Company and Its Critics in the Eighteenth Century," *Transactions of the Royal Historical Society* 20 (1970): 149–71.

16 Ruggles emphasizes the importance of the friendship between Dalrymple and Wegg for the HBC, arguing that "perhaps more than most others it would have been Alexander Dalrymple who in his discussions and proselytizing undoubtedly was of considerable influence on the geographic and cartographic education of Wegg, and on the gradual emergence of the more cartographic, exploratory, and overt policies of the Hudson's Bay Company during the latter half of this century ... They attended evening dinners together nearly a dozen times from 1768–1775, on the same occasions that Banks, Barrington, and Franklin were also frequent companions. From 1779 until 1799, when Wegg retired from Governorship, he and Dalrymple were at dinner together on approximately sixty-five occasions, which was the crucial period of stewardship of Company affairs by Wegg as Deputy and then Governor." Ruggles, "Governor Samuel Wegg," 193.

17 *Gentleman's Magazine,* "Review of a Journey from Prince of Wales Fort, in Hudson's Bay ...," *Gentleman's Magazine* 66, 6 (1796): 498 (emphasis added); *British Critic,* "Art. IX, a Journey from Prince of Wales Fort, in Hudson's Bay, to the Northern Ocean ..." *British Critic* 8 (1796): 54, 62.

18 Felix Driver, "Distance and Disturbance: Travel, Exploration and Knowledge in the Nineteenth Century," *Transactions of the Royal Historical Society* 14 (2004): 75. See also Janice Cavell, *Tracing the Connected Narrative: Arctic Exploration in British Print Culture, 1818–1860* (Toronto: University of Toronto Press, 2008), for a discussion of how writer and book editor John Hawkesworth's poorly received attempts to polish the writing of various explorers in the mid-eighteenth century led critics to favour first-person accounts by explorers. By the late eighteenth century, Cavell argues, "a narrative written by the commander of an expedition in a plain, honest style" had become "the paradigm for the best exploration literature," not in spite of its plainness, but precisely because this attested to the truth of the account. Ibid., 19.

19 *English Review,* "Review of a Journey from Prince of Wales's Fort in Hudson's Bay, to the Northern Ocean," *English Review of Literature, Science, Discoveries, Inventions, and Practical Controversies and Contests* 28 (1796): 1–2; *Critical Review,* "A Journey from Prince of Wales's Fort in Hudson's Bay, to the Northern Ocean," *Critical Review* 20 (1797): 139, 127. It is worth noting that the *Monthly Review,* which also published a celebratory article, was partly owned by A. Strahan, the publisher of *A Journey.* See Antonia Forster, "Griffiths, Ralph (1720?–1803)," *Oxford Dictionary of National Biography Online.*

20 *British Critic,* "Art. IX," 62.

21 See Alexander Dalrymple, *Plan for Promoting the Fur Trade, and Securing It to This Country, by Uniting the Operations of the East-India and Hudson's-Bay Companys* (London: George Bigg, 1789); Williams, "The Hudson's Bay Company," 170.

22 See, for example, *Critical Review,* "A Journey from Prince of Wales's Fort," 127.

23 See *Britannic Magazine,* "Customs and Manners of the Northern Indians," *Britannic Magazine* 5 (1797): 175–80; Kaleb, "Letter to the Editor, Re: Massacre of Esquimaux by the Indians," *Mirror of Literature, Amusement, and Instruction* 2, 60 (1823): 466–68; William Mavor, *Historical Account of the Most Celebrated Voyages, Travels, and Discoveries from the Time of Columbus to the Present Period,* vol. 17 (London: E. Newberry, 1797).

24 *Scots Magazine,* "Books."

25 *Critical Review,* "A Journey from Prince of Wales's Fort," 127. See also *Universal Magazine,* "Extraordinary Adventure and Resources of an Indian Woman," *Universal Magazine of Knowledge and Pleasure* 99 (1796): 317–19. The word "plain" can be read here as a reference to truthfulness: to write in a plain, unadorned manner was to write honestly and reliably. As Mary Louise Pratt observes, "travel literature did not remain immune to the professionalization of writing in the eighteenth century. Now that it had become a profitable business, traveler-writers and their publishers relied more and more on professional writers and editors to ensure a competitive product, often transforming manuscripts completely, usually in the direction of the novel. Debates about embellishment, seductiveness, naked truth, and the like are often debates about the role of these figures, and the compromises involved in writing for money." Mary Louise Pratt, *Imperial Eyes: Travel Writing and Transculturation* (London: Routledge, 1992), 88. See also Cavell, *Tracing the Connected Narrative.*

26 See, for example, Catherine Hall, *Civilising Subjects: Metropole and Colony in the English Imagination, 1830–1867* (Oxford: Polity Press, 2002); Roy Harvey Pearce, *Savagism and Civilization: A Study of the Indian and the American Mind* (Baltimore: Johns Hopkins University Press, 1967); Edward Said, *Orientalism* (New York: Pantheon, 1978).

27 *Critical Review,* "A Journey from Prince of Wales's Fort," 131, 132 (emphasis in original).

28 Seamus Deane, *The French Revolution and Enlightenment in England, 1789–1832* (Cambridge, MA: Harvard University Press, 1988); Tim Fulford, *Romantic Indians: Native*

Americans, British Literature, and Transatlantic Culture, 1756–1830 (Oxford: Oxford University Press, 2006); Haywood, *Bloody Romanticism;* Saree Makdisi, *Romantic Imperialism: Universal Empire and the Culture of Modernity* (Cambridge: Cambridge University Press, 1998); Robert Maniquis, "Filling Up and Emptying Out the Sublime: Terror in British Radical Culture," *Huntington Library Quarterly* 63, 3 (2000): 369–405; Carl Edward Thompson, *The Suffering Traveller and the Romantic Imagination* (Oxford: Oxford University Press, 2007).

29 Burke, quoted in Andrew McCann, *Cultural Politics in the 1790s: Literature, Radicalism, and the Public Sphere* (London: Macmillan, 1999), 57.

30 Hearne, *A Journey,* 150–51 (emphasis added).

31 Maniquis, "Filling Up and Emptying Out," 375; Makdisi, *Romantic Imperialism;* McCann, *Cultural Politics in the 1790s.*

32 McCann, *Cultural Politics in the 1790s,* 107. See also Jon Klancher, *The Making of English Reading Audiences, 1790–1832* (Madison: University of Wisconsin Press, 1987).

33 Haywood, *Bloody Romanticism,* 60, 61.

34 Linda Colley, *Captives: Britain, Empire, and the World, 1600–1850* (New York: Random House, 2002); Fulford, *Romantic Indians;* Haywood, *Bloody Romanticism.*

35 For an early assessment of Hearne's impact on Romantic poetry, see Lane Cooper, "A Dissertation upon Northern Lights," *Modern Language Notes* 21, 2 (1906): 44–46. See also Angela Byrne, *Geographies of the Romantic North: Science, Antiquarianism, and Travel, 1790–1830* (New York: Palgrave-Macmillan, 2013).

36 Ernest Hartley Coleridge, ed., *The Complete Poetical Works of Samuel Taylor Coleridge* (Oxford: Clarendon Press, 1975), 1:269.

37 Fulford, *Romantic Indians,* 165. See also Tim Fulford, "Slavery and Superstition in the Supernatural Poems," in *The Cambridge Companion to Coleridge,* ed. Lucy Newlyn (Cambridge: Cambridge University Press, 2002), 45–58.

38 Thompson, *The Suffering Traveller,* 227.

39 William Wordsworth, *The Excursion: Being a Portion of the Recluse, a Poem,* 2nd ed. (London: Longman, Hurst, Rees, Orme and Brown, 1820), 138.

40 Hearne, *A Journey,* 304, 340–41.

41 Ibid., 154.

42 McGhee, *The Last Imaginary Place,* 213. For an extended discussion of the association of savagery with a "lack of 'social affections'" and a tendency to "[glory] in hardship, cruelty, and torture," see Pearce, *Savagism and Civilization,* 86–87.

43 *Monthly Review,* "Review of Samuel Hearne, a Journey from Prince of Wales's Fort in Hudson's Bay, to the Northern Ocean 1769, 1770, 1771, 1772," *Monthly Review* 20 (1796): 250.

44 Fulford, *Romantic Indians,* 68–69.

45 Hearne, *A Journey,* 154–55.

46 Ted Boxer, "Memo to Chief, Program Policy and Planning Division Executive Secretariat, Re: Proposed Plaquing at Coppermine," 1973, 3, box 11, file 3, G-1993-007, Northwest Territories, Department of Culture and Communications fonds, Prince of Wales Northern Heritage Centre, Yellowknife, NT.

47 Hearne, *A Journey,* 340.

48 Ibid.

49 Dalrymple himself, upon reading Hearne's narrative, exclaimed that "whoever has read Mr. Hearne's Journal, must feel a strong desire, of correcting the brutality of the Indians,

truly called *Savage,* by introducing amongst them the Comforts and Humanity of civilized Life, and nothing will be more conducive, towards effecting that desirable Purpose, than establishing the Knowledge of God, and the Light of the Gospel, amongst them." Dalrymple, *Plan for Promoting the Fur Trade,* 32 (emphasis in original). See also Kerry Abel, *Drum Songs: Glimpses of Dene History* (Montreal and Kingston: McGill-Queen's University Press, 1993); Arthur Ray, *Indians in the Fur Trade: Their Role as Trappers, Hunters, and Middlemen in the Lands Southwest of Hudson Bay, 1660–1870* (Toronto: University of Toronto Press, 1974); Frank Tough, *As Their Natural Resources Fail: Native People and the Economic History of Northern Manitoba, 1870–1930* (Vancouver: UBC Press, 1996).

50 Michael Banton, "The Classification of Races in Europe and North America: 1700–1850," in *Race and Racialization: Essential Readings,* ed. Tania Das Gupta et al. (Toronto: Canadian Scholars' Press, 2007): 15–23.

51 For example, see Gustav Jahoda, "Towards Scientific Racism," in Das Gupta et al., *Race and Racialization,* 24–30, on the importance of travel narratives in shaping naturalist and race theorist Johann Blumenbach's work. C. Stuart Houston, Tim Ball, and Mary Houston trace extensive links between naturalists who operated in the Hudson Bay region and Linnaeus, Buffon, and others. C. Stuart Houston, Tim Ball, and Mary Houston, *Eighteenth-Century Naturalists of Hudson Bay* (Montreal and Kingston: McGill-Queen's University Press, 2003). In *Placing the Enlightenment* (Chicago: University of Chicago Press, 2007), Charles Withers considers the geographies of ideas about race through the late eighteenth century, including the varied ways in which travel narratives were taken up by readers. Specific evidence that late-eighteenth- and early-nineteenth-century racial theorists read *A Journey* has not been uncovered, but Charles Darwin certainly read it, and given its extensive circulation, commentary on its importance by Cook, La Pérouse, and others, and evidence of Hearne's correspondence with Andrew Pennant, it is highly likely that they did.

52 Terry Goldie, *Fear and Temptation: The Image of the Indigene in Canadian, Australian, and New Zealand Literatures* (Montreal and Kingston: McGill-Queen's University Press, 1989), 90, 95. This is, of course, a defining feature of colonial renderings of indigeneity. Ned Blackhawk explains, for instance, that Mark Twain's description of the Gochute as "the wretchedest type of mankind ... considerably inferior to even the despised Digger Indians of California, inferior to all races of savages on our continent" both misrecognized poverty as wretchedness and inferiority, and elided the causes of this poverty and suffering: imperial violence itself. Blackhawk, *Violence over the Land,* 11.

53 Ian S. MacLaren, "Exploring Canadian Literature: Samuel Hearne and the Inuit Girl," in *Probing Canadian Culture,* ed. P. Easingwood, K. Gross, and W. Klooss (Augsburg: AV-Verlag, 1991), 93, 106.

54 Hearne, *A Journey,* 154.

55 Robert E. Pinkerton, "The Far Away Metal River," *True: The Man's Magazine,* May 1947, 70.

56 Ibid., 68.

57 See, for example, Anne McClintock, *Imperial Leather: Race, Gender and Sexuality in the Colonial Contest* (New York: Routledge, 1995); Andrea Smith, *Conquest: Sexual Violence and American Indian Genocide* (Cambridge, MA: South End Press, 2005).

58 Pinkerton, "The Far Away Metal River," 80.

59 Don Gutteridge, *Coppermine: The Quest for the North* (Ottawa: Oberon Press, 1973). Consider, also, Peter C. Newman's 1986 retelling of the massacre in *Company of Adventurers:*

"Just after midnight on July 17 the massacre began. The Indians slithered right up to the tents and hurled themselves at the sleeping Eskimos. The scene was more reminiscent of an abattoir than of a battle, with the panic-stricken victims rearing out of their cozy tents and being impaled on out-thrust spears. More than twenty men, women and children, their faces still sweet from interrupted slumber, were slain within minutes, their death rattles despoiling the Arctic silence. A young Eskimo woman ran desperately towards Hearne, the one man not engaged in the killing. A Chipewyan wheeled and plunged a spear into her side." Quoted in MacLaren, "Exploring Canadian Literature," 91.

60 MacLaren, "Exploring Canadian Literature," 98.

61 Ian Baucom, "Spectres of the Atlantic," *South Atlantic Quarterly* 100, 1 (2001): 64, 65.

62 Samuel Hearne, quoted in MacLaren, "Exploring Canadian Literature," 94.

63 MacLaren, "Exploring Canadian Literature," 94. See also Charles Withers and Innes Keighren, "Travels into Print: Authoring, Editing and Narratives of Travel and Exploration, c. 1815-c. 1857," *Transactions of the Institute of British Geographers* 36, 4 (2011): 560–73.

Chapter 3: To Mourn

1 In Inuit epistemologies, plants are not given specific names unless they serve a particular purpose. Unlike Arctic cotton *(kanguuyat),* which is used as a wick in seal-oil lamps *(qudliit),* or capitate lousewort *(kukiujait),* which is edible, *Senecio lugens* has no edible, medicinal, or practical uses, and it therefore has no distinct name in Inuinnaqtun. Lucy Taipana, pers. comm., Kugluktuk, NU, 8 August 2007; see also Carolyn Mallory and Susan Aiken, *Common Plants of Nunavut* (Iqaluit: Nunavut Department of Education, 2004). Note, however, that it is not uncommon for there to be many terms in Inuktut for something that has just one name in English.

2 Technically, *lugeo* translates as "I mourn." In Latin, verbs are referred to in general terms by their first-person present indicative conjugation form.

3 Michael L. Charters, "California Plant Names: Latin and Greek Meanings and Derivations, a Dictionary of Botanical Etymology," 2003–05, http://www.calflora.net/botanical names/pageLH-LY.html; Edmund Carroll Jaeger, *A Source-Book of Biological Names and Terms,* 3rd ed. (Springfield, IL: Thomas, 1955), 145.

4 John Richardson in John Franklin, *Narrative of a Journey to the Shores of the Polar Sea, in the Years 1819, 20, 21, and 22 ...* (London: John Murray, 1823), 759.

5 This approach to truth is long-standing in a number of intellectual traditions. The way in which material objects figure in the production of truth has been of particular interest to actor-network scholars, who originally examined the production of scientific truth through laboratory practices but went on to consider the relational, material truth-effects generated in a range of other settings. How knowledge and things interweave to produce truth was also an enduring preoccupation of Michel Foucault, whose studies of how power targets "men in their relations [with things]" are more keenly attuned to the political stakes of producing truth. Michel Foucault, "Governmentality," in *The Foucault Effect: Studies in Governmentality,* ed. Graham Burchell, Colin Gordon, and Peter Miller (Chicago: University of Chicago Press, 1991), 93. See also Steven Shapin, *A Social History of Truth: Civility and Science in Seventeenth-Century England* (Chicago: University of Chicago Press, 1995).

6 Samuel Hearne, *A Journey from Prince of Wales's Fort, in Hudson's Bay, to the Northern Ocean ...* (London: Strahan and Cadell, 1795), 173.

7 [John Barrow], "Lord Selkirk, and the North-West Company," *Quarterly Review* 16 (October 1816): 167 (emphasis in original). Later, Hearne's inaccuracies were blamed on the imperfections of his instruments and particularly the unreliability of magnetic compasses at northern latitudes rather than his personal failings. See John Richardson, "Digression concerning Hearne's Route," in George Back, *Narrative of the Arctic Land Expedition to the Mouth of the Great Fish River ...* (London: John Murray, 1836), 144–55. For a more detailed discussion of the events leading up to the Franklin expedition, see Janice Cavell, *Tracing the Connected Narrative: Arctic Exploration in British Print Culture, 1818–1860* (Toronto: University of Toronto Press, 2008), particularly Chapters 2 and 4. See also Trevor Levere, *Science and the Canadian Arctic: A Century of Exploration, 1818–1918* (Cambridge: Cambridge University Press, 1993); Glyn Williams, *Arctic Labyrinth: The Quest for the Northwest Passage* (London: Allen Lane, 2009).

8 Lord Bathurst, quoted in Levere, *Science and the Canadian Arctic,* 105.

9 C. Stuart Houston, "New Light on Dr. John Richardson," *Canadian Medical Association Journal* 131 (1984): 653–60.

10 John Richardson, Letter from J. Richardson to W. Hooker, London, 8 May 1819, in *Sir W. Hooker's Letters to J. Richardson, 1819–1843,* 2b, 3, Kew Gardens Library and Archives, London.

11 Noah Heringman, "Introduction: The Commerce of Literature and Natural History," in *Romantic Science: The Literary Forms of Natural History,* ed. Noah Heringman (Albany: State University of New York Press, 2003), 1–22.

12 Londa Schiebinger, *Plants and Empire* (Cambridge, MA: Harvard University Press, 2004).

13 Janet Browne, "Botany in the Boudoir and Garden: The Banksian Context," in *Visions of Empire: Voyages, Botany, and Representations of Nature,* ed. David Philip Miller and Peter Hanns Reill (Cambridge: Cambridge University Press, 1996), 153–72; Theresa M. Kelley, "Romantic Exemplarity: Botany and 'Material' Culture," in Heringman, *Romantic Science,* 228–46; Gordon McOuat, "Cataloguing Power: Delineating 'Competent Naturalists' and the Meaning of Species in the British Museum," *British Journal for the History of Science* 34, 1 (2001): 1–28; Philip Rehbock, *The Philosophical Naturalists: Themes in Early Nineteenth Century British Biology* (Madison: University of Wisconsin Press, 1983).

14 Paul White has pointed out, moreover, that the religious beliefs of scientists may be less important to understanding nineteenth-century conflicts between religion and science than the ways in which various professional groups struggled to gain cultural authority against the Anglican Church. Paul White, *Thomas Huxley: Making the "Man of Science"* (Cambridge: Cambridge University Press, 2003), 101. John Hedley Brooke also provides a much more nuanced account of the relationship between religious belief and scientific practice. John Hedley Brooke, "Religious Belief and the Content of the Sciences," *Osiris,* 2nd ser., 16 (2001): 3–28. Charles Withers makes the important observation that Linnaeus "classified the human species as part of nature" but that "his was a static taxonomy in a God-given world. His emphasis on 'variety' paid little attention to the reasons for the different forms. Explanation of the variation mattered less than description of difference – 'to know these bodies ... by those marks imprinted on them by nature' as Linnaeus wrote." Charles W.J. Withers, *Placing the Enlightenment* (Chicago: University of Chicago Press, 2007), 144. In other words, Linnaeus's classificatory scheme did not require consideration of cause or origin, even if he himself understood this variation to be "God-given."

15 David Elliston Allen, *The Naturalist in Britain: A Social History* (London: Allen Lane, 1976), 54. See also Brooke, "Religious Belief."

16 On the history of objectivity, see Lorraine Daston and Peter Galison, *Objectivity* (New York: Zone Books, 2007).

17 John McIlraith, *Life of Sir John Richardson ...* (London: Longmans, Green, 1868), 4.

18 See, for example, C. Stuart Houston, *Arctic Ordeal: The Journal of John Richardson, Surgeon-Naturalist with John Franklin, 1820–22* (Kingston and Montreal: McGill-Queen's University Press, 1984).

19 See John Richardson, Letter to J. Franklin, 24 June 1823; John Richardson, Letter to J. Franklin, 6 July 1823; and John Richardson, Letter to J. Franklin, 22 July 1824, Kew Gardens Library and Archives, London, J. Richardson Letters to J. Franklin, 1823–42. See also John Richardson, Letter to Mary Richardson, 18 July 1821 [transcription], box 46, file 9, C.S. Houston fonds, Series VIII, University of Saskatchewan Archives, Saskatoon, SK. For discussion of Richardson's religious fervour, see Cavell, *Tracing the Connected Narrative.*

20 Richardson, Letter to Mary Richardson, 18 July 1821.

21 Richardson, Letter to J. Franklin, 22 July 1824, 23.

22 Rehbock, *The Philosophical Naturalists*; John Hedley Brooke, *Science and Religion: Some Historical Perspectives* (Cambridge: Cambridge University Press, 1991).

23 There was a precedent in the travel narrative genre for seeing signs of God's presence in plant life, particularly when confronted with personal hardship in "savage" settings. Much like Hearne's narrative, Mungo Park's *Travels in the Interior Districts of Africa* climaxes in a scene of absolute confrontation with savagery. Abandoned by his guides, pillaged by bandits, and left for dead, Park experienced what Mary Louise Pratt, *Imperial Eyes,* 75, describes as a "naturalist's epiphany." Park wrote, "Whatever way I turned, nothing appeared but danger and difficulty. I saw myself in the midst of a vast wilderness, in the depth of the rainy season, naked and alone, surrounded by savage animals, and men still more savage. I was five hundred miles from the nearest European settlement. At this moment, painful as my reflections were, the extraordinary beauty of a small moss in fructification irresistibly caught my eye ... Though the whole plant was not larger than the top of one of my fingers, I could not contemplate the delicate conformation of its roots, leaves, and capsule, without admiration. Can that Being, thought I, who planted, watered, and brought to perfection, in this obscure part of the world, a thing which appears of so small importance, look with unconcern upon the situation and sufferings of creatures formed after his own image? Surely not. I started up, and, disregarding both hunger and fatigue, travelled forward, assured that relief was at hand, and I was not disappointed." Mungo Park, *Travels in the Interior Districts of Africa ...* (London: Bulmer, 1799), 225.

24 These rules were not necessarily adhered to, even by Linnaeus. As Janet Browne points out, Linnaeus himself personified plants: for instance, he described plant fertilization as a form of marriage involving husbands, wives, and a marriage bed, Browne, "Botany in the Boudoir," 155–56. Richardson's personification of *Senecio lugens* as a grieving witness to the Bloody Falls massacre thus took its cue from Linnaeus as much as it subverted his naming protocol. See also Heringman, "Introduction: The Commerce of Literature"; Schiebinger, *Plants and Empire.*

25 Charters, "California Plant Names"; Jaeger, *A Source-Book,* 145.

26 Tim Fulford, Debbie Lee, and Peter J. Kitson, *Literature, Science, and Exploration in the Romantic Era* (Cambridge: Cambridge University Press, 2004); Ann Shteir, "Gender and 'Modern' Botany in Victorian England," *Osiris,* 2nd ser., 12 (1997): 29–38.

27 John Richardson, Letter to J. Franklin, 6 August 1823, Kew Gardens Library and Archives. Cavell claims that the expedition "achieved instant fame on its return to England in October 1822," owing in part to newspaper reports of the deaths of expedition members Robert Hood and Michel Teroahauté, published only days before. Cavell, *Tracing the Connected Narrative*, 88.

28 John Richardson, "Franklin's 1st Journey App," 1823, Kew Gardens Library and Archives, London. Thank you to D.J. Nicholas Hind at Kew Gardens for bringing this separately paginated appendix to my attention.

29 On the reading public for travel narratives at this time, see Janice Cavell, "Making Books for Mr Murray: The Case of Edward Parry's Third Arctic Narrative," *The Library: Transactions of the Bibliographical Society*, 7th ser., 14, 1 (March 2013): 45–69.

30 Janice Cavell, pers. comm., e-mail, Ottawa, 25 November 2013. Thank you to Janice Cavell for drawing my attention to the complexity of the image production process, the respective roles of Batty and Finden, and the importance of Back's original sketchbook, as well as for her careful reading of previous versions of this chapter.

31 Franklin, *Narrative of a Journey*, 175.

32 John Richardson in Houston, *Arctic Ordeal*, 77, 78.

33 Franklin, *Narrative of a Journey*, 174.

34 George Back, *Arctic Artist: The Journal and Paintings of George Back, Midshipman with Franklin, 1819–1822*, ed. C. Stuart Houston (Montreal and Kingston: McGill-Queen's University Press, 1994), 142.

35 George Back's original watercolour sketchbook is held by Library and Archives Canada (accession 1994–254-DAP). Thank you to Mary Margaret Johnston Miller at Library and Archives Canada for her assistance with consulting it. Back's sketchbook was acquired with the assistance of the Department of Canadian Heritage through the Canadian Cultural Property Export and Import Act, and with the aid of a grant from Hoechst-Celanese Canada. The sketch in question is reproduced as Figure 32 in *Arctic Artist*. As noted, Back did not sketch Bloody Falls in his own field sketchbook, and Hood's sketch probably formed the basis of the engraving (to which Back may have contributed). Stuart Houston claims that Hood's journals and sketches composed between 15 September 1820 and his death in October 1821 have been lost. See C. Stuart Houston, *To the Arctic by Canoe, 1819–1821: The Journal and Paintings of Robert Hood, Midshipman with Franklin* (Montreal and Kingston: McGill-Queen's University Press, 1994), xxxiv. See also Paul vanPeenen, "Arctic Artist: The Changing Nature of George Back's Arctic Land Expeditions, 1819–1835" (master's thesis, Simon Fraser University, 2008), 60.

36 Robin McGrath, "Samuel Hearne and the Inuit Oral Tradition," *Studies in Canadian Literature* 18, 2 (1993): 94–109; Denis St-Onge, "The Coppermine River: Art and Reality," *Canadian Geographic* 102, 4 (1982): 28–31.

37 Allen Niptanatiak, pers. comm., Kugluktuk, NU, 5 July 2006. St-Onge's argument about flooding is not very convincing. The location of the bones in the Back/Batty/Finden engraving, on the bluff overlooking the rapids, is not subject to flooding. Kugluktukmiut note that ice sometimes backs up behind the rapids and scours the landscape, but this process is more likely to displace materials at lower elevations, not at the bluff where the bones are placed. See also McGrath, "Samuel Hearne and the Inuit Oral Tradition."

38 Back, *Arctic Artist*, 142; Richardson in Houston, *Arctic Ordeal*, 77–78. Stuart Houston suggests that a rocky island several hundred yards downstream from the rapids "must have been the exact location of the massacre," but the expedition members' journals do not seem to support this claim. Back, *Arctic* Artist, 142.

39 Ian MacLaren, quoted in vanPeenen, "Arctic Artist," 26. See also Ian S. MacLaren, "The Aesthetic Map of the North, 1845–1859," *Arctic* 38, 2 (1985): 89–103.

40 Ian S. MacLaren, "From Exploration to Publication: The Evolution of a 19th Century Arctic Narrative," *Arctic* 47, 1 (1994): 48, 49.

41 Franklin, *Narrative of a Journey*, 350.

42 John Barrow to John Murray, 14 November 1821, quoted in Back, *Arctic Artist*, 382.

43 Dease and Simpson reported finding two skulls at Bloody Falls in 1838, "the sole remaining memorial of the atrocious massacre of the Esquimaux by Hearne's Chipewyans in 1772." Thomas Simpson, *Narrative of the Discoveries on the North Coast of America ...* (London: R. Bentley, 1843), 262. Historian Janice Cavell convincingly argues that though some Arctic explorers regularly and purposely misrepresented their experiences and findings, "extensive comparison of private and public writings by Franklin and Richardson shows that they were both remarkably reliable. Indeed, it is surprising how little either of them altered their journals during the publication process. Naturally, they were sometimes misled by cultural preconceptions or misinformed, but they did not deliberately distort things, even when they could have reaped considerable advantage from doing so." Janice Cavell, pers. comm., e-mail, Ottawa, 25 November 2013.

44 An informational placard at Bloody Falls points to *Senecio lugens* as a monument to the massacre, and current efforts to list the Coppermine as a federal "heritage river" also highlight the flower. See Nunavut Parks, *Coppermine River Nomination Document* (Kugluktuk, NU: Government of Nunavut, Parks and Tourism Division, 2002).

45 Williams, *Arctic Labyrinth*, 128.

46 Richardson, Letter to Mary Richardson, 18 July 1821.

47 Franklin, *Narrative of a Journey*, 174.

48 Back, *Arctic Artist*, 141.

49 Franklin, *Narrative of a Journey*, 226. See also Richardson's carefully worded statement regarding the extent of Hearne's reliability in his 1836 "Digression concerning Hearne's Route," 146–47: "But we should greatly mistake, if the detection of various instances of disingenuousness led us to consider him as entirely unworthy of credit ... We had an opportunity, on Sir John Franklin's first expedition, of conversing with several old men who had belonged to the party of Copper Indians, that met Hearne at Congecathewachaga. The leading facts of his journey are still current subjects of tradition among that tribe, as well as with the Northern Indians; and from all that we have been able to collect in the fur countries, as well as from an attentive examination of his narrative, we are led to conclude that he visited the various places marked in his map, in the order in which they stand; that all the rivers and lakes which he names actually exist; and that he has correctly described the general physical features of the country he traversed. His description of the lower part of the Coppermine River, in particular, is evidently that of one who had been on the spot." Note that Richardson avoids any reference to Hearne's credibility as witness to the massacre.

50 Ann Laura Stoler, *Along the Archival Grain: Epistemic Anxieties and Colonial Common Sense* (Princeton: Princeton University Press, 2009), 259 (emphasis in original); Jean-Paul Sartre, cited in ibid., 237.

51 Francis Spufford, *I May Be Some Time: Ice and the English Imagination* (London: Faber, 1996); John Wylie, "Becoming Icy: Scott and Amundsen's South Polar Voyages, 1910–1913," *cultural geographies* 9, 3 (2002): 249–65. But see Shane McCorristine, "'Involuntarily We Listen': Hearing the Aurora Borealis in Nineteenth-Century Arctic Exploration and Science," *Canadian Journal of History* 48, 1 (2013): 29–61.

52 This line comes from George Back's *Arctic Artist,* a lengthy poem describing the first Franklin expedition.

53 Houston, *Arctic Ordeal,* 156.

54 Franklin, *Narrative of a Journey,* 433.

55 D.J. Nicholas Hind, taxonomic specialist, pers. comm., Kew Gardens Herbarium, London, UK, 15 November 2007. See also Roger Hyam, *Plants and Their Names: A Concise Dictionary* (Oxford: Oxford University Press, 1994), 292.

56 John Richardson, "Dr. Richardson's Narrative," in Franklin, *Narrative of a Journey,* 342–44.

57 John Richardson, Letter to Mary Richardson, Slave Lake, April 1822 [transcription], box 46, file 9, C.S. Houston fonds, Series VIII, University of Saskatchewan Archives, Saskatoon, SK.

58 Ibid. (emphasis added).

59 Janice Cavell argues that the Franklin expedition members would have considered Michel Teroahauté an infidel; though probably baptized a Catholic, he appeared to have no religious principles and was thus understood to have failed to replace his Iroquois spiritual tradition with the Christian faith. Cavell, pers. comm., 25 November 2013.

60 Harriet Martineau, quoted in Janice Cavell, "Lady Lucy Barry and Evangelical Reading on the First Franklin Expedition," *Arctic* 63, 2 (June 2010): 135.

61 See Cavell, *Tracing the Connected Narrative,* Chapter 4.

62 See, for example, Richard Glover, "A Note on John Richardson's 'Digression concerning Hearne's Route,'" *Canadian Historical Review* 32, 3 (1951): 252–63; Ian S. MacLaren, "Notes on Samuel Hearne's Journey from a Bibliographical Perspective," *Papers/Cahiers of the Bibliographical Society of Canada* 31, 2 (1993): 21–45; Ian S. MacLaren, "Samuel Hearne's Accounts of the Massacre at Bloody Fall, 17 July 1771," *Ariel* 22, 1 (1991): 25–51; Robert McGhee, *The Last Imaginary Place: A Human History of the Arctic World* (Gatineau, QC: Canadian Museum of Civilization, 2004); Ken McGoogan, *Ancient Mariner: The Amazing Adventures of Samuel Hearne, the Sailor Who Walked to the Arctic Ocean* (Toronto: HarperFlamingoCanada, 2003); McGrath, "Samuel Hearne and the Inuit Oral Tradition"; Heather Rollason Driscoll, "The Genesis of 'A Journey to the Northern Ocean ...'" (PhD diss., University of Alberta, 2002); St-Onge, "The Coppermine River"; J. Tuzo Wilson, "New Light on Hearne," *Beaver Outfit* 280 (June 1949): 14–18.

63 J.B. Tyrrell, in Samuel Hearne, *A Journey from Prince of Wales's Fort in Hudson's Bay to the Northern Ocean ...,* ed. J.B. Tyrrell (Toronto: Champlain Society, 1911), 17.

64 Ibid., 15.

65 Ken McGoogan, in Samuel Hearne, *A Journey to the Northern Ocean: The Adventures of Samuel Hearne,* ed. Ken McGoogan (Victoria: Touchwood Books, 2007), xvi, xxiv, xi.

66 Janice Cavell, "The Hidden Crime of Dr. Richardson," *Polar Record* 43, 225 (2007): 155.

67 Glover, "A Note"; Richard Glover, "The Witness of David Thompson," *Canadian Historical Review* 31, 1 (1950): 25–38; M.A. MacLeod and Richard Glover, "Franklin's First Expedition as Seen by the Fur Traders," *Polar Record* 15, 98 (1971): 669–82.

68 Cavell, "The Hidden Crime," 156.

69 Ibid., 162.

70 Glover, "The Witness of David Thompson," 27. *Suppressio veri, suggestio falsi* means "in the suppression of truth is the suggestion of falsehood."

71 Ibid., 36.

72 Glover, "A Note," 252; Richard Glover, "Editor's Introduction," in *A Journey from Prince of Wales's Fort in Hudson's Bay to the Northern Ocean in the Years 1769, 1770, 1771, and 1772*, ed. Richard Glover (Toronto: Macmillan Press, 1958), xxx.

73 Donna Haraway, "A Game of Cat's Cradle: Science Studies, Feminist Theory, Cultural Studies," *Configurations* 2, 1 (1994): 62.

Chapter 4: Copper Stories

1 Millie Kuliktana, pers. comm., Kugluktuk, NU, 16 August 2007.

2 Samuel Hearne, "A Journal of Observations made on a Journey Inland from Prince of Wales's Fort in Latitude 58"50 North to Lat. 72" 00 Beginning 7th December 1770 ending June 30th 1772 by Samuel Hearne," 29, 31, transcription of Stowe Manuscript, c. 1791, MG21-Stowe MSS.307, MIKAN 104833, Library and Archives Canada, Ottawa.

3 Kerry Abel hints at this possibility in *Drum Songs,* noting that, as early as 1720, the "Chipewyan reported that a peace had been made with the Inuit and a trade for Inuit 'small Copper Lances & arrowheads had taken place.' At other times, relations were less tranquil. The famous massacre at Bloody Falls witnessed by Hearne in 1772 [sic] may have been part of the ongoing tensions." Kerry Abel, *Drum Songs: Glimpses of Dene History* (Montreal and Kingston: McGill-Queen's University Press, 1993), 31–32. Abel accepts that the Bloody Falls massacre actually did occur and lends credence to the notion that it was an act of war aimed at control of a particular resource. That is not precisely my suggestion here. I suggest, instead, that if one rejects Hearne's racialized framing of the Dene as motivated by some kind of inherent savagery (as well as more contemporary iterations of this assumption, in which it is taken for granted that Indigenous peoples warred against each other to secure control over resources and territories, in a kind of primitivized version of European wars), then some of the complex social, political, and economic relations informing the massacre can be considered.

4 David Morrison, "Thule and Historic Copper Use in the Copper Inuit Area," *American Antiquity* 52, 1 (1987): 3–12. See also Abel, *Drum Songs,* 32, which suggests that "the extent of copper use has probably been underestimated by archeologists and anthropologists."

5 See footnote by J.B. Tyrrell in Samuel Hearne, *A Journey from Prince of Wales's Fort in Hudson's Bay to the Northern Ocean ...*, ed. J.B. Tyrrell (Toronto: Champlain Society, 1911), 194–95.

6 John Richardson, quoted in ibid., 196.

7 John Franklin, *Narrative of a Journey to the Shores of the Polar Sea, in the Years 1819, 20, 21, and 22 ...* (London: John Murray, 1823), 130, 131, 132. The transcription was edited by Franklin.

8 Émile Petitot, *Traditions Indiennes du Canada Nord-Ouest* (Paris: Maisonneuve et C. Leclerc, 1886).

9 Walter Bayha comments on the importance of stories in Sahtú Dene contexts, in Walter Bayha, "Using Indigenous Stories in Caribou Co-Management," *Rangifer* 20 (2012): 25–29. Numerous anthropologists have also remarked on the importance of storytelling in northern Indigenous cultures. The phrase "good to think with" comes from Lévi-Strauss by way of Julie Cruikshank, *Do Glaciers Listen? Local Knowledge, Colonial Encounters, and Social Imagination* (Vancouver: UBC Press, 2005). As Cruikshank makes clear in her writing on oral traditions, storytelling is a key venue for teaching law and ethical conduct among the Tlingit and Tutchone peoples of the Yukon, an observation

that Keith Basso also makes about Western Apache storytelling practices. Keith Basso, *Wisdom Sits in Places: Landscape and Language among the Western Apache* (Albuquerque: University of New Mexico Press, 1996). Jean Briggs advances this point in reference to Inuit (though not through study in the Kitikmeot region), profiling, for example, the ways in which fantastical stories are used to teach children the boundaries of ethical conduct. Jean L. Briggs, *Inuit Morality Play: The Emotional Education of a Three-Year-Old* (New Haven: Yale University Press, 1998). Keavy Martin makes the crucial observation that though Inuit have, to date, not commented extensively or formally about the role of storytelling in their lives, "if we pay attention, most Inuit texts – whether oral or written, in Inuktitut or English – abound with these moments." Keavy Martin, *Stories in a New Skin* (Winnipeg: University of Manitoba Press, 2012), 119.

10 Rachel Qitsualik, "Skraeling," in *Our Story: Aboriginal Voices on Canada's Past* (Toronto: Doubleday, 2004), 38.

11 Collamer M. Abbott, "Colonial Copper Mines," *William and Mary Quarterly* 27, 2 (1970): 295–309; Elinore M. Barrett, "The King's Copper Mine: Inguarán in New Spain," *Americas* 38, 1 (1981): 1–29; Roger Burt, "The Transformation of the Non-Ferrous Metals Industries in the Seventeenth and Eighteenth Centuries," *Economic History Review* 48, 1 (1995): 23–45.

12 Burt, "The Transformation of the Non-Ferrous," 29.

13 Hearne, *A Journey,* 197.

14 Colin Adjun, pers. comm., Kugluktuk, NU, 20 August 2007; Joe Allen Evyagotailak, pers. comm., Kugluktuk, NU, 7 August 2007; Peter Taptuna, pers. comm., Kugluktuk, NU, 3 August 2007.

15 John Richardson, "Appendix 1: Geognostical Observations," in Franklin, *Narrative of a Journey,* 497–538. See also C. Stuart Houston, *Arctic Ordeal: The Journal of John Richardson, Surgeon-Naturalist with John Franklin, 1820–22* (Kingston and Montreal: McGill-Queen's University Press, 1984), 292.

16 J.B. Tyrrell, quoted in *Manitoba Free Press,* "The Barren Lands: They Are Not Valueless as Generally Supposed," *Manitoba Free Press* (Winnipeg), 15 June 1894, n.p.; J.B. Tyrrell, quoted in Imperial Mineral Resources Bureau, *The Mineral Industry of the British Empire and Foreign Countries, War Period, Copper (1913–1919)* (London: His Majesty's Stationery Office, 1922), 50.

17 Charles Camsell, *Son of the North* (Toronto: Ryerson Press, 1954), 122, 124, 125, 128–29. This was not the first time that Bloody Falls was linked to a violent event occurring elsewhere in the region. Although the murder of the two priests did not occur there, publicity at the time and more recent retellings of the story continue to localize it at the infamous rapids. See McKay Jenkins, *Bloody Falls of the Coppermine: Madness and Murder in the Arctic Barren Lands* (New York: Random House, 2006).

18 Camsell, *Son of the North,* 127. The ultimate outcome of Camsell and Bell's explorations was arguably of much greater historical significance. As a result of their survey, uranium mining would begin along the shores of Great Bear Lake, "which finally culminated in the release of atomic energy and the dropping of atomic bombs on Japan. It was from Great Bear Lake that much of the uranium came that went into the first atomic bombs." Ibid., 113. Camsell would go on to found the Royal Canadian Geographical Society in 1929, and upon publication of his biography in 1954, Prime Minister Louis St-Laurent expressed his "joy" that "this distinguished servant of our country has let his friends persuade him that his own story of the opening up of the North is a part of our history

and therefore belongs to Canada." Indeed, the interweaving of national interest, resource extraction, masculine adventure, and Indigenous encounter is a long-standing feature of "our history."

19 See Diamond Jenness, *Report of the Canadian Arctic Expedition, 1913–1918,* vol. 12, *The Life of the Copper Eskimo* (Ottawa: F.A. Acland, 1922), 19, 52; J.J. O'Neill, *Report of the Canadian Arctic Expedition, 1913–1918,* vol. 11, *Geology and Geography* (Ottawa: F.A. Acland, 1924), 60A.

20 This practice was not unique to Jenness, of course. When he conducted his studies, "folklore" was favoured over stories about current and recent experience, largely because of the influence of Franz Boas on anthropological research. See Wendy Wickwire, "To See Ourselves as the Other's Other: Nlaka'pamux Contact Narratives," *Canadian Historical Review* 75, 1 (1994): 1–20. Jenness included only a handful of what he termed "quasi-historical" stories in his official reports, including "Raids by White Men," told by Uloqsaq: "Near the Rae River there were three Eskimo settlements. A party of white men came from the west and completely destroyed both the first and the second. They would have killed all the Eskimos in the third settlement also, but the latter changed into musk-oxen and fled. Then the white men traveled about looking for more Eskimos to kill. A shaman named Kalupik, however, brought his magic to bear on them and prevented them from approaching his fellow-countrymen. A man cut off the legs of Kalupik one night as he lay sleeping. When he wakened in the morning he saw them lying on the floor where his enemy had thrown them down. He began to weep, but presently dried his eyes and by the power of his magic restored them into place." Story 74C by Uloqsaq, in Diamond Jenness, *Report of the Canadian Arctic Expedition, 1913–1918,* vol. 13, *Eskimo Folk-Lore* (Ottawa: F.A. Acland, 1924), 82A. Jenness dismissed the historical value of this series of stories by crafting footnotes that led the reader to similar accounts recorded by Boas in Cumberland Sound and along the west coast of Hudson Bay, in which the aggressors were identified as "Tornit" [Tuniit], not "Kablunaat." According to Robert McGhee, these were the Palaeo-Eskimo ancestors of contemporary Inuit. Robert McGhee, *Ancient People of the Arctic* (Vancouver: UBC Press, 2001), 135. Regardless of whether the story draws on traditions of storying Tuniit, it is clearly an evocative commentary on the power of Qablunaat, as is Jenness's effort to sidestep the story's significance.

21 Diamond Jenness, quoted in Stuart Jenness, ed., *Arctic Odyssey: The Diary of Diamond Jenness, Ethnologist with the Canadian Arctic Expedition in Northern Alaska and Canada, 1913–1916* (Hull, QC: Canadian Museum of Civilization, 1991), 556.

22 Ibid., 560, 599, 401.

23 For more on this dynamic in other contexts, see R. Cole Harris, *Making Native Space: Colonialism, Resistance, and Reserves in British Columbia* (Vancouver: UBC Press, 2002); Jake Kosek, *Understories: The Political Life of Forests in Northern New Mexico* (Durham, NC: Duke University Press, 2006); Tania Murray Li, *The Will to Improve: Governmentality, Development, and the Practice of Politics* (Durham, NC: Duke University Press, 2007); Hugh Raffles, *In Amazonia: A Natural History* (Princeton: Princeton University Press, 2002); Frank Tough, *As Their Natural Resources Fail: Native People and the Economic History of Northern Manitoba, 1870–1930* (Vancouver: UBC Press, 1996).

24 Vilhjalmur Stefansson, "The Stefánsson-Anderson Arctic Expedition of the American Museum: Preliminary Ethnological Report," *Anthropological Papers of the American Museum of Natural History* 14, 1 (1914): 1–395; Diamond Jenness, "The Cultural Transformation of the Copper Eskimos," *Geographical Review* 11, 4 (1921): 541–50; Diamond

Jenness, "Origin of the Copper Eskimos and Their Copper Culture," *Geographical Review* 13, 4 (1923): 540–51.

25 Donald Cadzow, *Native Copper Objects of the Copper Eskimo,* Indian Notes and Monographs (New York: Museum of the American Indian, 1920), 6, 22.

26 *Science News Letter,* "Airplanes Enable Geologists to Survey Arctic Copper," *Science News Letter* 20, 546 (1931): 204.

27 Maurice Métayer, *Unipkat: Tradition Esquimaude de Coppermine, Territoires-du-Nord-Ouest, Canada* (Quebec City: Université Laval, 1973), 3:785–86.

28 James Qoerhuk, "Texte 80," in Métayer, *Unipkat,* 2:565, 560–61.

29 Diavik Diamond Mines, *Diavik – Our Foundation, Our Future: The Story of the Diavik Diamonds Project* (Edmonton: Quality Colour Group, 2002), i.

30 Robert McPherson, *New Owners in Their Own Land: Minerals and Inuit Land Claims* (Calgary: University of Calgary Press, 2003), 265.

31 E.A. Schiller, "Noel Avadluk - Mackenzie Prospector," *North* 12, 1 (1965): 44, 45.

32 McPherson, *New Owners,* 265.

33 Ibid., 265–66.

34 The number of signatures on this petition calls into question Schiller's claim that prior to the staking rush of the 1960s, "few Eskimos in this part of the country were aware of prospecting for mineral deposits." Schiller, "Noel Avadluk," 44.

35 Peter Kulchyski and Frank Tester, *Kiumajut (Talking Back): Game Management and Inuit Rights, 1900–1970* (Vancouver: UBC Press, 2007), 240.

36 "Nunavut," which means "our land" in Inuktut, refers to both a territory within the Canadian federation and a comprehensive land claim agreement. Although Inuit insisted on the creation of the territory throughout their negotiation of the Nunavut Land Claim Agreement (NLCA), the territory was subject to a parallel negotiation process and was not secured until very late in the overall land claim negotiations, with associated effects on the coherency and harmonization of federal, territorial, and land claims governance structures. The territory of Nunavut is not exclusively Inuit – Inuit constitute 80 to 90 percent of Nunavut's population, and certain governance structures are modelled on their cultural values, but the territory's relationship with the federal government is similar to that of the Yukon or the Northwest Territories: Nunavut is a jurisdiction in the Canadian federation that is predominantly populated by Inuit and that roughly overlaps with the lands that they have traditionally occupied. The NLCA, on the other hand, outlines the rights and benefits of Inuit with respect to the settling of their claim to the territory. In exchange for converting the majority of their territory to Crown land, a cash settlement was made, Inuit surface and subsurface rights were determined for particular parcels of land, and rights to hunt and fish throughout the territory were articulated. For a fuller description of the land claim and the creation of Nunavut, see Jack Hicks and Graham White, "Nunavut: Inuit Self-Determination through a Land Claim and Public Government?" in *Nunavut: Inuit Regain Control of Their Lands and Their Lives,* ed. Jens Dahl, Jack Hicks, and Peter Jull (Copenhagen: International Work Group for Indigenous Affairs, 2000), 30–115. See also F. Abele et al., eds., *Northern Exposure: Peoples, Powers, and Prospects in Canada's North* (Montreal: Institute for Research on Public Policy, 2009).

37 Inuit Tapirisat of Canada, *Inuit Tapirisat of Canada: Speaking for the First Citizens of the Canadian Arctic* (Ottawa: Inuit Tapirisat of Canada, 1977), 4.

38 Neil McCrank, *Road to Improvement: The Review of the Regulatory Systems across the North* (Ottawa: Ministry of Indian Affairs and Northern Development, 2008), 34.

39 Nunavut Tunngavik Incorporated, *Mining Policy, Oyagakheoktin Maligakhaen* (Cambridge Bay, NU: Nunavut Tunngavik, 1997), 1. Nunavut Tunngavik Incorporated (NTI) was established to ensure that the NLCA is administered and implemented on behalf of its Inuit beneficiaries. Inuit in Nunavut are NTI shareholders.

40 As mentioned in Chapter 1 (note 56), Hearne is unclear regarding the exact composition of the massacre party, and though many emphasize that it was carried out by the ancestors of the Dënesųłiné (Chipewyan Dene), Sahtú and Tłı̨chǫ Dene leaders have also acknowledged that their ancestors may have played a role in hostilities. They also emphasize that the Bloody Falls massacre was just one of many conflicts between Inuit and Dene. According to George Mackenzie, former grand chief of the Tłı̨chǫ Dene Nation, the Tłı̨chǫ have not yet formally addressed the Bloody Falls massacre with Kugluktukmiut: "An apology may come later," he states, "but first we have to build good relations." George Mackenzie, pers. comm., Whitehorse, YK, 13 July 2009. See Chapter 6 for a fuller discussion of recent reconciliation efforts.

41 Quoted with permission from Janet Tamalik McGrath, "Isumaksaqsiurutigijakka: Conversations with Aupilaarjuk towards a Theory of Inuktitut Knowledge Renewal" (PhD diss., Department of Canadian Studies and Institute of Political Economy, Carleton University, 2011), 94–95, 409–10. The roman Inuktitut version (in ICI) follows:

Tamalik: A ... iqkiliit tusaumagakkit maligaqarmata ujararmigluunniit nanisikpata nunami piugilugu taimanna ikpiarjungmiutarituinnanngiluguguuq tunisivagiirluni tipaakimigluunniit tagva tigujungnaq&niuk ...

Aupilaarjuk: Ii ...

Tamalik: Ii ... Taimanna inuit maligaqarlalauqpat tamainnut uvvalu ilainnannginnut nunaup piqutinginnut ...?

Aupilaarjuk: Taimanna qaujimaluanngittakka taakkua kisiani uqaqtut ataatagalu uqaqpalauqtut kannujaruuq nanigupku qi'mimnguuq kajuqtuup mitquanut akiliriaqaqtara.

Tamalik: Hii ...

Aupilaarjuk: Tiguniarupku nunamit takanna aupaluktuq. Nanigupku pitaariniarupku qi'mirmik kajuqtuutiqaruma qi'mip kajuqtup mitqua akiliutinniaqparaguuq. Tagvuunaluaq tusaumajara taanna. Tamajjatuunngittualuugaluat. Pitaqauqtuq nalunanngittuugaluaq. Tamajja taimanna tusaq&git itqiliillu jalunaimi itqilirmik unikkaaqatauqattalaurama isumatari'lutigullu. Ilangit inuktituuttiaqattaqtut taipsumani tusaumajakka. Ilangit aakaugaluat.

Tamalik: Suuqa nunamik kamattiarasuk&tik ... iliqkusiqarmata ...

Aupilaarjuk: Hii.

Tamalik: Qaplunaatuunngimmata Qaplunaat atutuinnarasukpak&tik

Aupilaarjuk: Qaplunaatutuinnattiallari'mata kiinaujaaluk pijumanikualuk. Uvagulli nunaqaqkaangujutigut kiinaujaq pittailinngitaraluavut ikpigilaunnginnaptigulli. Kisiani inuusiqattiarniq nunalu mianirittiarninga taamnalu aksuruutiluarigaptigut.

42 McPherson, *New Owners,* xxiv, xxi.

43 Janet Tamalik McGrath's dissertation explores what she calls, for the purposes of her discussion, "Aupilaarjuk's triad," the three essential components to consider in the formulation of an Inuktitut theory of knowledge renewal: inuuqatigiingniq, inuusiqattiarniq, and niqiqainnarniq, translated as peoplehood, personhood, and livelihood. Niqiqainnarniq (livelihood) translates directly as "always having meat," the "benchmark for survival in

the Arctic traditional land-based economy." McGrath, "Isumaksaqsiurutigijakka," 196. McGrath writes that, as Aupilaarjuk explains, niqiqainnarniq today "also required *kiinaujaliurniq* – the ability to make money. This relates to the new circumstances that Inuit are situated within, in comparison to the days before settlements were established. Inuit have now transitioned to become reliant on the market economy to varying degrees, and thus the original meat economy of his youth now incorporates the concept and use of money." Ibid. Aupilaarjuk discusses at length how relations with hunting and meat rationing transfer to relations with money, and the need for Inuit youth to acquire strong skills in both.

44 Jackie Price, "Living Inuit Governance in Nunavut," in *Lighting the Eighth Fire: The Liberation, Resurgence, and Protection of Indigenous Nations,* ed. L. Simpson (Winnipeg: Arbeiter Ring Press, 2008), 128.

Chapter 5: Resistance Stories

1 Simon Taipana, Telegram to S.M. Hodgson, Commissioner, Government of the Northwest Territories, 4 August 1972, box 11, file 3, G-1993–007, Northwest Territories, Department of Culture and Communications fonds (DCC fonds), Prince of Wales Northern Heritage Centre, Yellowknife, NT (PWNHC).

2 Ted Boxer, "Memo to Chief, Program Policy and Planning Division Executive Secretariat, Re: Proposed Plaquing at Coppermine," 1973, 3, box 11, file 3, G-1993–007, DCC fonds, PWNHC.

3 In Indian-Eskimo Association, ed., *Coppermine Conference of Arctic Native People, July 14, 15, 16, 17, 18 1970* (Toronto: Indian-Eskimo Association, 1970), III-1.

4 Peter Cumming, "A Discussion Paper on Legal Rights," in Indian-Eskimo Association, *Coppermine Conference,* Appendix 1, 1–11.

5 Kirk Cameron and Graham White, *Northern Governments in Transition: Political and Constitutional Development in the Yukon, Nunavut and the Western Northwest Territories* (Montreal: Institute for Research on Public Policy, 1995), 47.

6 Cumming, "A Discussion Paper," 5.

7 Ultimately, the Nisga'a succeeded in their efforts, paving the way for modern land claims in Canada through their 1973 triumph in the *Calder* case. Following the *Calder* decision, the federal government's responses to Indigenous political movements shifted rapidly, as evidenced in its instigation of the Mackenzie Valley Pipeline Inquiry (Berger Inquiry) in 1974 and the settlement of various comprehensive claims such as the Inuvialuit Final Agreement in 1984 and the Nunavut Final Agreement in 1993. In an interview with James Arvaluk, Noel McDermott recalls a sudden and dramatic change in government attitudes toward Inuit in 1973, no doubt precipitated by its realization that "the writing was on the wall" with regard to Indigenous land claims. This shift had not yet occurred as the plaque dispute unfolded. James Arvaluk, *That's My Vision* (Iqaluit: Nunavut Arctic College, 2007), 69.

8 Peter Sidney, quoted in Indian-Eskimo Association, *Coppermine Conference,* II-9. The permits are referred to in Robert McPherson, *New Owners in Their Own Land: Minerals and Inuit Land Claims* (Calgary: University of Calgary Press, 2003), 51.

9 Agnes Semmler, quoted in Indian-Eskimo Association, *Coppermine Conference,* II-8–9.

10 Indian-Eskimo Association, *Coppermine Conference,* Appendix 2, 1.

11 Ibid., I-2.

12 McPherson, *New Owners,* 52.

13 Peter Kamingoak, quoted in Indian-Eskimo Association, *Coppermine Conference,* II-2.

14 David Tukutuk, quoted in Indian-Eskimo Association, *Coppermine Conference,* I-5.

15 Kamingoak, quoted in Indian-Eskimo Association, *Coppermine Conference,* II-4.

16 Boxer, "Memo to Chief," 3. Speaking during the Berger Inquiry regarding reactions to the Dene Declaration, Stephen Kakfwi observed a similar process at work: "Because we never wrote [our rights as a Dene Nation] down on paper before, the Government says we are being influenced by radical outsiders. We have always governed our lives before the Government came along. Long before Canada was formed, we governed our lives. We have always seen ourselves as Dene ... It is insulting to read narrow-minded people speak of us as being influenced by outsiders, as if our views have just been dreamed up a short while back." Quoted in Patrick Scott, ed., *Stories Told: Stories and Images of the Berger Inquiry* (Yellowknife: Edzo Institute, 2007), 16–17.

17 Inuit Tapirisat of Canada, *Inuit Tapirisat of Canada: Speaking for the First Citizens of the Canadian Arctic* (Ottawa: Inuit Tapirisat of Canada, 1977), 9 (emphasis in original). See also Peter Usher and Grahame Beakhurst, *Land Regulation in the Canadian North* (Ottawa: Canadian Arctic Resources Committee, 1973).

18 For discussion of settlement council activities in other communities, see Peter Kulchyski and Frank Tester, *Kiumajut (Talking Back): Game Management and Inuit Rights, 1900–1970* (Vancouver: UBC Press, 2007); McPherson, *New Owners.*

19 Louis St-Laurent, quoted in Mark Dickerson, *Whose North? Political Change, Political Development, and Self-Government in the Northwest Territories* (Vancouver: UBC Press, 1992), 63.

20 Dickerson, *Whose North?* 62. The salience of Dickerson's claim depends, of course, on how colonialism is defined, but it seems to me that the earlier interventions of the RCMP, missionaries, traders, and others must be considered as part of the colonial project, and that greater attention to the specific modalities of colonial intervention, domination, and dispossession that characterized different historical-geographical contexts is needed.

21 Michel Foucault, "Governmentality," in *The Foucault Effect: Studies in Governmentality,* ed. Graham Burchell, Colin Gordon, and Peter Miller (Chicago: University of Chicago Press, 1991), 93.

22 Samuel G. Ford, *The Book of Wisdom for Eskimo* (Ottawa: Bureau of Northwest Territories and Yukon Affairs, Land, Parks, and Forest Branch, Department of Mines and Resources, 1947). This is a fascinating document and has been a target of ridicule by Inuit for some time (see, for example, Bob Dawson, "The Book of Wisdom for Eskimo," YouTube video, 17 May 2011, https://www.youtube.com/watch?v=wXZCTfOAXCo). Its purpose is laid bare in the opening pages of the book: "The first part of this book is about how to be healthy and happy ... The second part contains advice about how to be prosperous." Ford, *The Book of Wisdom,* 1. Producing a healthy, happy, wage-earning population in the Arctic has preoccupied the federal government for some time. See also Paule McNichol, Frank Tester, and Peter Kulchyski, "Arctic Abstersion: The Book of Wisdom for Eskimo, Modernism and Inuit Assimilation," *Études/Inuit/Studies* 23, 1–2 (1999): 199–220.

23 Aqqaluk Lynge, *The Veins of the Heart to the Pinnacle of the Mind* (Montreal: International Polar Institute, 2008), 111.

24 David Scott, "Colonial Governmentality," *Social Text* 43 (2005): 215.

25 Peter Freuchen Ittinuar, *Teach an Eskimo How to Read: Conversations with Peter Freuchen Ittinuar* (Iqaluit: Nunavut Arctic College, 2008), 119; Arvaluk, *That's My Vision,* 146.

26 Aupilaarjuk, in Janet Tamalik McGrath, "Isumaksaqsiurutigijakka: Conversations with Aupilaarjuk towards a Theory of Inuktitut Knowledge Renewal" (PhD diss., Department of Canadian Studies and Institute of Political Economy, Carleton University, 2011).

27 Tania Murray Li, *The Will to Improve: Governmentality, Development, and the Practice of Politics* (Durham, NC: Duke University Press, 2007), 5.

28 Lynge, *The Veins of the Heart,* 111.

29 David Damas, *Arctic Migrants/Arctic Villagers: The Transformation of Inuit Settlement in the Central Arctic* (Montreal and Kingston: McGill-Queen's University Press, 2002); Frank Tester and Peter Kulchyski, *Tammarniit (Mistakes): Inuit Relocation in the Eastern Arctic, 1939–63* (Vancouver: UBC Press, 1994).

30 Tester and Kulchyski, *Tammarniit,* 3, 4.

31 Dickerson, *Whose North?* 62–63.

32 Richard G. Condon, *The Northern Copper Inuit: A History* (Toronto: University of Toronto Press, 1996); Peter Usher, *Fur Trade Posts of the Northwest Territories, 1870–1970* (Ottawa: Northern Science Research Group, Department of Indian Affairs and Northern Development, 1971). Inuinnait, who traditionally occupied the Central Arctic, were given the name "Copper Eskimo" by early anthropologists. Some Inuinnait settled in Kugluktuk (Coppermine), and the people of Kugluktuk are known as Kugluktukmiut. Others settled elsewhere. See "A Note on Language and Spelling" (pages xvii–xviii) and Béatrice Collignon, *Knowing Places: The Inuinnait, Landscapes, and the Environment* (Edmonton: Canadian Circumpolar Institute Press, 2006), 5.

33 Damas makes the important point that Coppermine was "virtually unique" among northern settlements in that patterns of caribou migration prompted Inuit to want to concentrate there around the same time that the government began aggressively promoting settlement, whereas migration and settlement were more coerced and even forced elsewhere in the North at this time. See Damas, *Arctic Migrants,* 80.

34 Condon, *The Northern Copper Inuit;* Dickerson, *Whose North?;* Kulchyski and Tester, *Kiumajut;* Tester and Kulchyski, *Tammarniit.*

35 Damas, *Arctic Migrants,* 75–79.

36 The nurse may well have been Betty Sperry, who married Reverend John Sperry in Coppermine in 1952. Betty "served for some time as the community nurse" during their stay, which ended in 1970. John Sperry, *Igloo Dwellers Were My Church* (Yellowknife: Outcrop, 2005), 112.

37 Ibid., 157.

38 John Amagoalik, *Changing the Face of Canada* (Iqaluit: Nunavut Arctic College, 2007), 39.

39 Kilikavioyak, quoted in Tester and Kulchyski, *Tammarniit,* 357.

40 Stuart Hodgson, quoted in Dickerson, *Whose North?* 88–89.

41 Amagoalik, *Changing the Face,* 59.

42 Arvaluk, *That's My Vision,* 134.

43 David Leonard, "Establishing the Archives of the North West Territories: A Regional Case Study in Legality," *Archivaria* 18 (1984): 70–83.

44 Boxer "Memo to Chief," 3, 1.

45 Ross Innes, Minutes, Discovery of the Coppermine River Meeting to Discuss Commemoration, 16 August 1972, box 11, file 3, G-1993-007, DCC fonds, PWNHC.

46 Hearne's "discovery" of the river was a somewhat banal event to commemorate. As he himself made clear, the river was useless as a shipping route, offered little in the way of copper reserves, and was of limited imperial value. In addition, Hearne "discovered" the river far inland, many miles upstream from the settlement of Coppermine. Choosing the river's discovery as a heritage moment seems to have been a political move to avoid direct reference to the Bloody Falls massacre, while still evoking it. Notably, interest in

commemorating the Coppermine as a heritage river is ongoing and provides an indirect mode of celebrating Arctic exploration and adventure without explicitly mentioning Bloody Falls. See Nunavut Parks, *Coppermine River Nomination Document* (Kugluktuk, NU: Government of Nunavut, Parks and Tourism Division, 2002).

47 L.H. Robinson, Letter to E.J. Boxer Re: 93/1 Discovery of the Coppermine, 1972, 1, box 11, file 3, G-1993–007, DCC fonds, PWNHC.

48 National and Historic Parks Branch, DIAND, Federal Plaque Inscription: Discovery of the Coppermine River, c. 1972, box 11, file 3, G-1993–007, DCC fonds, PWNHC.

49 Boxer "Memo to Chief," 1. For a brief biography of Lena Pedersen, see Library and Archives Canada, "Lena (Elizabeth Magdalena) Pedersen," *Canadian Women in Government,* 2000, http://www.collectionscanada.gc.ca/women/030001-1331-e.html.

50 Boxer, "Memo to Chief," 1; Innes, Minutes, Discovery, 2.

51 Government of the Northwest Territories, GNWT Internal Memo, "Memo to Commissioner, 1/9/72," box 11, file 3, G-1993–007, DCC fonds, PWNHC.

52 Red Pedersen, pers. comm., Kugluktuk, NU, 17 December 2013.

53 *Canadian Parliamentary Review,* "CPA Activities: The Canadian Scene," *Canadian Parliamentary Review* 10, 4 (1987–88): 41.

54 A.W.R. Carrothers, *Report of the Advisory Commission on the Development of Government in the Northwest Territories* (Ottawa: Department of Indian Affairs and Northern Development, 1966), 188, 89, 95.

55 Condon, *The Northern Copper Inuit;* Dickerson, *Whose North?*

56 Amagoalik, *Changing the Face,* 53; John Amagoalik, "The Last Colonial Czar," *Nunatsiaq News,* 8 March 1996, n.p.

57 Peter Kulchyski documents the persistence of this phenomenon in present-day northern Canada, where Indigenous peoples are still not deemed "ready" for self-government. See Peter Kulchyski, *Like the Sound of a Drum: Aboriginal Cultural Politics in Denendeh and Nunavut* (Winnipeg: University of Manitoba Press, 2005), 16.

58 Li, *The Will to Improve,* 17.

59 McPherson, *New Owners,* 95.

60 C.M. Drury, *Constitutional Development in the Northwest Territories: Report of the Special Representative* (Hull, QC: Supply and Services Canada, 1980), 34.

61 Amagoalik, *Changing the Face,* 42.

62 Ibid., 7.

63 Arvaluk, *That's My Vision;* Peter Irniq, "The Person I Was Supposed to Be and the Person I Have Become" (paper presented at the Sixteenth International Inuit Studies Conference, Winnipeg, 25 October 2008); Ittinuar, *Teach an Eskimo.*

64 Ittinuar, *Teach an Eskimo,* 119.

65 Arvaluk, *That's My Vision,* 146.

66 Tester and Kulchyski, *Tammarniit,* 356.

67 E.M. Cotterill, quoted in Dickerson, *Whose North?* 74–75.

68 Condon also documents Inuit recollections of housing conditions in Holman during this period, including comments by Joshua Oliktoak that he did not experience the housing as overcrowded: "It was fun. There was always some family there ... It was just part of life." Quoted in Condon, *The Northern Copper Inuit,* 166–67. Note, too, that missionaries and anthropologists had long complained about the "dirtiness" of igloos. Sperry offers his own observations of igloos in his memoir *Igloo Dwellers Were My Church.*

69 Innes, Minutes, Discovery, 1.

70 Kulchyski, *Like the Sound,* 268.

71 Collignon, *Knowing Places;* Allen Niptanatiak, pers. comm., Kugluktuk, NU, 5 July 2006; Peter Taptuna, pers. comm., Kugluktuk, NU, 3 August 2007.

72 Boxer, "Memo to Chief," 3.

73 Government of the Northwest Territories, "Application for Federal Crown Land," 24 April 1969, box 11, file 3, G-1993–007, DCC fonds, PWNHC.

74 Government of the Northwest Territories, "Application for Federal Crown Land," 8 May 1969, box 11, file 3, G-1993–007, DCC fonds, PWNHC.

75 Robert McGhee, Letter to Stuart Hodgson, 31 October 1968, 1, box 11, file 3, G-1993–007, DCC fonds, PWNHC.

76 Ibid. According to long-time Kugluktuk resident Larry Whittaker, there were only two cabins on the stretch of river between Bloody Falls and Coppermine when he arrived in 1970, his own and one used by Father Lapointe, but cabins quickly began to pop up during the ensuing years. These would have been built by Inuit. Larry Whittaker, pers. comm., Kugluktuk, NU, 26 July 2007.

77 Alice Ayalik, pers. comm., Kugluktuk, NU, 8 August 2007. Our conversation was interpreted by Mona Tiktalek.

78 Joe Allen Evyagotailak, pers. comm., Kugluktuk, NU, 7 August 2007.

79 Rosemarie Meyok, pers. comm., Kugluktuk, NU, 18 August 2007.

80 Simon Taipana, Telegram to S.M. Hodgson, Commissioner, Government of the Northwest Territories, 8 September 1972, box 11, file 3, Coll. G-1993–007, DCC fonds, PWNHC.

81 Li, *The Will to Improve,* 16.

82 John Sperry, Letter to S.M. Hodgson, 30 October 1972, box 11, file 3, Coll. G-1993–007, DCC fonds, PWNHC.

83 Li, *The Will to Improve,* 16–17.

84 Sperry to Hodgson, 30 October 1972.

85 L.H. Robinson, Letter to Ted Boxer from L.H. Robinson, Regional Director, Western Region, National and Historic Parks Branch, DIAND, 24 November 1972 (emphasis added), box 11, file 3, G-1993–007, DCC fonds, PWNHC.

86 John Sperry, Letter to Colin Adjun, Chairman, Coppermine Settlement Council, 30 October 1972, 1, box 11, file 3, G-1993–007, DCC fonds, PWNHC.

87 Marybelle Mitchell, *From Talking Chiefs to a Native Corporate Élite: The Birth of Class and Nationalism among Canadian Inuit* (Montreal and Kingston: McGill-Queen's University Press, 1996), 274.

88 Kerry Horn, pers. comm., Kugluktuk, NU, 17 August 2007. Excluding sport hunters and fishermen, who account for a large percentage of his business, Horn suggests that tourism makes up "less than 1 percent" of hotel stays. His comment must be contextualized, however; Kugluktuk experiences an annual influx of recreational tourists who arrive by canoe and who show great interest in Hearne and Bloody Falls. They tend not to stay at the Coppermine Inn because of its cost. But Horn's observations are nevertheless indicative of the limited importance of cultural-historical tourism in Kugluktuk.

89 Colin Adjun, Telex to Larry Elkin, Acting Secretary to the Executive Committee, GNWT, from Colin Adjun, Chairman, Coppermine Settlement Council, 25 April 1973, box 11, file 3, G-1993–007, DCC fonds, PWNHC.

90 P. Dixon, Memo from P. Dixon, Acting Chief of Program Policy and Planning, GNWT, to Acting Secretary to the Executive Committee, GNWT, 25 April 1973, with Annotations, box 11, file 3, G-1993–007, DCC fonds, PWNHC.

91 Larry Elkin, Memo from L. Elkin, Director, Executive Secretariat of the GNWT, to the Executive Committee, 16 July 1973, 1, box 11, file 3, G-1993–007, DCC fonds, PWNHC.

92 Boxer, "Memo to Chief," 5.

93 Larry Elkin, Letter from L. Elkin, Director, Executive Secretariat of the GNWT, to Randy Mitchell, Parks Branch, DIAND, 1 August 1973, box 11, file 3, G-1993–007, DCC fonds, PWNHC.

94 Michel Foucault, *The History of Sexuality*, vol. 1, *An Introduction* (New York: Random House, 1978), 95–96. See also Homi Bhabha, "Signs Taken for Wonders: Questions of Ambivalence and Authority under a Tree outside Delhi, May 1817," *Critical Inquiry* 12, 1 (1985): 144–65.

95 Lila Abu-Lughod, "The Romance of Resistance: Tracing Transformations of Power through Bedouin Women," *American Ethnologist* 17, 1 (1990): 47.

96 Scott, "Colonial Governmentality," 193 (emphasis in original).

97 As Amagoalik recalls, "The missionaries, in many ways, represented the government if there were no official representatives in the communities. They registered births and deaths, and in some cases handed out family allowances and that sort of thing." Amagoalik, *Changing the Face*, 36. A recent collection of Inuit elders' memories about the first missionaries in the North includes descriptions of the profound fear that some Inuit felt toward the missionaries and discusses their extensive influence on Inuit practices. See Victor Tungilik and Rachel Uyarasuk, *The Transition to Christianity*, ed. Jarich Oosten and Frédéric Laugrand (Iqaluit: Nunavut Arctic College, 1999). Abraham Okpik notes that as Inuit organized politically in the 1970s, they were actively discouraged by the clergy: "For a long time they said 'don't do that'. They said, 'We are going to keep them this way as long as we can.'" Abraham Okpik, *We Call It Survival* (Iqaluit: Nunavut Arctic College, 2005), 319. Tester and Kulchyski document the role of missionaries in distributing relief payments in communities through the 1950s and their willingness to use the payments to influence potential converts. Tester and Kulchyski, *Tammarniit*, 29, 248. Clearly, challenging someone like Sperry entailed both material and more metaphysical risks.

98 Ann Laura Stoler argues that "charmed stories" of imperialism and colonialism work from the "premise that we who study the colonial know both what imperial rule looks like and the dispositions of those it empowers." She points out that students of colonialism too often advance accounts wherein "good and evil" are understood as transcendent rather than historical categories, and in which the colonizers ("with whom we do *not* sympathize") are necessarily attributed "flat interiorities," whereas hazy subaltern figures are held up as heroic and resistant. See Ann Laura Stoler, *Along the Archival Grain: Epistemic Anxieties and Colonial Common Sense* (Princeton: Princeton University Press, 2009), 238 (emphasis in original).

99 A number of scholars have explored the importance of intimacy, trust, and friendship in colonial settings and made provocative arguments about the ways in which these more "tender ties" could both facilitate surveillance and coercion *and* provide openings for mutuality and more convivial forms of power. See, for example, Achille Mbembe, "The Intimacy of Tyranny," in *The Post-Colonial Studies Reader*, ed. Bill Ashcroft, Gareth Griffiths, and Helen Tiffin (New York: Routledge, 2006), 66–69; Adele Perry, "The Autocracy of Love and the Legitimacy of Empire: Intimacy, Power and Scandal in Nineteenth-Century Metlakahtlah," *Gender and History* 16, 2 (2004): 261–88; Ann Laura Stoler, *Carnal Knowledge and Imperial Power: Race and the Intimate in Colonial Rule* (Berkeley: University of California Press, 2002); Ann Laura Stoler, *Race and the Education of Desire* (Durham, NC: Duke University Press, 1995). See also Jennifer Robinson, "Power

as Friendship: Spatiality, Femininity and 'Noisy' Surveillance," in *Entanglements of Power: Geographies of Domination/Resistance,* ed. Joanne Sharp et al. (London: Routledge, 2000), 67–92.

100 Spivak, *A Critique,* 257.

101 Alice Ayalik recalls, for example, that she not only disputed the proposed plaques herself but also "agreed to say no with the other people ... We always have to agree with each other to say no, because if we keep saying yes to the white people if they want something with our land, then some day we'll have a hard time taking it back." Ayalik, pers. comm., 8 August 2007. Agreeing to say no, together, requires work and the nourishing of collective interests. Peter Kamingoak similarly emphasized the importance of speaking out and standing up for the people of Coppermine when asked about the plaque dispute, and went on to observe that the current MLA "needs to be a strong voice for the area and keep saying no when things aren't good for people here." Peter Kamingoak, pers. comm., Kugluktuk, NU, 8 August 2007. There are clear contemporary directives in these recollections.

102 Lena Pedersen, quoted in Mitchell, *From Talking Chiefs,* 240–41.

103 Amagoalik, *Changing the Face,* 43.

104 Jackie Price, "Tukisivallialiqtakka: The Things I Have Now Begun to Understand. Inuit Governance, Nunavut, and the Kitchen Consultation Model" (master's thesis, Department of Human and Social Development, University of Victoria, 2007), 52. See also Janet Tamalik McGrath, "Conversations with Nattilingmiut Elders on Conflict and Change: Naalattiarahuarnira" (master's thesis, Conflict Studies Program, Saint Paul University, 2005); McGrath, "Isumaksaqsiurutigijakka."

105 As Aupilaarjuk observes, "We now use the qablunaat *piqqusiq* [ways] in some regards, and it is evident that we will not leave that behind, it is certain that we will use some aspects of it. However our *inuuniq* [inuk-ness] needs always to be bigger, in our homeland. Our *inuuniq* is absolutely beautiful." Quoted in McGrath, "Isumaksaqsiurutigijakka," 371.

Chapter 6: Toward an Emerging Past

1 See, for example, Jackie Price, "Tukisivallialiqtakka: The Things I Have Now Begun to Understand: Inuit Governance, Nunavut, and the Kitchen Consultation Model" (master's thesis, University of Victoria, 2007); Rachel Qitsualik, "Inummarik: Self-Sovereignty in Classic Inuit Thought," in *Nilliajut: Inuit Perspectives on Security, Patriotism, and Sovereignty* (Ottawa: Inuit Qaujisarvingat, 2013), 23–34; Qikiqtani Inuit Association, *QTC Final Report: Achieving Saimaqatigiingniq* (Iqaluit: Qikiqtani Inuit Association, 2010); Inuit Circumpolar Council, *Declaration on Resource Development Principles in Inuit Nunaat* (Nuuk: Inuit Circumpolar Council, 2011); Janet Tamalik McGrath, "Isumaksaqsiurutigijakka: Conversations with Aupilaarjuk towards a Theory of Inuktitut Knowledge Renewal" (PhD diss., Carleton University, 2011); and Mariano Aupilaarjuk, Emile Imaruittuq, Akisu Joamie, Lucassie Nutaraaluk, and Marie Tulimaaq, *Perspectives on Traditional Law* (Iqaluit: Nunavut Arctic College, 1999).

2 See, for example, Victoria Lawson, "Geographies of Care and Responsibility," *Annals of the Association of American Geographers* 97, 1 (2007): 1–11; Doreen Massey, "Geographies of Responsibility," *Geografiska Annaler* 86, 1 (2004): 5–18; Jeff Popke, "Geography and Ethics: Spaces of Cosmopolitan Responsibility," *Progress in Human Geography* 31, 4 (2007): 509–18. For a different approach to responsibility in colonial contexts, see Gayatri Chakravorty Spivak, *A Critique of Postcolonial Reason: Toward a History of the Vanishing*

Present (Cambridge, MA: Harvard University Press, 1999); Gayatri Chakravorty Spivak, "Responsibility," *Boundary 2* 21, 3 (1994): 19–64. See also Parvati Raghuram, Clare Madge, and Pat Noxolo, "Rethinking Responsibility and Care for a Postcolonial World," *Geoforum* 40, 1 (2009): 5–13. Although not explicitly focused on colonial relations, Donna Haraway's exploration of how care and responsibility interweave with processes of "becoming" resonates with a turn toward understanding responsibility as an emergent, relational practice. See Donna Haraway, *When Species Meet* (Minneapolis: University of Minnesota Press, 2008).

3 Jackie Price, "Tukisivallialiqtakka," vii.

4 See, for example, Jaypetee Arnakak, "Commentary: What Is Inuit Qaujimajatuqangit?" *Nunatsiaq News,* 25 August 2000, http://www.nunatsiaqonline.ca/archives/nunavut000831/nvt20825_17.html; Digital Ingigenous Democracy, "Fact Sheet: Angiqatigiingniq - Deciding Together - Digital Indigenous Democracy," 5 May 2012, Isuma, http://s3.amazonaws.com/isuma.attachments/DIDOverview120504.pdf; Janet Tamalik McGrath, "Traditional Voices in Contemporary Inuit Governance: Perspectives on Conflict and Change" (paper presented at Fourteenth Annual Conflict Resolution Symposium, Faculty of Law, Carleton University, Ottawa, 2005); Natan Obed, "Inuit Values and the Implementation of the Land Claims Agreements," in *Northern Exposure: Peoples, Powers, and Prospects in Canada's North,* ed. F. Abele et al. (Montreal: Institute for Research on Public Policy, 2009), 511–14; Jackie Price, "Living Inuit Governance in Nunavut," in *Lighting the Eighth Fire: The Liberation, Resurgence, and Protection of Indigenous Nations,* ed. L. Simpson (Winnipeg: Arbeiter Ring Press, 2008), 127–38; Price, "Tukisivallialiqtakka"; Sheila Watt-Cloutier, "The Inuit Journey towards a POPs-Free-World," in *Northern Lights against POPs: Combatting Toxic Threats in the Arctic,* ed. D.L. Downie and T. Fenge (Montreal and Kingston: McGill-Queen's University Press for the Inuit Circumpolar Conference of Canada, 2003), 256–67.

5 Jenness was in the region from 1914 to 1916 but interacted most intensively with Jennie and her parents, Ikpukkuaq and Higilaq, during an eight-month stretch in 1915. See Stuart Jenness, ed., *Arctic Odyssey: The Diary of Diamond Jenness, Ethnologist with the Canadian Arctic Expedition in Northern Alaska and Canada, 1913–1916* (Hull, QC: Canadian Museum of Civilization, 1991).

6 Aime Ahegona, pers. comm., Kugluktuk, NU, 4 July 2006. Ptarmigan stories are discussed in greater detail in Chapter 7.

7 Thus, when Rosemarie Meyok suggests that, by the 1970s, people in Kugluktuk had "forgotten" about living in tents, she is referring to a sense of having lost some of the competency and facility, and perhaps some of the language and knowledge of the land, that go with tent living; she is not suggesting that Kugluktukmiut had no recollection of this time: "When Kugluktuk became a permanent settlement, it gathered people from all those places," she noted. Rosemarie was a teenager or older when her family moved in, and they brought a caribou-skin tent with them that they had lived in and erected in town to show people. She said that those who had gone to residential school "forgot about that" way of living, and her family also brought "so much dried meat which the people had also forgotten about." Rosemarie Meyok, pers. comm., Kugluktuk, NU, 18 August 2007.

8 Puiguqtunga means "I forget," but "she don't remember them quite well" was in many ways a more accurate and effective translation, as Nellie had indicated that she knew these stories but did not feel like telling them in full. Nellie Hikok, pers. comm., Kugluktuk, NU, 9 August 2007.

9 When providing transcriptions of stories recounted in translation, I insert a virgule "/" to indicate moments when interviewees paused in their Inuinnaqtun storytelling while the interpreter gave the English version.

10 Hikok, pers. comm., 9 August 2007.

11 The young man who killed himself on 8 August 2007 was the ninth suicide since July 2006 and the fifth since April 2007. The sudden increase in suicides during the summer of 2007 elicited national attention, including extended coverage on CBC Television's *The National.* Canadian Broadcasting Corporation, "Battling the Bottle," *CBC News: The National,* 22 October 2007. Media coverage, however, reproduced both the Qablunaaq expectation of suicide and suffering in northern Indigenous communities *and* what Jack Hicks describes as "a new simulacrum that exaggerates the rate of youth suicide among Inuit." Jack Hicks, "Toward More Effective, Evidence-Based Suicide Prevention in Nunavut," in Abele et al., *Northern Exposure,* 468; see also Emilie Cameron, "Life Going On," *The Walrus,* April 2008; Lisa Stevenson, "The Psychic Life of Biopolitics: Survival, Cooperation, and Inuit Community," *American Ethnologist* 39, 3 (2012): 592–613. (The earlier simulacrum to which Hicks refers is the widespread and incorrect belief among Qablunaat that, historically, it was common for Inuit elders to commit suicide as they aged, to avoid burdening their families.) A *Toronto Globe and Mail* editorial by Michael Byers, for example, claimed that "15 young men killed themselves in Kugluktuk" during a twelve-month period spanning 2006 and 2007, but the source for this claim is not cited, and it is in fact inaccurate. Michael Byers, "Unleashing the Human Potential in Canada's North," *Toronto Globe and Mail,* 19 August 2009. As Hicks comments, there is "no need to exaggerate the seriousness of what is happening with regard to suicide in Inuit societies — the facts speak for themselves." Indeed, as Upaluk Poppel states, "if the populations of 'mainland' Canada, Denmark and the United States had suicide rates comparable to those of their Inuit populations, national emergencies would be declared." Quoted in Hicks, "Toward More Effective," 467. Neither national nor territorial emergencies have been declared with respect to suicide in Nunavut, even though devastating rates of suicide continue in the territory. In 2013, for Inuit men aged fifteen to nineteen, the rate of death by suicide was forty times that of their peers Canada-wide. Jack Hicks, pers. comm., Ottawa, ON, 20 July 2014.

12 Kugluktuk Hamlet Council, public notice, 14 August 2007.

13 Millie Kuliktana, pers. comm., Kugluktuk, NU, 16 August 2007.

14 Marion Bolt, pers. comm., Kugluktuk, NU, 16 August 2007.

15 Joseph Niptanatiak, pers. comm., Kugluktuk, NU, 14 August 2007. Our conversation was interpreted by Mona Tiktalek.

16 Peter Kamingoak, pers. comm., Kugluktuk, NU, 8 August 2007.

17 Janet Tamalik McGrath, "Isumaksaqsiurutigijakka: Conversations with Aupilaarjuk towards a Theory of Inuktitut Knowledge Renewal" (PhD diss., Department of Canadian Studies and Institute of Political Economy, Carleton University, 2011), 301.

18 Joseph Niptanatiak, pers. comm., Kugluktuk, NU, 14 August 2007.

19 Marion Bolt, pers. comm., Kugluktuk, NU, 16 August 2007.

20 Alice Ayalik, pers. comm., Kugluktuk, NU, 8 August 2007.

21 Niptanatiak, pers. comm.

22 Rebecca Torretti, pers. comm., Kugluktuk, NU, 30 August 2008; Robert McGhee, pers. comm., Kugluktuk, NU, 19 March 2009; Rebecca Torretti, pers. comm., Kugluktuk, NU, 23 June 2009.

23 Blackfeather Focus Group A, Focus Group with Blackfeather Canoe Trippers, Kugluktuk, NU, 28 July 2007; Blackfeather Focus Group B, Focus Group with Blackfeather Canoe Trippers, Kugluktuk, NU, 13 August 2007. For a fuller discussion of this phenomenon, see Bruce Braun, *The Intemperate Rainforest: Nature, Culture, and Power on Canada's West Coast* (Minneapolis: University of Minnesota Press, 2002); Bryan Grimwood, "'Thinking Outside the Gunnels': Considering Natures and the Moral Terrains of Recreational Canoe Travel," *Leisure/Loisir* 35, 1 (2011): 49–69.

24 Millie Kuliktana, pers. comm., Kugluktuk, NU, 2 September 2008.

25 This statement reflects the active shifting of historical consciousness involved in building relations between Inuit and Dene communities in the region. Other Kugluktukmiut explicitly claim that Inuit blamed their Dene neighbours for the massacre, and point to the importance of formal schooling in teaching Inuit about Bloody Falls. Others suggest that any hostility toward Sahtú and Tłı̨chǫ is based on misinformation, and that the Chipewyan carried out the massacre. To my knowledge, there have not been any formal efforts on the part of Kugluktukmiut to address the massacre with Chipewyan (Dënesųłiné) communities.

26 Ron Doctor, pers. comm., Kugluktuk, NU, 30 March 2008.

27 George Mackenzie, Public Address, Kugluktuk, NU, 30 March 2008.

28 Joe Allen Evyagotailak, Public Address, Kugluktuk, NU, 30 March 2008.

29 Derrick Powers, George Mackenzie, and Delphus Baton, "Press Release: April 4 2008 – Inuit Sahtú and Tli Cho Gathering, Kugluktuk Nunavut," read publicly, Kugluktuk, NU, 3 April 2008.

30 Millie Kuliktana, presentation to Kugluktuk High School, Kugluktuk, NU, 28 March 2008.

31 Powers, Mackenzie, and Baton, "Press Release."

32 Ibid.

33 The Nunavut claim was settled in 1993, the Sahtú Dene and Metis claim was settled slightly later that year, and the Tłı̨chǫ agreement was settled in 2003. It is important to note, though, that today's rapprochement started long before the resolution of land claims. Anomak Pauline Niptanatiak (Pauline Plamondon) recalls that decades ago, when some men from Kugluktuk went to work at the mines in Port Radium, they interacted with Dene: "Some men wanted to marry Dene women but were told by their elders that 'it's not time to do that yet,' that there would be a time, but not yet. The Dene Elders told their women the same thing." Niptanatiak suggests that over the years, elders in both communities began telling stories about visiting and trading with the each other, "and that got people thinking they should have a visit." "The Dene liked tobacco," she said, and seal oil, "which is an excellent oil for preserving things in the winter ... Hearing these stories led people to start thinking about visiting." Anomak Pauline Niptanatiak (Pauline Plamondon), pers. comm., Kugluktuk, NU, 28 March 2008.

34 McPherson suggests, in fact, that the Parker Line was advanced to avoid "a Dene lawsuit over the issue." Robert McPherson, *New Owners in Their Own Land: Minerals and Inuit Land Claims* (Calgary: University of Calgary Press, 2003), 266.

35 Ibid., 266–67.

36 In the end, the border was drawn so as to provide the Tłı̨chǫ with a "window" on Contwoyto Lake by way of Fry Inlet, a southern wing of the lake, while the bulk of the lake remained in Nunavut (including the Lupin gold mine, which was active at the time and which employed a number of Kugluktukmiut). Note that the Coppermine

watershed spans Tłı̨chǫ and Inuit lands, as well as a small part of the Sahtú settlement area. A report prepared by William Wonders to address the issue of overlapping land use as it related to the settlement of comprehensive land claims contains extensive materials documenting Inuit and Dene land use in the region. Typically, he refers to the Bloody Falls massacre as a key moment in Inuit-Dene relations, but he also states that "local respondents in Coppermine said that their parents reported that until the 1950's they met Indians east of Great Bear Lake, travelled with them hunting and got along well with them." William Wonders, *Overlapping Land Use and Occupancy of Dene, Metis, Inuvialuit and Inuit in the Northwest Territories* (Ottawa: Indian and Northern Affairs, 1983), 60.

37 See Julie Cruikshank, *The Social Life of Stories* (Lincoln: University of Nebraska Press, 1998) and *Do Glaciers Listen?* Local Knowledge, Colonial Encounters, and Social Imagination (Vancouver: UBC Press, 2005); Paul Nadasdy, *Hunters and Bureaucrats: Power, Knowledge and Aboriginal-State Relations in the Southwest Yukon* (Vancouver: UBC Press, 2003); Keavy Martin, *Stories in a New Skin* (Winnipeg: University of Manitoba Press, 2012); and Nancy Wachowich, *Saqiyuq: Stories from the Lives of Three Inuit Women* (Montreal and Kingston: McGill-Queen's University Press, 2001).

38 Nellie Hikok, Public Address, Kugluktuk, Nunavut, 30 March 2008.

39 Elder from Behchokǫ̀, name unknown, 30 March 2008.

40 Colin Adjun, pers. comm., Kugluktuk, NU, 20 August 2007.

41 Daniel David Moses and Terry Goldie, eds., *An Anthology of Canadian Native Literature in English* (Toronto: Oxford University Press, 1992).

Chapter 7: Ptarmigan Stories

1 Métayer provides brief genealogical information about Louis Qajuina but no biographical material. It is possible that Qajuina was the same person as the "Kaiyuina" whom Diamond Jenness identified as a "Coronation Gulf Eskimo man, husband of Igeyaq, father of Hikkok, photographed at Bernard Harbour, 1916." Quoted in Stuart Jenness, ed., *Arctic Odyssey: The Diary of Diamond Jenness, Ethnologist with the Canadian Arctic Expedition in Northern Alaska and Canada, 1913–1916* (Hull, QC: Canadian Museum of Civilization, 1991), 644.

2 As far as I know, Robin McGrath was the first to search Métayer's work for stories that might relate to the Bloody Falls massacre. See Robin McGrath, "Samuel Hearne and the Inuit Oral Tradition," *Studies in Canadian Literature* 18, 2 (1993): 94–109.

3 Jenness did not dwell on Bloody Falls in his published work and only rarely referred to the massacre. His Canadian Arctic Expedition reports include occasional comments on Inuit-Dene relations, including the following statement: "The Copper Eskimos had no intercourse with the Indians of Great Bear lake until Mr. Stefansson brought them together in 1910; since then they have regularly visited the lake each summer and traded their dogs for guns and ammunition. Up to 1910 they were afraid of the Indians, and apparently never reached quite as far as Bear lake, its north end at least. They have a tradition that long ago some Indians came up from the south and massacred many of the Walliak natives, after which they went away west, carrying with them the Eskimos' pots. Possibly there is some reference in this to the massacre at Bloody fall. Higilak told me that the Eskimos never fought with the Indians, though the latter would steal their copper and pots." Diamond Jenness, *Report of the Canadian Arctic Expedition, 1913–1918*, vol. 12, *The Life of the Copper Eskimo* (Ottawa: F.A. Acland, 1922), 47.

4 Transliterated into ICI and translated into English by Janet Tamalik McGrath. For Métayer's spelling, see Maurice Métayer, *Unipkat: Tradition Esquimaude de Coppermine, Territoires-du-Nord-Ouest, Canada* (Quebec City: Université Laval, 1973), 2:472–76.

5 Patrick Wolfe, "Settler Colonialism and the Elimination of the Native," *Journal of Genocide Research* 8, 4 (2006): 388. See also Glen Coulthard, *Red Skin, White Masks: Rejecting the Colonial Politics of Recognition* (Minneapolis: University of Minnesota Press, 2014).

6 "In Nunavut, Harper Pledges $100M for Geomapping Scheme's Second Phase," *Nunatsiaq News,* 22 August 2013, http://www.nunatsiaqonline.ca/stories/article/65674in_nunavut_harper_announced_more_support_for_geo-mapping_of_the_north/.

7 Inuit managed to defeat a seismic-testing program in Lancaster Sound in 2010. As this book goes to press, the Hamlet of Clyde River is pursuing a legal challenge to the decision of the National Energy Board to permit a similar program in adjacent Baffin Bay and Davis Strait, against vociferous dissent on the part of Nunavummiut. See Warren Bernauer, "A Call to the South from Baffin Island," *Briarpatch Magazine,* 1 September 2014, http://briarpatchmagazine.com/articles/view/a-call-to-the-south-from-baffin-island1.

8 Michael Byers, *Who Owns the Arctic? Understanding Sovereignty Disputes in the North* (Toronto: Douglas and McIntyre, 2009).

9 Indigenous signatories across the country refute federal claims that they knowingly ceded their territorial claims through treaties, call upon the state to honour both the letter and spirit of these historical agreements, and reject the impostion of settler laws and jurisdiction over their lands. For a history of treaty making in Canada, including the differences between the early treaties negotiated by the British Crown and the later treaties negotiated by the Canadian state, see J.R. Miller, *Compact, Contract, Covenant: Aboriginal Treaty-Making in Canada* (Toronto: University of Toronto Press, 2009). For a history of treaty making in northern Canada, see René Fumoleau, *As Long As This Land Shall Last: A History of Treaty 8 and Treaty 11, 1870–1939* (Calgary: University of Calgary Press, 2004). For an examination of how settler jurisdiction was asserted, see Shiri Pasternak, "Jurisdiction and Settler Colonialism: Where Do Laws Meet?" *Canadian Journal of Law and Society* 29, 2 (2014): 145–61.

10 *House of Commons Debates,* 22nd Parl., 1st Sess, no. 1 (8 December 1953): 717. Sincere thanks to Janice Cavell for drawing my attention to this speech.

11 Ibid., 719.

12 Ibid.

13 Ibid., 720. Drew's wish was not granted. Although the new ministry did take on Eskimo affairs, Indian affairs continued to be administered under Citizenship and Immigration until 1966, when the Department of Indian Affairs and Northern Development was created and both Indian and Eskimo administration came to fall under the same ministry, where they remain today.

14 Diamond Jenness, *The Indians of Canada* (Ottawa: National Museum of Canada, 1932); Wade Davis, in Arctic Circle Panel, "How We Misunderstand the Canadian North," *Globe and Mail,* 20 January 2014, http://www.theglobeandmail.com/news/national/the-north/arctic-circle-panel-how-we-misunderstand-the-canadian-north/article16404201/?page=all.

15 Comprehensive land claim negotiations begin with the recognition that Indigenous peoples hold pre-existing, unceded Aboriginal title to their lands. But the agreements require Indigenous signatories to permanently cede, surrender, and release this title to the Crown (or agree to modify or "not assert" it) in exchange for fee simple title over

specific parcels of land and other negotiated rights and responsibilities. For further discussion, see Miller, *Compact, Contract, Covenant*; for a critique of past and present efforts to extinguish Indigenous territorial claims, see Russell Diabo, "Harper Launches Major First Nations Termination Plan: As Negotiating Tables Legitimize Canada's Colonialism," *First Nations Strategic Bulletin* 10, 7–10 (June-October 2012) 1–9; Peter Kulchyski and Warren Bernauer, "Modern Treaties, Extraction, and Imperialism in Canada's Indigenous North: Two Case Studies," *Studies in Political Economy* 93 (Spring 2014): 3–23; and Shiri Pasternak, "How Capitalism Will Save Colonialism: The Privatization of Reserve Lands in Canada," *Antipode* (forthcoming).

16 See, for example, Glen Coulthard, "From Wards of the State to Subjects of Recognition? Marx, Indigenous Peoples, and the Politics of Dispossession in Denendeh," in *Theorizing Native Studies,* ed. Audra Simpson and Andrea Smith (Durham, NC: Duke University Press, 2009), 56–98.

17 Sandra Inutiq, "Makita Co-President Sandra Inutiq's Speech to the Government of Nunavut's Public Forum on Uranium Mining," 17 March 2011, http://makitanunavut.files.wordpress.com/2012/03/inutiq_gn_forums.pdf. Nunavummiut Makitagunarningit (the people of Nunavut can rise up) is an independent, non-profit organization of Nunavummiut concerned about uranium development in the territory. In addition to intervening in formal environmental assessment processes, Makita's goals include promoting public awareness and education; promoting accountability and transparency in Nunavut's public and land claims organizations; protecting environmental, health, social, and harvesting rights and well-being; and promoting Inuit Qaujimajatuqangit in decision making around uranium development.

18 Jaypeetee Arnakak, "Incorporation of Inuit Qaujimanituqangit or Inuit Traditional Knowledge into the Government of Nunavut," *Journal of Aboriginal Economic Development* 3, 1 (2002): 35. Although the established term today is "Inuit Qaujimajatuqangit" (that which Inuit have always known to be true), Arnakak suggests that many advocated replacing this term with "Inuit Qaujimanituqangit." The former term was inherited from the GNWT's Traditional Knowledge Policy ("which deals with 'traditional knowledge' largely in isolation from contemporary realities" [35]). The latter was preferred by many because the infix "-niq-" implies a more active, ongoing relationship with what Inuit have always known and reinforces the contemporary importance of IQ as a "living technology."

19 Ibid., 34.

20 Ibid.

21 IQ Task Force, *The First Annual Report of the Inuit Qaujimajatuqanginnut (IQ) Task Force* (Iqaluit: Government of Nunavut, 2002), 4.

22 Sandra Inutiq, "Makita Co-President Sandra Inutiq's Speech."

23 See Warren Bernauer, "The Uranium Controversy in Baker Lake," *Canadian Dimension* 46, 1 (2012), https://canadiandimension.com/articles/view/the-uranium-controversy-in-bakerlake. The forum was a key demand from Makita and one of many attempts to promote transparent and democratic decision making regarding uranium development.

24 See Government of Nunavut, *What Was Said About Uranium in Nunavut: Public Forum on Uranium, Summary Report* (Ottawa: Brubacher Development Strategies Incorporated, 2011).

25 Inuit Circumpolar Council, *Declaration on Resource Development.*

26 Laakkuluk Williamson Bathory, "Naamaleqaaq! Idle No More in the Arctic," *Northern Public Affairs* 1, 3 (Spring 2013): 39.

27 See Jackie Price, "Tukisivallialiqtakka"; Jackie Price, "But You're Inuk, Right?" (paper presented to the University of Victoria, Indigenous Governance Program, 13 February 2013), https://www.youtube.com/watch?v=W36cGxXpjWw); Coulthard, "From Wards of the State" and *Red Skin, White Masks*. See also Paul Nadasdy, *Hunters and Bureaucrats: Power, Knowledge and Aboriginal-State Relations in the Southwest Yukon* (Vancouver: UBC Press, 2003) and "Boundaries among Kin: Sovereignty, the Modern Treaty Process, and the rise of Ethno-Territorial Nationalism among Yukon First Nations," *Comparative Studies in Society and History* 54, 3 (2012): 499–532; Kulchyski and Bernauer, "Modern Treaties."

28 Jackie Price, "But You're Inuk, Right?"

29 Digital Indigenous Democracy, "Fact Sheet: Angjqatigiingniq - Deciding Together - Digital Indigenous Democracy," 5 May 2012, Isuma, http://www.isuma.tv/DID/DIDoverview5May2012.

30 Zacharias Kunuk, "My Inuit Point of View" (submission to Nunavut Impact Review Board, Igloolik, Nunavut, 8 June 2012), http://www.isuma.tv/did/zacharias-kunuk-formal-intervention-to-nirb-written-submission-june-8-2012.

31 Terry Audla and Duane Smith, "Letter to the Editor: A Principled Approach to Research and Development in Inuit Nunangat Starts with the People," *Arctic* 67, 1 (2014); 120–21. Audla and Smith were responding to an attempt by Qablunaaq scientists to articulate a vision for future research in the North without any consultation with Inuit and without reference to the multiple statements and guidelines Inuit have issued regarding northern research.

32 Aime Ahegona, pers. comm., Kugluktuk, NU, 4 July 2006.

33 Nellie Hikok, pers. comm., Kugluktuk, NU, 9 August 2007.

34 Mark Kalluak, *How Kabloonat Became and Other Inuit Legends* (Yellowknife: Government of Northwest Territories, Department of Education, 1974), 130–31. Ptarmigan sound like they are crying "Nauk! Nauk!" when they vocalize, and this means "where" in Inuktitut.

35 Ibid., 131.

36 Sandra Pikujak Katsak, quoted in Nancy Wachowich, in collaboration with Apphia Agalakti Awa, Rhoda Kaukjak Katsak, and Sandra Pikujak Katsak, *Saqiyuq: Stories from the Lives of Three Inuit Women* (Montreal and Kingston: McGill-Queen's University Press, 2001), 250–51.

Glossary

ACRONYMS

DIAND: Department of Indian Affairs and Northern Development (now AANDC, Aboriginal Affairs and Northern Development Canada)

GNWT: Government of the Northwest Territories

HBC: Hudson's Bay Company

ICI: Inuit Cultural Institute

ITK: Inuit Tapiriit Kanatami (national Inuit organization, preceded by Inuit Tapirisat of Canada, or ITC)

IQ: Inuit Qaujimajatuqangit

NLCA: Nunavut Land Claim Agreement

NTI: Nunavut Tunngavik Incorporated. Corporation established to ensure that the NLCA is administered and implemented on behalf of its Inuit beneficiaries. Inuit in Nunavut are shareholders of NTI

NWT: Northwest Territories

INUKTUT TERMS

Angmagiaat: capelin (a small fish)

Biffi: dried fish

Inuinnait: (literally, "the real people") Inuit who traditionally occupied the Central Arctic region. Inuinnait were described by early anthropologists as "Copper Eskimo"

Inuinnaqtun: Inuit language spoken in the Central Arctic, particularly the Kitikmeot region of Nunavut

Inuit Nunangat: Inuit lands

Inuit Qaujimajatuqangit (IQ): "That which Inuit have always known to be true"; often defined as Inuit traditional knowledge but Inuit emphasize that IQ is a living technology that is both more broad and of greater contemporary relevance than the "traditional"

Inuktitut: Inuit language spoken in the Eastern Arctic, particularly the Kivalliq and Qikiqtani regions of Nunavut

Inuktut: umbrella term for Inuit languages spoken across Canada, including Inuinnaqtun, Inuktitut, Inuvialuktun, Inuttitut, and Inuttut

Inummarik: a "real" Inuk

Itqiliq: singular term for a non-Inuk Indigenous person; in the Kitikmeot region of Nunavut, *Itqiliq* typically refers to a Dene person (plural *Itqiliit*)

Kakivak: a particular kind of fish spear (plural *kakivaat*)

Kugluk: accepted in Kugluktuk as "rapids," but in ICI, *rapids* is spelled qurluq, and *Kugluk* means "to startle"

Kugluktukmiut: people of Kugluktuk

Nalunaruirumaaqtuq: Nattilingmiut Inuktitut expression for "confusion usually resolves itself" or "things come clear eventually"

Nautsiaq: flower

Nuna: land; refers to totality of land, sea, and ice regions

Nunavummiut: people of Nunavut

Onoagahiovik place to stay all night and fish

Pilimmaksaq-: verb form of *pilimmaksarniq*, one of the six IQ principles, referring to the importance of engaging and learning in order to become more competent and skilful.

Qablunaanguniq: the features, characteristics, and entitlements associated with being Qablunaaq (close to "whiteness")

Qablunaaq: singular term for a non-Inuk, non-Indigenous person (plural Qablunaat)

Qablunaatitut: English language

Qajaq: kayak (plural *qajait*)

Bibliography

Archival and Other Primary Sources

Boxer, Ted. "Memo to Chief, Program Policy and Planning Division Executive Secretariat, Re: Proposed Plaquing at Coppermine," 1973. Box 11, file 3, G-1993–007, Northwest Territories, Department of Culture and Communications fonds, Prince of Wales Northern Heritage Centre, Yellowknife, NT.

Carefoot, E.H. "Matonabbee: A Play in Twenty Scenes." 1980. 25th Street Theater fonds, University of Saskatchewan Archives, Saskatoon, SK.

Dixon, P. Memo from P. Dixon, Acting Chief of Program Policy and Planning, GNWT, to Acting Secretary to the Executive Committee, GNWT, 25 April 1973, with Annotations. Box 11, file 3, G-1993–007, Northwest Territories, Department of Culture and Communications fonds, Prince of Wales Northern Heritage Centre, Yellowknife, NT.

–. Memo from P. Dixon, Acting Chief of Program Policy and Planning, GNWT, to Stuart Hodgson, Commissioner, GNWT, 10 July 1973. Box 11, file 3, G-1993–007, Northwest Territories, Department of Culture and Communications fonds, Prince of Wales Northern Heritage Centre, Yellowknife, NT.

Elkin, Larry. Letter from L. Elkin, Director, Executive Secretariat of the GNWT, to Randy Mitchell, Parks Branch, DIAND, 1 August 1973. Box 11, file 3, G-1993–007, Northwest Territories, Department of Culture and Communications fonds, Prince of Wales Northern Heritage Centre, Yellowknife, NT.

–. Memo from L. Elkin, Director, Executive Secretariat of the GNWT, to the Executive Committee, 16 July 1973. Box 11, file 3, G-1993–007, Northwest Territories, Department of Culture and Communications fonds, Prince of Wales Northern Heritage Centre, Yellowknife, NT.

Evyagotailak, Joe Allen. Public Address. Kugluktuk, NU, 30 March 2008.

Government of the Northwest Territories. "Application for Federal Crown Land," 8 May 1969. Box 11, file 3, G-1993–007, Northwest Territories, Department of Culture and Communications fonds, Prince of Wales Northern Heritage Centre, Yellowknife, NT.

–. "Application for Federal Crown Land," 24 April 1969. Box 11, file 3, G-1993–007, Northwest Territories, Department of Culture and Communications fonds, Prince of Wales Northern Heritage Centre, Yellowknife, NT.

–. GNWT Internal Memo, "Memo to Commissioner, 1/9/72." Box 11, file 3, G-1993–007, Northwest Territories, Department of Culture and Communications fonds, Prince of Wales Northern Heritage Centre, Yellowknife, NT.

Hearne, Samuel. "A Journal of Observations made on a Journey Inland from Prince of Wales's Fort in Latitude 58"50 North to Lat. 72" 00 Beginning 7th December 1770 ending June 30th 1772 by Samuel Hearne." Transcription of Stowe Manuscript, c. 1791. MG21-Stowe MSS.307, MIKAN 104833, Library and Archives Canada, Ottawa.

–. "Samuel Hearne Letter, Etc., to A. Strahan, 1792." Coll. 48800–48918, ff. 51, Strahan Papers, British Library, London, UK.

–. Samuel Hearne to HBC, 28 August 1772. Folder 17405, HBCA A.11/14, London Inward Correspondence from HBC Posts – Churchill, 1723–87, HBC Archives, Winnipeg, MN.

Innes, Ross. Minutes, Discovery of the Coppermine River Meeting to Discuss Commemoration, 16 August 1972. Box 11, file 3, G-1993–007, Northwest Territories, Department of Culture and Communications fonds, Prince of Wales Northern Heritage Centre, Yellowknife, NT.

Irons, Joanne, ed. *Coppermine - A Community Remembers Its Past.* Coppermine, NT: Canada Council, Oral Traditions Program, 1990. Prince of Wales Northern Heritage Centre, Yellowknife, NT.

Kugluktuk Hamlet Council. Public Notice. 14 August 2007.

Kuliktana, Millie. Presentation to Kugluktuk High School. Kugluktuk, NU, 28 March 2008.

Mackenzie, George. Public Address. Kugluktuk, NU, 30 March 2008.

McGhee, Robert. Letter to Stuart Hodgson, 31 October 1968. Box 11, file 3, G-1993–007, Northwest Territories, Department of Culture and Communications fonds, Prince of Wales Northern Heritage Centre, Yellowknife, NT.

National and Historic Parks Branch, DIAND. Federal Plaque Inscription: Discovery of the Coppermine River, c. 1972. Box 11, file 3, G-1993–007, Northwest Territories, Department of Culture and Communication fonds, Prince of Wales Northern Heritage Centre, Yellowknife, NT.

Powers, Derrick, George Mackenzie, and Delphus Baton. "Press Release: April 4 2008 – Inuit Sahtú and Tli Cho Gathering, Kugluktuk Nunavut." Read publicly, Kugluktuk, NU, 3 April 2008.

Richardson, John. "Franklin's 1st Journey App. 2nd ed." 1823. Kew Gardens Library and Archives, 1823.

–. Letter to J. Franklin, 24 June 1823. *Richardson, J. Letters to J. Franklin, 1823–1842.* Kew Gardens Library and Archives, London, UK.

–. Letter to J. Franklin, 6 August 1823. *Richardson, J. Letters to J. Franklin, 1823–1842.* Kew Gardens Library and Archives, London, UK.

–. Letter to W. Hooker, London, 8 May 1819. In *Sir W. Hooker's Letters to J. Richardson, 1819–1843.* Kew Gardens Library and Archives, London, UK.

–. Letter to Mary Richardson, 18 July 1821 [transcription]. Box 46, file 9, C.S. Houston fonds, Series VIII, University of Saskatchewan Archives, Saskatoon, SK.

–. Letter to Mary Richardson, Slave Lake, April 1822 [transcription]. Box 46, file 9, C.S. Houston fonds, Series VIII, University of Saskatchewan Archives, Saskatoon, SK.

Robinson, L.H. Letter to E.J. Boxer Re: 93/1 Discovery of the Coppermine, 1972. Box 11, file 3, G-1993–007, Northwest Territories, Department of Culture and Communications fonds, Prince of Wales Northern Heritage Centre, Yellowknife, NT.

–. Letter to Ted Boxer from L.H. Robinson, Regional Director, Western Region, National and Historic Parks Branch, DIAND, 24 November 1972. Box 11, file 3, G-1993–007, Northwest Territories, Department of Culture and Communications fonds, Prince of Wales Northern Heritage Centre, Yellowknife, NT.

Sperry, John. Letter to Colin Adjun, Chairman, Coppermine Settlement Council, from J.R. Sperry, 30 October 1972. Box 11, file 3, G-1993–007, Northwest Territories, Department of Culture and Communications fonds, Prince of Wales Northern Heritage Centre, Yellowknife, NT.

–. Letter to S.M. Hodgson, 30 October 1972. Box 11, file 3, G-1993–007, Northwest Territories, Department of Culture and Communications fonds, Prince of Wales Northern Heritage Centre, Yellowknife, NT.

Taipana, Simon. Telegram to S.M. Hodgson, Commissioner, Government of the Northwest Territories, 4 August 1972. Box 11, file 3, G-1993–007, Northwest Territories, Department of Culture and Communications fonds, Prince of Wales Northern Heritage Centre, Yellowknife, NT.

–. Telegram to S.M. Hodgson, Commissioner, Government of the Northwest Territories, 8 September 1972. Box 11, file 3, G-1993–007, Northwest Territories, Department of Culture and Communications fonds, Prince of Wales Northern Heritage Centre, Yellowknife, NT.

Other Sources

Abbott, Collamer M. "Colonial Copper Mines." *William and Mary Quarterly* 27, 2 (1970): 295–309. http://dx.doi.org/10.2307/1918655.

Abel, Kerry. *Drum Songs: Glimpses of Dene History.* Montreal and Kingston: McGill-Queen's University Press, 1993.

Abu-Lughod, Lila. "The Romance of Resistance: Tracing Transformations of Power through Bedouin Women." *American Ethnologist* 17, 1 (1990): 41–55. http://dx.doi.org/10.1525/ae.1990.17.1.02a00030.

Ahmed, Sara. *The Cultural Politics of Emotion.* Edinburgh: University of Edinburgh Press, 2004.

–. "Declarations of Whiteness: The Non-Performativity of Anti-Racism." *Borderlands* 3, 2 (2004).

Akulukjuk, Tommy. "Looking Up through the Microscope." *Études/Inuit/Studies* 28, 2 (2004): 211–12. http://dx.doi.org/10.7202/013204ar.

Alfred, Taiaiake. *Wasáse: Indigenous Pathways of Action and Freedom.* Peterborough: Broadview, 2005.

Alfred, Taiaiake, and Jeff Corntassel. "Being Indigenous: Resurgences against Contemporary Colonialism." *Government and Opposition* 40, 4 (2005): 597–614. http://dx.doi.org/10.1111/j.1477–7053.2005.00166.x.

Allen, David Elliston. *The Naturalist in Britain: A Social History.* London: Allen Lane, 1976.

Amagoalik, John. *Changing the Face of Canada.* Iqaluit: Nunavut Arctic College, 2007.

–. "The Last Colonial Czar." *Nunatsiaq News,* 8 March 1996, n.p.

Anderson, Kay. *Race and the Crisis of Humanism.* London: Routledge, 2007.

–. "Science and the Savage: The Linnean Society of New South Wales, 1874–1900." *Ecumene* 5, 2 (1998): 125–43. http://dx.doi.org/10.1191/096746098701555602.

Archibald, Joanne. *Indigenous Storywork.* Vancouver: UBC Press, 2008.

Arnakak, Jaypeetee. "Commentary: What Is Inuit Qaujimajatuqangit?" Nunatsiaq News, 25 August 2000. http://www.nunatsiaqonline.ca/archives/nunavut000831/nvt20825_17.html.

–. "Incorporation of Inuit Qaujimaniarnaktuqangit or Inuit Traditional Knowledge into the Government of Nunavut." *Journal of Aboriginal Economic Development* 3, 1 (2002): 33–39.

Arvaluk, James. *That's My Vision.* Iqaluit: Nunavut Arctic College, 2007.

Ashcroft, Bill, Gareth Griffiths, and Helen Tiffin. *The Empire Writes Back: Theory and Practice in Post-Colonial Literature.* New York: Routledge, 1989. http://dx.doi.org/10.4324/9780203426081.

Audla, Terry, and Duane Smith. "Letter to the Editor: A Principled Approach to Research and Development in Inuit Nunangat Starts with the People." *Arctic* 67, 1 (2014): 120–21.

Aupilaarjuk, Mariano, Emile Imaruittuq, Akisu Joamie, Lucassie Nutaraaluk, and Marie Tulimaaq. *Perspectives on Traditional Law.* Iqaluit: Nunavut Arctic College, 1999.

Back, George. *Arctic Artist: The Journal and Paintings of George Back, Midshipman with Franklin, 1819–1822,* ed. C. Stuart Houston. Montreal and Kingston: McGill-Queen's University Press, 1994.

Banton, Michael. "The Classification of Races in Europe and North America: 1700–1850." In *Race and Racialization: Essential Readings,* ed. Tania Das Gupta, Carl E. James, Roger C.A. Maaka, Grace-Edward Galabuzi, and Chris Andersen, 15–23. Toronto: Canadian Scholars' Press, 2007.

Barrett, Elinore M. "The King's Copper Mine: Inguarán in New Spain." Americas (Academy of American Franciscan History) 38, 1 (1981): 1–29. http://dx.doi.org/10.2307/981079.

[Barrow, John.] "Lord Selkirk, and the North-West Company." *Quarterly Review* 16 (October 1816): 129–72.

Basso, Keith. *Wisdom Sits in Places: Landscape and Language among the Western Apache.* Albuquerque: University of New Mexico Press, 1996.

Baucom, Ian. "Spectres of the Atlantic." *South Atlantic Quarterly* 100, 1 (2001): 61–82. http://dx.doi.org/10.1215/00382876-100-1-61.

Bayha, Walter. "Using Indigenous Stories in Caribou Co-Management." *Rangifer* 20 (2012): 25–29.

Benjamin, Walter. *The Arcades Project.* Trans. Howard Eiland and Kevin McLaughlin. Cambridge, MA: Belknap Press, 1999.

–. "Edward Fuchs, Collector and Historian." In *Walter Benjamin: Selected Writings.* Vol. 3, *1935–1938,* ed. Michael W. Jennings, 260–302. Cambridge, MA: Harvard University Press, 2002.

–. "On the Concept of History." In *Walter Benjamin: Selected Writings.* Vol. 4, *1938–1940,* ed. Michael W. Jennings, 389–400. Cambridge, MA: Harvard University Press, 2003.

Bennett, John R., and Susan Rowley, eds. *Uqalurait: An Oral History of Nunavut.* Montreal and Kingston: McGill-Queen's University Press, 2004.

Bernauer, Warren. "A Call to the South from Baffin Island." *Briarpatch Magazine,* 1 September 2014. http://briarpatchmagazine.com/articles/view/a-call-to-the-south-from-baffin-island1.

–. "The Uranium Controversy in Baker Lake." *Canadian Dimension* 46, 1 (2012): https://canadiandimension.com/articles/view/the-uranium-controversy-in-bakerlake.

Bhabha, Homi. *Nation and Narration.* London: Routledge, 1990.

–. "Signs Taken for Wonders: Questions of Ambivalence and Authority under a Tree outside Delhi, May 1817." *Critical Inquiry* 12, 1 (1985): 144–65. http://dx.doi.org/10.1086/448325.

Blackhawk, Ned. *Violence over the Land: Indians and Empires in the Early American West.* Cambridge, MA: Harvard University Press, 2006.

Blomley, Nicholas. "Law, Property, and the Geography of Violence: The Frontier, the Survey, and the Grid." *Annals of the Association of American Geographers* 93, 1 (2003): 121–41. http://dx.doi.org/10.1111/1467–8306.93109.

Bloom, Lisa. *Gender on Ice: American Ideologies of Polar Expeditions.* Minneapolis: University of Minnesota Press, 1993.

Bonesteel, Sarah. *Canada's Relationship with Inuit: A History of Policy and Program Development.* Ottawa: Indian and Northern Affairs Canada, 2006.

Braun, Bruce. "Environmental Issues: Inventive Life." *Progress in Human Geography* 32, 5 (2008): 667–79. http://dx.doi.org/10.1177/0309132507088030.

–. *The Intemperate Rainforest: Nature, Culture, and Power on Canada's West Coast.* Minneapolis: University of Minnesota Press, 2002.

Briggs, Jean L. *Inuit Morality Play: The Emotional Education of a Three-Year-Old.* New Haven: Yale University Press, 1998.

Britannic Magazine. "Customs and Manners of the Northern Indians." *Britannic Magazine* 5 (1797): 175–80.

British Critic. "Art. IX, a Journey from Prince of Wales Fort, in Hudson's Bay, to the Northern Ocean ..." *British Critic* 8 (1796): 54–62.

Brody, Hugh. "Eskimo Politics: The Threat from the South." *New Left Review* 79 (1973): 60–68.

–. *The People's Land: Eskimos and Whites in the Eastern Arctic.* Markham: Penguin, 1975.

Brooke, John Hedley. "Religious Belief and the Content of the Sciences." *Osiris,* 2nd ser. 16 (2001): 3–28.

–. *Science and Religion: Some Historical Perspectives.* Cambridge: Cambridge University Press, 1991.

Brown, Bill. "Thing Theory." *Critical Inquiry* 28, 1 (2001): 1–22. http://dx.doi.org/10.1086/449030.

Brown, Wendy. *States of Injury: Power and Freedom in Late Modernity.* Princeton: Princeton University Press, 1995.

Browne, Janet. "Botany in the Boudoir and Garden: The Banksian Context." In *Visions of Empire: Voyages, Botany, and Representations of Nature,* ed. David Philip Miller and Peter Hanns Reill, 153–72. Cambridge: Cambridge University Press, 1996.

Burt, Roger. "The Transformation of the Non-Ferrous Metals Industries in the Seventeenth and Eighteenth Centuries." *Economic History Review* 48, 1 (1995): 23–45.

Butler, Judith. *Precarious Life: The Powers of Mourning and Violence.* London: Verso, 2004.

Byers, Michael. "Unleashing the Human Potential in Canada's North." *Toronto Globe and Mail,* 19 August 2009. http://www.theglobeandmail.com/globe-debate/unleashing-the-human-potential-in-canadas-north/article1201517/.

–. *Who Owns the Arctic? Understanding Sovereignty Disputes in the North.* Toronto: Douglas and McIntyre, 2009.

Byrd, Jodi. *The Transit of Empire: Indigenous Critiques of Colonialism.* Minneapolis: University of Minnesota Press, 2011.

Byrne, Angela. *Geographies of the Romantic North: Science, Antiquarianism, and Travel, 1790–1830.* New York: Palgrave-Macmillan, 2013. http://dx.doi.org/10.1057/9781137311320.

Cadzow, Donald. *Native Copper Objects of the Copper Eskimo.* Indian Notes and Monographs. New York: Museum of the American Indian, 1920.

Cameron, Emilie. "Copper Stories: Imaginative Geographies and Material Orderings of the Central Canadian Arctic." In *Rethinking the Great White North: Race, Nature, and the Historical Geographies of Whiteness in Canada,* ed. A. Baldwin, L. Cameron, and A. Kobayashi, 169–90. Vancouver: UBC Press, 2011.

–. "Life Going On." *The Walrus,* April 2008.

–. "New Geographies of Story and Storytelling." *Progress in Human Geography* 36, 5 (2012): 572–91.

–. "Securing Indigenous Politics: A Critique of the Vulnerability and Adaptation Approach to the Human Dimensions of Climate Change in the Canadian Arctic." *Global Environmental Change* 22, 1 (2012): 103–14. http://dx.doi.org/10.1016/j.gloenvcha.2011.11.004.

–. "'To Mourn': Emotional Geographies and Natural Histories in the Canadian Arctic." In *Emotion, Place, and Culture,* ed. L. Bondi, L. Cameron, J. Davidson, and M. Smith, 163–86. London: Ashgate, 2009.

Cameron, Kirk, and Graham White. *Northern Governments in Transition: Political and Constitutional Development in the Yukon, Nunavut and the Western Northwest Territories.* Montreal: Institute for Research on Public Policy, 1995.

Cameron, Laura. *Openings: A Meditation on History, Method, and Sumas Lake.* Montreal and Kingston: McGill-Queen's University Press, 1997.

Camsell, Charles. *Son of the North.* Toronto: Ryerson Press, 1954.

Canadian Broadcasting Corporation. "Battling the Bottle." *CBC News: The National,* 22 October 2007.

–. *Canada, a People's History.* Episode 6, *The Pathfinders.* Toronto: CBC, 2001.

Canadian Parliamentary Review. "CPA Activities: The Canadian Scene." *Canadian Parliamentary Review* 10, 4 (1987–88): 40–42.

Carrothers, A.W.R. *Report of the Advisory Commission on the Development of Government in the Northwest Territories.* Ottawa: Department of Indian Affairs and Northern Development, 1966.

Castree, Noel. "Commodity Fetishism, Geographical Imaginations and Imaginative Geographies." *Environment and Planning A* 33, 9 (2001): 1519–25. http://dx.doi.org/10.1068/a3464.

–. "False Antitheses? Marxism, Nature, and Actor-Networks." *Antipode* 34, 1 (2002): 111–46. http://dx.doi.org/10.1111/1467–8330.00228.

Cavell, Janice. "The Hidden Crime of Dr. Richardson." *Polar Record* 43, 225 (2007): 155–64. http://dx.doi.org/10.1017/S0032247407006183.

–. "Lady Lucy Barry and Evangelical Reading on the First Franklin Expedition." *Arctic* 63, 2 (June 2010): 131–40.

–. "Making Books for Mr Murray: The Case of Edward Parry's Third Arctic Narrative." *The Library: Transactions of the Bibliographical Society,* 7th ser., 14, 1 (March 2013): 45–69.

–. *Tracing the Connected Narrative: Arctic Exploration in British Print Culture, 1818–1860.* Toronto: University of Toronto Press, 2008.

Charters, Michael L. "California Plant Names: Latin and Greek Meanings and Derivations, a Dictionary of Botanical Etymology." 2003–05. http://www.calflora.net/botanicalnames/pageLH-LY.html.

Clayton, Daniel. "Critical Imperial and Colonial Geographies." In *Handbook of Cultural Geography*, ed. Kay Anderson, Mona Domosh, Steve Pile, and Nigel Thrift, 354–68. London: Sage, 2003. http://dx.doi.org/10.4135/9781848608252.n25.

Coleridge, Ernest Hartley, ed. *The Complete Poetical Works of Samuel Taylor Coleridge*. Vol. 1. Oxford: Clarendon Press, 1975.

Colley, Linda. *Captives: Britain, Empire, and the World, 1600–1850*. New York: Random House, 2002.

Collignon, Béatrice. *Knowing Places: The Inuinnait, Landscapes, and the Environment*. Edmonton: Canadian Circumpolar Institute Press, 2006.

Condon, Richard G. *The Northern Copper Inuit: A History*. Toronto: University of Toronto Press, 1996.

Cook, James. *A Voyage to the Pacific Ocean Undertaken by Command of His Majesty for Making Discoveries in the Northern Hemisphere* ... Vol. 4. London: Printed for John Stockdale et al., 1784.

Cooper, Lane. "A Dissertation upon Northern Lights." *Modern Language Notes* 21, 2 (1906): 44–46. http://dx.doi.org/10.2307/2917735.

Coulthard, Glen. "From Wards of the State to Subjects of Recognition? Marx, Indigenous Peoples, and the Politics of Dispossession in Denendeh." In *Theorizing Native Studies*, ed. Audra Simpson and Andrea Smith, 56–98. Durham, NC: Duke University Press, 2009.

–. *Red Skin, White Masks: Rejecting the Colonial Politics of Recognition*. Minneapolis: University of Minnesota Press, 2014.

–. "Subjects of Empire: Indigenous Peoples and the 'Politics of Recognition' in Canada." *Contemporary Political Theory* 6, 4 (2007): 437–60. http://dx.doi.org/10.1057/palgrave.cpt.9300307.

Critical Review. "A Journey from Prince of Wales's Fort in Hudson's Bay, to the Northern Ocean." *Critical Review* 20 (1797): 127–39.

Cronon, William. "A Place for Stories: Nature, History, and Narrative." *Journal of American History* 78, 4 (1992): 1347–76. http://dx.doi.org/10.2307/2079346.

Cruikshank, Julie. *Do Glaciers Listen? Local Knowledge, Colonial Encounters, and Social Imagination*. Vancouver: UBC Press, 2005.

–. *The Social Life of Stories*. Lincoln: University of Nebraska Press, 1998.

Cumming, Peter. "A Discussion Paper on Legal Rights." In *Coppermine Conference of Arctic Native People, July 14, 15, 16, 17, 18 1970*, ed. Indian-Eskimo Association, Appendix 1, 1–11. Toronto: Indian-Eskimo Association, 1970.

Dalrymple, Alexander. *A Letter from Mr. Dalrymple to Dr. Hawkesworth, Occasioned by Some Groundless and Illiberal Imputations in His Account of the Late Voyages to the South*. London: Printed for J. Nourse et al., 1773.

–. *Memoir of a Map of the Lands around the North-Pole, Scale 1/10 of an Inch to 1°. of Latitude*. London: n.p., 1789.

–. *Plan for Promoting the Fur Trade, and Securing It to This Country, by Uniting the Operations of the East-India and Hudson's-Bay Companys*. London: George Bigg, 1789.

Damas, David. *Arctic Migrants/Arctic Villagers: The Transformation of Inuit Settlement in the Central Arctic*. Montreal and Kingston: McGill-Queen's University Press, 2002.

Daston, Lorraine, and Peter Galison. *Objectivity.* New York: Zone Books, 2007.

Davis, Wade. "How We Misunderstand the Canadian North." Arctic Circle Panel, *Globe and Mail,* 20 January 2014. http://www.theglobeandmail.com/news/national/the-north/arctic-circle-panel-how-we-misunderstand-the-canadian-north/article16404201/?page=all.

de Leeuw, Sarah, Emilie S. Cameron, and Margo L. Greenwood. "Participatory and Community-Based Research, Indigenous Geographies, and the Spaces of Friendship: A Critical Engagement." *Canadian Geographer* 56, 2 (2012): 180–94. http://dx.doi.org/10.1111/j.1541–0064.2012.00434.x.

Deane, Seamus. *The French Revolution and Enlightenment in England, 1789–1832.* Cambridge, MA: Harvard University Press, 1988.

Derrida, Jacques. *Archive Fever: A Freudian Impression.* Trans. Eric Prenowitz. Chicago: University of Chicago Press, 1995.

Diabo, Russell. "Harper Launches Major First Nations Termination Plan: As Negotiating Tables Legitimize Canada's Colonialism." *First Nations Strategic Bulletin* 10, 7–10 (June-October 2012): 1–9.

Diavik Diamond Mines. *Diavik – Our Foundation, Our Future: The Story of the Diavik Diamonds Project.* Edmonton: Quality Colour Group, 2002.

Dickerson, Mark. *Whose North? Political Change, Political Development, and Self-Government in the Northwest Territories.* Vancouver: UBC Press, 1992.

Digital Indigenous Democracy. "Fact Sheet: Angjqatigiingniq - Deciding Together - Digital Indigenous Democracy." 5 May 2012, Isuma. http://www.isuma.tv/DID/DIDoverview5May2012.

Driver, Felix. "Distance and Disturbance: Travel, Exploration and Knowledge in the Nineteenth Century." *Transactions of the Royal Historical Society* 14 (2004): 73–92.

Drury, C.M. *Constitutional Development in the Northwest Territories: Report of the Special Representative.* Hull, QC: Supply and Services Canada, 1980.

Dyer, Richard. *White.* New York: Routledge, 1997.

English Review. "Review of a Journey from Prince of Wales's Fort in Hudson's Bay, to the Northern Ocean." *English Review of Literature, Science, Discoveries, Inventions, and Practical Controversies and Contests* 28 (1796): 1–8.

Fanon, Frantz. *The Wretched of the Earth.* Trans. Richard Philcox. New York: Grove Press, 2004. (Orig. pub. 1963.)

Fienup-Riordan, Ann. *Hunting Tradition in a Changing World: Yup'ik Lives in Alaska Today.* New Brunswick, NJ: Rutgers University Press, 2000.

Flaherty, Martha. "Freedom of Expression or Freedom of Exploitation?" *Northern Review* 14 (1995): 178–85.

Foucault, Michel. *Discipline and Punish: The Birth of the Prison.* New York: Vintage Books, 1979.

–. "Governmentality." In *The Foucault Effect: Studies in Governmentality,* ed. Graham Burchell, Colin Gordon, and Peter Miller, 87–104. Chicago: University of Chicago Press, 1991.

–. *The History of Sexuality.* Vol. 1, *An Introduction.* New York: Random House, 1978.

–. "On the Genealogy of Ethics: An Overview of Work in Progress." In *The Foucault Reader,* ed. Paul Rabinow, 340–72. New York: Pantheon, 1984.

–. *The Order of Things: An Archeology of the Human Sciences.* London: Routledge, 2002. (Orig. pub. 1970.)

–. *Power/Knowledge: Selected Interviews and Other Writings, 1972–77*, ed. Colin Gordon. Brighton: Harvester House, 1980.

–. *Security, Territory, Population: Lectures at the Collège de France 1977–1978*. New York: Picador, 2009.

–. *"Society Must Be Defended": Lectures at the Collège de France, 1975–1976*. New York: Picador, 2003.

Frankenburg, Ruth. *White Women, Race Matters: The Social Construction of Whiteness*. Minneapolis: University of Minnesota Press, 1993.

Franklin, John. *Narrative of a Journey to the Shores of the Polar Sea, in the Years 1819, 20, 21, and 22 ...* London: John Murray, 1823.

Freeman, Minnie Aodla. *Life among the Qallunaat*. Edmonton: Hurtig, 1978.

Fry, Howard Tyrrell. *Alexander Dalrymple (1737–1808) and the Expansion of British Trade*. Toronto: University of Toronto Press, for the Royal Commonwealth Society, 1970.

Fulford, Tim. *Romantic Indians: Native Americans, British Literature, and Transatlantic Culture, 1756–1830*. Oxford: Oxford University Press, 2006.

–. "Slavery and Superstition in the Supernatural Poems." In *The Cambridge Companion to Coleridge*, ed. Lucy Newlyn, 45–58. Cambridge: Cambridge University Press, 2002. http://dx.doi.org/10.1017/CCOL0521650712.004.

Fulford, Tim, Debbie Lee, and Peter J. Kitson. *Literature, Science, and Exploration in the Romantic Era*. Cambridge: Cambridge University Press, 2004.

Fumoleau, René. *As Long as This Land Shall Last: A History of Treaty 8 and Treaty 11, 1870–1939*. Calgary: University of Calgary Press, 2004.

Gedalof, Robin. *Paper Stays Put: A Collection of Inuit Writing*. Edmonton: Hurtig, 1980.

Geller, Peter. "Visions of a Northern Nation: Richard Finnie's Views of Natives and Development in Canada's 'Last Frontier.'" *Film History* 8, 1 (1996): 18–43.

Gentleman's Magazine. "Review of a Journey from Prince of Wales Fort, in Hudson's Bay ..." *Gentleman's Magazine* 66, 6 (1796): 497–99.

Gibson-Graham, J.K. *A Postcapitalist Politics*. Minneapolis: University of Minnesota Press, 2006.

Glover, Richard. "Editor's Introduction." In *A Journey from Prince of Wales's Fort in Hudson's Bay to the Northern Ocean in the Years 1769, 1770, 1771, and 1772*, ed. Richard Glover, vii–xliii. Toronto: Macmillan Press, 1958.

–. "A Note on John Richardson's 'Digression concerning Hearne's Route.'" *Canadian Historical Review* 32, 3 (1951): 252–63. http://dx.doi.org/10.3138/CHR-032–03–04.

–. "The Witness of David Thompson." *Canadian Historical Review* 31, 1 (1950): 25–38. http://dx.doi.org/10.3138/CHR-031–01–02.

Goldie, Terry. *Fear and Temptation: The Image of the Indigene in Canadian, Australian, and New Zealand Literatures*. Montreal and Kingston: McGill-Queen's University Press, 1989.

Government of Canada. *Canada's Northern Strategy: Our North, Our Heritage, Our Future*. Ottawa: Ministry of Indian Affairs and Northern Development, 2009.

–. "Prime Minister Harper Delivers on Commitment to the 'New North.'" Press release. Office of the Prime Minister, 10 March 2008. http://pm.gc.ca/eng/news/2008/03/10/prime-minister-harper-delivers-commitment-new-north.

Government of Nunavut. *What Was Said about Uranium in Nunavut: Public Forum on Uranium, Summary Report*. Ottawa: Brubacher Development Strategies Incorporated, 2011.

Grace, Sherrill. *Canada and the Idea of North.* Montreal and Kingston: McGill-Queen's University Press, 2002.

Graham, Andrew. *Andrew Graham's Observations of Hudson's Bay, 1767–1791,* ed. Glyndwr Williams. London: Hudson's Bay Record Society, 1969.

Greenfield, Bruce. "The Idea of Discovery as a Source of Narrative Structure in Samuel Hearne's *Journey to the Northern Ocean.*" *Early American Literature* 21 (1986–87): 189–208.

Gregory, Derek, and Allen Pred, eds. *Violent Geographies: Fear, Terror, and Political Violence.* London: Routledge, 2007.

Gumboots. *Search for a Passage.* Sound recording. Yellowknife, NT: Gumboots, 2000.

Gutteridge, Don. *Coppermine: The Quest for the North.* Ottawa: Oberon Press, 1973.

Hall, Catherine. *Civilising Subjects: Metropole and Colony in the English Imagination, 1830–1867.* Oxford: Polity Press, 2002.

Haraway, Donna. "A Game of Cat's Cradle: Science Studies, Feminist Theory, Cultural Studies." *Configurations* 2, 1 (1994): 59–71. http://dx.doi.org/10.1353/con.1994.0009.

–. "Situated Knowledges: The Science Question in Feminism and the Privilege of Partial Perspectives." *Feminist Studies* 14, 3 (1988): 575–99. http://dx.doi.org/10.2307/3178066.

–. *When Species Meet.* Minneapolis: University of Minnesota Press, 2008.

Hardt, Michael, and Antonio Negri. *Empire.* Cambridge, MA: Harvard University Press, 2000.

Harris, R. Cole. "How Did Colonialism Dispossess? Comments from an Edge of Empire." *Annals of the Association of American Geographers* 94, 1 (2004): 165–82. http://dx.doi.org/10.1111/j.1467–8306.2004.09401009.x.

–. *Making Native Space: Colonialism, Resistance, and Reserves in British Columbia.* Vancouver: UBC Press, 2002.

Harvey, David. *Justice, Nature, and the Geography of Difference.* Oxford: Blackwell, 1995.

Hawkesworth, John. *An Account of the Voyages Undertaken by the Order of His Present Majesty for Making Discoveries in the Southern Hemisphere ...* London: Strahan and Cadell, 1773.

Haywood, Ian. *Bloody Romanticism: Spectacular Violence and the Politics of Representation.* New York: Palgrave Macmillan, 2006. http://dx.doi.org/10.1057/9780230596795.

Hearne, Samuel. *A Journey from Prince of Wales's Fort in Hudson's Bay, to the Northern Ocean ...* London: Strahan and Cadell, 1795.

–. *A Journey from Prince of Wales's Fort in Hudson's Bay to the Northern Ocean ...,* ed. J.B. Tyrrell. Toronto: Champlain Society, 1911.

–. *A Journey to the Northern Ocean: The Adventures of Samuel Hearne,* ed. Ken McGoogan. Victoria: Touchwood Books, 2007.

Heringman, Noah. "Introduction: The Commerce of Literature and Natural History." In *Romantic Science: The Literary Forms of Natural History,* ed. Noah Heringman, 1–22. Albany: State University of New York Press, 2003.

Hicks, Jack. "Toward More Effective, Evidence-Based Suicide Prevention in Nunavut." In *Northern Exposure: Peoples, Powers, and Prospects in Canada's North,* ed. F. Abele, T.J. Courchene, F.L. Seidle, and F. St-Hilaire, 467–98. Montreal: Institute for Research on Public Policy, 2009.

Hicks, Jack, and Graham White. "Nunavut: Inuit Self-Determination through a Land Claim and Public Government?" In *Nunavut: Inuit Regain Control of Their Lands and Their Lives,* ed. Jens Dahl, Jack Hicks, and Peter Jull, 30–115. Copenhagen: International Work Group for Indigenous Affairs, 2000.

Holdstock, Pauline. *Into the Heart of the Country*. Toronto: Harper Collins, 2011.

Houston, C. Stuart. *Arctic Ordeal: The Journal of John Richardson, Surgeon-Naturalist with John Franklin, 1820–22*. Kingston and Montreal: McGill-Queen's University Press, 1984.

–. "New Light on Dr. John Richardson." *Canadian Medical Association Journal* 131 (1984): 653–60.

–. *To the Arctic by Canoe, 1819–1821: The Journal and Paintings of Robert Hood, Midshipman with Franklin*. Montreal and Kingston: McGill-Queen's University Press, 1994.

Houston, C. Stuart, Tim Ball, and Mary Houston. *Eighteenth-Century Naturalists of Hudson Bay*. Montreal and Kingston: McGill-Queen's University Press, 2003.

Hulan, Renée. *Northern Experience and the Myths of Canadian Culture*. Montreal and Kingston: McGill-Queen's University Press, 2002.

Hutchings, Kevin. "Writing Commerce and Cultural Progress in Samuel Hearne's *A Journey ... to the Northern Ocean*." *Review of International English Literature* 28, 2 (1997): 49–78.

Hyam, Roger. *Plants and Their Names: A Concise Dictionary*. Oxford: Oxford University Press, 1994.

Imperial Mineral Resources Bureau. *The Mineral Industry of the British Empire and Foreign Countries, War Period, Copper (1913–1919)*. London: His Majesty's Stationery Office, 1922.

Indian-Eskimo Association, ed. *Coppermine Conference of Arctic Native People, July 14, 15, 16, 17, 18 1970*. Toronto: Indian-Eskimo Association, 1970.

Inuit Circumpolar Council. *A Circumpolar Inuit Declaration on Sovereignty in the Arctic*. Inuit Circumpolar Council, on behalf of Inuit in Greenland, Canada, Alaska, and Chukotka, 2009.

–. *Declaration on Resource Development Principles in Inuit Nunaat*. Nuuk, Greenland: Inuit Circumpolar Council, 2011.

Inuit Tapirisat of Canada. *Inuit Tapirisat of Canada: Speaking for the First Citizens of the Canadian Arctic*. Ottawa: Inuit Tapirisat of Canada, 1977.

Inutiq, Sandra. "Makita Co-President Sandra Inutiq's Speech to the Government of Nunavut's Public Forum on Uranium Mining," 17 March 2011. http://makitanunavut.files.wordpress.com/2012/03/inutiq_gn_forums.pdf.

Ipellie, Alootook. *Arctic Dreams and Nightmares*. Penticton: Theytus Books, 1993.

–. "Thirsty for Life: A Nomad Learns to Write and Draw." In *Echoing Silence: Essays on Arctic Narrative*, ed. John Moss, 93–102. Ottawa: University of Ottawa Press, 1997.

Irniq, Peter. "The Person I Was Supposed to Be and the Person I Have Become." Paper presented at the Sixteenth International Inuit Studies Conference, Winnipeg, 25 October 2008.

Ittinuar, Peter Freuchen. *Teach an Eskimo How to Read: Conversations with Peter Freuchen Ittinuar*. Iqaluit: Nunavut Arctic College, 2008.

IQ Task Force. *The First Annual Report of the Inuit Qaujimajatuqanginnut (IQ) Task Force*. Iqaluit: Government of Nunavut, 2002.

Jaeger, Edmund Carroll. *A Source-Book of Biological Names and Terms*. 3rd ed. Springfield, IL: Thomas, 1955.

Jahoda, Gustav. "Towards Scientific Racism." In *Race and Racialization: Essential Readings*, ed. Tania Das Gupta, Carl E. James, Roger C.A. Maaka, Grace-Edward Galabuzi, and Chris Andersen, 24–30. Toronto: Canadian Scholars' Press, 2007.

Jenkins, McKay. *Bloody Falls of the Coppermine: Madness and Murder in the Arctic Barren Lands*. New York: Random House, 2006.

Jenness, Diamond. "The Cultural Transformation of the Copper Eskimos." *Geographical Review* 11, 4 (1921): 541–50. http://dx.doi.org/10.2307/208249.

–. *The Indians of Canada*. Ottawa: National Museum of Canada, 1932.

–. "Origin of the Copper Eskimos and Their Copper Culture." *Geographical Review* 13, 4 (1923): 540–51. http://dx.doi.org/10.2307/208162.

–. *Report of the Canadian Arctic Expedition, 1913–1918*. Vol. 12, *The Life of the Copper Eskimo*. Ottawa: F.A. Acland, 1922.

–. *Report of the Canadian Arctic Expedition, 1913–1918*. Vol. 13, *Eskimo Folk-Lore*. Ottawa: F.A. Acland, 1924.

Jenness, Stuart, ed. *Arctic Odyssey: The Diary of Diamond Jenness, Ethnologist with the Canadian Arctic Expedition in Northern Alaska and Canada, 1913–1916*. Hull, QC: Canadian Museum of Civilization, 1991.

Justice, Daniel Heath. *Our Fire Survives the Storm: A Cherokee Literary History*. Minneapolis: University of Minnesota Press, 2006.

Kaleb. "Letter to the Editor, Re: Massacre of Esquimaux by the Indians." *Mirror of Literature, Amusement, and Instruction* 2, 60 (1823): 466–68.

Kalluak, Mark. *How Kabloonat Became and Other Inuit Legends*. Yellowknife: Government of Northwest Territories, Department of Education, 1974.

Kelley, Theresa M. "Romantic Exemplarity: Botany and 'Material' Culture." In *Romantic Science: The Literary Forms of Natural History*, ed. Noah Heringman, 228–46. Albany: State University of New York Press, 2003.

King, Thomas. *The Truth about Stories: A Native Narrative*. Toronto: House of Anansi Press, 2003.

Klancher, Jon. *The Making of English Reading Audiences, 1790–1832*. Madison: University of Wisconsin Press, 1987.

Kosek, Jake. *Understories: The Political Life of Forests in Northern New Mexico*. Durham, NC: Duke University Press, 2006. http://dx.doi.org/10.1215/9780822388302.

Kulchyski, Peter. *Like the Sound of a Drum: Aboriginal Cultural Politics in Denendeh and Nunavut*. Winnipeg: University of Manitoba Press, 2005.

Kulchyski, Peter, and Warren Bernauer, "Modern Treaties, Extraction, and Imperialism in Canada's Indigenous North: Two Case Studies." *Studies in Political Economy* 93 (Spring 2014): 3–23.

Kulchyski, Peter, and Frank Tester. *Kiumajut (Talking Back): Game Management and Inuit Rights, 1900–1970*. Vancouver: UBC Press, 2007.

Kunuk, Zacharias. "My Inuit Point of View." Submission to Nunavut Impact Review Board, Igloolik, Nunavut, 8 June 2012. http://www.isuma.tv/did/zacharias-kunuk-formal-intervention-to-nirb-written-submission-june-8-2012.

Kuokkanen, Rauna. *Reshaping the University: Responsibility, Indigenous Epistemes, and the Logic of the Gift*. Vancouver: UBC Press, 2007.

Kuptana, Rosemarie. "Ilira: Or Why It Is Unthinkable for Inuit to Challenge Qallunaat Authority." *Inuit Art Quarterly* 8 (1993): 5–7.

Lallemand, A.J.N. "À La Pérouse." In *Voyage De Samuel Hearne, Du Fort Du Prince De Galles ...*, Paris: Imprimerie de Patris, 1799.

Lambert, David, and Alan Lester, eds. *Colonial Lives across the British Empire: Imperial Careering in the Long Nineteenth Century*. Cambridge: Cambridge University Press, 2006.

Latour, Bruno. *The Pasteurization of France.* Trans. Alan Sheridan and John Law. Cambridge, MA: Harvard University Press, 1988.

–. *Reassembling the Social.* Oxford: Oxford University Press, 2005.

–. *We Have Never Been Modern.* Cambridge, MA: Harvard University Press, 1993.

Laut, Agnes. *Pathfinders of the West: Being the Thrilling Story of the Adventures of the Men Who Discovered the Great Northwest.* New York: Macmillan, 1918.

Law, John. *After Method: Mess in Social Science Research.* New York: Routledge, 2004.

–. *Aircraft Stories: Decentering the Object in Technoscience.* Durham, NC: Duke University Press, 2002.

–. "On the Subject of the Object: Narrative, Technology, and Interpellation." *Configurations* 8, 1 (2000): 1–29. http://dx.doi.org/10.1353/con.2000.0003.

–. *Organizing Modernity.* Oxford: Blackwell, 1994.

Law, John, and Vicky Singleton. "Performing Technology's Stories: On Social Constructivism, Performance, and Performativity." *Technology and Culture* 41, 4 (2000): 765–75. http://dx.doi.org/10.1353/tech.2000.0167.

Lawson, Victoria. "Geographies of Care and Responsibility." *Annals of the Association of American Geographers* 97, 1 (2007): 1–11. http://dx.doi.org/10.1111/j.1467–8306.2007.00520.x.

Leacock, Stephen. "Reflections on the North." *Beaver Outfit* 267, 3 (1936): 9–12.

Leonard, David. "Establishing the Archives of the North West Territories: A Regional Case Study in Legality." *Archivaria* 18 (1984): 70–83.

Levere, Trevor. *Science and the Canadian Arctic: A Century of Exploration, 1818–1918.* Cambridge: Cambridge University Press, 1993.

Li, Tania Murray. "Indigeneity, Capitalism, and the Management of Dispossession." *Current Anthropology* 51, 3 (2010): 385–414. http://dx.doi.org/10.1086/651942.

–. "To Make Live or Let Die? Rural Dispossession and the Protection of Surplus Populations." *Antipode* 41, S1 (2009): 66–93.

–. *The Will to Improve: Governmentality, Development, and the Practice of Politics.* Durham, NC: Duke University Press, 2007. http://dx.doi.org/10.1215/9780822389781.

Library and Archives Canada. "Lena (Elizabeth Magdalena) Pedersen." *Canadian Women in Government,* 2000. http://www.collectionscanada.gc.ca/women/030001-1331-e.html.

Livingstone, David. *The Geographical Tradition: Episodes in the History of a Contested Enterprise.* Oxford: Blackwell, 1992.

–. *Putting Science in Its Place: Geographies of Scientific Knowledge.* Chicago: University of Chicago Press, 2003. http://dx.doi.org/10.7208/chicago/9780226487243.001.0001.

Lorimer, Hayden. "Herding Memories of Humans and Animals." *Environment and Planning D, Society and Space* 24, 4 (2006): 497–518. http://dx.doi.org/10.1068/d381t.

–. "Telling Small Stories: Spaces of Knowledge and the Practice of Geography." *Transactions of the Institute of British Geographers* 28, 2 (2003): 197–217. http://dx.doi.org/10.1111/1475–5661.00087.

Luste, George J. "History, Travel, and Canoeing in the Barrens." In *Nastawgan: The Canadian North by Canoe and Snowshoe,* ed. Bruce W. Hodgins and Margaret Hobbs, 38–55. Weston, ON: Betelgeuse Books, 1985.

Lutz, John Sutton, ed. *Myth and Memory: Stories of Indigenous-European Contact.* Vancouver: UBC Press, 2007.

Mack, Johnny. "Hoquotist: Reorienting through Storied Practice." In *Storied Communities: Narratives of Contact and Arrival in Constituting Political Community,* ed. Hester Lessard, Rebecca Johnson, and Jeremy Webber, 287–307. Vancouver: UBC Press, 2011.

MacKinnnon, C.S. "Hearne, Samuel." *Dictionary of Canadian Biography Online,* 2000. http://www.biographi.ca/en/bio.php?BioId=36065.

MacLaren, Ian S. "The Aesthetic Map of the North, 1845–1859." *Arctic* 38, 2 (1985): 89–103. http://dx.doi.org/10.14430/arctic2117.

–. "Exploring Canadian Literature: Samuel Hearne and the Inuit Girl." In *Probing Canadian Culture,* ed. P. Easingwood, K. Gross, and W. Klooss, 87–106. Augsburg: AV-Verlag, 1991.

–. "From Exploration to Publication: The Evolution of a 19th Century Arctic Narrative." *Arctic* 47, 1 (1994): 43–53.

–. "Notes on Samuel Hearne's Journey from a Bibliographical Perspective." *Papers/Cahiers of the Bibliographical Society of Canada* 31, 2 (1993): 21–45.

–. "Samuel Hearne's Accounts of the Massacre at Bloody Fall, 17 July 1771." *Ariel* 22, 1 (1991): 25–51.

MacLeod, M.A., and Richard Glover. "Franklin's First Expedition as Seen by the Fur Traders." *Polar Record* 15, 98 (1971): 669–82. http://dx.doi.org/10.1017/S0032247400061775.

Makdisi, Saree. *Romantic Imperialism: Universal Empire and the Culture of Modernity.* Cambridge: Cambridge University Press, 1998. http://dx.doi.org/10.1017/CBO97805 11549779.

Mallory, Carolyn, and Susan Aiken. *Common Plants of Nunavut.* Iqaluit: Nunavut Department of Education, 2004.

Maniquis, Robert. "Filling Up and Emptying Out the Sublime: Terror in British Radical Culture." *Huntington Library Quarterly* 63, 3 (2000): 369–405. http://dx.doi.org /10.2307/3817749.

Manitoba Free Press. "The Barren Lands: They Are Not Valueless as Generally Supposed." *Manitoba Free Press* (Winnipeg), 15 June 1894, n.p.

Martin, Keavy. *Stories in a New Skin.* Winnipeg: University of Manitoba Press, 2012.

Massey, Doreen. "Geographies of Responsibility." *Geografiska Annaler* 86, 1 (2004): 5–18. http://dx.doi.org/10.1111/j.0435–3684.2004.00150.x.

Mavor, William. *Historical Account of the Most Celebrated Voyages, Travels, and Discoveries from the Time of Columbus to the Present Period.* Vol. 17. London: E. Newberry, 1797.

Mbembe, Achille. "The Intimacy of Tyranny." In *The Post-Colonial Studies Reader,* ed. Bill Ashcroft, Gareth Griffiths, and Helen Tiffin, 66–69. New York: Routledge, 2006.

McCann, Andrew. *Cultural Politics in the 1790s: Literature, Radicalism, and the Public Sphere.* London: Macmillan, 1999.

McClintock, Anne. *Imperial Leather: Race, Gender and Sexuality in the Colonial Contest.* New York: Routledge, 1995.

McCorristine, Shane. "'Involuntarily We Listen': Hearing the Aurora Borealis in Nineteenth-Century Arctic Exploration and Science." *Canadian Journal of History* 48, 1 (2013): 29–61.

McCrank, Neil. *Road to Improvement: The Review of the Regulatory Systems across the North.* Ottawa: Ministry of Indian Affairs and Northern Development, 2008.

McEwan, Cheryl. "Material Geographies and Postcolonialism." *Singapore Journal of Tropical Geography* 24, 3 (2003): 340–55. http://dx.doi.org/10.1111/1467–9493.00163.

McGhee, Robert. *Ancient People of the Arctic.* Vancouver: UBC Press, 2001.

–. *The Last Imaginary Place: A Human History of the Arctic World.* Gatineau, QC: Canadian Museum of Civilization, 2004.

McGoogan, Ken. *Ancient Mariner: The Amazing Adventures of Samuel Hearne, the Sailor Who Walked to the Arctic Ocean.* Toronto: HarperFlamingoCanada, 2003.

McGrath, Janet Tamalik. "Conversations with Nattilingmiut Elders on Conflict and Change: Naalattiarahuarnira." Master's thesis, Conflict Studies Program, Saint Paul University, 2005.

–. "Isumaksaqsiurutigijakka: Conversations with Aupilaarjuk towards a Theory of Inuktitut Knowledge Renewal." PhD diss., Department of Canadian Studies and Institute of Political Economy, Carleton University, 2011.

–. "Remembering Mariano Aupilarjuk." *Inuktitut* 113 (Summer 2013): 22–33.

McGrath, Robin. *Escaped Domestics.* St. John's: Killick Press, 1998.

–. "Samuel Hearne and the Inuit Oral Tradition." *Studies in Canadian Literature* 18, 2 (1993): 94–109.

McIlraith, John. *Life of Sir John Richardson ...* London: Longmans, Green, 1868.

McKeon, Lauren. "Walk of Peace." *Yellowknifer* 20 (May 2009).

McNichol, Paule, Frank Tester, and Peter Kulchyski. "Arctic Abstersion: The Book of Wisdom for Eskimo, Modernism and Inuit Assimilation." *Études/Inuit/Studies* 23, 1–2 (1999): 199–220.

McOuat, Gordon. "Cataloguing Power: Delineating 'Competent Naturalists' and the Meaning of Species in the British Museum." *British Journal for the History of Science* 34, 1 (2001): 1–28.

McPherson, Robert. *New Owners in Their Own Land: Minerals and Inuit Land Claims.* Calgary: University of Calgary Press, 2003.

Mearns, Rebecca. "Nunavut, Uqausivut, Piqqusivullu Najuqtiarlavut (Caring for Our Land, Language and Culture): Exploring Land Camps as an Educational and Research Tool in Gjoa Haven, Nunavut." Paper presented at ArcticNet Conference, Ottawa, Ontario, 10 December 2014.

Métayer, Maurice. *Unipkat: Tradition Esquimaude de Coppermine, Territoires-du-Nord-Ouest, Canada.* 3 vols. Quebec City: Université Laval, 1973.

Miller, J.R. *Compact, Contract, Covenant: Aboriginal Treaty-Making in Canada.* Toronto: University of Toronto Press, 2009.

Milligan, Richard, and Tyler McCreary. "Inscription, Innocence, and Invisibility: Early Contributions to the Discursive Formation of the North in Samuel Hearne's *A Journey to the Northern Ocean.*" In *Rethinking the Great White North: Race, Nature, and the Historical Geographies of Whiteness in Canada,* ed. Andrew Baldwin, Laura Cameron, and Audrey Kobayashi, 147–68. Vancouver: UBC Press, 2011.

Minh-ha, Trinh T. *Woman, Native, Other: Writing Postcoloniality and Feminism.* Bloomington: University of Indiana Press, 1993.

Minh-ha, Trinh T., in conversation with Annamaria Morelli. "The Undone Interval." In *The Post-Colonial Question: Common Skies, Divided Horizons,* ed. Iain Chambers and Lidia Curti, 3–16. London: Routledge, 1998.

Mitchell, Marybelle. *From Talking Chiefs to a Native Corporate Élite: The Birth of Class and Nationalism among Canadian Inuit.* Montreal and Kingston: McGill-Queen's University Press, 1996.

Mitchell, Timothy. *Rule of Experts: Egypt, Techno-Politics, Modernity.* Berkeley: University of California Press, 2006.

Mitchell, W.J.T. *What Do Pictures Want? The Lives and Loves of Images.* Chicago: University of Chicago Press, 2005.

Monthly Review. "Review of Samuel Hearne, a Journey from Prince of Wales's Fort in Hudson's Bay, to the Northern Ocean 1769, 1770, 1771, 1772." *Monthly Review* (New York) 20 (1796): 246–51.

Morrison, David. "Thule and Historic Copper Use in the Copper Inuit Area." *American Antiquity* 52, 1 (1987): 3–12. http://dx.doi.org/10.2307/281056.

Moses, Daniel David, and Terry Goldie, eds. *An Anthology of Canadian Native Literature in English*. Toronto: Oxford University Press, 1992.

Mowat, Farley. *Coppermine Journey: An Account of a Great Adventure – Selected from the Journals of Samuel Hearne*. Toronto: McClelland and Stewart, 1958.

Nadasdy, Paul. "Boundaries among Kin: Sovereignty, the Modern Treaty Process, and the Rise of Ethno-Territorial Nationalism among Yukon First Nations." *Comparative Studies in Society and History* 54, 3 (2012): 499–532.

–. *Hunters and Bureaucrats: Power, Knowledge and Aboriginal-State Relations in the Southwest Yukon*. Vancouver: UBC Press, 2003.

Nagy, Murielle. "Comment les Inuvialuit parlent de leur passé." *Anthropologie et sociétés* 26, 2–3 (2002): 193–213. http://dx.doi.org/10.7202/007055ar.

Newhouse, David. "Telling Our Story." In *Walking a Tightrope: Aboriginal People and Their Representations*, ed. U. Lischke and D.T. McNab, 42–52. Waterloo: Wilfrid Laurier University Press, 2005.

Nunavut Parks. *Coppermine River Nomination Document*. Kugluktuk, NU: Government of Nunavut, Parks and Tourism Division, 2002.

Nunavut Tunngavik Incorporated. *Mining Policy, Oyagakheoktin Maligakhaen*. Cambridge Bay, NU: Nunavut Tunngavik, 1997.

Nungak, Zebedee. "History in the Making: Thoughts on Self-Government in Our Land." *Inuktitut Magazine* 66 (Spring 1987): 71–80.

–. "Qallunaat 101." *Utne Reader* (March–April 2004).

Obed, Natan. "Inuit Values and the Implementation of the Land Claims Agreements." In *Northern Exposure: Peoples, Powers, and Prospects in Canada's North*, ed. F. Abele, T.J. Courchene, F.L. Seidle, and F. St-Hilaire, 511–14. Montreal: Institute for Research on Public Policy, 2009.

Ogborn, Miles. *Indian Ink: Script and Print in the Making of the English East India Company*. Chicago: University of Chicago Press, 2007.

Okalik, Looee. "Inuujunga: The Intricacy of Indigenous and Western Epistemologies in the Arctic." In *Indigenous Pathways into Social Research*, ed. D. Mertens, F. Cram, and B. Chilesa, 239–48. Vancouver: Left Coast Press, 2013.

Okpik, Abraham. *We Call It Survival*. Iqaluit: Nunavut Arctic College, 2005.

O'Neill, J.J. *Report of the Canadian Arctic Expedition, 1913–1918*. Vol. 11, *Geology and Geography*. Ottawa: F.A. Acland, 1924.

Park, Mungo. *Travels in the Interior Districts of Africa* ... London: Bulmer, 1799.

Pasternak, Shiri. "How Capitalism Will Save Colonialism: The Privatization of Reserve Lands in Canada." *Antipode* (forthcoming).

–. "Jurisdiction and Settler Colonialism: Where Do Laws Meet?" *Canadian Journal of Law and Society* 29, 2 (2014) 145–61.

Payne, Michael. *Prince of Wales' Fort: A Social History, 1717–1782*. Parks Canada Manuscript Report No. 371. Ottawa: Parks Canada, 1979.

Pearce, Roy Harvey. *Savagism and Civilization: A Study of the Indian and the American Mind*. Baltimore: Johns Hopkins University Press, 1967.

Perry, Adele. "The Autocracy of Love and the Legitimacy of Empire: Intimacy, Power and Scandal in Nineteenth-Century Metlakahtlah." *Gender and History* 16, 2 (2004): 261–88. http://dx.doi.org/10.1111/j.0953–5233.2004.00341.x.

Petitot, Émile. *Traditions Indiennes du Canada Nord-Ouest.* Paris: Maisonneuve et C. Leclerc, 1886.

Petrone, Penny. *Northern Voices: Inuit Writing in English.* Toronto: University of Toronto Press, 1988.

Podruchny, Carolyn. "Werewolves and Windigos: Narratives of Cannibal Monsters in French-Canadian Voyageur Oral Tradition." *Ethnohistory* (Columbus, OH) 51, 4 (2004): 677–700. http://dx.doi.org/10.1215/00141801-51-4-677.

Popke, Jeff. "Geography and Ethics: Spaces of Cosmopolitan Responsibility." *Progress in Human Geography* 31, 4 (2007): 509–18. http://dx.doi.org/10.1177/0309132507077090.

Pratt, Geraldine. "Circulating Sadness: Witnessing Filipina Mothers' Stories of Family Separation." *Gender, Place and Culture* 16, 1 (2009): 3–22. http://dx.doi.org/10.1080/09663690802574753.

Pratt, Mary Louise. *Imperial Eyes: Travel Writing and Transculturation.* London: Routledge, 1992.

Price, Jackie. "The Arctic Is My Home: Affirming the Art of Inuit Governance." *Fuse* 35, 2 (2012): 2–3

–. "But You're Inuk, Right?" Paper presented to the University of Victoria, Indigenous Governance Program, 13 February 2013. https://www.youtube.com/watch?v=W36cGxXpjWw.

–. "Living Inuit Governance in Nunavut." In *Lighting the Eighth Fire: The Liberation, Resurgence, and Protection of Indigenous Nations,* ed. L. Simpson, 127–38. Winnipeg: Arbeiter Ring Press, 2008.

–. "Tukisivallialiqtakka: The Things I Have Now Begun to Understand. Inuit Governance, Nunavut, and the Kitchen Consultation Model." Master's thesis, Department of Human and Social Development, University of Victoria, 2007.

Pringle, Heather. "New Respect for Metal's Role in Ancient Arctic Cultures." *Science* 277, 5327 (1997): 766–67. http://dx.doi.org/10.1126/science.277.5327.766.

Qikiqtani Inuit Association. *QTC Final Report: Achieving Saimaqatigiingniq.* Iqaluit: Qikiqtani Inuit Association, 2010.

Qitsualik, Rachel. "Inummarik: Self-Sovereignty in Classic Inuit Thought." In *Nilliajut: Inuit Perspectives on Security, Patriotism, and Sovereignty*, 23–34. Ottawa: Inuit Qaujisarvingat, 2013.

–. "Is It 'Eskimo' or 'Inuit'?" *Indian Country Today,* 11 February 2004. http://indiancountrytodaymedianetwork.com/ictarchives/2004/02/11/qitsualik-is-it-eskimo-or-inuit-89951.

–. "Nalunaktuq." Canadian Broadcasting Corporation, 31 August 2006. No longer available on website.

–. "Skraeling." In *Our Story: Aboriginal Voices on Canada's Past,* by Tantoo Cardinal, Tomson Highway, Basil Johnston, Thomas King, Brian Maracle, Lee Maracale, Jovette Marchessault, Rachel A. Qitsualik, and Drew Hayden Taylor, 36–66. Toronto: Doubleday, 2004.

Qoerhuk, James. "Texte 80." In Maurice Métayer, *Unipkat: tradition Esquimaude de Coppermine, Territoires-du-Nord-Ouest, Canada,* 555–67. Quebec City: Université Laval, 1973.

Raffles, Hugh. *In Amazonia: A Natural History.* Princeton: Princeton University Press, 2002.

–. "'Local Theory': Nature and the Making of an Amazonian Place." *Cultural Anthropology* 14, 3 (1999): 323–60. http://dx.doi.org/10.1525/can.1999.14.3.323.

Raghuram, Parvati, Clare Madge, and Pat Noxolo. "Rethinking Responsibility and Care for a Postcolonial World." *Geoforum* 40, 1 (2009): 5–13. http://dx.doi.org/10.1016/j.geoforum.2008.07.007.

Ray, Arthur. *Indians in the Fur Trade: Their Role as Trappers, Hunters, and Middlemen in the Lands Southwest of Hudson Bay, 1660–1870.* Toronto: University of Toronto Press, 1974.

Regan, Paulette. *Unsettling the Settler Within: Indian Residential Schools, Truth Telling, and Reconciliation in Canada.* Vancouver: UBC Press, 2010.

Rehbock, Philip. *The Philosophical Naturalists: Themes in Early Nineteenth Century British Biology.* Madison: University of Wisconsin Press, 1983.

Richardson, John. "Appendix 1: Geognostical Observations." In John Franklin, *Narrative of a Journey to the Shores of the Polar Sea, in the Years 1819, 20, 21, and 22 ...*, 497–538. London: John Murray, 1823.

Ricoeur, Paul. *Memory, History, Forgetting.* Chicago: University of Chicago Press, 2004. http://dx.doi.org/10.7208/chicago/9780226713465.001.0001.

Robinson, Jennifer. "Power as Friendship: Spatiality, Femininity and 'Noisy' Surveillance." In *Entanglements of Power: Geographies of Domination/Resistance,* ed. Joanne Sharp, Paul Routledge, Chris Philo, and Ronan Paddison, 67–92. London: Routledge, 2000.

Roediger, David. *The Wages of Whiteness: Race and the Making of the American Working Class.* London: Verso, 1991.

Rollason Driscoll, Heather. "The Genesis of 'A Journey to the Northern Ocean ...'" PhD diss., University of Alberta, 2002.

Ruggles, Richard. "Governor Samuel Wegg: Intelligent Layman of the Royal Society." *Notes and Records of the Royal Society of London* 32, 2 (1978): 181–99. http://dx.doi.org/10.1098/rsnr.1978.0015.

Said, Edward. *Culture and Imperialism.* New York: Knopf, 1993.

–. *Orientalism.* New York: Pantheon, 1978.

–. *The World, the Text, and the Critic.* Cambridge, MA: Harvard University Press, 1983.

Saldanha, Arun. "Actor-Network Theory and Critical Sociology." *Critical Sociology* 29, 3 (2003): 419–32. http://dx.doi.org/10.1163/156916303322591130.

Santos, Boaventura de Sousa. "A Critique of Lazy Reason: Against the Waste of Experience." In *The Modern World-System in the Longue Durée,* ed. Immanuel Wallerstein Organization, 157–97. London: Paradigm, 2004.

Schaffer, Simon. "Visions of Empire: Afterword." In *Visions of Empire: Voyages, Botany, and Representations of Nature,* ed. David Philip Miller and Peter Hanns Reill, 335–52. Cambridge: Cambridge University Press, 1996.

Schiebinger, Londa. *Plants and Empire.* Cambridge, MA: Harvard University Press, 2004.

Schiller, E.A. "Noel Avadluk – Mackenzie Prospector." *North* (Department of Northern Affairs and Natural Resources, Ottawa) 12, 1 (1965): 44–46.

Science News Letter. "Airplanes Enable Geologists to Survey Arctic Copper." *Science News Letter* 20, 546 (1931): 204.

Scots Magazine. "Books: Cook's *Voyage to the Pacific Ocean.*" *Scots Magazine* 46 (June 1784): 309–17.

Scott, David. "Colonial Governmentality." *Social Text* 43 (2005): 191–220.

Scott, James. *Weapons of the Weak: Everyday Forms of Peasant Resistance.* New Haven: Yale University Press, 1985.

Scott, Patrick, ed. *Stories Told: Stories and Images of the Berger Inquiry.* Yellowknife: Edzo Institute, 2007.

Shapin, Steven. *A Social History of Truth: Civility and Science in Seventeenth-Century England.* Chicago: University of Chicago Press, 1995.

Shields, Rob. "The True North Strong and Free." In *Places on the Margin: Alternative Geographies of Modernity,* 162–206. London: Routledge, 1991.

Shteir, Ann. "Gender and 'Modern' Botany in Victorian England." *Osiris,* 2nd ser., 12 (1997): 29–38. http://dx.doi.org/10.1086/649265.

Simpson, Audra. "Mohawk Interruptus." Paper presented to to the University of Victoria, Indigenous Governance Program, Victoria, BC, 7 November 2012. https://www.youtube.com/watch?v=FWzXHqGfH3U.

–. "Settlement's Secret." *Cultural Anthropology* 26, 2 (2011): 205–17.

Simpson, Leanne. "Anticolonial Strategies for the Recovery and Maintenance of Indigenous Knowledge." *American Indian Quarterly* 28, 3–4 (2004): 373–84.

–. *Dancing on Our Turtle's Back: Stories of Nishnaabeg Re-creation, Resurgence, and a New Emergence.* Winnipeg: Arbeiter Ring Publishers, 2011.

Simpson, Thomas. *Narrative of the Discoveries on the North Coast of America* ... London: R. Bentley, 1843.

Smith, Andrea. *Conquest: Sexual Violence and American Indian Genocide.* Cambridge, MA: South End Press, 2005.

Smith, Linda Tuhiwai. *Decolonizing Methodologies.* London: Zed Press, 1999.

Sparke, Matthew. "Political Geography – Political Geographies of Globalization III: Resistance." *Progress in Human Geography* 32, 3 (2008): 423–40. http://dx.doi.org/10.1177/0309132507086878.

Sperry, John. *Igloo Dwellers Were My Church.* Yellowknife: Outcrop, 2005.

Spivak, Gayatri Chakravorty. "Can the Subaltern Speak?" In *Marxism and the Interpretation of Culture,* ed. Cary Nelson and Lawrence Grossberg, 271–313. Urbana: University of Illinois Press, 1988.

–. *A Critique of Postcolonial Reason: Toward a History of the Vanishing Present.* Cambridge, MA: Harvard University Press, 1999.

–. *The Post Colonial Critic: Interviews, Strategies, Dialogues.* New York: Routledge, 1990.

–. "Responsibility." *Boundary 2* 21, 3 (1994): 19–64. http://dx.doi.org/10.2307/303600.

Spufford, Francis. *I May Be Some Time: Ice and the English Imagination.* London: Faber, 1996.

St-Onge, Denis. "The Coppermine River: Art and Reality." *Canadian Geographic* 102, 4 (1982): 28–31.

Stefansson, Vilhjalmur. *My Life with the Eskimo.* New York: Macmillan, 1993 [1913].

–. "The Stefánsson-Anderson Arctic Expedition of the American Museum: Preliminary Ethnological Report." *Anthropological Papers of the American Museum of Natural History* 14, 1 (1914): 1–395.

Stevenson, Lisa. "The Psychic Life of Biopolitics: Survival, Cooperation, and Inuit Community." *American Ethnologist* 39, 3 (2012): 592–613. http://dx.doi.org/10.1111/j.1548-1425.2012.01383.x.

Stoler, Ann Laura. *Along the Archival Grain: Epistemic Anxieties and Colonial Common Sense.* Princeton: Princeton University Press, 2009.

–. *Carnal Knowledge and Imperial Power: Race and the Intimate in Colonial Rule.* Berkeley: University of California Press, 2002.

–. *Race and the Education of Desire.* Durham, NC: Duke University Press, 1995.

Tagaq, Tanya. Interview with Jian Ghomeshi. *Q.* CBC Radio One, 24 September 2014.

Tester, Frank, and Peter Irniq. "Inuit Qaujimajatuqangit: Social History, Politics and the Practice of Resistance." *Arctic* 61, 1 (2008): 48–61.

Tester, Frank, and Peter Kulchyski. *Tammarniit (Mistakes): Inuit Relocation in the Eastern Arctic, 1939–63.* Vancouver: UBC Press, 1994.

Thomas, Nicholas. *Entangled Objects: Exchange, Material Culture, and Colonialism in the Pacific.* Cambridge, MA: Harvard University Press, 1991.

Thompson, Carl Edward. *The Suffering Traveller and the Romantic Imagination.* Oxford: Oxford University Press, 2007. http://dx.doi.org/10.1093/acprof:oso/9780199259984.001.0001.

Tough, Frank. *As Their Natural Resources Fail: Native People and the Economic History of Northern Manitoba, 1870–1930.* Vancouver: UBC Press, 1996.

Tungilik, Victor, and Rachel Uyarasuk. *The Transition to Christianity,* ed. Jarich Oosten and Frédéric Laugrand. Iqaluit: Nunavut Arctic College, 1999.

Universal Magazine. "Extraordinary Adventure and Resources of an Indian Woman." *Universal Magazine of Knowledge and Pleasure* 99 (1796): 317–19.

Usher, Peter. "Environment, Race and Nation Reconsidered: Reflections on Aboriginal Land Claims in Canada." *Canadian Geographer* 4 (2003): 365–82.

–. *Fur Trade Posts of the Northwest Territories, 1870–1970.* Ottawa: Northern Science Research Group, Department of Indian Affairs and Northern Development, 1971.

–. *Economic Basis and Resource Use of the Coppermine-Holman Region, NWT.* Ottawa: Department of Northern Affairs and National Resources, 1965.

Usher, Peter, and Grahame Beakhurst. *Land Regulation in the Canadian North.* Ottawa: Canadian Arctic Resources Committee, 1973.

vanPeenen, Paul. "Arctic Artist: The Changing Nature of George Back's Arctic Land Expeditions, 1819–1835." Master's thesis, Simon Fraser University, 2008.

Venema, Kathleen. "Mapping Culture onto Geography: 'Distance from the Fort' in Samuel Hearne's Journal." *Studies in Canadian Literature* 23, 1 (1998): 9–31.

–. "'Under the Protection of a Principal Man': A White Man, the Hero, and His Wives in Samuel Hearne's Journey." *Essays on Canadian Writing* 70 (2000): 162–90.

Wachowich, Nancy, in collaboration with Apphia Agalakti Awa, Rhoda Kaukjak Katsak, and Sandra Pikujak Katsak. *Saqiyuq: Stories from the Lives of Three Inuit Women.* Montreal and Kingston: McGill-Queen's University Press, 2001.

Wainwright, Joel. *Decolonizing Development: Colonial Power and the Maya.* Malden: Blackwell, 2008. http://dx.doi.org/10.1002/9780470712955.

Warkentin, Germaine, ed. *Canadian Exploration Literature: An Anthology.* Toronto: Oxford University Press, 1993.

Watt-Cloutier, Sheila. "The Inuit Journey towards a POPs-Free-World." In *Northern Lights against POPs: Combatting Toxic Threats in the Arctic,* ed. D.L. Downie and T. Fenge, 256–67. Montreal and Kingston: McGill-Queen's University Press for the Inuit Circumpolar Conference of Canada, 2003.

Wenzel, George. *Animal Rights, Human Rights: Ecology, Economy, and Ideology in the Canadian Arctic.* Toronto: University of Toronto Press, 1991.

–. "The Harp-Seal Controversy and the Inuit Economy." *Arctic* 31 (March 1978): 3–6.

White, Hayden. *The Content of the Form: Narrative Discourse and Historical Representation.* Baltimore: Johns Hopkins University Press, 1987.

White, Paul. *Thomas Huxley: Making the "Man of Science."* Cambridge: Cambridge University Press, 2003.

Wickwire, Wendy. "To See Ourselves as the Other's Other: Nlaka'pamux Contact Narratives." *Canadian Historical Review* 75, 1 (1994): 1–20. http://dx.doi.org/10.3138/CHR-075-01-01.

Widdowson, Frances, and Albert Howard. *Disrobing the Aboriginal Industry: The Deception behind Indigenous Cultural Preservation.* Montreal and Kingston: McGill-Queen's University Press, 2008.

Wiegman, Robyn. "Whiteness Studies and the Paradox of Particularity." *Boundary* 26, 3 (1999): 115–50.

Williams, Glyndwr. *Arctic Labyrinth: The Quest for the Northwest Passage.* London: Allen Lane, 2009.

–. "The Hudson's Bay Company and Its Critics in the Eighteenth Century." *Transactions of the Royal Historical Society* 20 (1970): 149–71. http://dx.doi.org/10.2307/3678766.

Williamson Bathory, Laakkuluk. "Naamaleqaaq! Idle No More in the Arctic." *Northern Public Affairs* 1, 3 (Spring 2013): 39–41.

Wilson, J. Tuzo. "New Light on Hearne." *Beaver Outfit* 280 (June 1949): 14–18.

Wilson, Shawn. *Research Is Ceremony: Indigenous Research Methods.* Halifax: Fernwood, 2008.

Withers, Charles, and Innes Keighren. "Travels into Print: Authoring, Editing and Narratives of Travel and Exploration, c. 1815-c. 1857." *Transactions of the Institute of British Geographers* 36, 4 (2011): 560–73. http://dx.doi.org/10.1111/j.1475-5661.2011.00437.x.

Withers, Charles W.J. "Eighteenth-Century Geography: Texts, Practices, Sites." *Progress in Human Geography* 30, 6 (2006): 711–29. http://dx.doi.org/10.1177/0309132506071515.

–. *Placing the Enlightenment.* Chicago: University of Chicago Press, 2007.

Wolfe, Patrick. "Settler Colonialism and the Elimination of the Native." *Journal of Genocide Research* 8, 4 (2006): 387–409.

–. *Settler Colonialism and the Transformation of Anthropology: The Politics and Poetics of an Ethnographic Event.* London: Cassell, 1999.

Wonders, William. *Overlapping Land Use and Occupancy of Dene, Metis, Inuvialuit and Inuit in the Northwest Territories.* Ottawa: Indian and Northern Affairs, 1983.

Wordsworth, William. *The Excursion: Being a Portion of the Recluse, a Poem.* 2nd ed. London: Longman, Hurst, Rees, Orme and Brown, 1820.

Wylie, John. "Becoming Icy: Scott and Amundsen's South Polar Voyages, 1910–1913." *cultural geographies* 9, 3 (2002): 249–65. http://dx.doi.org/10.1191/1474474002eu247oa.

Index

Note: "(i)" after a page number indicates an illustration. For acronyms used in subentries, please see page 233 of the Glossary.

Printed and bound in Canada by Friesens
Set in Garamond by Apex CoVantage, LLC
Copy editor: Deborah Kerr
Indexer: Cheryl Lemmons
Cartographer: Eric Leinberger